Roman Perspectives on Linguistic Diversity

Roman Perspectives on Linguistic Diversity

Guardians of a Changing Language

Edited by
ADAM GITNER

OXFORD
UNIVERSITY PRESS

Oxford University Press is a department of the University of Oxford. It furthers the University's objective of excellence in research, scholarship, and education by publishing worldwide. Oxford is a registered trade mark of Oxford University Press in the UK and certain other countries.

Published in the United States of America by Oxford University Press
198 Madison Avenue, New York, NY 10016, United States of America.

© Oxford University Press 2023

All rights reserved. No part of this publication may be reproduced, stored in a retrieval system, or transmitted, in any form or by any means, without the prior permission in writing of Oxford University Press, or as expressly permitted by law, by license, or under terms agreed with the appropriate reproduction rights organization. Inquiries concerning reproduction outside the scope of the above should be sent to the Rights Department, Oxford University Press, at the address above.

You must not circulate this work in any other form
and you must impose this same condition on any acquirer.

Library of Congress Cataloging-in-Publication Data
Names: Gitner, Adam, editor.
Title: Roman perspectives on linguistic diversity : guardians of a changing language / edited by Adam Gitner.
Description: New York : Oxford University Press, 2023. | Includes bibliographical references and index.
Identifiers: LCCN 2022053536 (print) | LCCN 2022053537 (ebook) | ISBN 9780197611975 (hardcover) | ISBN 9780197612002 | ISBN 9780197611999 (epub)
Subjects: LCSH: Kaster, Robert A. | Classical philology—Study and teaching—Rome—History. | Latin language—History. | Education, Ancient. | Education—Rome—History. | Language teachers—Rome. | Sociolinguistics—Rome.
Classification: LCC PA53.R66 2023 (print) | LCC PA53 (ebook) | DDC 470.9—dc23/eng/20230106
LC record available at https://lccn.loc.gov/2022053536
LC ebook record available at https://lccn.loc.gov/2022053537

DOI: 10.1093/oso/9780197611975.001.0001

Printed by Integrated Books International, United States of America

ROBERTO A. KASTER
DONO DEDIMVS
sermonis exactori optimo et magistro dilecto,
qui in studiis tam grammaticis quam litterariis novas semitas patefecit,
vetera scripta sospitavit,
affectus antiquorum male intellectos pervestigavit.

Contents

Preface	ix
Adam Gitner	
Acknowledgments	xix
Contributors	xxi
Short Title Abbreviations	xxiii

INTRODUCTION

1. Counterfeit and Coinage: Gresham's Law and the Grammarian   3
   James E. G. Zetzel

PART I: VARRO

2. Varro the Conservative?   23
   Katharina Volk

3. Varro and the Sabine Language in the *De lingua Latina*   33
   Wolfgang D. C. de Melo

4. Varro's Word Trees   47
   Andreas T. Zanker

PART II: PROFESSIONAL GRAMMARIANS

5. The Use of Greek in Diomedes' *Ars grammatica*   73
   Bruno Rochette

6. The Grammarian Consentius on Language Change
   and Variation   99
   Tommaso Mari

7. *Antiquus = squalidus*? Pompeius' Attitude toward Antiquity   115
   Anna Zago

viii CONTENTS

8. T(w)o Be or Not T(w)o Be?: The *dualis numerus* according to
   Latin Grammarians Up to the Early Middle Ages   131
   Tim Denecker

9. Anonymous Grammatical Scholarship: Insights from an
   Annotated Juvenal Codex from Egypt   143
   Alessandro Garcea and Maria Chiara Scappaticcio

PART III: SCHOLARS AND INTELLECTUALS

10. Civic Metaphors for Lexical Borrowing from Seneca to Gellius   169
    Adam Gitner

11. Grammar and Grammarians, Linguistic and Social Change
    from Gellius to Macrobius   191
    Leofranc Holford-Strevens

12. Language Variation and Grammatical Theory in Roman
    Legal Texts   199
    Rolando Ferri

    Epilogue

    The (Very Fragile) Origins of *Guardians of Language*   225
    Robert A. Kaster

    Prosopographical Addenda to Known Ancient Grammarians   232
    Robert A. Kaster

Bibliography   243
General Index   261
Index of Notable Passages   271

Preface

Adam Gitner

1. Orientation: Roman Perspectives on Linguistic Diversity

Robert Kaster's *Guardians of Language* (1988) broke new ground by exploring how fully ancient grammarians were embedded in the late antique social order and how actively they participated in maintaining it. They were, in Kaster's words, "one of antiquity's great middlemen . . . poised between town and country, between distinct levels in urban society, between the family and the community, or between the cultures of prestige, classical and Christian" (*Guardians* 7). It can fairly be considered three different books in one: the first half is a synoptic historical analysis, including case studies of individual grammarians; the second half is a prosopography of all known (and several unknown) grammarians; and embedded within the prosopography are close readings of multiple late antique poetic and epistolary corpora where grammarians play a role (e.g., the *Anthologia Graeca*, Ausonius, Isidore of Pelusium, Libanius, Sidonius Apollinaris, and many epigraphic and papyrological texts). It is an extraordinary achievement, all the more remarkable since it is only a small part of the wider range of interests that Kaster has pursued over the course of his career.[1] After three decades

---

[1] In the Epilogue, which describes the genesis of *Guardians*, Bob compares his scholarly trajectory to "that of a pinball in mid-play." Vast stretches of that pinball table hardly come into play in this volume, but they deserve to be mentioned here. His work on ancient grammarians includes, in addition to *Guardians of Language*, his edition and commentary of Suetonius' *De grammaticis et rhetoribus* (1995) and its companion textual study (1992) as well as his completion of Charles Murgia's edition of Servius' commentary on *Aeneid* Books 9–12 (2018). Furthermore, Bob has produced critical editions of Macrobius' *Saturnalia* (OCT: 2011a; textual study 2010; Loeb translation 2011b) and of Suetonius' *De vita Caesarum* (OCT: 2016a, including a revised *De grammaticis et rhetoribus*; with companion textual study 2016b). Another key leitmotif of his work has been ancient emotions, including *Emotion, Restraint, and Community in Ancient Rome* (2005), which relates to his translation of Seneca's *Dialogues* 3–5 (in *Anger, Mercy, Revenge*, 2010, with M. Nussbaum) and the edited volume *Hope, Joy, and Affection in the Classical World* (2016 with R. Caston). He has also published several translations of Cicero, including the *Pro Sestio* (2006) and the *Brutus* and *Orator* (2020), and a travelogue-*cum*-historical and cultural essay on the Appian Way (2012). For his work on the Carolingian manuscripts of Virgil, published as *The Tradition of the Text of the Aeneid in the Ninth Century* (1990), see the Epilogue.

X PREFACE

of flourishing research on ancient grammar and linguistic thought, which has included much foundational work on the text and interpretation of these authors, it is worth returning to some of the sociological themes emphasized by *Guardians*.[2]

The present book develops one of *Guardian*'s line of inquiry by focusing on one particular point of contact between ancient linguistic thought and ancient society: namely, how Roman grammarians—as well as scholars and intellectuals more broadly—described, made sense of, and sometimes resisted linguistic diversity within the Roman Republic and Empire. This diversity includes social and diachronic variation within Latin as well as multilingual contact with Greek and other Mediterranean languages, sociolinguistic topics that have recently gained attention (e.g., Adams 2003, 2007, 2013; Dickey and Chahoud 2010). "Diversity" thus refers to both innerlinguistic differences within a single language, Latin, as well as to a lesser extent differences between Latin and other languages.[3] In pursuing this line of investigation, the present volume builds on recent publications exploring ancient linguistic thought from several complementary angles.[4] It is in some

---

[2] It is impossible to survey the range of significant publications on ancient grammar that have appeared since 1988, but a helpful guide to the Roman material is provided by Zetzel's overview, *Critics, Compilers, and Commentators* (2018) and the online bibliography to the *Grammatici Latini*, maintained by Garcea (https://cgl.hypotheses.org/). On the Latin side there has been much high-quality textual scholarship, particularly in the "Collectanea Grammatica Latina" series under the direction of De Nonno (including, e.g., Zago's Pompeius 2017b and Spangenberg Yanes's *De nominibus dubiis* 2020), De Gruyter's "Sammlung griechischer und lateinischer Grammatiker," and the online *Corpus Grammaticorum Latinorum* and *Grammatici disiecti* projects, directed by Garcea. On Varro, see n. 10; on Priscian, n. 12. Grammatical scholia have also not been neglected: Clausen and Zetzel's *Commentum Cornuti* (2004), Cioffi's work on Donatus' commentaries (2017, 2018), and Murgia and Kaster's Servius *Aen.* 8–12 (2018), to name just a few publications. Also significant is the amount of research dedicated to Latin instruction in a Greek milieu: for example, Bonnet's edition of the bilingual Dositheus (2005), Dickey's *Colloquia pseudodositheana* (2012–15), Scappaticcio's publication of grammatical fragments on papyri (2015), and Fressura's *Vergilius Latinograecus* (2017). De Paolis' edition of Macrobius' *De verborum Graeci et Latini differentiis vel societatibus excerpta* (1990) is especially relevant to the themes of this volume. Not least, Schad's *Lexicon of Latin Grammatical Terminology* (2007) has made all this material more intelligible and accessible.

[3] Roman references to *diversitas* (or *varietas*) *linguarum* refer exclusively to the latter type of differences, i.e., between languages. To my knowledge the phrase occurs only twice in Classical sources: Plin. *nat.* 11.271 (about physical differences in the human voice) *hinc illa gentium totque linguarum toto orbe diversitas*; and Quint. *inst.* 11.3.87 (about the use of hands to communicate) *ut in tanta per omnis gentes nationesque linguae diversitate hic mihi omnium hominum communis sermo videatur*. Diversity among languages becomes a much more frequent topic of reflection in Christian sources beyond the scope of this volume, partly because of Babel and the xenolalia of Pentecost: see Denecker (2017, Chs. 4–6). By contrast, Roman grammarians do sometimes use *diversitas* (without genitive *linguae*) to discuss intra-linguistic difference: see *TLL* V.1 1573.66–73 (Hey); on the grammatical use of *varietas* see Schad (2007) s.v.

[4] Particularly relevant for the intellectual orientation of this volume are Desbordes (2007), Basset et al. (2007), Ferri (2011), Ferri and Zago (2016), Denecker (2017, especially Part 2 "Language Diversity"), and the philosophically inflected work on ancient linguistic thought developed by Pezzini and Taylor (2019) and Taylor (2020).

PREFACE   xi

respects both narrower and broader than *Guardians*, as explained below, but it shares with Kaster's study an emphasis on the social and historical contexts in which ancient scholars operated.

Roman grammarians in particular played a two-sided role in relation to linguistic diversity. On the one hand, they actively spread and helped to maintain a remarkably uniform vision of Latin over the diverse terrain of the Roman Empire and across many centuries of use, certainly well into the sixth century (the end-point for *Guardians* is circa 565). Löfstedt called this "Received Standard Imperial Latin" (1959, 48; see *Guardians* 194–95).[5] The exceptional, long-term stability of grammatical knowledge was one of the central questions *Guardians* sought to address. The answer it develops has to do with the embeddedness of grammarians within local and municipal structures, the mutually reinforcing collaboration between the grammarians and the local elites from whom they often came (see particularly *Guardians*, Ch. 6).

On the other hand, since grammarians and their allies were the guardians patrolling the boundaries of *Latinitas*, they were also among the best surviving witnesses to the actual diversity of Latin, not all of which is clearly attested in surviving written sources. For Latin, after all, did continue to change over these centuries, despite the diligent labor of the grammarians, as Jerome, for example, attests (*Gal.* 2.2 p. 382[C] *cum . . . et ipsa Latinitas et regionibus cotidie mutetur et tempore*).[6] The grammarians in fact have quite a lot to say, sometimes directly and sometimes implicitly, about diachronic differences between their own contemporary Latin and the classical Latin of the *auctores* they taught (see esp. Zetzel, Chapter 1).[7] They also teach us about regional differences (see Mari, Chapter 6, on Consentius) and—if we a cast

[5] Remarkably uniform, that is, by the standards of a pre-modern empire before the advent of printing, but the gap between the view of Latin promoted by the grammarians and acceptable usage, as found in official and quasi-official documents, could be considerable. On the standardization of Latin see, e.g., Adams (2007, 13–17) and Clackson (2015), who emphasizes the differences between *Latinitas* (and the source on which it was calqued, Ἑλληνισμός) and the modern conception of a standardized language.

[6] See Denecker (2017, 238) on this passage, where Jerome notes an affinity between the (Celtic) languages spoken by the Galatians and Treviri and also between Punic and Phoenician. Earlier remarks on diachronic change in Latin are found in, e.g., Varro *ling.* 5.3 *neque omnis impositio verborum exstat, quod vetustas quasdam delevit* (noting semantic change to *hostis*); and Quintilian *inst.* 8.3.26 (noting the obsolence of words such as *oppido* "certainly," *antegerio* "very," and *aerumna* "grief") *totus prope mutatus est sermo*. Ancient accounts of linguistic change are discussed by Müller (2003) and Denecker (2017, 288–303). Zair (2019) discusses the grammarians' use of postulated or reconstructed etyma.

[7] A classic example of a grammatical source that illustrates linguistic change implicitly is the *Appendix Probi*, not discussed here (see, e.g., Powell 2011).

xii PREFACE

a glance to a neighboring professional group, the jurists—also about pragmatic and sociolinguistic differences (see Ferri, Chapter 12).[8] Furthermore, they are aware of Latin in contact with other languages, such as the Italic languages (see de Melo, Chapter 3, on what Varro calls "Sabellic") and especially Greek (see Rochette, Chapter 5, on Diomedes).

Nevertheless, the main focus of this book is not on Roman scholars and grammarians as sources of linguistic information about non-standard Latin. The emphasis instead falls on their perspectives toward linguistic diversity as recorded in their works: in other words, the conceptual models they employed, their habits of thought and expression, modes of understanding, and habitual metaphors. It is in this conceptual space where some of the tensions inherent in the grammarian's line of work were expressed and negotiated: in particular, the difficulty of maintaining a unified front to Latinity despite ongoing, observable change, and the difficulty of using a fairly rigid system of inherited grammatical knowledge to describe a linguistic reality that was sometimes more complex (see Denecker, Chapter 8, on the long-lived notion of the Latin "dual," inherited from Greek grammarians; Zanker, Chapter 4, on Varro's tree metaphors; and Gitner, Chapter 10, on metaphors for lexical borrowing). Also relevant are the scholars' positioning of themselves in relation to antiquity, as explored in two of the chapters (Volk on Varro, Chapter 2, and Zago on Pompeius, Chapter 7).[9] More generally, the variety of ancient perspectives can sometimes be linked to changing historical circumstances, as well as different professional roles and audiences.

This emphasis entails two significant departures from *Guardians of Language*.

First, the camera has zoomed out somewhat from a close-up on the professional grammarian to take in ancient scholars and other experts more generally, partly in order to place professional and non-professional views of language in dialogue with each other. This dialogue has proved to open a particularly rich vein of analysis: especially in the chapters by Zetzel (Chapter 1), describing a central tension between simplified, pedagogical models of Latin (*grammatica*), typically aimed at students, and more complex, sophisticated descriptions (*Latinitas*), and by Holford-Strevens (Chapter 11), who describes the socially inflected criticism directed by amateur scholars, such

---

[8] On grammarians' discussion of colloquial Latin see Probert and Ferri (2010).

[9] On representations of antiquity more widely see the papers in Rocchi and Mussini (2017; esp. the chapter by De Nonno).

PREFACE   xiii

as Gellius, at professional grammarians. Ferri's exploration (Chapter 12) of reflection on language found in ancient legal sources reveals fascinating new terrain, where grammatical concepts interact with practical, legal problems.

Secondly, the chronological frame has been widened from late antiquity (third to sixth centuries) to include sources from earlier Roman antiquity that do not stand entirely within the mainstream of professional grammatical literature. The Late Republic is represented mainly through Varro's *De lingua Latina*, an unrivalled source for Roman linguistic reflection (see Chapters 2–4).[10] Other scholarly but non-professional voices have been included from the Principate, such as Seneca, Suetonius, and Aulus Gellius (discussed in Chapters 10 and 11). However, the sixth-century cut-off remains roughly the same as in *Guardians*. The latest source discussed at length is the sixth-century Juvenal codex from Antinoë whose scholastic annotations are newly presented and discussed by Maria Chiara Scappaticcio and Alessandro Garcea (Chapter 9). Nevertheless, Tim Denecker's essay on the Latin dual (Chapter 8) makes some adventurous forays even later into the early medieval grammatical tradition (the seventh-century *Ars Ambrosiana* and the ninth-century Smaragdus of Saint-Mihiel). Their misunderstanding of vowel quantity (apparently confusing the perfect *legēre* with the infinitive *legĕre*) incidentally reveals an important discontinuity with respect to earlier grammarians, which would seem to support regarding the end of the sixth century as an important turning point in Latin linguistic thought (but certainly not a cut-off).

This broadening of the frame also involves some significant losses and exclusions. The choice to focus on Latin and its grammatical tradition entails the loss of Greek voices, who were well represented in *Guardians* and made among the most profound contributions to linguistic thought during the Roman Empire (in particular, Apollonius Dyscolus).[11] One native Greek speaker who is represented here is the fourth-century grammarian Diomedes, who despite writing a Latin grammar in Latin drew extensively on Greek literary quotations and his knowledge of Greek more generally in order

---

[10] The new edition and commentary by de Melo (2019b) puts the study of this work on a new, firmer footing. The upsurge of interest in Varro is represented by, e.g., Butterfield (2015), MacRae (2016), Arena and Mac Góráin (2017), Nelsestuen (2017), Leonardis (2019), and Spencer (2019).

[11] Valuable recent surveys of Greek linguistic scholarship can be found in Dickey (2007), Montanari, Matthaios and Rengakos (2015), Matthews (2019), and Montanari (2020). Exemplary both textually and interpretively is Roussou's recent edition of Pseudo-Arcadius' Epitome of Herodian's *De prosodia catholica* (2018). The value of seeing Latin and Greek sources in contact is amply demonstrated by Probert's recent study of Roman grammarians on the Latin accent (2019).

xiv PREFACE

to communicate effectively with his Greek-speaking audience (Rochette, Chapter 5). The considerable intellectual debt of Roman grammarians to their Greek predecessors and contemporaries is also highlighted by the peculiar notion of the Latin dual number, inherited from Greek grammar but adapted in creative ways to Latin (Denecker, Chapter 8). Furthermore, Scappaticcio and Garcea (Chapter 9) show Greek speakers interacting with a Latin literary text in their exploration of the multiple layers of bilingual annotation in a sixth-century Juvenal codex of eastern provenance.

Nor for practical reasons could everything valuable within the Latin linguistic tradition be included or discussed. Keeping with Kaster's choice to "remain in the intellectual foothills of the profession" and "resist... the temptation to make for the summit (say, Priscian)" (*Guardians* 138), this volume has likewise omitted Priscian, whose *Institutiones grammaticae* both crown the grammatical tradition and point forward to the Middle Ages.[12]

Christian and philosophical perspectives are also given little direct attention in this volume, partly in accordance with the focus of *Guardians* and partly because both topics have been the subject of outstanding recent research. As *Guardians* shows, Christianity hardly disrupted the long-term professional and institutional continuity of the ancient grammarian, despite his growing interaction with new ecclesiastical sources of power;[13] nevertheless, Christianity did play a significant role in changing ideas about language, especially in theological sources, as demonstrated by Denecker's *Ideas on Language in Early Latin Christianity* (2017). Ancient philosophical perspectives on language have also been explored by recent publications, particularly Pezzini and Taylor's excellent collection of essays on Roman linguistic naturalism (2019) and Taylor's volume on Lucretius (2020).

2. Structure and Content

The volume opens with Zetzel's introductory survey, "Counterfeit and Coinage: Gresham's Law and the Grammarian," which establishes many of the themes and parameters explored in detail in subsequent chapters.

---

[12] This painful absence is somewhat counterbalanced by an ongoing Priscian renaissance, exemplified by the ERC Project *PAGES: Priscian's Ars Grammatica in European Scriptoria*, led by Rosellini, as well as by the translations of the Groupe *Ars Grammatica*. For an overview see *CCC* 309–11.

[13] For example, as Kaster notes (*Guardians* 154), the only evidence of Pompeius' Christianity is that he comments on the grammatical number of the word *Pascha*.

Whereas modern writers take language change for granted, ancient writers tended to think about language change as a form of corruption. To illustrate the ancient viewpoint, Zetzel invokes the economic notion of Gresham's Law: bad money drives out good. The paper explores these ideas using several examples: the explanations of inflectional morphology in treatises on *Latinitas*, the alternative treatment of syllable division employed in treatises *De finalibus* to cope with changes in prosody, and the redefinition of solecism as stylistic virtuosity in analyses of *vitia et virtutes orationis* and in such works as Aemilius Asper's *Grammatica Vergiliana*.

The division of the rest of the book follows the three main types of sources discussed. Varro occupies a place of honor as the subject of the first category, with three contributions devoted to different aspects of his linguistic thought. The second category "Professional Grammarians" includes contributions about individual grammarians (Diomedes, Consentius, Pompeius), grammatical doctrine (the Latin dual number), and grammatical annotations (the Antinoë codex of Juvenal). The final category "Scholars and Intellectuals" moves beyond the turf of the professional grammarian to consider men of letters, including Seneca, Suetonius, and Gellius, as well as the Roman jurists.

The first of the three essays on Varro, "Varro the Conservative?" by Katharina Volk, provides an important counterpoint to Zetzel's argument as well as an introduction to the intellectual and cultural context of Varro of Reate. According to one traditional view, Varro was an arch-conservative, who was born among the backward-looking Sabines and hankered after an ideal past. Along these lines, his linguistic scholarship would be an attempt to reconstruct and revive practices and usages from this paradise lost of "pure Latinity." On the contrary, Volk argues that Varro is remarkably sanguine about historical and linguistic change, viewing it as a natural aspect of human life generally. Varro thus provides a valuable contrast to the view of later scholars and grammarians, particularly from the Augustan age onward, who yearned more overtly for the revival of an idealized linguistic past. The second essay, "Varro and the Sabine Language in the *De lingua Latina*," by Wolfgang de Melo, investigates in more detail one particular element of Varro's cultural background: his understanding of the Italic language he calls "Sabine." This raises the issue of language contact as a phenomenon that Roman intellectuals had to address and confront within the multilingual Mediterranean, which recurs throughout the volume. De Melo shows that Varro portrays it more as a dialect of Latin than a language in its own right, underlining the extent to which the social dominance of Latin colors

Varro's experience of language diversity. The last paper in the series, Andreas Zanker's "Varro's Word Trees," builds on de Melo's contribution by focusing on one particular but extremely common metaphor used by Varro to describe bilingual interaction: the word as tree. Zanker shows how a careful investigation of metaphor illuminates cultural assumptions and also reveals connections between Varro's linguistic and agricultural interests.

The next section is devoted to professional grammarians, with five contributions in roughly chronological order. The first three contributions form a series of case studies addressing individual grammarians in depth. "The Use of Greek in Diomedes' *Ars grammatica*," by Bruno Rochette, emphasizes the bilingual environment of ancient scholarship. Like many Roman grammarians, Diomedes, who was active after Charisius and Donatus in the latter half of the fourth century, explicitly addressed an audience of Greeks learning Latin. Rochette surveys the many different functions that Greek served for such a bilingual readership. The next paper, "The Grammarian Consentius on Language Change and Variation" by Tommaso Mari, addresses the fifth-century Consentius. His *Ars de barbarismis et metaplasmis* is the longest extant treatise on the so-called vices and virtues of speech, and thus directly addresses linguistic variety. Mari, who has recently completed an edition of the work (2021), shows how Consentius' understanding of *barbarismus* differs from modern conceptions of linguistic error, and he illustrates the geographic and social categories that Consentius uses to describe them, which he relates to the grammarian's social context in the elite society of fifth-century Gaul. The third paper, Anna Zago's "*Antiquus = squalidus*? Pompeius' Attitudes towards Antiquity," turns to the more flamboyant Pompeius, one of the figures Kaster memorably brought to life in *Guardians*. As a recent editor of Pompeius' work (2017b), she makes a signal contribution here by reconstructing and discussing the prologue to his *Commentum artis Donati*, which has until recently not been published in its entirety. The prologue shows Pompeius engaging polemically with Caesar's grammatical work, which reveals a surprisingly negative attitude toward antiquity more generally.

The fourth and fifth papers on grammarians take different approaches. Instead of focusing on a single author, Tim Denecker's "T(w)o Be or Not T(w)o Be: The *dualis numerus* according to Latin Grammarians up to the Early Middle Ages" traces the development of a grammatical topic throughout the entire corpus of Roman grammarians. Specifically, he studies the imaginary concept of a Latin dual number, supposedly distinct from

PREFACE xvii

the singular and plural. This is a case where the conceptual and terminological framework developed to describe Greek grammar led to productive friction when applied to Latin. By tracing this idea from Quintilian to the early medieval grammarians, Denecker illustrates a range of strategies employed by grammarians to discuss an unusual linguistic feature, as well as changing views of authority and normativity. The fifth paper, "Anonymous Grammatical Scholarship: Insights from an Annotated Juvenal Codex from Egypt" by Maria Chiara Scappaticcio and Alessandro Garcea, takes us almost into the classroom of an ancient grammarian. Examining the marginalia found on the sixth-century Antinoë fragment of Juvenal, they identify several different annotators interacting with each other in order to explain the linguistic difficulties of a complex literary author. By sheer luck of survival, this portion of Juvenal involves a lengthy complaint about ancient instruction (7.149–98), making it especially relevant to the sociological themes of *Guardians*.

The final section turns from grammarians to Roman scholars and nonprofessional men of letters who are nevertheless deeply engaged with language. Three contributions discuss literary authors, including Seneca, Suetonius, Gellius, and the Roman jurists. The inclusion of such authors marks a difference from *Guardians of Language*, but also a form of continuity since the emphasis remains on the social context in which Roman linguistic thought developed. The first of these contributions, "Civic Metaphors for Lexical Borrowing from Seneca to Gellius" by Adam Gitner, concentrates on a distinctively Roman metaphor used to understand loanwords borrowed into Latin from other languages: the notion that they gain linguistic "citizenship" (*civitas*). A survey of such passages, mainly found in literary authors from Seneca to Gellius, reveals how changing conceptions of Roman citizenship informed the vocabulary and perspectives used to understand linguistic contact. Next, Leofranc Holford-Strevens considers in detail the linguistic views of this gentleman scholar in "Grammar and Grammarians, Linguistic and Social Change from Gellius to Macrobius." Gellius tends to speak in a tone of gentlemanly superiority toward professional grammarians. Accordingly, he is dismissive of their normative and dogmatic approach to language, which relies on simplistic rules that are not actually supported by the ancient authors. Gellius instead adopts a more nuanced position, showing awareness that older Latin was not uniform and that the gulf between the literary standard and contemporary everyday speech was continuing to widen in the second century.

xviii PREFACE

The final contribution considers views about language among a different, highly influential group of Roman professionals: Roman jurists. Rolando Ferri in "Language Variation and Grammatical Theory in Roman Legal Texts" identifies many points of contact between the writings of *grammatici* and the jurists who put their theories to use in resolving concrete legal difficulties. Particularly noteworthy are the jurists' discussion of lexical meaning, regional differences, the pragmatics of spoken communication, and speakers' linguistic errors.

As is fitting for a volume that addresses the social context of ancient scholarship, the book concludes by turning an eye toward the historical setting of modern scholarship. An autobiographical epilogue by Robert Kaster describes the social and intellectual origins of *Guardians of Language* and provides a personal look inside a modern-day scholar's workshop. Kaster also provides an appendix of Prosopographical Addenda, supplementing the original prosopography found in *Guardians of Language*.

Acknowledgments

This book began as a conference held at the University of Cologne in July 2018 to celebrate the thirtieth anniversary of the publication of *Guardians of Language* (1988), a work that pioneered the study of ancient grammarians as social agents. For many of his students, Bob Kaster is not just a guardian of language in the best sense but a model human being, whose generosity with his time, sane advice, and deep sense of fairness have been an inspiration. In any future prosopography of latter-day grammarians, he will surely be enrolled as both *clarissimus* and *humanissimus*.

This volume and the conference on which it is based would not have been possible without the generous collaboration of Jan Felix Gaertner, my host at the University of Cologne, the Wilhelm von Humboldt Foundation, which funded the conference and my research stay in Cologne, and the Department of Altertumskunde, which provided both organizational support and a friendly community of outstanding researchers. Special thanks are owed to Martin Stöckinger for his logistical know-how and to the departmental secretaries Birgit Overmann and Christiane Kaduk. The volume has been much improved by the press, thanks in particular to the sharp-eyed anonymous reviewers and the support of Stefan Vranka.

I am deeply grateful to everyone who participated in the conference and for their generosity and patience throughout the process of publication. In keeping with his wish not to have a Festschrift, the conference was focused on one aspect only of Bob's scholarship, and it cannot pretend to represent the wide circle of scholars whom Bob has influenced. One participant, in particular, at every single panel stood out: Laura Kaster, without whose encouragement I suspect Bob might not have consented to this undertaking. To both of them above all I am delighted to say: thank you.

Adam Gitner
Munich
December 2021

Contributors

Tim Denecker obtained his PhD from KU Leuven and is a Publishing Manager at Brepols & Corpus Christianorum (Turnhout, Belgium). His research and publications mainly focus on conceptions about language and grammar in the Latin West during late antiquity and the early Middle Ages.

Rolando Ferri is Professor of Latin at the University of Pisa. He has worked on Horace (*I dispiaceri di un Epicureo*, 1993) and Senecan tragedy (*Octavia: A Play Attributed to Seneca*, Cambridge, 2003). His interest in the history of the Latin Language, with a focus on its informal and lower registers, has led him to work on Latin lexicography and bilingual glossaries and on the application of politeness theory to Latin texts.

Alessandro Garcea is Full Professor of Latin language and literature at the Sorbonne Université (Paris). His research interests include: epistolary genre, passions, Cicero, Varro, Caesar, Aulus Gellius, and ancient linguistic theories. He is the project director of the following online corpora: *Corpus Grammaticorum Latinorum* and *Grammatici disiecti*.

Adam Gitner is a lexicographer at the *Thesaurus linguae Latinae* (Bavarian Academy of Sciences) and docent at Ludwig-Maximilians-Universität. He received his PhD at Princeton University (*Horace and the Greek Language: Aspects of Literary Bilingualism*, 2012) and has published on Horace, Greco-Latin bilingualism, and ancient linguistic thought.

Leofranc Holford-Strevens was until retirement Consultant Scholar-Editor at Oxford University Press. He is the author of *Aulus Gellius: An Antonine Scholar and his Achievement* (2003) and *Gelliana* (2019), a companion volume to his Oxford Classical Text, and the co-editor with Amiel Vardi of *The World of Aulus Gellius*. He has also written extensively on calendars and computistics.

Robert A. Kaster is Kennedy Foundation Professor of Latin Language and Literature, emeritus, and Professor of Classics, emeritus, at Princeton University. His scholarship has largely been devoted to Roman rhetoric, the history of ancient education, Roman ethics, and textual criticism.

Tommaso Mari is a cultural officer at the Italian Ministry of Foreign Affairs and International Cooperation. He has edited Consentius' *De barbarismis et metaplasmis* and the Carolingian treatise *Pauca de barbarismo*, and has recently worked on the minutes of late antique church councils as evidence of spoken Latin and Greek.

xxii CONTRIBUTORS

Wolfgang de Melo is Professor of Classical Philology at the University of Oxford. He has published a monograph on the early Latin verb system and has edited Plautus for the Loeb Classical Library. His most recent work is a critical edition of Varro's *De lingua Latina*, with introduction, translation, and commentary.

Bruno Rochette is Professor of Classics at the University of Liège (Belgium). His research concerns mainly Greco-Latin bilingualism. He is the author of a book about Latin in the Greek world and of many contributions about various aspects of this large problematic. He is currently working on Latin grammars for a Greek-speaking audience.

Maria Chiara Scappaticcio is Professor of Latin at the University of Naples "Federico II." Her research focuses on Latin literary texts transmitted by papyrus, especially in her role as editor of the new *Corpus of Latin Texts on Papyrus* (six volumes, Cambridge University Press, 2023/4), funded by an ERC grant. Her current research also concerns the *Commentariolum petitionis* and electoral propaganda in the Roman world.

Katharina Volk is Professor of Classics at Columbia University and the author of monographs on Latin didactic poetry, Manilius, Ovid, and the intellectual history of the Late Republic.

Anna Zago is Lecturer at the University of Pisa. Her research focuses on the manuscript tradition and the ecdotics of late antique and medieval texts, with a particular concentration on grammatical and exegetical works. She also works on the history of ancient linguistic thought as well as schooling in ancient Rome. She has published critical editions of Latin grammatical texts (Servius, Pompeius).

Andreas T. Zanker is Assistant Professor of Classics at Amherst College. He has written books on the Greek and Latin vocabularies of meaning and Homeric metaphor, and has co-edited a volume on the relationship between Horace and Seneca.

James E. G. Zetzel is Anthon Professor of Latin emeritus at Columbia University. His scholarly interests include Cicero and the history of classical scholarship. His *Critics, Compilers, and Commentators: An Introduction to Roman Philology, 200 BCE–800 CE* appeared in 2018, and *The Lost Republic: Cicero's De oratore and De re publica* appeared in 2022.

Short Title Abbreviations

Abbreviated citations of Latin texts follow the conventions of the *Thesaurus linguae Latinae* unless otherwise indicated (these, along with information about the relevant critical editions, can be found in the online *Index auctorum*: https://www.thesaurus. badw.de/tll-digital/index/a.html). Though less familiar to Anglophone readers, these conventions provide exhaustive and unambiguous coverage of all Latin texts, including late antiquity. Abbreviated work titles have been kept in lower case even when they would typically be capitalized in English prose, but the commas as separators have been converted into dots.

Citations of Roman grammarians likewise generally conform to *TLL* conventions. These typically include a reference to the volume, page, and line number(s) in H. Keil's *Grammatici Latini* (7 volumes, Leipzig, 1855–80; with a supplemental volume by H. Hagen, 1870), here abbreviated "*gramm.*" Thus "Vel. *gramm.* VII 74.16–75.5" refers to Velius Longus' orthographic treatise in Keil, volume 7, page 74, line 16 to page 75, line 5. (NB: the "*gramm.*" in references to Charisius refers to Barwick's edition; this can be distinguished from a reference to Keil by the absence of a volume number.)

Abbreviations of Greek sources are based on Liddell–Scott–Jones' *Greek Lexicon* (maintained and expanded by the *Diccionario Griego-Español*: http://dge.cchs.csic. es/lst/lst4.htm).

Additionally the following abbreviations are used:

AE	*L'Année épigraphique*. Paris 1888–.
BGU	*Aegyptische Urkunden aus den Königlichen Museen zu Berlin.* Berlin 1895–.
CCC	J. E. G. Zetzel, *Critics, Compilers, and Commentators: An Introduction to Roman Philology 200 BCE–800 CE*. Oxford 2018.
CGL	G. Goetz et al., *Corpus glossariorum Latinorum*. Leipzig 1888–1923.
CIL	*Corpus inscriptionum Latinarum*. Berlin 1862–.
CLE	F. Buecheler and E. Lommatzsch, *Anthologia latina, pars posterior: Carmina latina epigraphica*. Leipzig 1895–1930.
DGE	F. R. Adrados et al. (ed.), *Diccionario Griego-Español*. Madrid 1980–.
FDS	K. Hülser, *Die Fragmente zur Dialektik der Stoiker: neue Sammlung der Texte mit deutscher Übersetzung und Kommentaren*. Stuttgart, 1987–1988.

xxiv SHORT TITLE ABBREVIATIONS

Guardians R. A. Kaster, *Guardians of Language: The Grammarian and Society in Late Antiquity*. Berkeley 1988.

GG *Grammatici Graeci*. Leipzig 1855–1880.

gramm. See paragraph above.

GRF G. Funaioli, *Grammaticae Romanae fragmenta*. Leipzig 1907.

ICVR J. B. de Rossi, A. Silvagni, et al., *Inscriptiones christianae urbis Romae*. Rome 1922–1985.

IG *Inscriptiones Graecae*. Berlin 1873–.

ILS H. Dessau, *Inscriptiones Latinae selectae*. Berlin 1892–1916.

LGGA F. Montanari, F. Montana, and L. Pagani (eds.), *Lexicon of Greek Grammarians of Antiquity*. Brill Online.

OED *Oxford English Dictionary*, 3rd edn. online. Oxford 2001–.

OLD P. W. Glare (ed.), *Oxford Latin Dictionary*, 2nd edn. Oxford 2012.

PCBE Mandouze, A. et al., *Prosopographie chrétienne du Bas-Empire*. Paris 1982–.

PLRE J. R. Martindale, *The Prosopography of the Later Roman Empire*. Cambridge 1971–1992.

RE A. Pauly, G. Wissowa, G. Kroll, et al. (eds.), *Paulys Real-Encyclopädie der classischen Altertumswissenschaft*. Stuttgart 1893–1997.

SB *Sammelbuch griechischer Urkunden aus Aegypten*. Berlin and Wiesbaden 1913–.

SEG *Supplementum Epigraphicum Graecum*. Leiden 1923–.

SIG W. Dittenberger, *Sylloge inscriptionum Graecarum*. Leipzig 1914–24.

SVF H. von Arnim, *Stoicorum veterum fragmenta*. Leipzig 1903–5.

TLL *Thesaurus linguae Latinae*. Leipzig 1900–.

INTRODUCTION

1

Counterfeit and Coinage

Gresham's Law and the Grammarian

James E. G. Zetzel

Dicimus magistris magistris
grammaticis ut vale- valeant,
duris qui capistris capistris
et os et fauces colli- colligant.
o Latinitas,
quot et quanta das
gaudia et carmina cum fidi- fidibus.

W. Stroh/Jan Novák

The guardians of language who stand on sentry duty in Rober Kaster's magnificent book of that title were, as he showed so clearly, protecting both the society to which they to some extent controlled entry and the correct language that was, so to speak, the key to the gate of social acceptability.[1] I have nothing to add to what *Guardians* has said about grammar as a social institution or about the grammarian's uncomfortable liminal position as a figure of relatively low status whose instruction and approval were essential for students to attain a much higher status than their teachers; indeed, this paper will for the most part steer clear of the authors Kaster so memorably discussed. The problems addressed here are slightly different: to continue with the metaphor of Kaster's title, are the guardians keeping language

---

[1] There are only two footnotes in this paper to Kaster 1988, but my debt to it (and to its author) should be evident throughout. I am indebted also to Katharina Volk for reading a draft, to Adam Gitner for valuable editorial improvements, and to the participants in Cologne for their comments. The metaphor of my title was suggested by a headline in *The Onion* on March 19, 2008: "Black Guy Asks Nation For Change" (https://politics.theonion.com/black-guy-asks-nation-for-change-181 9569703).

James E. G. Zetzel, *Counterfeit and Coinage* In: *Roman Perspectives on Linguistic Diversity*. Edited by Adam Gitner, Oxford University Press. © Oxford University Press 2023. DOI: 10.1093/oso/9780197611975.003.0001

4   INTRODUCTION

locked up and imprisoned, or are they keeping it safe from outside attacks? And what do you do when you are guarding a prisoner whose shape is constantly shifting, who keeps escaping from your control? To abandon metaphor if only briefly, how does the grammarian cope with language change, and how do others react to the methods used by the grammarian to keep language fixed?

Let me start from what ought to be fairly obvious, and presumably was to students of language in antiquity too: language is neither uniform nor fixed. Even aside from social or regional variations, there are diachronic variations: there are changes in phonology, there are changes in morphology, there are changes in syntax, there are changes in the meanings of words. Worse than that, there is synchronically often more than one perfectly legitimate and grammatical way to say something. For Latin—both for us and for our ancient grammarian predecessors—it is even more problematic that much of the regularity of the classical language was a very artificial construction: a deliberate choice to label as correct one declension of a given noun, one spelling, one pronunciation. Whose deliberate choice it was I will not even try to consider, for there was clearly more than one chooser, and therefore more than one acceptable (to one person or another) choice. James Adams, for instance, in his recent reader of informal Latin, has emphasized that the rules that Cicero and Caesar use to govern their speech allow for a narrower range of "correct" possibilities than those used by some of their equally literate contemporaries.[2] And that does not even touch the problem of poetic diction and style.

None of this should be surprising: we experience different levels of style and grammar in our own languages every day, and although we may grit our teeth at some of the barbarities we hear from our students or deans, we can still, unfortunately, understand them perfectly well most of the time, and our sensitivity to barbarism (in all senses), even if we recognize it, diminishes over time. I no longer even notice the misuse of "due to" for "owing to"; I wince at but rarely correct the use of "gift" or "loan" as verbs; but I still try to insist that "data" are (or was that "is"?) plural, not singular. As some of the examples discussed below may suggest, the same feeling of resignation may have affected ancient teachers too—again, if they even recognized what was wrong. In the practice of teaching a classical language and a classical literature—as we do, as the ancient *grammaticus* also did—we have considerable difficulty in accepting change, even though we know we must: to use the metaphor

---

[2] On Vitruvius' divergences from classical practice, see Adams (2016, 191); more generally 641–2.

of my title, we view change as something counterfeit, and currency a mixed blessing. While we have to recognize Gresham's Law—the economic principle of entropy, that bad coinage drives out good—we do not have to like it.[3] Or rather, as *grammatici* we live by both aspects of the rule. What Gresham's Law is usually taken to mean is that true quality is always replaced by something worse. But it also means—what Gresham himself meant—that the good coin disappears because it is being hoarded as something valuable that is no longer available. And for gold, in the Roman grammarian's currency, read Virgil or Cicero. Even *grammatici*, however, occasionally recognize that language is not as fixed as we might like it to be: I want to suggest, in fact, that the grammarian is made by various critics to be more reactionary than he really was.

It is not merely as *laudator temporis acti* or as guarantor of social continuity that the *grammaticus* focuses his instruction on the great literature of the past; there is also a practical aspect to the focus on what is changeless rather than what is current. Students of language, whether children receiving formal instruction in their native language or people of any age learning a second language—a category that became ever larger for Latin instructors from the third century on—need clarity. They do not need to be told that there is more than one spelling of *maximus*; they do not need to know that the declension of third-declension nouns is often variable; they do not want too much information about the changes in Latin prosody or the increasing use of prepositions or (God forbid) that some people use the wrong case with various prepositions. We simplify. We tell lies. And we sympathize when the *grammaticus* offers his students a clearer, more uniform Latin than we know, or he knew, from real life.

There is, however, a problem with this: real life itself. What the grammarian teaches is an ideal language, or at least a simplified one, and sooner or later students inevitably learn that we have not been telling the whole truth. They recognize that there is a certain dissonance (often quite literally) between the language they learn in school and the language they hear on the street; equally problematic, particularly for someone teaching the *Aeneid*, is that they learn that even the literary language does not always conform to what they are being taught.[4] What then? There are of course multiple answers

---

[3] Gresham's Law was so named by Macleod (1858, 475–6): " . . . the illustrious Gresham, who has the great merit as far as we can discover, of being the first who discerned the great fundamental law of the currency, that good and bad money cannot circulate together."

[4] Or for someone teaching Juvenal, as shown by the fifth-century annotated manuscript of Juvenal discussed by Garcea and Scappaticcio in this volume (Chapter 9).

6 INTRODUCTION

to that question, depending on the specific aspect of Latin that is being assailed; this paper will concern only of a few of them, first from the side of the grammarian (how does the emperor respond when the students see that he has no clothes?), and then from the other side, other people's response to grammarians' rejection of linguistic variety and change. That point of view is well represented by my epigraph, taken from Wilfried Stroh's *carmen*, written originally for the *Ludi Latini* of 1983.[5]

Examples of practical responses by ancient grammarians to genuine linguistic change are fairly rare, but they exist. As we know, the sounds of Latin changed. From fairly early times, Latin stress patterns led to the weakening of unstressed vowels, to iambic shortening, the correption of final -ō and other alterations, some phonetic, some morphological. It is not difficult to find numerous examples of such changes in early Latin, but after the language became more formalized in the first century BCE they are less evident in literary texts. Quintilian complains that people swallow the ends of words and lengthen the beginnings.[6] Donatus views it as barbarism if people pronounce *deos* with long ē and short ŏ.[7] And, indeed, beginning with Servius, a new type of writing about syllables appears: instead of assuming that students would know the natural quantity of vowels and offering only an explanation of the reasons why syllables are long, short, or common, treatises *De finalibus* show pupils how to know whether a syllable is long or short, because they no longer knew it automatically.[8] And along with that, beginning with Donatus, syllables begin to be defined in a new way: instead of going through all the mute-liquid variations, grammarians start to define the syllable as always beginning with a vowel, thus reducing the number of ways a vowel can be long from seven to four.[9] That is a practical response to a genuine problem: if students were expected to speak and even write classical Latin correctly, including verses that scanned and prose with quantitative clausulae rather than the rhythmical *cursus* of contemporary usage, they needed help to navigate the differences between spoken and written language.

---

[5] I cite the text from http://stroh.userweb.mwn.de/novak/nov_texte/cantlat.htm. For the printed version see Novák 1985, 88–9 (no. XLIII).

[6] Quint. *inst.* 11.3.33 *dilucida vero erit pronuntiatio primum si verba tota exierint, quorum pars devorari, pars destitui solet, plerisque extremas syllabas non perferentibus dum priorum sono indulgent.*

[7] Don. *gramm. mai.* 3.1 p. 654.5 *ut si quis deos producta priore syllaba et correpta posteriore pronuntiet.*

[8] The basic discussions of treatises *De finalibus* are those of Leonhardt (1989, 24–71) and De Nonno (1990); for further references, see *CCC* 178.

[9] On this see Leonhardt (1989, 46–50).

COUNTERFEIT AND COINAGE   7

Nowhere, however, is the gap between literary Latin and the real world clearer than in poetry. There are obvious differences in prosody—the long *I* of *Italia*, the double *-ll-* of *relliquiae*—and making words fit the hexameter created morphological problems as well. One of the most familiar examples, and one of the earliest in the grammatical tradition, begins from Virgil's use (once in the *Eclogues*, twice in the *Georgics*) of the plural *hordea* for "barley." An early Vergiliomastix, quoted as "Bavius and Maevius" by the longer form of Servius and as "Cornificius Gallus" by the grammarian Cledonius, attacked this with the verse *hordea qui dixit, superest ut tritica dicat* ("someone who says barleys might just as well say spelts").[10] The broader grammatical question of *singularia tantum* and *pluralia tantum* is even older than Virgil: an important fragment of Caesar, *De analogia* already identified *triticum* and *harena* as singular only and *quadrigae* as plural only.[11] Quintilian treats the problem of *hordea* as old hat, and worries only whether it should be considered a barbarism because it is only the change of one or two letters within a word or a solecism because it is a grammatical mistake (*inst.* 1.5.6):

> absurdum forsitan videatur dicere barbarismum, quod est unius verbi vitium, fieri per numeros aut genera sicut soloecismum: scala tamen et scopa contraque hordea et mulsa, licet litterarum mutationem detractionem adiectionem habeant, non alio vitiosa sunt quam quod pluralia singulariter et singularia pluraliter efferuntur.

> It may seem ridiculous to say that a barbarism (a flaw in a single word) is made through [errors in] number or gender like a solecism, but *scala* and *scopa* and contrariwise *hordea* and *mulsa*, even if they have only a change, removal, or addition of letters, are not faulty for any reason other than that plurals are used as singular and singulars as plural.

Quintilian of course is perfectly well aware (as was Varro too) that poets get some leeway (1.5.11):

> scire autem debet puer haec apud scriptores carminum aut venia digna aut etiam laude duci.

---

[10] Serv. auct. *georg.* 1.210; Cledon. *gramm.* V 43.2.
[11] Caes. *anal.* frg. 11 Garcea (= Gell. 19.8.1–8). This long fragment (together with Garcea's commentary) has much else of interest.

8   INTRODUCTION

> Boys should know that such things in poetic authors are felt to deserve for-
> giveness or even praise.

Grammarians, according to Quintilian, should avoid using poetic citations as examples of barbarism because in context they are not wrong.

This passage of Quintilian alludes to, but does not define as carefully as the later grammarians do, the problem of poetic language. Virgil uses *hordea* rather than *hordeum* for metrical reasons: second-declension neuter nouns with a trochee before the final syllable can, in high-style poetry, only be used in the forms ending in *-a*. Such uses of the poetic plural (and various other grammatical peculiarities I am not concerned with) *metri causa* are classed not as barbarism, because that would lower the students' respect for the poet, but as metaplasm, which Donatus defines as the alteration of the shape of a proper prose word in poetry *metri ornatusve causa* (*gramm. mai.* 3.4 p. 660.8–9).[12] There is a set of very familiar problems of poetic prosody and morphology found in many of the fifth-century grammars, but the problems themselves are much earlier, and go back to the first century and before.[13]

Poetic language is not a very good example of linguistic change, but Virgil's *hordea* is useful because it is not simply a matter of "poetic plural" *metri gratia*, but a real question of social variation. As Courtney points out in his commentary on *hordea qui dicit, superest ut tritica dicat*, Virgil is using *hordea* not to mean "barley" as a collective noun, but to mean a bunch of individual barley corns or stalks of barley.[14] And that use of plural for individual members of a collective substance is, as Paul Maas observed more than a century ago, notably rustic and agricultural in its associations. As he says, whoever wrote this verse was accusing Virgil of transplanting his father's farmyard to Augustus' court.[15] That is one possible legitimate response to poetic metaplasm: it can at times be seen as an appropriation of specialized diction rather than simply a mistake. On the other hand, that is

---

[12] The basic distinction is given by Donatus as: *barbarismus est una pars orationis vitiosa in communi sermone, in poemate metaplasmus* (*gramm. mai.* 3.1 p. 653.2–3).

[13] Useful recent discussions of the texts on barbarism and metaplasm may be found in Mari (2017b, 31–46) and Zago (2017b, 131–73, 271–98). On Consentius' discussion of plurals *hordea* and *vina* as licensed by authority, see also Mari in this volume (Chapter 6, §2).

[14] Courtney (1993, 285–6).

[15] Maas (1973 [originally published 1902], 550): "Der Hohn scheint gegen den Bauernsohn aus Mantua gerichtet zu sein, der jene Formen von dem Gehöfte seines Vaters an den Hof des Augustus verpflanzt hatte."

COUNTERFEIT AND COINAGE 9

rare. Another response, of which we possess only one sample, is to recognize that Virgil's language is remarkably odd, particularly in its syntax. Agrippa's remark (if it is his) preserved in Donatus' life of Virgil about Virgil's new kind of *cacozelia* is one of the sharpest pieces of ancient literary criticism, but it was left to Aemilius Asper in the late second century to demonstrate its truth in his (very fragmentary) *Grammatica Vergiliana*: it is a list of differences between Virgil and normal Latin.[16] That may not be satisfactory in the long run because it admits, at least implicitly, that Virgil is not a suitable text for students who want to learn normal Latin. The most familiar response, documented for Servius in detail by Kaster in *Guardians*,[17] is to recognize Virgil's deliberate and necessary deviation from a norm *metri causa*, which the pupil should admire, but (at least when speaking prose) not copy.

There are other kinds of linguistic variation than the problems raised by poetic diction, and they come closer to the practical problems of teaching a changing language. One of the traditional forms of grammatical or rhetorical instruction was word lists, in particular lists of synonyms (which will not concern me here) and *differentiae*, which will.[18] A fair number of these lists survive, and in parts they clearly go back to the early empire or beyond. They are, in origin, aids to refinement of vocabulary: they offer distinctions between words of similar meaning, such as: *inter abstinentiam et continentiam: abstinentia est, quae ab alienis abstinet, continentia, quae continet a suis* (*diff.* ed. Beck A5); or *inter absolutum et dimissum: absolutus est, qui cum accusaretur innocens, liberatus est a crimine . . . ; dimissus est, qui sine crimine est tamquam aliquis ab amico aut servus* (*diff.* ed. Beck A6). These examples come from the list known as *inter absconditum et absconsum*, preserved in a ninth-century mainly glossographic manuscript (Montpellier, Bibliotheque Interuniversitaire H 306).[19] Another list has, for example: *inter metum et timorem et pavorem* (*diff. gramm. suppl.* p. 275.1) or *inter tacere et silere* (*diff. gramm. suppl.* p. 275.10).[20] Such lists also include some words that sound alike, such as *pellax* and *fallax* (*diff. gramm. suppl.* p. 283.13)

[16] See *CCC* 138–9.

[17] *Guardians* 168–96.

[18] Fuller discussion of the collections of *differentiae* in *CCC* 104–6, 235–6. In general, see Brugnoli (1955).

[19] Published in Beck (1883); entries are cited here according to Beck's numeration. In the manuscript the collection is ascribed to Cicero: see Brugnoli (1955, 153–82); on the manuscript, probably from Auxerre, see Bischoff (1998–2014, II: nr. 2857).

[20] Published by Hagen (1870 = *gramm. supp.*, 275–90) from three Bern manuscripts in one of which it too is ascribed to Cicero.

10   INTRODUCTION

or *officere* and *inficere* (*diff. gramm. suppl.* p. 282.7). As time goes on and Latin becomes fuzzier, the *differentiae* become more elementary: between *disertum* and *desertum* (*diff.* ed. Beck D32) or between *sus* and *suus* (*diff.* ed. Beck S34) or between *quo* and *ubi* (ps.-Caper *gramm.* VII 92.1). Sound changes come in, such as the perennial problem of *b* and *v*: Agroecius and many other glossaries explain the difference between *acervus* and *acerbus* (*gramm.* VII 114.16 = 6 Pugliarello [1978]);[21] so too between *abitum* and *habitum* (Agroec. *gramm.* VII 114.17 = 8 P.; *diff.* ed. Beck A8) or *notum* and *nothum* (*diff.* ed. Beck. N14) or *quaeritur* and *queritur* (Agroec. *gramm.* VII 116.18 = 34 P.; *diff.* ed. Beck Q2).

But then there are others. When Agroecius explains the difference between *praemium* with a diphthong and *pretium* or *precor* with a short *ĕ*, he tells his pupils that the *veteres* wanted important words to have diphthongs and be written *quadam dignitate*.[22] The difference between the vowels of *praemium* and *pretium* is found in a number of grammatical texts, but the dignity of diphthongs appears to be Agroecius' very own invention, just as there is no parallel known to me for his explanation of *s* as a liquid being the result of the weak *s* among the Etruscans (*gramm.* VII 118.7–13 = 42 P.; my translation is at best impressionistic):

> quaeritur ab aliquantis, quare s littera inter liquidas posita sit, cum vel sola facere syllabam videatur ac per hoc dicta sit "suae cuiusdam potestatis est," aliae autem liquidae in ipso concursu litterarum et sermonum ita conglutinentur, ut paene interire videantur. haec ratio est: apud Latium, unde Latinitas orta est, maior populus et magis egregiis artibus pollens Tusci fuerunt, qui quidem natura linguae suae s litteram raro exprimunt. haec res eam fecit haberi liquidam.

> Some people wonder why the letter *s* is classified as a liquid, since on its own it seems able to make a syllable and for that reason it is said "to have a certain power of its own," while other liquids are so stuck together in the meeting of letters and words that they almost seem to disappear. This is the reason: in Latium, where Latinity came from, a large population with

---

[21] See also *diff.* ed. Beck A20; Prob. *app. gramm.* IV 200.22. This part of the *Appendix Probi* is also found in Montpellier H 306, the source of the ascription to Probus.

[22] Agroec. *gramm.* VII 114.21–115.2 = 10–11 P.: *praemium cum diphthongo scribendum; pretium, precor sine diphthongo. veteres enim maioris rei sermones cum diphthongo et quadam dignitate scribi voluerunt.* For grammarians' discussion of *e*/*ae*, see Adams (2013, 75–80).

COUNTERFEIT AND COINAGE   11

strong and outstanding skills were the Tusci, who according to the nature of their language rarely pronounce the letter *s*. That made it be considered a liquid.

We all try to give our students some interesting means of remembering things that make no sense to them. Similarly, Ps.-Caper tells his pupils that no native Latin words use the letter *y* "so you can make fun of people who say *gyla*."[23]

There is a further stage in this process, less entertaining perhaps but quite significant: when the grammarians invent distinctions between words that are in fact the same. The problem of the final vowel of the noun whose genitive is *roboris* (is it *robur* or *robor*?) appears as early as Quintilian, but it is not until Agroecius that we get the explanation that *robur* has to do with *virtus*, and *robor* belongs to trees.[24] Or that *periculum* refers to *discrimen*, and *periclum* to *experimentum*.[25] Or (in the Montpellier glossary) that *accersere* is *vocare*, but *arcessere* is *accusare*.[26] The word *cohors* (or *cors* or *chors*) had several spellings, and was used in different contexts. Beck's glossary gives the *differentia* as follows: *cortes sunt rusticorum, chortes militum castra* (C36). That is wrong, but it is very old (with one spelling or another): a trace of a double etymology appears in Varro (*ling.* 5.88), although he does not seem to accept it, and Velius Longus, in the early second century CE, reports that *grammatici* make a distinction between *coortes* in the countryside, derived from *coorior*, and *cohortes* in the army, derived from *cohortatione*. Velius rejects this and derives the military use from the fact that soldiers are drafted from *rustici* and it is the same word (*gramm.* VII 74.16–75.5):

> talis quaestio est <et> circa cohortes et coortes, ubi diversam voluerunt significationem esse grammatici, ut coortes sint villarum, unde homines cooriantur pariter . . ., at cohortes militum a mutua cohortatione. nam chortes audimus quidem vulgo, sed barbare dici. de superiore differentia mihi aliud videtur . . .: nam tam militum quam rusticorum cohortes sunt, siquidem et milites e rusticis et ex eiusdem regionis hominibus conscribebantur, ut et agnoscere et tueri invicem possent.

---

[23] Ps.-Caper *gramm.* VII 105.17: *y litteram nulla vox nostra adsciscit. ideo insultabis gylam dicentibus.*

[24] Agroec. *gramm.* VII 118.19 = 47 P.: *rubor coloris est, robur virtutis, robor arboris*; cf. Quint. *inst.* 1.6.22.

[25] Agroec. *gramm.* VII 124.24 = 128 P.

[26] *diff.* ed. Beck A13. Fuller (and slightly different) discussions of *accersere/arcessere* in Char. *gramm.* 335.20–336.7 and Diom. *gramm.* I 379.11–13.

12 INTRODUCTION

There is a similar question involving *cohortes* and *coortes*, where the grammarians want there to be different meanings, that *coortes* belong to farms, from which men arise together . . . but *cohortes* of soldiers from their mutual exhortation. We often hear *chortes*, but that is a spoken barbarism. As far as the *differentia* above is concerned, I have a different opinion . . .: there are *cohortes* of soldiers as well as of countryfolk, seeing that soldiers were drafted from countryfolk and from men of the same region, so that they could recognize and protect one another.

These distinctions are of course bogus, as are many others: they suppress the possibility of phonological change or variation by positing different origins or meanings for two forms of the same word.

One last example of this kind of technique—what might be called *differentiae* without a difference—is also very old, and again is attested in Velius Longus as well as several other sources. That is the problem of the word for "shield," *clipeus*—or *clupeus* or *clipeum* or *clupeum*; take your pick. The earliest extant full discussion appears in Charisius, almost certainly taken from Julius Romanus at the beginning of the third century, but citing the elder Pliny (Char. *gramm.* p. 98.1–16):

clipeus masculino genere in significatione scuti ponitur, ut Labienus ait, neutro autem genere imaginem significat. sed Asinius pro Vrbiniae heredibus imaginis clipeum masculine dixit, "clipeus praetextae imaginis positus." et Livius in significatione scuti neutraliter saepius et Pomponius in Capella, cum ait "clipeum in medium fixum est." quare <Plinius> dubii sermonis II indistincto genere dici ait, sed littera differre, ut pugnatorium per i clipeum dicamus, quia est clipeus <ἀπὸ τοῦ κλέπτειν>, id est celare, dictus, imaginem vero per u a cluendo. sed haec differentia mihi displicet propter communionem i et u litterarum. nam et maximus et maxumus dicimus et optimus et optumus, nec tamen illa differentia secernimus.

Clipeus in the masculine is used with the meaning "shield" according to Labienus, and in the neuter it means an image. But Asinius in his speech "On Behalf of the Heirs of Urbinia" has masculine *clipeus* meaning "image": *clipeus praetextae imagine positus*. And Livy frequently uses the neuter meaning "shield" and Pomponius in *Capella*, when he says *clipeum in medium fixum est*. That is why Pliny in Book 2 of *Dubius Sermo* says that the gender doesn't matter but that there is a different spelling, so that we speak of

COUNTERFEIT AND COINAGE 13

a military shield as *clipeus* (because *clipeus* comes from the Greek κλέπτειν meaning to conceal) while for the image we spell it with a *u*, from *cluere*. But I don't like this *differentia*, since the letters *i* and *u* are shared: we say *maximus* and *maxumus* and *optimus* and *optumus*, and we don't call that a *differentia*.

There are two problems: one is the gender of the word, the other is its first vowel. And there are two possible meanings: as the Montpellier glossary puts it, "A *clipeus* is what you take into battle, i.e. *scutum*; a *clupeus* is that on which *imagines* are placed"—in other words, as we learn from other sources, round plaques with portraits on them.[27] There are also different etymologies: the word for shield is derived from *celare* or Greek κλέπτειν, to conceal, while the word for portrait plaque comes from *cluendo* or (implicitly, in Pliny's account in *nat.* 35.13) from Greek γλύφειν, to sculpt. This is, of course, learned nonsense, and some people knew that it was nonsense, as the end of the quotation from Charisius given above shows.[28] And as with *cohors*, Velius Longus says that we should pay no attention to the dumb distinction of grammarians (*vanam ... differentiam*) who derive one word from *clependo* the other from *cluendo*.[29]

Velius Longus is an interesting figure. He is, quite clearly, a class traitor, a grammarian criticizing grammarians, but while grammarians themselves do not often criticize other grammarians in their books (we do not know about the classroom, where *odium philologicum* is perhaps more unrestrained), there exists a fair amount of criticism of grammarians for being too picky, too normative, and too unwilling to welcome variation, variety, or change. It is perhaps no surprise that most such criticisms, at least the ones I have found, come from the early empire, and from people who quite clearly would rather distinguish their own scholarship from the work of mere grammarians.

One such text comes from far outside the normal grammatical canon. In one of his epigrams accompanying a gift, Martial, along with a fancy spoon (at least I think that's what it is), writes as follows (14.120):

> quamvis me ligulam dicant equitesque patresque,
> dicor ab indoctis lingula grammaticis.

---

[27] *diff.* ed. Beck C25: *inter clipeum et clupeum: "clipeus" dicitur qui ducitur in proelium, id est scutum; "clupeus" autem, in quo imagines ponuntur.* For the plaques, see Plin. *nat.* 35.13.

[28] I hesitate to assign an author to this comment; given the source problem, it could be said by Pliny, Romanus, or Charisius himself. It is probably Romanus.

[29] Vel. *gramm.* VII 68.11: *idem puto et in "clipeo" per i scripto observandum, nec audiendam vanam grammaticorum differentiam, qui alterum a clependo, <alterum a cluendo> putant dictum.*

14   INTRODUCTION

Knights and senators call me *ligula*, but I am called *lingula* by ignorant grammarians.

The only dumb grammarian who does this is Romanus (in Charisius), who is in fact not at all dumb and who makes the question slightly more complicated than Martial suggests by distinguishing the two meanings of the word and ingeniously giving them different etymologies (Char. *gramm*. p. 132.14–16):

lingula cum n a linguendo dicta est in argento; in calceis vero ligula a ligando. sed usus ligulam sine n frequentat.

Lingula with *n*, derived from *lingere* ["to lick"], is used for silverware; in the footware department it is *ligula* derived from *ligare* ["to tie"]. But in common usage *ligula* without *n* is more common [i.e., in both meanings].

Unfortunately, this tidy distinction appears to be wrong; at least Varro derived the name of a sword (related in shape to the tongue of a shoe, not to a skimming spoon) from *lingua* (*ling*. 7.107), and it appears (from a search in PHI) that while *ligula* always refers to the spoon, *lingula* has a much wider range of reference. Of course, editors may be following Martial rather than the manuscripts, and the two forms are too close palaeographically to be distinguished with any certainty. In any case, Martial's epigram reveals the same social snobbery that we find in Gellius (which Kaster has discussed),[30] and in fact it turns up in a number of passages in Charisius, which come from Romanus, who in turn has probably (I say hesitantly) taken many of them from Flavius Caper or the Elder Pliny. Old Pliny's scorn of *grammatici* is clear from the preface to the *Natural Histories* (*praef.* 28), and it appears in several passages of Charisius/ Romanus. Pliny, for instance, rejects the grammarians' rule that the accusative plural of *funis* ought to be *funeis*.[31] He seems scornful of some grammarians' idea (*quidam grammatici ita dicendum putant*) that the nominative singular of *iugera* is *iuger* like *tuber* (third declension, not second declension *iugerum*; both are found).[32] And he is contemptuous of grammarians' prescriptions when he says that we don't really know the genitive plurals of *pax* and *lux* because the grammarians have not yet made rules about monosyllables.[33]

---

[30] See *Guardians* 50–60.
[31] Plin. *dub. serm.* frg. 56 della Casa (= Char. *gramm*. p. 164.30–165.7).
[32] Plin. *dub. serm.* frg. 76 della Casa (= Char. *gramm*. p. 170.26–32).
[33] Plin. *dub. serm.* frg. 79 della Casa (= Char. *gramm*. p. 178.24–9).

COUNTERFEIT AND COINAGE   15

I am not going to try to disentangle the sources of Romanus or Charisius. Beyond the three passages that cite the Elder Pliny, there are fifteen more in which the author reports, and generally takes exception to, some rule of the grammarians, along with four more in the treatise *De nominibus dubiis*, which goes back to a relatively early source, and two more in Asper's *grammatica Vergiliana*, besides the two in Velius Longus. Not all of them are detailed enough to be useful, and some of them repeat others: Virgil's *hordea* (along with *pluralia/singularia tantum* in general, such as *scopae* and *scalae* in *De nominibus dubiis*) is (or are) a source of disgust or discussion with antecedents going back at least to Caesar; the spelling, gender, and meaning of *clupeus* get repeated; and Velius was also exercised by the broader question of the orthography and pronunciation of the *sonus medius*.

Consider, for instance, the grammarians' rule that adjectives in -*us* should not have adverbs ending in -*er*. What about *naviter, humaniter, largiter, and duriter*? The grammarians say that they belong to *antiquitas*, but are perfectly capable of regularity, *secundum suam rectam analogiam* (Char. *gramm.* p. 145.11–12; all the following citations are from Charisius). The grammarians say that *sales* in the plural can only mean *facetiae*, but Fabianus used it to mean salt (p. 135.17–136.1). Why do the grammarians say that Latin nouns ending in -*es* don't change in the genitive? I (whoever "I" is) don't understand it, unless they mean nouns ending in short -*es* (p. 168.23–7). Grammarians say that we shouldn't say *russeus* but *russus*, like *albus* and *prasinus* (p. 91.22– 4; both forms are attested). Grammarians reject the word *neptis*, because nouns ending in -*os* (*nepos*) have no alternative feminine form: see Ennius. But *consuetudo* has created *nepos* in the masculine and *neptis* in the feminine (p. 114.23–7). Grammarians say that *quis* is interrogative and *qui* is relative, *quod tamen auctores non observaverunt* (p. 115.14–15). Grammarians say that *oliva* is the tree and *olea* the fruit, *sed veteres hoc non observaverunt* (p. 125.23–4). Grammarians say that *insomnia* plural means the same as *somnia* (and cite Virgil) and in the singular (feminine) means *vigilia* (and cite Pacuvius). But Virgil... (p. 129.1–12). Some grammarians think you can make adverbs from participles and pronouns and verbs, but I think they're wrong. They think *sapienter* comes from a participle, but *sapiens* is a noun as well as a participle. Any adverbs that come from pronouns only exist in books by grammarians, *in consuetudine non videmus*. If they ever existed, they are obsolete *consensu publici usus* (p. 240.31–241.1).

Detailed examination of one problematic area will suffice, the various rules governing the relationship of the nominative and the genitive

16   INTRODUCTION

of third-declension nouns. One rule governs Greek names ending in *-is*. According to Romanus (p. 113.8–11), grammarians say that all Greek names ending in *-is* ought to be one syllable longer in the genitive than in the nominative: thus the genitive of *Sarapis* is *Sarapidis*, not *Sarapis*, and of *Iris* it is *Iridis* (the same rule appears verbatim at p. 169.13–19 in the chapter on analogy, where Romanus discusses the use of *Irim* in *Aen*. 9.2). Yet, he adds, "since we can decline them in Latin, there is no need to shape *consuetudo* by *ratio*, especially since we have authorities . . . ," and he cites Varro and Virgil, the latter using not only *Irim*, but *Parim* et *Tigrim*.[34] Two things about this are worth noting. One is the almost explicit equation of *ratio* and *grammaticus* as parallel opponents of *consuetudo*, to which I will return; the other is that in fact the only other grammarian to talk about the declension of *Iris*, Sacerdos (an identical account in Probus' *Catholica*), classifies nouns differently and says simply that nouns in the third declension ending in *-ris* have either *-ris* or *-dis* in the genitive, and that both *Iridis* and *Iris* are correct (Sacerd. *gramm*. VI 478.19 = Prob. *gramm*. IV 27.27).

The other problematic grammarian's rule concerning the genitive is the claim that no genitive should be more than one syllable longer than its nominative. A few words break this rule, notably *anceps* (and *praeceps*), *iter*, *iecur*, and *supellex*. The last of these seems to be the biggest problem, and *supellex* is one of the most frequently discussed words in Charisius. First, in a section of the grammar that is not based on Romanus, Charisius gives the rule: "all masculine and feminine nouns in the singular grow by no more than one syllable, and so I think we should say *supellectilis*, not *supellex* and *ancipes* rather than *anceps*."[35] This is helpfully contradicted in the chapter on analogy according to Romanus, where there are two not quite adjacent entries for *supellex* that discuss the problem, but solve it by applying two quite different rules. The first tells us that the grammarians have thought that this is an exception, contrary to the above stated rule, because its genitive is *supellectilis*.

---

[34] Char. *gramm*. p. 113.8–17: *Sarapis Sarapidis volunt grammatici genitivo caso dici, non Sarapis, quia omnia nomina Graecae figurae is terminata in genitivo syllaba crescere debent, ut Iris Iridis. . . . sed cum et Latine declinari possint, non est necesse consuetudinem ratione reformare, praesertim cum adsit auctoritas . . .*

[35] Char. *gramm*. p. 58.26–30: *omnia masculini et feminini generis vocabula singulari numero in declinatione non plus quam una syllaba increscunt, unde mihi videtur non supellex, sed supellectilis esse dicendum, et <ancipes> ancipitis <potius> quam anceps*. With this, see also Char. *gramm*. p. 110.26–111.4: *supellex magis auctoritate dicitur quam ratione. nam non debet duabus syllabis plus crescere a nominativo genetivus. quam rationem ut custodirent veteres, multa dure protulerunt, ut ancipes pro anceps et praecipes pro praeceps. nec tamen quisquam haec supellectilis dicere ausus est, et ideo rectius est cum pluribus stare et quod speciosius est in loquendo proferre*. Note that after *praeceps* Putschius (followed by Barwick) added *et supellectilis pro supellex*, which is rightly deleted by Uría (2009).

COUNTERFEIT AND COINAGE   17

Then, seemingly unconnected, comes the observation "But their ending is -*gis*, as in *gregis regis remigis*."[36] This last sentence identifies the rule in question, which appears a page earlier under the rubric *supellectilis*: "This is the one exception to the rule that genitives should grow by one syllable, both because it shouldn't be shorter than the dative and because the nominative ends in -*x*, which is a double letter."[37] The rule (which also appears elsewhere) is that nouns ending in -*x*, because it is a double consonant, grow by one syllable in the genitive, as in *rex, regis*.[38]

The second discussion of *supellex* does not mention the grammarians explicitly, but is quite opinionated: "*Supellex*. They say that some people have claimed that a nominative *supellectilis* is possible, so that the genitive not grow by two syllables. But we (Charisius himself? Romanus?) have not yet found a suitable example of people talking that way, like *ancipes* and *praecipes*, which antiquity has disgustingly produced in accordance with *ratio*."[39] *Ratio* here looks back to the other, more common rule, that nouns should not grow by more than one syllable. And what about this alleged nominative *supellectilis*? Only one grammarian, Priscian, supports it, and he does so by citing a fragment from the Elder Cato, which can, in fact, as easily be construed as genitive as it can as nominative.[40] Charisius, or Romanus, is quite right to say that he has never found it, and that it is just a rancid grammarian's rule, as elsewhere (110.29) he calls it *dure* (not *duriter*) and says that *supellex* has *auctoritas* rather than *ratio*.

There are more references to *grammatici* in the *Grammatici Latini*, but I need not go further in listing them. References to generic *grammatici* are

---

[36] Char. *gramm*. p. 182.18–21: *supellex. et hoc inter excepta esse praeter regulam supra scriptam notandum grammatici putaverunt. nam supellectilis facit. gis autem finiuntur ut gregis regis remigis.*

[37] Char. *gramm*. p. 181.20–3: *supellectilis. genetivus una syllaba crescere debet excepto hoc nomine, et quia dativo minor esse non debet et qua nominativus in x littera, quae duplex est, terminatur.*

[38] There is another exception, *senex*, but it presents a different problem, and I will not discuss it here.

[39] Char. *gramm*. p. 182.27–183.4: *supellex. quosdam nominativo haec supellectilis posse dici temptasse rettulerunt, ne genetivus duabus syllabis cresceret. sed necdum nobis idoneum proin loquentis occurrit exemplum, velut ancipes et praecipes, quod vetustas cum ratione rancidum protulit.* With this, see also Char. *gramm*. p. 58.21, 59.27, 60.2, 111.15. The passage is also discussed by Zago in this volume (text no. 7).

[40] Prisc. *gramm*. II 279.15–18: *supellex supellectilis (vetustissimi tamen etiam haec supellectilis nominativum proferebant. Cato adversum Tiberium Sempronium Longum [= orat. 161]: "si posset auctio fieri de artibus tuis, quasi supellectilis solet")* . . . . One other grammarian's note on the subject, this time anonymous, is incompletely preserved in Festus (p. 378.11–20 L. = p. 294 M.), using the rule about words in -*x* "*Supellectilis* and *senis* used to be said (*dicebantur*) in the nominative, but now are seen to be contrary to the rule of analogy according to which words ending in -*x* get another syllable in oblique cases. These two have seceded from the rule [corrupt text] but that should not weaken the principle." Festus gives no example of nominative *supellectilis*.

18 INTRODUCTION

virtually always critical, and they are critical for the same reason: grammarians posit rules that are rigid and artificial; they represent *ratio* and analogy. They at times invent rules that have no examples, such as *supellectilis*, and even more often they invent rules that are contrary to the practice of earlier writers (*auctoritas*) and to what people do in fact say (*consuetudo*). The vocabulary used here—*ratio, consuetudo, auctoritas*—has a very familiar context: these are the standard criteria, mutually inconsistent, but omnipresent, for *Latinitas*.[41]

And it is with the fraught relationship between *Latinitas* and *grammatica* that I want to conclude. Although virtually all the material I have talked about that attacks grammarians comes from grammars, that peculiarity reflects the fact that the larger late antique grammars are the heirs of two very different traditions of talking about language, each of which views itself as a guardian of language (to use Kaster's title) against (to use my own title) counterfeiting, bad coinages, and Gresham's Law. Each tradition portrays itself as beleaguered, but the enemies they are warding off, and probably their own social positions in the war for linguistic purity, are very different. From the point of view of the *grammaticus*, the enemy is the decline to barbarism, in both senses of that word: quantities must be preserved; endings must be correct; speakers of Latin should not put singular-only words into the plural. This is normative grammar, and it is directed to students in the classroom. In aid of that, the grammarian creates helpful rules to guide beginners in the creation of correct forms: nouns can grow by no more than one syllable in the oblique cases. *Quis* is interrogative, *qui* is relative. Nouns ending in *-os* are of common gender and have no separate feminine. All second-declension adjectives in *-us* have adverbs in *-e*. The grammarian is the agent or enforcer of *ratio*, and for a good reason: as I said before, students need clarity and order. We don't teach elementary classes the exceptions and the variables: we teach them the rules that they will later learn do not always apply. You don't start teaching the third conjugation with *fero*.

But *Latinitas* is something very different. Where the grammarian is defending against ignorance, the Latinist (there is no better name for him) is defending against impoverishment. The Latinist, at least the most prominent examples of the breed, is not a grammarian by profession. Pliny the Elder, Caper, Romanus: the first certainly, the others almost certainly, never saw

---

[41] For discussion of the language of *Latinitas* see Zetzel (2019); on the relationship between (normative) grammar and (descriptive) *Latinitas* see also Zetzel (2015).

COUNTERFEIT AND COINAGE   19

an elementary classroom, any more than Aulus Gellius or Fronto did.[42] They are amateurs, lovers of the Latin language. They relish the exceptions; they hunt out exquisite lections; and their rhetoric makes the *grammaticus* into a figure of fun, rigidity, and stupid rules that are fine for children, but not for gentlemen. For the grammarian, language is a synchronic system that needs regularity and correctness to function; for the Latinist, language embodies history, change, and variety, and is to be savored as well as understood. The grammarian guards against future decline; the Latinist laments past losses. In the late antique battle to define Latin, the grammarian was very clearly the winner: the simplifying, regularizing, and analytic Donatus exists in hundreds of manuscripts, while not a single work *De Latinitate* survives complete. That story is of course not complete: a remarkable new version of *Latinitas* arose, represented most memorably in Gregory the Great's injunction: it is shameful to constrain the oracle of heaven by the rules of Donatus.[43] But instead of the multiplicity and charm of Republican Latin literature, it is the vulgar Latin of the Vulgate that is opposed to the grammarian's commands.[44] I cannot help thinking, with a degree of regret, that this is one more instance of the operation of Gresham's Law.

[42] On these authors see Holford-Strevens in this volume (Chapter 11).

[43] Greg. M. *moral. epist.* 5: *non metacismi collisionem fugio, non barbarismi confusionem devito, situs modosque etiam et praepositionum casus servare contemno, quia indignum vehementer existimo, ut verba caelestis oraculi restringam sub regulis Donati.*

[44] See also *CCC* 83–8 for further discussion of treatises on *Latinitas* and 214–17 on Christian ideas of Latinity.

PART I
VARRO

2

Varro the Conservative?

Katharina Volk

Marcus Terentius Varro, we are told, was an archconservative.[1] Born in Reate, among the backward-looking Sabines, the great polymath, so Hellfried Dahlmann surmises, was raised "in den alten strengen Auffassungen der *mores maiorum*"[2] and, witnessing the unraveling of the Roman Republic, kept hankering after the ideal past his etymological and antiquarian studies aimed to uncover. In the words of Andrew Drummond, "his preoccupation with the threatened or actual loss of Rome's past, traditional values, and identity undoubtedly represents a reaction, by a man of profoundly conservative outlook, to what he saw as a deep contemporary crisis."[3] Being, in the assessment of Eduard Norden, "ein echtes Kind der Romantik,"[4] Varro composed what Manfred Fuhrmann has labeled "Vergangenheitsliteratur,"[5] backward-looking writing, with the help of which he aimed, thus again Dahlmann, to lead his fellow citizens back "zu den großen alten Zeiten der Vergangenheit."[6] Exhibiting, according to Elizabeth Rawson, a "perpetual tendency to assume that the *maiores* were all-wise and all-knowing"[7] and generally viewing Rome's past greatness as a kind of paradise lost, he aimed to reconstruct and

---

[1] I am grateful to Adam Gitner for inviting me to contribute to the Cologne conference and this volume. I am grateful to Jim Zetzel for comments on a draft. But I am most grateful, for his friendship and support through so many years, to Bob Kaster, *amicissimus* and γραμματικώτατος. This paper, which retains some festures of its original oral delivery, is part of my exploration, across a number of publications (Volk 2016; 2019; and 2021, 182–200, 211–24), of Varro's intellectual *modus operandi*. I refer the reader to these other publications for more in-depth discussion of many of the issues I can mention only briefly here.

[2] Dahlmann (1935, 1173).

[3] Drummond (2013, 416).

[4] Norden (1901, 254). Norden views Varro as representative of a general spirit of nostalgic romanticism in the Late Republic, but is somewhat perplexed to observe "daß unter dem Mantel des gläubigen und positivistischen Romantikers so oft der Pferdefuß des Rationalisten hervorsieht" (ibid.).

[5] Fuhrmann (1987, 141), generally on Roman literature from the Middle Republic to the Augustan Age that treats the past "im Dienst einer vor allem mit moralischen Kriterien operierenden Zeitkritik" (142).

[6] Dahlmann (1935, 1181). Similar ideas are found in, e.g., Tarver (1997) and Peglau (2003).

[7] Rawson (1972, 35); cf. her comment on the same page that "[t]he new antiquarianism of the fifties proclaimed its conservative political ends frankly." See also Rawson (1985, 236–47).

Katharina Volk, *Varro the Conservative?* In: *Roman Perspectives on Linguistic Diversity*. Edited by Adam Gitner, Oxford University Press. © Oxford University Press 2023. DOI: 10.1093/oso/9780197611975.003.0002

24 VARRO

revive past practices and linguistic usage, and found in the archaic forms of Latin the holy grail of "die reine Latinitas."[8] These quotations span over a century and attest to a view of Varro that has remained remarkably stable: in the most recent volume of papers on the man from Reate, the editors in their introduction still state as a matter of course that "Varro represented his time as one of crisis, lamenting the loss of past traditions."[9]

The picture that emerges, in short, is that of a man who diagnoses a decline that has led Rome to a moment of crisis; turns to the study of the past to uncover the state of things in earlier, unspoiled times; and intends his work as part of an effort to restore this past glory and bring about a return of at least some version of the good old days. This portrait of Varro as a nostalgic, romantic, conservative, or even reactionary *laudator temporis acti* has, on the face of it, a lot of plausibility. Roman authors in general and those of the Late Republic in particular do tend toward narratives of decline, and as the archetypal antiquarian, Varro through much of his work focused on research into the past. The idea that his backward-looking scholarship was motivated by disenchantment with the present also fits well with larger narratives about the birth of critical thinking at Rome from a feeling of crisis in the socially and politically turbulent period of the Late Republic.[10] The question remains, is this view of Varro as a conservative actually correct?

The short answer is that we do not know. Unlike in the case of, say, Cicero and Sallust, we have very little sense of Varro's opinions. With the exception of *De re rustica*, no complete work of his survives, and we are sadly bereft of prefatory material that might have given us some idea of what Varro thought he was doing. There are no letters, and even if there were, it might not be so easy to interpret them: Varro's correspondent Cicero apparently found it challenging to get a grip on his cryptic and difficult contemporary.[11] As a result, we must tease out any evidence from the bits and pieces of Varro's fragmentary works and have to live with the very real possibility that we might be completely missing the point.

---

[8] Dahlmann (1935, 1207): "Mit der Klarlegung der Herkunft, der Etymologie der alten Wörter ... verfolgt er ganz praktische Zwecke, insofern er in dem alten Sprachidiom die reine Latinitas sieht"; similarly Grebe (2001, 142).

[9] Arena and Mac Góráin (2017, 3). See also Leonardis (2019) for a sustained recent argument for Varro's conservatism. A related Varronian stereotype is the author's supposed love of all things Sabine, on which see de Melo, Chapter 3 in this volume.

[10] See Fuhrmann (1987); Moatti (1997; "birth of critical thinking" comes from the title of the 2015 English translation of her book).

[11] On the not always easy relationship of Cicero and Varro, see Kumaniecki (1962) and Rösch-Binde (1998).

VARRO THE CONSERVATIVE? 25

Before coming to the putative conservatism of Varro's work, let me point out briefly that he was not necessarily a political conservative. Of course, like Cicero he supported Pompey in Greece, and after the Battle of Pharsalus and Caesar's pardon found himself in a somewhat awkward situation at Rome. Unlike Cicero, however, he had been a lifelong supporter of Pompey, served on Caesar's land commission in 59, and during Caesar's rule dedicated his *Antiquitates rerum divinarum* to him and was tapped by the dictator for organizing his planned public library. If Cicero was a moderate some-time optimate, Varro might perhaps be described as a lapsed *popularis*.[12] Needless to say, political affiliation, such as it was in the Late Republic, need not map onto any larger worldview: the Caesarian Sallust bemoaned Rome's political disintegration and moral decline as much as the reactionary Cato.

As for Varro the writer, it is impossible for me in this paper to survey every single one of his extant and fragmentary works. There are certainly individual places where the author or a speaker appear to deplore some kind of decline, but especially in the fragments, context is difficult to assess, and the work's topic and genre must be taken into account. Thus, for example, there is a lot of griping about deteriorated morality in the *Menippean Satires*—but these represent exactly the kind of writing where we would expect a display of curmudgeonly conservatism.[13] Generally speaking, it is not that Varro never plays the "decline card"; it is just that it is only one of the many in his deck.

Apart from this, it is a fair bet that a *diligentissimus investigator antiquitatis* (Cic. *Brut.* 60) has a certain interest in or even enthusiasm for the past. Large parts of the Varronian corpus focus on *antiquitates* in one way or another, whether archaic word forms, old Roman cults, the origins of Latin drama, the genealogy of ancient *gentes*, or the prehistory of the Roman people itself.[14] In

---

[12] This does not mean that "Cicero and Varro were on opposite sides of an ideological divide" or that Varro was a committed champion of the rights of the Roman people, as suggested by Wiseman (2009, 107–29; quotation at 112). As so much else about him, Varro's political views are ultimately unknowable. He has often been thought to have been a kind of career politician and general, who did his job without larger ambitions; Dahlmann (1935, 1176) suggests that "[e]r war im Grunde eine durchaus unpolitische Natur."

[13] On the putative conservatism of the *Satires*, see Leonardis (2014; who, however, unlike me takes them as serious expressions of Varro's own opinion); by contrast, Scholz (2003) finds no nostalgic hankering for the good old days and sees Varro as the proponent of a "in der zeitgenössichen Lebenswirklichkeit praktizierbare Ethik der Mitte" (184). Another work that might have featured (a) narrative(s) of decline is Varro's "biography" of the Roman people, *De vita populi Romani*: a number of (typically context-less) fragments appear to refer to the influx of *luxuria* or other developments with negative connotations. The history of agriculture in *De re rustica* features elements of both progress and decline, as shown by Nelsestuen (2017).

[14] For Varro's focus on and approaches to the past, see Schröter (1963), Moatti (1997, 143–5), Romano (2003), Piras (2017), Leonardis (2019), and Volk (2019).

26   VARRO

the few passages, mostly in *De lingua Latina*, where Varro talks about his scholarly, especially etymological efforts, it becomes clear that he views his task as one of recovering a past that has become obliterated through the passage of time, *vetustas*. As he observes, "few things have not been distorted by *vetustas*, many have been removed," and it is thus his goal "to dig up as best I can what has become covered up by the passage of time."[15]

But does engaging in historical research and reconstruction automatically entail dissatisfaction with the present and a wish to bring back a superior past state of things? In the case of Varro, much depends on how one views the ravages of *vetustas*.[16] Is the passage of time simply a natural process that erodes earlier stages and our knowledge of them, or is the development by which the past becomes increasingly forgotten and irrecoverable caused by human failing? The following famous passage from the *Antiquitates rerum divinarum* is the prime—and pretty much only—piece of evidence for the posited Varronian ambition for a restoration of the past (frg. 2a = Aug. *civ.* 6.2)[17]:

> se timere ne pereant (*sc.* dei), non incursu hostili, sed civium neglegentia, de qua illos velut ruina liberari a se . . . et in memoria bonorum per eius modi libros recondi atque servari utiliore cura, quam Metellus de incendio sacra Vestalia et Aeneas de Troiano excidio penates liberasse praedicatur.

> [Varro says] that he is afraid that the gods will perish, not because of an enemy attack but because of the citizens' neglect. From this [he says] he is liberating them as from a collapse and committing them to the memory of good men through his books of this kind, saving them in a more useful fashion than Metellus is said to have saved the sacred implements of Vesta from conflagration and Aeneas the Penates from the fall of Troy.

According to this assessment, the collapse (*ruina*) of religious knowledge at Rome is caused by *civium neglegentia*. Varro to the rescue: he will "liberate" the forgotten gods just as Metellus saved the Palladium and Aeneas the Penates.

But to what purpose? Varro does not apparently envisage a restoration of old cults and temples (he is no Augustus), but simply wishes to remind his

---

[15] *ling.* 5.5 *vetustas pauca non depravat, multa tollit*; 6.2 *quae obruta vetustate ut potero eruere conabor.*

[16] On this issue, compare Romano (2003, 102–8).

[17] All fragments of *ARD* are quoted from the edition of Cardauns (1976).

VARRO THE CONSERVATIVE? 27

fellow citizens of each god's character and sphere of influence, so that they can invoke the right one when need be (*ARD* frg. 3 = Aug. *civ.* 4.22):

> pro ingenti beneficio . . . iactat praestare se civibus suis, quia non solum commemorat deos, quas coli oporteat a Romanis, verum etiam dicit, quid ad quemque pertinet. quoniam nihil prodest . . . hominis alicuius medici nomen formamque nosse, et quod sit medicus ignorare, ita . . . nihil prodesse scire deum esse Aesculapium, si nescias eum valetudini opitulari atque ita ignores, cur ei debeas supplicare.

> [Varro] boasts that he is doing an immense service to his fellow citizens by telling them not only which gods ought to be worshiped by the Romans, but also which of them is in charge of what. For just as it is of no use to know the name and looks of a certain man who is a doctor, but not to know that he *is* a doctor, thus it is useless to know that Aesculapius is a god if you don't know that he is in charge of health, and are thus ignorant of why you should pray to him.

Varro thus presents himself as a pragmatic benefactor (see *beneficio*) who is making himself useful (see *utiliore cura* in *ARD* frg. 2a) by telling the Romans which god is in charge of what.

Taken together, the two passages hardly amount to a sustained program of deploring the present, elevating the past, and spearheading a return to the glory that was Rome once upon a time. Criticism of the present is muted: the citizens have neglected the gods, but is this a sign of decline or just the way of the world? No more is said about this, at least not in the fragments we possess. There is something desirable about the past, namely the fact that people still knew their gods. But here the problems start: which past and which gods? When did religious *neglegentia* set in, in Varro's own time or long ago? When was the past to which this is the present? Is Varro going to tell us about the gods of our grandfathers' time—or about those of the period of the kings? As even a cursory reading of the *Antiquitates rerum divinarum* shows, Roman religion is and has always been in flux: different kings and civic leaders established different cults and imported more and more gods; Rome went from aniconic worship to the use of cult images; foreign religious practices made their way into the city, and occasionally were kicked out again;[18] temples were built and torn down. It would be hard to pin down a moment when Roman

---

[18] For Varro's treatment of oriental cults across his works, see Rolle (2017).

28 VARRO

religion was in an ideal state—and Varro does not seem to be interested in doing so. Rather, he tells it how it was and is, warts and all, including even such questionable aspects of Roman religious life as theatrical festivals.[19]

Varro's point thus does not seem to be to celebrate let alone bring back the past, but simply to teach his fellow Romans about it. In the *Academica*, Cicero puts into Varro's mouth the following statement of his scholarly goals: "I endeavored, as much as I could, to make known to our countrymen those things that no one had taught before and that those interested were not able to learn from any other source."[20] This seems to be a reasonable description of what Varro is doing in the *Antiquitates*: telling the Romans about their gods, recovering the knowledge that *vetustas* and *neglegentia* have obscured. While he advertises the practical usefulness of his work—people may now be able to pray to the gods much more efficiently—there is no sense that Varro himself intends to lead a religious revival, and the *Antiquitates* proclaims no do's and don't's. The antiquarian provides the information; this information is potentially useful; but any use that people want to make of it is up to them.

But in keeping with this volume's theme, let us finally move on to language and language change. Is it the case that, as Dahlmann surmised, Varro was on a quest for "die reine Latinitas" and aimed, as it were, at purifying the language of the tribe? Once again, it is fairly clear that Varro just *loved* old words and enjoyed unraveling their hidden meaning or obscured morphology. But does this mean that he thought that older was better and that the Latin language had declined?

Any such putative nostalgia is complicated by the fact that like Roman religion, the Latin language does not have one past, but many.[21] Even if a thousand *verba primigenia* were established through the original *impositio* of such royal *onomatothetai* as Latinus and Romulus, it is clear that they are not the only source of Latin vocabulary and also that there have been numerous

---

[19] Augustine is indignant about Varro's discussion of *ludi scaenici* in a work on religion (*civ.* 4.1 = Varro *ARD* Bk. 10 testimonia Cardauns; *civ.* 4.31 = Varro *ARD* frg. 12 Cardauns), but as his quotations show, Varro's attitude was exactly that he had to describe the actual religious practices of the Romans and not construct an ideal religion from scratch. For further discussion, see Volk (2016; 2019; and 2021, 211–18).

[20] Cic. *ac.* 1.8 *quae autem nemo adhuc docuerat nec erat unde studiosi scire possent, ea quantum potui...feci ut essent nota nostris.*

[21] As Romano (2003) shows, "ancient" (*antiquum* or *vetus*) is a relative term for Varro: something is "old" by virtue of being older than something else, and there is always a past deeper than the one previously established; compare Piras (2017). Varro throughout his work likes to explore remote strata of time, e.g., tracing back the *origo gentis Romanae* in his eponymous work not to Romulus and Remus or Aeneas but to the Ogygian flood. Generally on Varro's ideas of prehistory, see Della Corte (1976).

VARRO THE CONSERVATIVE? 29

developments since.[22] Words have been borrowed from Greek, Sabine, and other languages; new *impositiones* are taking place even now; *declinatio voluntaria* continuously derives new words from old ones; and poets keep enriching the language with their own inventions and formations.[23] When exactly was there an ideal state of pure Latinity?

By definition, the part of *De lingua Latina* most directly concerned with Latin's past were the books on etymology, of which we still possess three. At the beginning of the first of these, Varro defines the task of the etymologist remarkably similarly to that of the religious antiquarian as described in the *Divine Antiquities* (*ling.* 5.5):

> illa quae iam maioribus nostris ademit oblivio, fugitiva secuta sedulitas Muci et Bruti retrahere nequit. non, si non potuero indagare, eo ero tardior, sed velocior ideo, si quivero. non mediocris enim tenebrae in silva ubi haec captanda neque eo quo pervenire volumus semitae tritae, neque non in tramitibus quaedam obiecta quae euntem retinere possent.

> What forgetting took away already from our ancestors, the eagerness of Mucius and Brutus cannot bring back, even though it pursued the fugitives. But even if I cannot track them down, I will not therefore follow them any more slowly, but even more quickly if there is a chance that I will succeed. For there is not inconsiderable darkness in the forest where one must catch them, nor are there welltrodden paths on which to reach the place where we want to go, and there are many obstacles in the road that can hold up the traveler.

Once again, the Romans have been affected by *oblivio*, and once again, Varro sets out to recover what has been lost or even run away. The image initially seems to be that of a fugitive slave,[24] though the evocation of the woods shifts the metaphor into one of tracking down and hunting animals. The darkness and obstacles on the path are caused by language change, the various

---

[22] Number of *verba primigenia*: *ling.* 6.36–7; royal namegivers: *ling.* 5.9.

[23] On *declinatio*, see Zanker, Ch. 4 in this volume; on Varro's view of Latin's relationship to Greek, see Gitner (2015); on his ideas about things Sabine, see de Melo, Chapter 3 in this volume; on his possible intuition of cognate relationships (in the modern sense) among Greek, Latin, and Sabellic, see Ferriss-Hill (2014); on the diverse origins and non-static nature of Latin according to Varro, see Dench (2005, 316–21).

[24] This idea is reinforced by the joking reference to two famous lawyers, Mucius (Scaevola) and (M. Iunius) Brutus (it is not clear which Scaevola Varros is referring to; more than one of them excelled as a jurist).

30 VARRO

processes that render words phonetically and morphologically unrecognizable and semantically incomprehensible. Varro has no illusions about how much Latin has changed over time (*ling.* 5.3):

> quae ideo sunt obscuriora, quod neque omnis impositio verborum exstat, quod vetustas quasdam delevit, nec quae exstat sine mendo omnis imposita, nec quae recte est imposita, cuncta manet (multa enim verba litteris commutatis sunt interpolata), neque omnis origo est nostrae linguae e vernaculis verbis, et multa verba aliud nunc ostendunt, aliud ante significabant (ut hostis: nam tum eo uerbo dicebant peregrinum qui suis legibus uteretur, nunc dicunt eum quem tum dicebant perduellem).

> These matters are rather unclear because (i) not every introduced word still exists and the passage of time has destroyed some; (ii) not every word that exists was established flawlessly; (iii) not every one that was established correctly remains whole (for many words have been altered because letters were changed); (iv) not all the vocabulary of our language consists of native words; and (v) many words now denote something different from their original meaning, e.g., *hostis*: in the past, they used this for a foreigner living by his own laws, now they refer with it to the kind of person they used to call a *perduellis* [enemy].

This change, however, is not a terrible thing. Varro views it as a natural process, akin to human aging and the succession of generations (*ling.* 5.5):

> quem puerum vidisti formosum, hunc vides deformem in senecta. tertium seculum non videt eum hominem quem vidit primum.

> The man you saw handsome as a boy, you see disfigured in old age. The third generation does not see the same man the first one saw.

Of course, one might grieve over the physical deterioration of individual human beings or feel wistful at the turnover of generations, but there is no point getting upset about it, nor is it anyone's fault. If you are a member of the third generation, you cannot bring back the man from the first, nor do you want to—just as you do not want to start again using *hostis* to mean "stranger" if all your contemporaries employ it to say "enemy." What you can do, and what Varro wants to do, is find out what happened in those earlier generations of words—and how we got from there to here.

VARRO THE CONSERVATIVE?   31

But even Varro knows that the past is too deep and that we cannot always recover the true origin of a word. He famously expresses his doubts as to whether he will ever gain knowledge of the fourth and final step of etymology (*ling.* 5.8–9) and declares himself satisfied with elucidating the myriad processes of *declinatio* without understanding what lies behind each and every *impositio*.[25] It would be nice, for example, to know where *equus* comes from, but the inability to do so does not detract from the achievement of the etymologist who can explain that *equus* has given rise to *eques*, and *eques* to *equitatus*.[26] After all, you do not even know the name of your great-great-great-grandfather's mother, so why would you expect that even someone as learned as Varro can elucidate the gobbledygook of the *carmen Saliare* for you?[27] There is so much to learn about the past; it does not matter if some things just have to remain unknown.

To move toward a conclusion: no, I do not think Varro was a conservative. There is little evidence that he generally thought of his own time as one of decline; that he believed that things were always better in the past; or that he wanted to restore some earlier, better stage of religious or linguistic practice, or even to preserve the present state for future generations. What he wanted is to *know* about the past, know as much as possible, and pass it on to his fellow Romans. That is the *beneficium* he envisages: rendering the Romans more informed about their own language and culture, furnishing them with a knowledge that might have practical uses but that also has a much wider cultural significance. In Cicero's famous homage in the *Academica*, Varro's works for the first time make the Romans feel at home in their own city and enable them to "know who [they] are."[28] It is not about the greatness of Rome,

[25] On this issue, see further Zanker, Ch. 4 in this volume.

[26] *ling.* 7.4 *qui ostendit equitatum esse ab equitibus, equites ab equite, equitem ab equo neque equus unde sit dicit, tamen hic docet plura et satisfacit grato* ("Whoever shows that *equitatus* comes from *equites, equites* from *eques*, and *eques* from *equus*, but does not say where *equus* is from, nevertheless imparts much knowledge and satisfies a grateful student.").

[27] *ling.* 7.3 *cur scriptoris industriam reprehendas qui herois tritavum, atavum non potuerit reperire, cum ipse tui tritavi matrem dicere non possis? quod intervallum multo tanto propius nos, quam hinc ad initium Saliorum, quo Romanorum prima verba poetica dicunt Latina* ("Why would you find fault with a writer's diligence if he cannot find out who the great-great-great-grandfather or great-great-grandfather of some hero was, when you yourself cannot name your great-great-great-grandfather's mother? That's much closer to us in time than from today back to the composition of the Salian Hymn, which they say was the earliest Latin poetic text of the Romans.").

[28] Cic. *ac.* 1.9 *nam nos in nostra urbe peregrinantis errantisque tamquam hospites tui libri quasi domum deduxerunt, ut possemus aliquando qui et ubi essemus agnoscere* ("For when we were wandering disoriented in our own city like strangers, your books led us home, as it were, so that we were finally able to understand who and where we were.").

32   VARRO

whether in the past or the present, it is about Rome's *identity*, in all its synchronic and diachronic intricacy and messiness.

The programmatic fragment 3 of the *Antiquitates rerum divinarum*, partly quoted above, ends with the jocular comment that as a result of Varro's religious research, "we" (i.e, Varro and his readers) will not "do what the mime actors do and ask Liber for water and the Lymphae for wine."[29] The point here can hardly be that mime dialogue reflects a general state of religious decline at Rome or that Varro's readers really did not know of what beverage Liber was in charge. What is wrong with the characters in the mime, and what makes them funny, is not that they are bad but that they are *ignorant*—and it is ignorance that Varro is endeavoring to dispel. To quote once more from the related fragment 2a, Varro's mission is to establish, by means of his books, knowledge *in memoria bonorum*. Who are these *boni*? Are they Cicero's right-thinking republicans? Are they good men? The best and brightest? The cool people? They are clearly members of the elite, the upper-class Romans for whom Varro is writing. At the same time, it seems to me that Varro is using the adjective proleptically: it is through Varro's books that his readers become *boni*: people who know, who are aware of the past, who are at home in their own city.

Thus Varro is not a guardian of language, or Roman religion, or any other closed, fixed, and idealized set of data or area of expertise. Rather than defining and delimiting knowledge, he is continuously expanding and exploding it. In the weird and wonderful school of Varro, there is always so much more to learn.

---

[29] *ARD* frg. 3 . . . *ne faciamus, ut mimi solent, et optemus a Libero aquam, a Lymphis vinum.*

3
Varro and the Sabine Language in the *De lingua Latina*

Wolfgang D. C. de Melo

1. Misleading First Impressions

I had the idea for this chapter when I read Gitner (2015), a clear and convincing piece that examines how Varro envisaged the relationship between Greek and Latin. I felt that a similar piece was needed for Sabine and Latin in his *De lingua Latina*. After all, Varro was born in Reate, on Sabine territory, was already referred to as *Reatinus* in ancient times, and mentions the Sabines and the Sabine language regularly. My main worry was that I might have too much material for a single article.

I soon realized that I need not have worried. First impressions can be misleading, and the idea that Varro is in any way preoccupied with Sabine is such a misleading first impression, albeit one that has become enshrined in the secondary literature, where much has been made of Varro's Sabine origins, local pride, and his ideas about the relationship between Latin and Sabine (see for example Poucet 1967 or, to a lesser extent, Terrosi Zanco 1961).[1] This emphasis in itself makes it worthwhile looking at the *De lingua Latina* afresh, so that we can correct or at least modify older views that have now become the *communis opinio*.

In this chapter, I want to answer three questions. First, to what extent has Varro's enthusiasm for the Sabine language been overstated? How prominent is Sabine in the *De lingua Latina* compared with other languages like Greek or Gaulish?[2] Here, some basic figures and statistics will be helpful. Second, how

---

[1] Burman (2017, 179) discusses thirty-nine Varronian glosses, of which only fifteen come from Varro, and rightly notes that it is only in modern times that Varro came to be regarded as the ultimate source of some of the others.

[2] In *rust.* 3.1.6, Varro also discusses a word still in use in the Sabine territory, *tebae* "hill"; he believes that this word started as a Pelasgian Greek loan in Sabine. Later sources, such as Velius Longus and the *Liber de praenominibus*, ascribe a number of further Sabine glosses to Varro; these are

34 VARRO

does Varro envisage the relationship between Sabine and Latin? A different angle on this question is provided by Zanker, also in this volume (Chapter 4). And third, what precisely is Sabine? Is it a separate language for Varro or a dialect, and how does it fit into our modern conception of the Italic language family? The evidence is limited, but enough to draw some conclusions.

Before I try to answer these questions, I shall briefly explore how linguistic misconceptions can come about, and then look at Greek in the *De lingua Latina*, as this is a more complex issue that can provide us with certain avenues for our Sabine questions.

2. The Genesis of Misconceptions

Linguistic misconceptions most commonly arise in two ways: first, when we look at a specific phenomenon in isolation, without taking alternatives into consideration, and second, and worse, when our own interests blind us to these alternatives so that we are not even aware of them.

Since Varro was the greatest scholar of Plautus in antiquity, I may illustrate the first problem with a Plautine example (from de Melo 2009). In early Latin, there are different forms of the imperfect and the simple future in the fourth conjugation. Thus, next to classical *audiebam* "I heard" and *audiam* "I shall hear," we find *audibam* and *audibo*. The general impression one gets when reading Plautus without a concordance is that the types *audibam* and *audibo* are both common in his comedies, and that especially the future type *audibo* is normal. These forms stick out for a classicist trained in the literature of the first century BCE. However, this is a misconception that vanishes when we look at the alternatives. In the imperfect, forms in *-ibam* are still normal: there are seventeen tokens, but there are only three of forms in *-iebam*, which means that the archaic forms in *-ibam* amount to 85 percent of the total. In the future, forms in *-ibo* are frequent in absolute terms, with forty-six tokens. However, these forty-six tokens contrast with 184 in *-iam*, so that forms in *-ibo* amount to only 20 percent of the total. What is more, the future in *-ibo* shows signs of fossilization in that it is especially common with the verb *scire* "to know," where *-i-* is part of the verb root. First impressions are misleading: we learn classical Latin before we turn to early and late texts,

---

not discussed here because in the passages in question, there is no discussion of the linguistic relationship between Sabine and Latin.

VARRO AND THE SABINE LANGUAGE   35

and so we notice *audibam* and *audibo* easily because they deviate from what we use ourselves. But unless we contrast these forms with their classical equivalents, we cannot assess realistically what should count as normal or linguistically neutral within Plautus.

If we now return to Varro, we find a similar problem in nominal inflection. Gellius (4.16.1) comments on the genitive of the fourth declension:

> M. Varronem et P. Nigidium, viros Romani generis doctissimos, comperimus non aliter elocutos esse et scripsisse quam "senatuis" et "domuis" et "fluctuis," qui est patrius casus ab eo quod est "senatus," "domus," "fluctus."

> We have discovered that Marcus Varro and Publius Nigidius, the most learned men of the Roman race, exclusively said and wrote *senatuis* and *domuis* and *fluctuis*, which is the genitive case of *senatus* ["senate"] *domus* ["house"] and *fluctus* ["wave"].

This is an interesting statement, but is it actually true? Gellius was an intelligent reader of ancient texts, not a corpus linguist. He was bound to notice divergent forms of the genitive case in the fourth declension, but he was equally bound to overlook the "regular" forms in *-us* that he would have used himself. I am uncertain to what extent we can believe Gellius when he makes such a sweeping statement. The manuscript evidence for the genitive in *-uis* is meagre, but then again, manuscripts tend to normalize deviant morphology. Ultimately, we do not know.[3]

The second problem is worse, but nobody is immune to it, as we all have conscious and unconscious biases. In antiquity, Varro was called *Reatinus* not because he spoke a different language or because of any political allegiance, but simply in order to distinguish him from his contemporary, the minor poet (Publius) Terentius Varro Atacinus. In continental scholarship, this epithet, *der Reatiner / le Réatinien / il Reatino*, is often used so as not to repeat the name *Varro* endlessly, a habit that, to me, is stylistically more annoying because the overuse of an epithet is more tedious than the overuse of a simple name. However, the overuse of the epithet had a side-effect that is far worse than annoying those of a sensitive disposition: scholars have come to see every mention of Reate and the Sabines as significant, as part of Varronian identity politics. Sadly, I have also been misled, in part also because I am

---

[3] For more details than I can provide here, see especially Garcea (2012, 223–8).

36 VARRO

interested in the Italic languages. I shall rectify this error in what follows; but let us first look at Greek.

3. The Relationship between Latin and Greek

Varro understands that Greek has influenced Latin in various ways. The most obvious of these is through lexical borrowing. Maltby (1993, 50) estimates that 12–13 percent of Varro's etymologies derive Latin words from Greek ones. In many cases, modern etymologists agree, although there are a few tokens where Varro fails to recognize such loans, as in 5.118 or 5.120. In 5.118, Varro derives *cilliba*, a type of table with four legs, from *cibus* "food," while we today consider it a loan from κιλλίβας (derived from κίλλος "donkey").[4] The metaphor came about because both things have four legs, but perhaps it was not an obvious one. In 5.120, Varro derives *magida*, a type of plate, from *magnitudo* "large size," whereas modern etymologists think of it as a loan from μαγίς, or rather, its Hellenistic form μαγίδα. Here, Varro presumably failed to make the connection because he was more familiar with the classical language than with the contemporary Hellenistic variety. What is much more common than cases where Varro fails to notice Greek origin are those instances where he thinks of loans, while we today acknowledge parallel developments from Indo-European. Thus, *ovis* "sheep" and ὄις both go back to Indo-European, whereas Varro believes the Latin word to be a loan from Greek (*ling.* 5.96; cf. Prisc. *gramm.* II 253.19).

Varro even acknowledges the existence of Greek case endings in loan words and discusses to what extent such words should be nativized (10.69–71).

But when it comes to the origins of the Latin language, Varro "accounted for certain morphological similarities between Latin and Greek not in terms of a genetic relationship, but rather by convergent development that was due to the independent response of speakers of both languages to similar linguistic demands" (Gitner 2015, 48–9).

Does the relationship between Sabine and Latin go deeper than this for Varro? In what follows, I shall look at the distribution of *Sabinus* and related words over the entirety of Varro's *De lingua Latina*, before assessing the individual passages and then attempting to answer my original questions.

---

[4] For more details on this passage and others discussed here from Varro's *De lingua Latina*, please see my commentary (2019) *ad loc.*

VARRO AND THE SABINE LANGUAGE 37

4. The Distribution of *Sabinus* and Related Concepts over the *De lingua Latina*

Varro's *De lingua Latina* originally consisted of twenty-five volumes, with a tripartite structure: an introductory volume was followed by six books on etymology, six on morphology, and twelve on syntax. Some of the remaining syntactic fragments indicate that the later syntactic books also discussed topics that today would fall under sentential semantics.

The six books on etymology and the six books on morphology were further divided into two halves of equal length; the first halves dealt with the theoretical side and the second halves, with the practical applications. What has come down to us in direct transmission is books 5–10, that is, the practical etymologies and the theory of morphology. We have a limited number of fragments from the other books, preserved in various grammarians, but these are not sufficient to allow us to reconstruct the remaining books with any degree of accuracy.

It is interesting to see that *Sabinus* is not distributed evenly over the remaining corpus. The word is attested twenty-seven times, in twenty passages, to be discussed in what follows. Eleven of these passages are in book 5, a further five are in book 6, and four are in book 7. The distribution over the etymological books is fairly even if we consider the fact that book 5 is twice as long as book 6 or book 7. However, what is remarkable is that *Sabinus* is not attested at all in the books on morphology or in the fragments. For Varro, the Sabines are relevant in the etymological part because some Latin words come from there, or perhaps also because of a deeper genetic relationship between Sabine and Latin. But the Sabine language is not relevant to synchronic morphology.

One might expect a similar distribution pattern for other languages, with the exception of Greek; Latin has a fair number of loan words from many sources, but morphologically, only Greek is relevant, either through borrowed endings or through grammatical doctrine. However, this expectation is not entirely borne out by the facts. In 5.100, *tigris* "tiger" is classified as a loan from Armenian, and *camelus* is said to have come into Latium with a Syriac name. Neither language is mentioned elsewhere in the *De lingua Latina*. On the other hand, the languages of the Egyptians, Phoenicians, and Gauls are mentioned in 8.65, in connection with nominal morphology: Egyptian and Phoenician have only one case, that is, they lack a case system, while Gaulish has a more complex system. Egyptian is not

38   VARRO

mentioned again at all, while Phoenician comes up in 5.113 in connection with the name for purple dye, and Gaulish comes up in 5.167 in connection with *reno* "garment made from animal skin (reindeer?)," a word that we nowadays classify as Germanic in origin based on the sound changes it underwent. This means that Sabine did not only not influence Latin morphology, it is not even considered useful for comparative purposes. We can only speculate why that is; perhaps it was considered to be too similar in its case system to warrant a mention.

Words connected with Sabine show a very similar distribution pattern. *Oscus* is found four times in the etymological books, once in book 5 and three times in book 7. There are no attestations in the direct transmission of the morphological books, and there is only one in the fragments. Here, in frg. 5 Kent, where Gellius (2.25.5–10) is paraphrasing lost parts of book 8, Varro does not talk about Oscan morphology, but about the word *Oscus* and how its Latin adverb is *Osce*, while from *Maurus* "North African" we get *Maurice*.

Lucanus/Lucanicus/Lucas/Luca is found an astonishing sixteen times. Three attestations are in two passages of book 5, and the remainder are in book 7, but it has to be said that these thirteen items in book 7 are all in one single passage, 7.39–40, where Varro discusses the old word for "elephant," *Luca bos*.

And finally, *Reate/Reatinus* occurs four times, once in book 5 (5.53), once in book 6 (6.5), and twice in 8.83. As with *Oscus*, no claim is made about deviant morphology in Reate in this last passage. Varro merely points out that from the toponym *Reate*, the adjective *Reatinus* is derived, and that this adjective can be used as a name for a freedman; other examples for this derivation process are provided as well.

We have now seen that *Sabinus* and connected words are almost restricted to the etymological books. What we need to look at next is how important Sabine and similar varieties are for Varronian etymology.

5. A Closer Look at the Twenty Passages in Which *Sabinus* Is Attested

In what follows, I shall look at the twenty passages in which *Sabinus* is attested, as well as the attestations of *Oscus* and similar words in the etymological books. I shall move from the least relevant to the most significant passages.

VARRO AND THE SABINE LANGUAGE   39

5.1 Passages without Linguistic Interest

Not all passages in which *Sabinus* occurs are relevant to Varronian linguistics. We can compare 5.41:

> hic mons ante Tarpeius dictus a virgine Vestale Tarpeia, quae ibi ab Sabinis necata armis et sepulta; cuius nominis monimentum relictum, quod etiam nunc eius rupes Tarpeium appellatur saxum.

> This hill was called the *Tarpeius* ["Tarpeian"] before, from the Vestal virgin *Tarpeia*, who was killed by the Sabines with their shields and buried there. A reminder of her name is left, because even now its cliff is called the *Tarpeium saxum* ["Tarpeian rock"].

The Sabines are mentioned because they killed the Vestal virgin Tarpeia. The Sabines did perhaps not behave in the most honorable way imaginable, but neither was Tarpeia a model of good morals. Varro presents the episode in neutral language, without taking sides. The passage is of historical or mythological significance, but is linguistically irrelevant.

Other passages are equally insignificant. In 5.32, *Sabini* "the Sabines / Sabine land" and *Lucani* "the Lucanians / Lucanian land" are mentioned as the names of territories, because places can be named after the inhabitants. In 6.20, Varro tells us that at the feast of Consus there is a play depicting the abduction of the Sabine women. And in 5.149, Varro states that according to Piso's *Annals*, the *lacus Curtius* was named after the Sabine Mettius Curtius, who fought in the war between Romulus and Tatius. What is interesting in this last passage is that alternative accounts by other historians are presented in 5.148 and 5.150, and again Varro remains neutral, showing no preference for one of the stories.

At first sight, 5.66 looks like a more linguistic passage, but it is probably also unimportant. Here, Varro informs us that his teacher, Aelius Stilo, equated the Latin Dius Fidius with the Sabine Sancus and the Greek Hercules; but this is a purely functional equivalence and does not imply common origin or borrowing in any way—in fact, Aelius derives *Dius Fidius* from *Diouis filius* "son of Jupiter."

Similarly, several of the passages containing related words are not of linguistic interest. The *ager Reatinus* is mentioned in 5.53, but only as the territory from which the Palatines originated. The same *ager Reatinus* reappears

40 VARRO

in 6.5 in connection with a naming convention: in and around Reate, those born *prima luce* "at the first light" are called *Lucii*. The same convention existed in and around Rome at some point in the past as well. Annoyingly, we do not know whether the form of the name *Lucius* was exactly the same in Reate as in Rome or whether Varro has adapted it phonologically and morphologically.

Of the adjectives associated with Lucania, we have already seen the attestation in 5.32, where *Lucani* is used as the name of the Lucanian territory. In 5.111, the *Lucanica* is mentioned, a type of sausage first encountered by Roman soldiers when they were in Lucanian territory and named after the tribe by the Romans. A typological parallel would be our "frankfurters." The remaining thirteen adjectives are in the passage 7.39–40, where Varro deals with the *luca bos* "elephant." Three theories are advanced: Vergilius argues that *lucas / luca* is derived from *Lucanus*; Cornelius believes it to be from *Libycus* "Libyan," as elephants are not native to Lucania, but rather to North Africa; and Varro himself connects the adjective with *lux* "light" because elephants wear gilded shields that reflect the light. Modern etymology is of course in agreement with Vergilius: Romans first encountered elephants in Lucania, when Pyrrhus brought them over from North Africa, and as they had never encountered animals of this type, they called them Lucanian cows, just as the Dutch call the orange *sinaasappel / appelsien* "Chinese apple." The original adjective was **Loukanos*, which in Latin yielded *Lucanus*, but in Oscan, with regular syncope, **lovkans*. In *lucas bos*, the adjective was borrowed from Oscan, but adapted phonologically to Latin, with monophthongization of the diphthong and loss of nasal before *-s*. This is an odd morphological shape for a Latin adjective to have, so *lucas* became *luca*. Varro, who objects to Vergilius' theory vehemently, is correct in his derivation only indirectly, insofar as the *Lucani* are connected with *lux* etymologically.

5.2 Loans from Sabine and Oscan

We can move on to passages that are more interesting for our purposes. In quite a few cases, Varro assumes straightforward loans from Sabine. Modern scholars may not always agree, but these passages show that Varro believed there to have been significant language contact, with borrowings into Latin. It is possible that he also thought certain words to be loans from Latin into

VARRO AND THE SABINE LANGUAGE   41

Sabine, but the *De lingua Latina* is about Latin rather than Sabine, so this topic is never discussed.

In 5.97, Varro assumes loans from Sabine:

> "hircus," quod Sabini "fircus." quod illic "fedus," in Latio rure "hedus," qui in urbe ut in multis "a" addito "haedus."

> The *hircus* ["he-goat"] got its name because the Sabines say *fircus*. What is a *fedus* ["kid"] there, is a *hedus* in Latium in the countryside, which in the city is a *haedus* with an added *a*, as in many words.

Quod is unlikely to be relative here ("that which"): it is against Varronian practice merely to adduce parallels; he is only interested in sources in the etymological books. Modern etymologists would say that the words are cognate rather than loans, and that *h-* is original, while *f-* is a hypercorrection that came about when initial *f-* began to turn into *h-*. The sound change and its hypercorrection are both attested for Middle Faliscan (see Wallace and Joseph 1991 for details).

Loans are also assumed in 5.107, where cookies are called *lixulae* and *similixulae*, *vocabulo Sabino* "with a Sabine word," as these are so common there. The form *simi-* "half" is interesting: in Osco-Umbrian, original *$\bar{e}$* (preserved in Latin *semi-*) and *$\bar{\imath}$* merged in quality (though not in quantity) prehistorically, and the result was closed vowels that must have sounded similar to what a Roman would represent with the letter *I*. In 5.159, the *vicus cuprius* "good row (of houses)" is assumed to come from Sabine *cupro* (ablative), glossed as *bonum* "good"; an adjective *kuprom* with this meaning is attested in Oscan. Incidentally, our main manuscript has *cyprius* and so on, presumably because the scribe confused the name with Cyprus and Cypriote. In 6.5 (and also in 7.77), *crepusculum* "dusk" is considered to be Sabine, and connected with the name *Crepuscus*, given to people in Amiternum who were born at dusk. Whether the word is really Sabine is unclear; we could be dealing with cognates or a loan in the other direction. The same is true of *catus*, glossed as *acutus* "sharp" in 7.46, and treated as Sabine by Varro.

There is also one passage in which a straightforward loan from Oscan is assumed. In 7.54, we learn that Naevius refers to the dirt in wool that has not yet been carded as *asta*, "from the Oscans." The word may well be corrupt, but the fact that Naevius has such a word makes it likely that other Romans understood it and that it was a reasonably well-established borrowing. 7.29 is more complicated. In Atellan farces staged in Latin rather than Oscan, the

42 VARRO

character of the old man is called *Pappus*, and Varro tells us that in Oscan he is referred to as *casnar* (from **kasnāros*, with syncope, cognate with Latin *canus* "gray"). Varro is talking about words like *cascus* "old," so he may simply be adducing a word that he felt to be cognate in some way; alternatively, the word may have been used as a name in Atellan farce when staged in Latin.

When Varro is uncertain about an etymology, he is not averse to advancing two alternatives. Sometimes, one of these alternatives is derivation from Sabine or some other language. In 5.68, *sol* "sun" is considered to be either a loan word from Sabine or a derivation of *solus* "alone" (as the one who alone causes day). Similarly, in 5.73, *Mars* comes from the *mares* "men" who go to war, or from Sabine *Mamers*. It is nice to see that Sabine has the same reduplicated form of the name that we find in Oscan. In 5.97, *porcus* "pig" is considered a loan from Sabine (*aprunum porcum* is cited in the accusative) or from Greek (with a parallel from religious texts). And in 6.28, the *Idus* "Ides" are considered to be from Etruscan *itus* or from a Sabine form that is transmitted as *idus*. To the modern etymologist, the Etruscan form must be a loan from Latin or some other Italic language, with the normal rendition of *d* as *t*; if the word had come from Etruscan, Latin as a language that has both sounds would have preserved *t*. The Sabine form can hardly have been identical with the Latin one, otherwise Varro would not have cited Etruscan at all, or would not have cited it before Sabine. We thus have to emend, but whether we should emend to an Oscan-style *eidus* or to an Umbrian-style *edus* or to something else entirely is unclear. At any rate, borrowing from Sabine is always considered a possibility in these examples. We also find one double etymology involving Oscan. The *supparus* or *supparum*, a type of garment, may ultimately be a loan from Greek. For Varro, in 5.131, it is derived from *supra* "above," as an outer garment, or from Oscan, where apparently the same form was in use.

5.3 More Complex Cases

There remain five passages which are more complicated for various reasons. The first of these is 6.57, where compounds of *loqui* "to speak" are discussed. The terms *eloqui* "to speak forth" and *reloqui* "to speak back" are said to be used in Sabine shrines for those speaking from the sanctuary of a deity.[5]

---

[5] For a defense of the reading *eloqui*[*um*] see de Melo (2019b) *ad loc.*

VARRO AND THE SABINE LANGUAGE   43

Neither word can be of Osco-Umbrian origin, as the labiovelar shows, which in Osco-Umbrian would correspond to -*p*- (compare *quinque* "five" and Oscan *pompe*, as in the originally Oscan town of *Pompeii* "fifth city"). In fact, both words are perfectly normal Latin compounds that have simply acquired special religious meanings in Sabine shrines.

In 6.13, we learn that the Sabines call a purification *februm*, and that this word is also known from Roman ceremonies; the ancient Romans called a piece of goat-hide *februm*. Varro does not specify the relationship between Sabine and Latin here, but one gets the impression that the two terms are considered cognates and that we are not dealing with a loan from Sabine into Latin or *vice versa*. *Februm* is preserved in Sabine, but is an archaism in Latin.

In 5.123, Varro mentions the vessel called *lepesta*. This term seems to have fallen out of use in Latin, but is preserved in religious usages among the Sabines. Varro notices that the Greeks have a δεπέστα; and he argues that the roots came from there into the Sabine territory as well as into the Latin one.[6] For Varro, then, we have a word that is identical in Sabine and Latin, yet not because of borrowing between these two or because the two languages are cognate, but rather because we are dealing with independent loans from Greek. This is a very sophisticated way of looking at the situation.

We have already seen part of 7.29. But there is more to that passage. In 7.28, Varro glosses the Ennian *cascus* as *vetus* "old" and says that the origin of the word is Sabine, a language *quae usque radices in Oscam linguam egit* "which drove its roots all the way into the Oscan language." Then, in 7.29, we learn that the Samnites, descendants of the Sabines, had a town *Casinum*, with a related name, and that this town was referred to by *nostri* "our people" as *Forum Vetus* "Old Market" even in Varro's time. Obviously, the old name never disappeared completely, hence modern *Cassino*, but what is of interest is not so much the supposed loan *cascus* or the translation of *Casinum*, but rather the linguistic relationships outlined here. Oscan was clearly still a distinct language in Varro's day. The Samnites are only mentioned in three places: here; in 5.142, where Varro talks about a type of gladiator wearing Samnite dress; and in 5.29, where Varro argues that in principle, the river *Volturnus* is irrelevant to the Latin etymologist, as it starts in Samnium and has its name from there, but that we nevertheless examine such words because the town *Volturnum* is now Roman. This indicates that the Samnite language was also to be considered a separate language (today we classify

---

[6] On this metaphor see Zanker (Chapter 4, §2) in this volume.

44 VARRO

it as part of the Oscan dialect continuum). Whatever Sabine was, it was not simply a type of Oscan, and it did not only influence Latin, but also Oscan and Samnite.

One long passage remains that deserves to be quoted in full (5.74):

> "Feronia," "Minerva," "Novensides" a Sabinis. paulo aliter ab eisdem dicimus haec: "Palem," "Vestam," "Salutem," "Fortunam," "Fontem," "Fidem." et arae Sabinum linguam olent, quae Tati regis voto sunt Romae dedicatae. nam, ut annales dicunt, vovit "Opi," "Florae," "Vediovi," "Saturno"que, "Soli," "Lunae," "Volcano," et "Summano," itemque "Larundae," "Termino," "Quirino," "Vortumno," "Laribus," "Dianae," "Lucinae"que; e quis nonnulla nomina in utraque lingua habent radices, ut arbores quae in confinio natae in utroque agro serpunt. potest enim "Saturnus" hic de alia causa esse dictus atque in Sabinis, et sic "Diana," de quibus supra dictum est.

> *Feronia, Minerva*, and the *Novensides* come from the Sabines. Slightly differently from the same people, we say the following: *Pales, Vesta, Salus* ["salvation"], *Fortuna* ["Luck"], *Fons* ["Fountain"], *Fides* ["Faith"]. The altars too, which by the vow of King Tatius were dedicated in Rome, have the smell of the language of the Sabines. For, as the annals state, he vowed altars to *Ops* ["Wealth"], *Flora, Vediovis*, and *Saturnus, Sol* ["Sun"], *Luna* ["Moon"], *Volcanus*, and *Summanus*, and likewise to *Larunda, Terminus, Quirinus, Vortumnus*, the *Lares, Diana*, and *Lucina*. Among these, some names have roots in each language, like trees that have sprung up on a boundary and extend into each field. For *Saturnus* may have got his name here for a different reason than among the Sabines, and so also *Diana*; about these there was a discussion above.

Here, a distinction is made between three categories of theonyms. First, we have three that are considered direct loans. Their etymologies are not taken up again. Next, there are six that are slightly different in the two languages and are thought to be either adapted loans or, more likely, independent developments from the same origins. I am leaning toward this second hypothesis for two reasons. On the one hand, two words are given native etymologies elsewhere: Varro connects *Fons* with *fundere* "to pour out," and *Fides* with the Fetial priests and with *foedus* "treaty." And on the other hand, there is still our third category, which has to be somehow distinct from our second one, and it is this category consisting of fifteen deities where

VARRO AND THE SABINE LANGUAGE   45

Varro says explicitly that we cannot decide between loans and independent developments. For *Sol*, already dealt with earlier, Varro states in 5.68 that it could be a loan or derived natively from *solus* "alone." For other words, we find purely native explanations elsewhere: *Ops* is said to be from *opus* "work" and *opus* "need" (5.64); *Saturnus*, from *satus* "sowing" (5.64); *Luna*, from *lucere* "to shine" and *noctu* "at night" (5.68); *Volcanus*, from *vis* "force" and *violentia* "violence" (5.70); *Quirinus*, from the *Quirites* (5.73); *Diana*, from *Diviana*, that is, *dis-* "apart" or *de-* "from" and *via* "way" (5.68); and *Lucina*, from *lux* (5.69). For the *Lares*, no native etymology is given, but Varro points out that the older form was *Lases* (6.2), and that *pauper* "poor" is from *paulus* "little" and *Lar*. *Terminus* is derived from *terere* "to rub, wear down," or could be a loan from Greek τέρμων (5.21). And in 5.46, Varro calls *Vortumnus* the chief deity of the Etruscans, so he is presumably a loan in Sabine and Latin, although he might have made it into Latin via Sabine.

6. Conclusions

It is time to draw some conclusions. At the beginning of this piece I asked three questions. The first was whether Varro's enthusiasm for Sabine was overstated. The answer to this is most definitely in the affirmative. The Sabines and Sabine itself are found in only twenty passages. Several of these are of no linguistic interest, and Varro does not even seem interested in emphasizing the historical importance of the Sabines. He reports neutrally. Whatever local pride he may have had, he did not let it influence his historical judgment.[7] Linguistically, Varro does not consider the Sabines of any morphological significance for Latin; whatever their language was like, it was not suitable for comparisons with Latin and did not influence Latin inflection or derivation. Lexically, he accepts some Latin words as Sabine loans, but these instances are not numerous. Maltby (1993, 50) shows that only 4 percent of all Varronian etymologies are to do with languages other than Greek, while supposed Greek origins account for 12–13 percent of our material. The Sabine material among these 4 percent is very limited, and even here we often find double etymologies, as among the theonyms, where Sabine origin is one option, but parallel development is another. Oscan and the Lucanians are almost irrelevant from a linguistic perspective.

---

[7] See Volk (Chapter 2) in this volume on Varro's relationship to the past.

46   VARRO

The second question was how Varro envisaged the relationship between Sabine and Latin. The relationship between Greek and Latin is discussed on occasion; for instance, in 5.21 Varro tells us that Evander was an Arcadian and brought Arcadian words with him. The relationship between Sabine and Latin seems to be one of lexical borrowings and parallel developments. Very rarely is Varro more explicit. When he says, in 7.29, that the Sabine language drove its roots into Oscan and Latin, this need not mean that Sabine is older, or that it had a deep morphological influence on either language; the passage could be interpreted in purely lexical terms, with loan words entering Oscan and Latin from Sabine. What is interesting is that most of the potential loans are theonyms, with a few animal names added into the mix.

Our final question is what Sabine actually was, for Varro and from a modern perspective. To begin with the modern perspective, and judging from the lexical items transmitted in our work, it seems to have been no more than a dialect of Latin. *Eloqui* and *reloqui* cannot be Osco-Umbrian because of the preserved labiovelar, and the same goes for *Quirinus*. Forms like *fedus* and *fircus* are later on ascribed to the "ancients," but similar forms can actually be found in Middle and Late Faliscan (as hypercorrections after the change of initial *f* to *h*). They may be dialectal Latin, but have no parallels in Osco-Umbrian. *Cuprum* is an Oscan word, as is *Mamers*, and we may tentatively conclude that an originally Osco-Umbrian-speaking area had become almost completely Latinized, but that certain lexical items survived Latinization. Varro speaks of the Sabine *lingua*, but that does not mean that he thought of it as a separate language in the modern sense; he may simply have been referring to a language variety that struck him as divergent from Roman Latin.[8]

---

[8] Burman (2017, 186) takes a more agnostic view, but this is because she also takes into account Sabine glosses by other authors, which need not refer to the same language variety that Varro calls Sabine.

4
Varro's Word Trees

Andreas T. Zanker*

1. Introduction

Varro's word trees are a prominent feature of the polymath's *De lingua Latina*;[1] in spite of the existence of numerous other metaphors, similes, and analogies for word derivation,[2] this particular image shows uncommon elaboration in the remnants of Varro's text. Varro's word trees are, as we will see, composites constructed out of more basic metaphors buried deep in the Roman terminology for grammatical categories. Much of the Latin grammatical vocabulary was calqued on the Greek one, and Varro was undoubtedly relying on previous Greek and Roman thinkers (e.g., the Stoics) for some of his metaphors for language,[3] but the Roman intellectual appears to have exploited the figurative qualities of this vocabulary in particularly creative ways. In what follows, I will be building on the work of Adam Gitner, who was the first to truly bring out the importance of the image of the tree in Varro. Adam focused primarily on the notion of the word tree's roots and their role in determining word affiliation; in this paper I would like to focus on its branches, in line with some recent comments by Jim Zetzel and Wolfgang de Melo.

It would be nice if the individual descriptions of words as trees were consistent with each other in *De lingua Latina*, yet Varro does not simply offer a

---

* This is for Bob—a teacher and scholar whose clarity is matched only by his integrity, patience, and kindness.

[1] The word tree has been discussed by Gitner (2014) and MacDonald (2018), as well as by Dench (2005, 317), Spencer (2011a; 2011b; 2015b), *CCC* 41, and Blank (2019). I am grateful to Wolfgang de Melo for sharing the proofs of his edition of *De lingua Latina* (2019b) with me; I follow his text (only indicating major textual interventions) and translation, occasionally offering alternate translations in square brackets. For Varro's *Res rusticae* I use the edition of Flach (2006), broadly following the Loeb translation.

[2] On metaphor in Varro's *De lingua Latina*, see Blank (2008, 62–3), Spencer (2011a; 2011b; 2015a; 2015b, 81–2), Gitner (2014), MacDonald (2016; 2018), Volk (2019).

[3] E.g., Varro *may* suggest that Chrysippus made use of the paternal metaphor for word derivation in the following: *ling.* 10.59 *nam nonnunquam alterum ex altero videtur, ut Chrysippus scribit, quemadmodum pater ex filio et filius ex patre...*

Andreas T. Zanker, *Varro's Word Trees* In: *Roman Perspectives on Linguistic Diversity.* Edited by Adam Gitner, Oxford University Press. © Oxford University Press 2023. DOI: 10.1093/oso/9780197611975.003.0004

single, unified version of the analogy to his reader. As we shall see, the image of the tree performs a multitude of tasks, and its instantiations often have different emphases and even conflict with each other. We might think of the tree as serving as a prototypical template from which Varro could derive a suitable image for the discussion at hand: for example, as Carolyn MacDonald has argued, an emphasis on word forms as the tree's roots affords the possibility of digging them up in the process of antiquarian research, whereas, as Wolfgang de Melo has pointed out, the notion of words as branches "falling" (*casus*) and "leaning away" (*declinatio*) offers a clear image by which Varro's readership could envision inflection and word derivation.[4] Different elements of the word tree could therefore be "profiled" as required. One might, for example, prefer to focus on the roots or the fruit in order to make a specific point, thus selecting one of the two trees in the following diagram:[5]

Trees are usefully complicated entities, with a variety of parts and functions, and are versatile as a source domain. They moreover have the virtue of being widely understood for all their complexity: Varro could expect his ancient

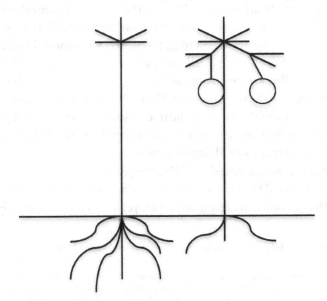

Figure 4.1 Different profiling of word trees

---

[4] MacDonald (2018), de Melo (2019b, 214–15).
[5] My diagrams throughout are designed for the purpose of clarifying the scenarios depicted in the text, not as true representations.

VARRO'S WORD TREES   49

readers to be aware of trees and their metaphorical affordances (even if some of these details are unfamiliar to his modern readership). The source domain would have come naturally to Varro, who had direct knowledge of farming from his childhood in Sabine Reate and his experience of running his own farms,[6] from his reading (as revealed in *Res rusticae*) and observation of different climates while in the military,[7] and from his time spent on Caesar's commission for the provision of land grants to veterans in Campania in 59 BCE.[8] Varro would have been able to draw on arboreal analogues and imagery with considerable confidence and sophistication.

2. Roots

As mentioned, I shall not focus on the *radices*, or roots, of Varro's word trees, as Adam Gitner and Carolyn MacDonald have already discussed them; they are the most difficult examples. While the instances differ among themselves in significant ways, they all use the notion of roots in order to get at the question of affiliation of one kind or another. Early on in the surviving books of *De lingua Latina*, for example, Varro describes a word as a tree that has roots spreading across a border that divides two different properties. Varro has just established a four-fold division of items in both the real world and the lexicon: *locus, corpus, tempus,* and *actio* ("place," "body," "time," and "action"). All words, and the things they describe, can be divided into these categories, and Varro states his intention to structure the subsequent books of *De lingua Latina* in accordance with them, covering *corpus* and *locus* in book 5 (in sequence), *tempus* and *actio* in book 6. If he were to divide his text up exclusively by this division, Varro would only discuss words that relate to place in the part of book 5 of *De lingua Latina* that covers *locus*, or conversely words that relate to bodies in the part devoted to *corpus*; however, he notes that every so often he will disregard the division he has just imposed (*ling.* 5.13):[9]

> **sed qua cognatio eius erit verbi quae radices egerit extra fines suas,**
> **persequemur. saepe enim ad limitem arboris radices sub vicini**

[6] On Varro's youth and land-holdings, see Della Corte (1954, 13–21).

[7] For instance, his time spent serving under Pompey against Sertorius gave him the opportunity to observe Spanish vineyards, where vines were allowed to grow on the ground rather than upright on sticks (see *rust.* 1.8.1); Della Corte (1954, 58–60).

[8] See Della Corte (1954, 88–9).

[9] Taylor (1974, 69–71).

50   VARRO

prodierunt segetem. quare non, cum de locis dicam, si ab "agro" ad "agrarium hominem," ad "agricolam" pervenero, aberraro.

But where the kin of the word under discussion is, even when it [i.e., the word's kin] has driven its roots beyond its territory, we shall follow. For often the roots of a tree near a boundary have advanced under the neighbor's field. Hence when I am speaking about places, I shall not go astray if from *ager* ["field"] I come to an *agrarius homo* ["landowner"] and to an *agricola* ["farmer"] (cf. *ling.* 7.5).

That is to say—when talking about the derivations from a given word, Varro will not always stick to the class of word/thing under discussion: the importance of the kindred relationship between *ager, agrarius* (*homo*), and *agricola* overrides the fact that the first is a *locus* and the latter two are *corpora*.[10] When it comes to the image itself, it appears that the words *agrarius* and *agricola* are to be pictured as trees related (cf. *cognatio*) to the term *ager* that are planted on the boundary between properties; while *ager* stands squarely within the field of *locus*, the derivative terms *agrarius* and *agricola* have thrust their roots into the field of *corpus* (the border between the categories is marked by a broken line in the following diagram):

The notion of "roots" allows Varro to emphasize the obscurity and hidden nature of the relationship between the different terms and the categories to which they belong: beginning from the tree that has given rise to other words, Varro will follow (*persequemur*) the derived terms that have spread their roots into a different field (*radices sub vicini prodierunt segetem*).

Later in book 5, Varro uses a similar image of sunken roots in surveying foreign words for divinities. Here, however, it is the origin of the words, their etymology, that is at issue rather than their affiliation within a conceptual category (*ling.* 5.74):

et arae Sabinum linguam olent, quae Tati regis voto sunt Romae dedicatae. nam, ut annales dicunt, vovit "Opi," "Florae," "Vediovi," "Saturno"que, "Soli," "Lunae," "Volcano," et "Summano," itemque "Larundae," "Termino," "Quirino," "Vortumno," "Laribus," "Dianae," "Lucinae"que; **e quis nonnulla nomina in utraque lingua habent radices, ut arbores quae in confinio**

---

[10] Taylor (1974, 102), points out the appropriateness of the choice of the agricultural examples (*ager, agricola, agrarius*). See also the discussion of *lego* below.

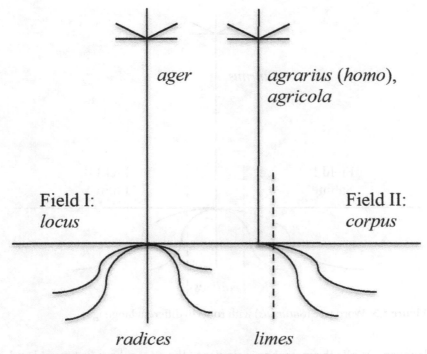

Figure 4.2 Derivatives of *ager* ("field") with roots moving across a category border

natae in utroque agro serpunt. potest enim "Saturnus" hic de alia causa esse dictus atque in Sabinis, et sic "Diana," de quibus supra dictum est.

The altars too, which by the vow of King Tatius were dedicated in Rome, have the smell of the language of the Sabines. For, as the annals state, he vowed altars to *Ops* ["Wealth"], *Flora*, *Vediovis*, and *Saturnus*, *Sol* ["Sun"], *Luna* ["Moon"], *Volcanus*, and *Summanus*, and likewise to *Larunda*, *Terminus*, *Quirinus*, *Vortumnus*, the *Lares*, *Diana*, and *Lucina*. Among these, some names have roots in each language, like trees that have sprung up on a boundary and extend into each field. For *Saturnus* may have got his name here for a different reason than among the Sabines, and so also *Diana*; about these there was a discussion above.

Here the forms of the words *Saturnus* and *Diana* are the same in both Sabine and Latin, yet they have different etymologies, an *alia causa*, in each

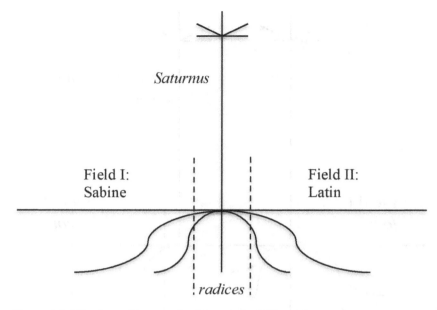

Figure 4.3 Word tree (*Saturnus*) with roots in different languages

language. While the metaphor is similar to the one we have just considered, the idea that it communicates is quite different. A word tree may have different roots/*etyma* on either side of a linguistic border (in the following diagram the border between the two languages lies inside the two broken vertical lines).[11]

Varro states that *Saturnus* can be used in Latin for a different *causa* than among the Sabines: the form of the word may be identical even when the reasons for its existence differ. The notion may seem obscure, but Gitner has shown persuasively that Varro is here engaging with the notion of language convergence—the way in which two languages may "grow together."

The question of how languages relate to each other re-emerges later on in the fifth book of *De lingua Latina*. Here, in studying words relating to liquid, Varro notes how the word *lepesta* ("wine-jar") is found in Sabine, Greek, and Latin (*ling.* 5.123):

> item dictae "lepestae," quae etiam nunc in diebus sacris Sabinis vasa vinaria in mensa deorum sunt posita. apud antiquos scriptores Graecos inveni

---

[11] On this difficult passage, see Gitner (2014) and de Melo in this volume (Chapter 3, §5.3).

VARRO'S WORD TREES   53

appellari poculi genus δεπέσταν; **quare vel inde radices in agrum Sabinum et Romanum sunt profectae.**

Likewise, the wine vessels were called *lepestae* which are placed on the table of the gods on the sacred days of the Sabines even now. In the ancient Greek writers I have found that a kind of cup was called a δεπέστα; **hence its roots probably set out from there into the Sabine territory [= field] and the Roman one.**

Again, languages are portrayed as fields, yet here three of them are in play; the roots set off from Greek, which appears to be where the term first originated (so much seems to be suggested by *apud antiquos scriptores Graecos inveni*), and from there (*inde*) enter Sabine and Latin.[12] Here, the term *radix* underscores not so much the etymology of a term but rather the term's presence in a language as a standard word. The single idealized word-form now has roots in a number of different languages and therefore belongs to them all, even if in this case its ultimate origin is Greek (the broken vertical lines in the following diagram again demarcate the different languages).[13]

Conversely, in book 7 Varro mentions the word *subulo* ("piper"), used by Ennius, whose roots are in Etruria rather than Latium: the word is Etruscan and does not really count as a Latin term, since it has not struck roots in the Latin field.[14]

In these last examples—which deal with the affiliation of words present in different languages—Varro is attempting to describe how a single word tree can exist in different language-fields simultaneously, or otherwise fail to be truly incorporated into a host language. Citing the Roman jurist Gaius (*dig.* 41.1.7.13), Gitner has pointed out that if a tree sprouted roots that moved into another's field, the tree was the common property of the two property holders; on his reading, "words with roots in two languages are no longer the possession of any single language but have become common property

---

[12] On this passage see also de Melo (Chapter 3, §5.3). Gitner (2014) prefers a metaphor of immigration, and may well be correct: "[the *radices*] are described as 'setting out' like travelers for a foreign land." Nevertheless, the language of the roots' "travel" is frequent in such excerpts, and paralleled in Varro's *Res rusticae*: compare, for instance, *rust.* 1.23.6 *antequam radices longius procedere possint, alii conserunt hortos, alii quid aliud.*

[13] Collart (1954, 241–2) suggests that the Sabine language serves as the intermediary between Greek and Latin; see, however, de Melo, Chapter 3 in this volume. Cf. *ling.* 7.28 *primum "cascum" significat "vetus"; secundo eius origo Sabina, quae usque radices in Oscam linguam egit.*

[14] Cf. *ling.* 7.35 *"subulo" dictus, quod ita dicunt tibicines Tusci. quocirca radices eius in Etr<ur>ia, non Latio quaerendae.*

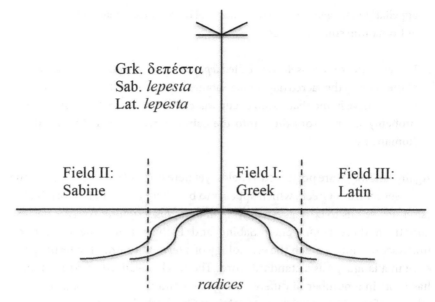

Figure 4.4 Movement of a word from Greek into Sabine and Latin

(*communis*)." Even though there is only one word-form, it is possible for it to have different etymologies in different languages (*de alia causa esse dictus*). Before moving on, we should take stock and emphasize how different these last applications of the metaphor of word roots are from the first example we studied, where the emphasis was on the word's affiliation in the categories of *locus* and *corpus*: already we can see the word tree being used for different, potentially incompatible, ends.

3. Branches

Besides the notion of roots by themselves, Varro manipulates the configuration of the tree for other emphases—ones that are perhaps more familiar to us. Toward the middle of book 5, he claims that names for artisans are derived not from the verb itself but rather from an intermediate form (*ling.* 5.93):

> artificibus maxima causa ars, id est, ab "arte medicina" ut sit "medicus" dictus, a "sutrina" "sutor," non a "medendo" ac "suendo," quae omnino ultima vice **earum rerum radices, ut in proxumo libro aperietur.**

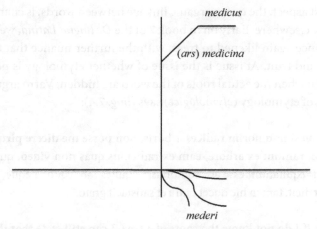

Figure 4.5 Relationship of the derived term *medicus* ("doctor") to its root

For craftsmen the main reason for their names is their craft, that is, that from the *ars medicina* ["medical art"] the *medicus* ["medical doctor"] is named and from the *ars sutrina* ["shoemaker's art"] the *sutor* ["shoemaker"], and not from *mederi* ["to cure"] and *suere* ["to sew"], which, however, in the last resort are the roots of these things, as will be revealed in the next book.[15]

Unfortunately, Varro does not in fact go into this in depth in the following book; what he suggests in this passage, however, is that verb forms such as *mederi* and *suere* serve as the roots of their respective word trees; from them, other words are derived. In the "last resort," *ultima vice*, these are the roots of the derived terms:[16]

As in the examples above, the roots need to be unearthed, yet in this case the image lays emphasis neither on a categorical principle (e.g., *corpus* versus *locus*) nor linguistic affiliation (e.g., Sabine versus Latin) but rather on the generative properties of the roots as pre-forms, that is, how they give rise to other forms. It also links individual terms in a chain of derivation; *mederi* is basic, the adjectival (*ars*) *medicina* is derived from that, and finally we arrive at the name for the profession *medicus*.

---

[15] There is a textual issue in the middle of the key phrase; for ease of reading, I have simplified the de Melo's text from *ultima [h]uic[r]e[i]* to *ultima vice*. See de Melo's apparatus for Collart's emendation.
[16] Cf. *ling.* 8.53 *hoc fere triplices habet radices, quod et a vocabulo oritur, ut a "venatore" "venabulum," et a nomine, ut a "Tibure" "Tiburs," et a verbo, ut a "currendo" "cursor."*

56 VARRO

This last aspect, the quasi-organic linkage between words, is characterized more fully elsewhere. Early on in book 7 of the *De lingua Latina*, we see word families once again likened to trees, with the further nuance that they have branches and fruit. At issue is the issue of whether etymology is possible or useful even when the actual roots of the word are hidden; Varro argues that it is. The art of etymology (*etymologice*) says (*ling.* 7.4):

> ... neque si non norim radices arboris, non posse me dicere pirum esse ex ramo, ramum ex arbore, eam ex radicibus quas non video. quare qui ostendit "equitatum" esse ab "equitibus," "equites" ab "equo," neque "equus" unde sit dicit, tamen hic docet plura et satisfacit grato.

> ... that if I do not know the roots of a tree, I can still state that the pear is from the branch, the branch is from the tree, and the tree from roots which I cannot see. Hence, a man who shows that *equitatus* ["cavalry"] is from *equites* ["cavalrymen"], and *eques* from from *equus* ["horse"], but does not say where *equus* is from, still teaches several things and satisfies a grateful person.

The image is here highly explicit: although the roots are hidden (*non norim*), the tree produces a pear (*pirum*), which hangs from a branch (*ex ramo*), which in turn hangs from a tree (*ex arbore*). The analogy is therefore notable for apparently depicting at least some words in terms of fruit hanging from a tree;[17] again, the image appears to be adopted for the purpose of ad hoc visualization rather than designed to be either internally coherent (for instance, why do some words correspond with fruit, others with branches?) or aligned with the other word trees in *De lingua Latina*.

4. Shoots

Why is the branch structure of the tree, discussed in the previous examples, an appropriate image for the relationship between words? In part, the image's aptness is due to the Latin vocabulary employed for grammatical inflection and derivation, that is, *declinatio* and *casus*: a tree's branches, like declensions

---

[17] The idea of derived words as fruit is not unparalleled; after making the point that certain words may be similar in form but different in meaning, Varro uses the following analogy at *ling.* 9.92: *itaque saepe gemina facie mala negamus esse similia, si sapore sunt alio.*

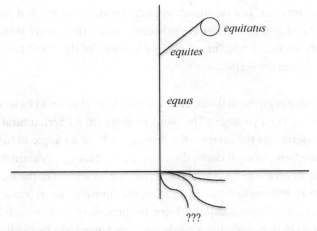

Figure 4.6 Relationship of the derived term *equitatus* ("cavalry") to an unknown root

and cases, "lean down/away" and represent "fallings."[18] Here we must go into what Varro meant by *declinatio* in a bit of depth. Varro used the term more broadly than the later grammarians; on the one hand, it could describe the mechanical inflection of both nouns and verbs (we would use the terms "declension" and "conjugation" respectively).[19] On the other, the term could encompass the creative act of deriving a new word from an earlier one. Varro called the former (1) *declinatio naturalis* ("natural derivation") and the latter (2) *declinatio voluntaria* ("voluntary derivation" *ling.* 8.21).

The first, (1) *declinatio naturalis*, operates by the mechanism of analogy in order to provide, for example, case endings to nouns; the noun forms "lean down," they decline, from the main trunk of the word tree from the *casus rectus* ("upright case"), that is, the nominative.[20] At the beginning of book 8, Varro uses *homo* ("man") as an example (*ling.* 8.1):

> ut **propago** omnis natura secunda, quod prius illud rectum, unde ea, sic **declinata**. itaque **declinatur in verbis**, rectum "homo," obliquum "hominis," quod declinatum a recto.

---

[18] See the terminological discussion in the introduction of de Melo (2019b).
[19] See Taylor (1974, particularly 12–13).
[20] Elsewhere, the term *declinare* is used of heavenly bodies, rivers, and the Lucretian swerve, as at Lucr. 2.221–2 *quod nisi* **declinare** *solerent, omnia deorsum / imbris uti guttae caderent per inane profundum*. On the terms *natura* and *naturalis* in their grammatical senses, see de Melo (2019a).

As every **offshoot** is a secondary growth, because that vertical part from which it comes is first, so are **the inflected forms. Thus, there is inflection in words**: vertical *homo* "man," oblique *hominis* "of the man," because it is inflected from the vertical.

Varro here draws an explicit link between the physical tree and its lexical equivalent (it is a crucial passage). The word *propago* (in its agricultural meaning, "shoot") determines the image—the *propagines* lie at an angle to the first, upright *Stammform*. In such cases, the term *casus* ("falling," "grammatical case") comes into its own—just as shoots on a tree, the variations of the word branch down, that is, *nascuntur* (*ling.* 7.16), from the "upright" form (*casus rectus*) to the declined ones (*casus obliqui*).[21] Here, the process of declension is automatic (i.e., natural) in the sense that a newly imported word will be readily declined in Latin if only the nominative form is ascertained (*ling.* 8.6).

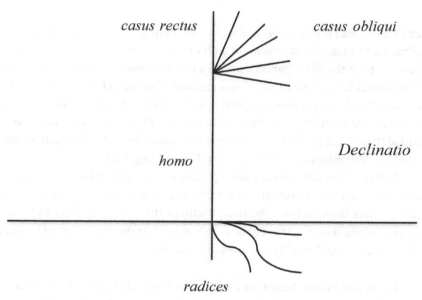

Figure 4.7 Natural declension of the noun *homo* ("man")

---

[21] Ancient scholarship knew of a number of accounts for why the cases (πτώσεις, *casus*) were so named; for instance, a scholion to Dionysius Thrax (*GG* I.3 231.16–27) asserts that the nominative is a "case" ("falling") even though it is described as upright (εὐθεῖα/ὀρθή). It bids us imagine someone grasping a pen and releasing it: even if it should stand straight upon impact, it will still have fallen. In the same way, a word in the nominative may be considered a "falling." For other explanations, see Thorp (1989), Robins (1993, 66–7), Brandenburg (2014). On the question of the Stoic conception of "case," see Frede (1994).

VARRO'S WORD TREES

The metaphor of the tree branches out in other ways as well. For instance, Varro distinguishes between two types of word—one of them is productive of declined forms (*fecundum*), such as *lego*, (*legis, legit*), while the other is sterile (*sterile*) in that it produces (*parit*) no forms beyond its upright form; these are the indeclinables (*ling.* 8.9):

> duo enim genera verborum, **unum fecundum, quod declinando multas ex se parit disparilis formas,** ut est "lego," "legi," "legam," sic alia, **alterum genus sterile, quod ex se parit nihil,** ut est "et," "iam," "vix," "cras," "magis," "cur."

> For there are two classes of words, **one fertile, because it produces many different forms from itself by inflecting,** such as is *lego* ["I am reading"], *legi* ["I have read"], *legam* ["I shall read"] and likewise others, **and another barren class, because it produces nothing from itself,** such as is *et* ["and"], *iam* ["now"], *vix* ["hardly"], *cras* ["tomorrow"], *magis* ["more"], *cur* ["why"].

The situation might be depicted thus (where the left side of the word tree represents "sterile" words, the right side "fertile" ones such as *lego*):

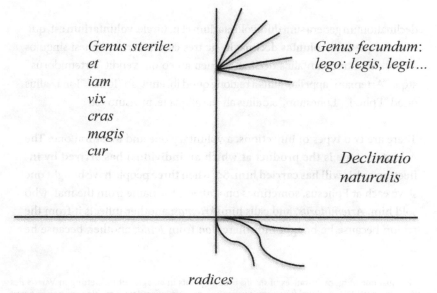

Figure 4.8 Sterile (left side) and fertile (right side) word trees

60 VARRO

The terms *fecundus*, *sterilis*, and *pario* are of course appropriate to a tree metaphor, as is the notion that a great number of words has "died" (*interierit*), found within a subsequent discussion at *ling.* 8.59 of how deponent verb forms fail to create a present participle distinguishable from the active forms (e.g., *loquor* yields a present participle with an active ending, *loquens*):[22]

> non est ergo analogia, praesertim cum tantus numerus vocabulorum in eo genere **interierit** quod dicimus . . .

> Thus, there is no analogy, especially since such a great number of nouns [e.g., present participles] **has perished** in this class which we are talking about.

The forms have apparently wilted on the word tree. Appropriate too are the references to *natura* as the motivation for the *declinatio* throughout the text: for *declinatio naturalis*, the forms will be produced of themselves, unless a human being "perverts it [i.e., nature] on account of his/her inept usage" (*ling.* 10.60). The productivity of both trees and words is regulated by nature.

The second type of *declinatio*, (2) *declinatio voluntaria*, involves the derivation of one term from another by human design. Again, there appears to be a horticultural metaphor at work in the term *declinatio*, whereby the new term is "bent down" from an earlier form (*ling.* 8.21):

> declinationum genera sunt duo, voluntarium et naturale. **voluntarium est, quo ut cuiusque tulit voluntas declinavit.** sic tres cum emerunt Ephesi singulos servos, nonnunquam alius declinat nomen ab eo qui vendit "Artemidorus," atque "Artemam" appellat, alius a regione quod ibi emit, ab "Ionia" "Iona," alius quod "Ephesi" "Ephesium," sic alius ab alia aliqua re, ut visum est.

> There are two types of inflections, a voluntary one and a natural one. **The voluntary type is the product at which an individual has arrived by inflection as his will has carried him.** So, when three people have bought one slave each at Ephesus, sometimes one inflects the name from the man who sold him, *Artemidorus*, and calls him *Artemas*; another inflects it from the region because he bought him there, *Ion* from *Ionia*; another, because he

---

[22] For just one of many instances of *sterilis* used of plants in an agricultural setting in Varro's *Res rusticae*, see *rust.* 1.31.3: *eiuncidum enim sarmentum propter infirmitatem* **sterile** *neque ex se potest eicere vitem . . .*

VARRO'S WORD TREES   61

bought him at *Ephesus*, calls him *Ephesius*; in this way everyone names him
after some other thing, as seems appropriate.

Here, the process of word derivation is neither mechanical nor automatic,
as in the cases of verb conjugation and noun declension, but terms are instead derived by human choices in naming. The process is unpredictable,
non-systematic, and sometimes confusing, in that people may assign words
to things in an inexpert way. While *natura* itself had served as the guiding
principle in the case of *declinatio naturalis*, in the example above, which
involves the creation of a slave name, we see the artificial *voluntas* of a human
directing the way in which the word is derived.[23]

5. "First Born" and "Leaned Down" Words

Both inflection and derivation, that is *declinatio naturalis* and *declinatio
voluntaria*, depend on a base form. In book 6 of *De lingua Latina*, we learn
that terms that cannot be derived from other words (e.g., verbs such as
lego, *scribo*, and *sto*), but that have their own roots (*radices*), are said to be
primigenia ("first born"), while subsidiary forms, namely those that come
into being from another form (6.37 *quae ab alio quo oriuntur*), are said to
be declined from these first born terms.[24] In order to demonstrate this,
Varro takes as his example the word *lego* ("I gather"); this is the *primigenium
verbum*, and from it are *declinata* ("leaned down") its inflected forms and
derivatives. Varro notes (*ling.* 6.36) that the "leanings down" include (a) terms
with both temporal qualities and cases (participles), (b) terms with temporal
qualities but no cases (finite verbs), (c) terms with cases but no temporal
qualities (nouns), and (d) terms with neither temporal qualities nor cases
(adverbs). The following tree diagram can be constructed:

[23] Natural derivation will however occur once these names have been set down: e.g., speakers will
naturally create the forms *Artemidori*, *Ionis*, and *Ephesi* for the genitive case form of the new names
(*ling.* 8.22). Some scholars have seen the example of the naming of slaves for *declinatio voluntaria*
as problematic in its context; see Dahlmann (1940, 86–7) and Fehling (1957, 71–3), who argue
that the example belongs properly in the lost portion on etymology rather than in the section on
declinatio voluntaria: in the words of Fehling (1957, 72), "[d]as Beispiel zeigt also nicht die Willkür
der gewählten Ableitungsform, sondern die Willkür der Namensgebung."
[24] These terms correspond to the πρωτότυπα ("prototypes") and παράγωγα ("derivative forms") in
Dionysius Thrax *GG* I.1 25.3–5 εἴδη δὲ δύο, πρωτότυπον καὶ παράγωγον. πρωτότυπον μὲν οὖν ἐστι
τὸ κατὰ τὴν πρώτην θέσιν λεχθέν, οἷον Γῆ. παράγωγον δὲ τὸ ἀφ᾽ ἑτέρου τὴν γένεσιν ἐσχηκός, οἷον
Γαιήϊος ("there are two forms, the prototype and the derivative form. The protoype is that which is
said at the first imposition [of the word], e.g., Γῆ ['earth']. But the derivative form is that which has its
origin from another [word], e.g., Γαιήϊος ['sprung from Gaia']"). Cf. Dahlmann (1932, 81 n. 2).

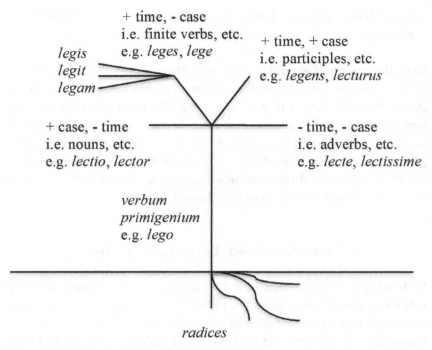

Figure 4.9 *Declinata* of the verb *lego* ("I gather")

As an aside, we might also note the use of *lego* ("collect," "pick," "read") in such examples; Varro himself derived *lego* in the sense "read" from "gather."[25] The use of this particular example in the context of fertile and sterile word trees would therefore seem appropriate and intentional.[26] The instance is not unique, and, as Taylor has noted, there is also something quizzical about the relationship between the example *ager* in *De lingua Latina* 5.13 and the image in which it is embedded (see Section 2): Varro clearly wants to play with the term "field" in this context, in that the kin of the word tree of *ager* ("field") is in fact forcing its "roots" into a neighbor's property. While they are admittedly common example-words in Varro, both *ager* and *lego* have ties to the agricultural quality of the word

---

[25] Cf. *ling.* 6.66 *"legere" dictum, quod "leguntur" ab oculis litterae*.
[26] In his *Res rusticae*, for instance, Varro speaks of "gathering" olives and grapes (e.g., *rust.* 1.34.2 *uvas... legere*).

VARRO'S WORD TREES 63

tree: Varro was seemingly not unaware of the figurative aspects of the material he was presenting.

6. Planting Words

How did the *primigenia* (or "first words") emerge? Throughout *De lingua Latina*, we read of words being *imposita rebus* ("set upon things"), and the expression in fact appears in the very first passage of our surviving text (*ling.* 5.1):

> **quemadmodum vocabula essent imposita rebus** in lingua Latina, sex libris exponere institui.

> In what way **names are applied to** [= set upon] **concepts** [= **things**] in the Latin language, I have undertaken to set out in six books.[27]

An unprefixed form, *ponere*, was also used: at the beginning of the seventh book, Varro states his intention to explain the words *posita* ("set down") by the Roman poets (*ling.* 7.5):[28]

> dicam in hoc libro de verbis quae a poetis sunt **posita**.

> In this book I shall speak about the words which have been **employed** [= set down] by the poets.

The noun *impositio* is the standard Latin translation of the Greek θέσις ("imposition"), yet Varro appears to incorporate the term into the tree metaphor with a particular enthusiasm; in proceeding to discuss poetic words at the beginning of book 7, for example, he states the following (*ling.* 7.2):

> **cum haec amminicula addas ad eruendum voluntatem impositoris, tamen latent multa.** quod si poetice <quae> in carminibus servavit multa prisca quae essent, sic etiam cur essent posuisset, **fecundius poemata ferrent fructum.**

---

[27] There are many such expressions; e.g., *ling.* 8.9 *causa, inquam, cur eas ab* **impositis** *nominibus declinarint, quam ostendi.*

[28] Cf. *ling.* 6.60 *quibus ea novissent, nomina* **ponebant**.

64 VARRO

> Even though you employ these aids in order to unearth the will of the
> man who invented [= set down] a word, still much remains hidden. But
> if the art of poetry, which has preserved much that is old in compositions,
> had in this way also set out why those words exist, **poems would bear fruit
> more abundantly.**

The metaphor of "digging" of course suggests that the intention of the placer (*impositor*) is located "under" the word; elsewhere as well, the meanings of words are figuratively to be found "beneath" the word.[29] The reference to "bearing fruit" further brings in the agricultural metaphor and suggests the notion that a poem is a grove of word trees. Exactly why it might bear more fruit once the intentions of its *impositor* are known is of course left unanswered (although I think we can put forward a conjecture for this based on what follows).

The terms *ponere* and *imponere* (and by extension *impositor*) can themselves be linked to the tree metaphor by turning to Varro's manual on how to run a farm, the *Res rusticae*, where they could mean "to plant." Consider the section that concerns the proper laying-out of trees on a property in order to produce the maximum amount of fruit: trees should be *posita* ("planted") in a quincunx pattern, so that they do not shield each other from the sunlight (*rust.* 1.7.2):[30]

> itaque maiores nostri ex arvo aeque magno, sed male consito et minus
> multum et minus bonum faciebant vinum et frumentum, **quod quae suo
> quidque loco sunt posita**, ea minus loci occupant, et minus officit aliud alii
> ab sole ac luna ac vento.

> Therefore our ancestors produced wine and grain in lesser quantity and
> quality from a property that was equally large yet less well laid-out: **since
> those things that are planted each in its own space** take up less space and
> do not shield each other so much from the sun, moon, and wind.

The prefixed form could be used in a similar manner (e.g., *rust.* 1.26 *alternos ordines imponunt* "they plant alternate rows [of cypresses]"). Although Varro

---

[29] E.g., *ling.* 7.1 *non reprehendum igitur in illis qui in scrutando verbo litteram adiciunt aut demunt, quo facilius **quid sub ea voce** subsit videri possit.* Compare Epicurus, *Ep. Herod.* 37, where what is arranged under the vocalizations is the πρῶτον ἐννόημα.

[30] The usage was common; cf. e.g., Hor. *carm.* 2.13.1–3 *ille et nefasto te **posuit** die, / quicumque primum, et sacrilega manu / produxit, arbos.* The noun *positio* was used in the sense "planting" by, e.g., Columella; cf. *OLD* s.v. *positio* 1.

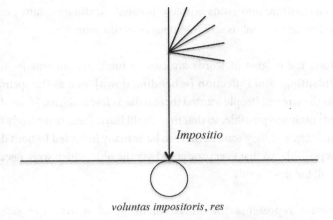

Figure 4.10 Placement (*impositio*) of a word on a thing (*res*)

shows a marked preference for the verb *sero* ("to sow") in the *Res rusticae*, from excerpts such as these we can ascertain that the term (*im*)*ponere* was used for the planting of trees in Varronian Latin as well as for the imposition of names upon things.

I would therefore suggest that the notion of planting was at least in the back of Varro's mind when he used terms such as *impositio*. In addition to the idea of "bending down" words to create derived terms, we have the prior procedure of a basic word being "planted" on top of the thing (*res*) it is to designate (the arrow at the base of the tree illustrates the implied movement):[31]

7. Propagating Word Trees

At the beginning of book 8 (8.5), Varro clearly distinguishes *impositio* from *declinatio* (note the use of the river metaphor for "derivation" here applied):

duo igitur omnino verborum principia, **impositio <et declinatio>, alterum ut fons, alterum ut rivus. imposita** nomina esse voluerunt

---

[31] The precise meaning of *res* is debated; Varro seems to be able to use it to denote the external referent (the item being referred to), the *signifié* (the concept in the speaker's mind), and the "grammatical substance" of the term (e.g., plurality when it comes to nouns). See Roesch (1999); compare de Melo (2019b, 229). I prefer the neutral translation "thing."

66   VARRO

quam paucissima, quo citius ediscere possent, **declinata** quam plurima, quo facilius omnes quibus ad usum opus esset dicerent.

Therefore, the origins of words are two in total, **assignment [= setting down/planting] and inflection [= bending down]**, one as the spring, the other as the stream. People wanted there to be as few **assigned [= set down/planted]** nouns as possible, so that they could learn them completely all the more quickly, and they wanted there to be as many **inflected [= bent down]** ones as possible, so that everyone could say the ones which were necessary for use all the more easily.

The *impositio* represents the initial planting of words, the subsequent derivations (both natural and voluntary) fall under the heading of *declinatio*. Yet this is where things become a bit dicey for our understanding of the tree, in that the *impositio*, or planting, of words on things appears in some contexts to be the same thing as *declinatio voluntaria*, the intentional derivation of one term from another in order to name something.[32] At such moments, the two can essentially be synonyms, and indeed, occasionally both expressions are used in conjunction: in discussing why names sometimes appear to be derived from other terms almost randomly, Varro suggests that the reason is that language users "plant" (*imponunt*) words on things by "bending them down" (*declinantes*) ineptly (*ling.* 10.16):

quare proinde ac simile conferri non oportet ac dicere, ut sit ab "Roma" "Romanus," sic ex "Capua" dici oportere "Capuanus," quod in consuetudine vehementer natat, **quod declinantes imperite rebus nomina imponunt**, a quibus cum accepit consuetudo, turbulenta necesse est dicere.

Thus one ought not to set up a comparison of similarity and say that, as from *Roma* comes *Romanus* so from *Capua* one ought to say *Capuanus*, something which is subject to considerable fluctuation in usage, **because those who inflect [= bend down] assign names to [= set/plant names on] objects without skill.** When usage has adopted these names, one cannot help saying them in a confused way.[33]

---

[32] Cf. Dahlmann (1940, 86–7).

[33] The confusion about the relationship between *imponere* and *declinare* is also apparent at, e.g., *ling.* 9.34 and 10.15.

VARRO'S WORD TREES   67

How can these two things be reconciled? How can the "leaning down" of a term, which would appear to occur on the tree itself, at the same time constitute a "planting" of a new tree on top of a *res* ("thing")? It might be of course be argued that Varro is simply being irregular in his use of the terminology, but I would like to suggest two ways of resolving the terminological clash in such passages.

The first involves looking once again at Varro's own manual on how to run a farm, the *Res rusticae*. In the first book of his agricultural text, Varro discusses how to transfer shoots cut from a tree into the ground in order to create a new tree; this is the third of the four different ways of creating a new plant (*rust.* 1.40.4):

> tertium genus seminis, quod ex arbore per surclos **defertur** in terram, si in humum **demittitur**, in quibusdam, cum est, videndum, ut eo tempore sit deplantatum, quo oportet—id fit tum, antequam gemmare aut florere quid incipit—et quae de arbore transferas ut ea deplantes potius quam defringas, quod plantae solum stabilius, **quo latius aut radices facilius mittit.**

> If the third type of planting, which consists in **carrying** shoots **down** to the earth from the tree, **is sent down** into the earth, you must in certain cases watch out that the shoot has been removed at the right time (and that this occurs before it has begun to bud or blossom). And that you pull out rather than snap off the shoots that you are transferring from the tree, since the more stable the bottom of the plant is, **the more broadly or easily it sends out its roots.**

Varro, then, was aware of the method by which a cutting is removed from a tree in order to create a new plant; is it possible that this was in the back of his mind when it came to the integration of the terms *declinatio* and *impositio*? The word tree metaphor that capitalized on the terms *declinatio* and *casus*, *ramus* and *radix*, *sterilis* and *fecundus*, would thereby be extended to include more artificial and (at least to the layperson) more exotic modes of planting than the usual one. On this interpretation, the process depicted in *ling.* 10.16, where *declinare* and *imponere* are apparently equated, would be the following: the derived term (*propago*) is first "bent away" (*declinantes*) before being removed and set in the ground (*imponunt*) on top of the thing it designates (*rebus*):

The image is of course flawed (and there is no explicit reference to the act of removing the word-shoot from the mother word tree in Varro's *De lingua*

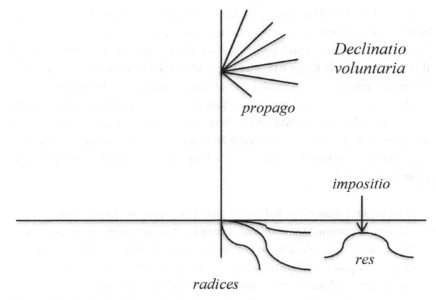

Figure 4.11 Planting (*impositio*) of a cutting from a word tree

Latina), but it is one possible way of reconciling *declinatio voluntaria* with *impositio*, and it has the virtue of being prompted by an agricultural work written by Varro himself.

There is, however, a further relevant mode of creating new trees from old ones. "Layering" is the process by which an uncut shoot from a tree or grapevine is buried in the soil with its tip exposed and allowed to take root, while still remaining attached to the "mother" tree. Eventually, the new tree can be severed from its mother and take on an existence of its own. Varro never describes the process of layering in the *Res rusticae*, yet he was doubtless aware of it: it is described by Cato the Elder in *De agri cultura* (*agr.* 32.1, 51–2), whom Varro cites frequently in his own agricultural writing, and subsequently by Columella (see, e.g., *Res rustica* 4.15 and *De arboribus* 7). Here is Cato (*agr.* 51):[34]

> propagatio pomorum, aliarum arborum. ab arbore abs terra pulli qui nascentur, eos in terram deprimito extollitoque primorem partem, uti radicem capiat: inde biennio post effodito seritoque.

[34] For further references, see Thurmond (2017, 85–6).

Layering of fruit trees, and of other trees: press down into the earth the sprouts that spring from the ground around the tree, and raise up the tip, so that it may take root. Two years later, dig [the new tree] up and plant [it elsewhere].[35]

The process may seem obscure, but it is still used today in (for example) the traditional propagation of mastic trees in southern Chios (φύτεμα με καταβολάδες).[36] It may be depicted in the following way:
It thereby offers an analogy for the process of word derivation and imposition:

On this model, the *propago* led into the soil will become a word tree in its own right once it has been severed from its mother, and the process will begin afresh. The image is again imperfect, in that it does it does not explain why a word has moved from the branches to form roots of its own, but it does offer a way of avoiding the conflict between the standard terms for derivation (*declinatio voluntaria* and *impositio*) while remaining within the bounds of the metaphor. I suggest that in such examples Varro is still working with word trees.

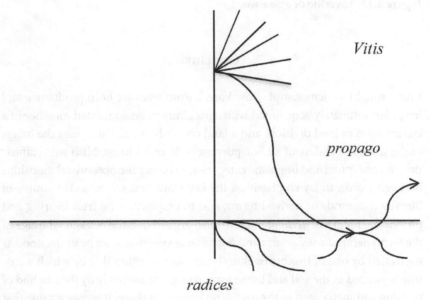

Figure 4.12 Layering of a tree

[35] At Columella *Res rustica* 4.15, the layered shoot is called a *mergus* "diver."
[36] While used frequently in the propagation of vines in the ancient world, the technique of layering has become rare in modern viticulture due to the spread of Phylloxera; it is still sometimes used in Phylloxera-free wine regions, such as the Coonawarra in South Australia.

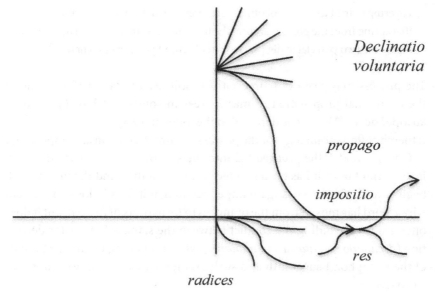

Figure 4.13 Layering of a new word

8. Conclusion

I have sought to demonstrate how Varro's word trees are both productive and irregular: intimately acquainted with agriculture as an appointed member of a commission of land division, and a land owner himself, Varro uses the image of the tree for a variety of ad hoc purposes—in order to establish word affiliation to conceptual and linguistic categories, to depict the obscure relationships between words, to lay emphasis on the key word that served as the source of literally thousands of derived terms, and to emphasize the fruit-bearing and productive nature of *declinatio*. I have also argued that the occasional usage of the terms *declinatio voluntaria* and *impositio* as synonyms can be understood as motivated by one of two horticultural metaphors—either that by which a cutting is planted in the soil and left to form roots, or conversely by the method of training a branch down to the earth and burying it there. It is conceivable that the lost sections on syntax, *coniunctio*, may have continued to apply the metaphor: trellised vines were, after all, described as *iugata* in the agricultural writers. In any case, Varro's word trees, be they original or not (and it is possible that others had already used the image), represent an important moment in the history of linguistics, a field in which the image of the tree has been highly fruitful.

PART II
PROFESSIONAL GRAMMARIANS

5

The Use of Greek in Diomedes'
Ars grammatica

Bruno Rochette

1. Introduction

Diomedes' *Ars grammatica*—together with the grammars of Dositheus, Charisius, the so-called *Anonymus Bobiensis*, and later Eutyches and Priscian—belongs to a group of late antique Latin textbooks composed for native speakers of Greek, probably in the context of an eastern city such as Constantinople or Antioch.[1] All these grammatical treatises, which do not give the impression of being handbooks for elementary Latin teaching, share at least two assumptions about their readers: that they know at least some Latin already and that they also know Greek.[2] Many of these readers would have aspired toward a stronger command of Latin in order to advance in their careers in the civil, juridical, or military spheres of Roman administration.[3] Diomedes' likely use of Charisius and the specific forms of address point to a date at the end of the fourth century and before the middle of the fifth, when he is cited by Rufinus (e.g., *gramm.* VI 555.5–10; see *Guardians* 271).[4]

---

[1] On these bilingual Latin grammars in general see Dionisotti (1984), Schenkeveld (2007), and Rochette (2015). Overviews of Diomedes are found in *Guardians* 270–2 (no. 47) and *CCC* 294–5. For Dositheus see the recent edition of Bonnet (2005) and Lenoble, Swiggers, and Wouters (2000), and for the *Anonymus Bobiensis* see De Nonno (1982). References to Diomedes (= Diom.) are to the edition of Keil (*gramm.* I 199.1–529.28) with page and line number.

[2] Another kind of handbook existed for learning the rudiments of Latin: Hermeneumata (see Dickey 2016b, 4–6).

[3] On the audience and motivations for learning Latin in the Eastern empire, see Dickey (2016b, 1–4).

[4] By contrast, Mazhuga (1998) argues for the dependence of Charisius on Diomedes, but his arguments have not found widespread agreement. Dammer (2001, 43–7, and esp. 170–2) strongly reaffirms Diomedes' direct use of Charisius (along with one of Charisius' main sources) and Donatus.

Bruno Rochette, *The Use of Greek in Diomedes'* Ars grammatica In: *Roman Perspectives on Linguistic Diversity*. Edited by Adam Gitner, Oxford University Press. © Oxford University Press 2023.
DOI: 10.1093/oso/9780197611975.003.0005

74   PROFESSIONAL GRAMMARIANS

Who was Diomedes and in what sociolinguistic context did he live? Information about him has been collected in the prosopographical section of Robert Kaster's *Guardians of Language*, where Diomedes appears as number 47 (see also *CCC* 294–5). No external evidence about his life is preserved. The preface of his *Ars* gives a general but imprecise idea of the orientation of his grammar. Following the model of Charisius' *praefatio*, which takes the form of a dedicatory epistle to the writer's son, Diomedes' *Ars* also begins with a letter, addressed to a certain Athanasius (299.1–8):[5]

> Diomedes Athanasio salutem dicit. artem merae Latinitatis puraeque eloquentiae magistram sub incude litteraria dociliter procudendo formatam humanae sollertiae claritas expolivit. hanc cum cognovissem excellentem facundiam tuam plurimi facere, desiderio tuo libenter indulgens summo studio, quantum mediocris admodum ingenii mei qualitas capere patiebatur, trino digestam libello dilucideque expeditam censui esse mittendam, quia ipsos aurium meatus audita scientia conplere absentia denegatum est.

> Diomedes sends greetings to Athanasius. The art of undiluted Latinity and the instructor of pure eloquence, having been formed at the literary anvil with gentle hammering, have been polished up by the brilliance of human expertise. When I learned that Your Outstanding Eloquence regarded this art very highly, gladly indulging in your desire with the greatest care, as much as the quality of my mediocre intelligence was able to absorb, I resolved that it should be sent to you, compiled and lucidly arranged in three books, since absence forbade me to fill the channels of your ears with oral knowledge.

We do not know anything about this Athanasius, but we can infer from Diomedes' wording that he must have held a high position in Roman society and was interested in Latin grammatical theory. Diomedes addresses him as *excellens facundia tua* (299.4) and elsewhere as *prudentia tua* (473.3–4), expressions that "may indicate that he was a member of a learned profession—esp. a rhetorician or advocate—or belonged to a branch of the imperial service that recruited heavily from the learned professions"

---

[5] Discussed by Schenkeveld (2007, 183). Uría (2006) analyzes Charisius' *praefatio*, and Dammer (2001, 59–63) compares this with Diomedes' *praefatio*.

THE USE OF GREEK IN DIOMEDES' *ARS GRAMMATICA*   75

(*Guardians* 272).[6] Similar formulae of solemn address are commonplace and can be found also in Priscian (e.g., *gramm.* III 405.14–15 *sapiens eloquentia vestra*). Diomedes, who seems to have been a professional grammarian, dedicated to Athanasius a text in three parts (299.9–10 *collatio tripertita*), each book corresponding to different age of his school audience (299.10 *secundum trina aetatis gradatim legentium spatia*). The material and arrangement suggest the author was a professional grammarian.[7] Perhaps Diomedes was a teacher in an aristocratic family, who in the name of his private pupil recommended his book to a wider public.

Certainly the names Diomedes and Athanasius point to a Greek-speaking context, and the highly abstract style of his Latin, which is amply on display in the preface, may suggest a native Greek speaker (*CCC* 294).[8] Furthermore, the books contain many references to the Greek language. This contribution provides an analysis of such passages, focusing on examples where Greek and Latin are compared and where code-switching occurs.[9]

A useful point of comparison is Charisius' *Ars grammatica*.[10] Already at the beginning, in the chapter *De litteris*, Charisius mentions the differences between the vowels of Greek and Latin (*gramm.* p. 4.17–5.4). In the next chapter, *De syllabis*, the Greek etymology of the word *syllaba* is discussed (*gramm.* p. 8.9–14 παρὰ τὸ συλλαμβάνειν τὰ γράμματα). In the ninth chapter, the absence of the dual in Latin is noted in contrast to Greek (*gramm.* p. 15.22–3).[11] Furthermore, Greek equivalents of Latin words are given throughout the work. In the long list of *singularia tantum and pluralia tantum* (*gramm.* p. 32.19–39.23), almost every item is followed by a Greek equivalent and sometimes with an explanation. There are far fewer of these simple Greek glosses in Diomedes. Instead, as we shall see, Diomedes has

---

[6] On *prudentia tua* (*vestra*) as a formal address in later Latin, see *TLL* X.2 2380.71–2381.9 (for proconsuls, bishops, praetorian prefects, etc.). Dammer (2001, 56–8) accepts Kaster's view.

[7] For instance, professional Latin grammarians are attested in Constantinople from around 360 CE onward: Evanthius (*Guardians* no. 54) and Chrestus (*Guardians* no. 27); see further Lemerle (1971, 64 and n. 55); Schamp (2009, 260).

[8] Dammer (2001, 369) collects some constructions that may indicate Diomedes' first language was Greek (e.g., *quidem . . . vero* as a calque on μὲν . . . δέ, *est* + infinitive to express possibility, and an apparent genitive absolute at 439.29–30 *ipsorum . . . scientium*). It is now generally agreed that Diomedes was mainly writing for Greeks, but earlier scholars such as Tolkiehn supposed a mainly Latin audience (on the history of this question: Dammer 2001, 56–8).

[9] Lacerda Faria Rocha and Fortes (2016, 242–7) also discuss multilingualism and code-switching in Diomedes, restricting their corpus to intra-sentential switches. A few of the same examples are also discussed under category four below.

[10] Stoppie (2005) analyzes Charisius' use of Greek in detail; Schenkeveld (2007) discusses similarities and differences between the two grammarians.

[11] On the dual in the Roman grammarians more generally, see Denecker (Chapter 8).

76 PROFESSIONAL GRAMMARIANS

tended to integrate his knowledge of Greek (and of Greek sources) more thoroughly into the content of the *Ars*.

2. The Nature of Diomedes' *Ars grammatica*

Quellenforschung on the relationship among Charisius, Diomedes, and Dositheus has led to the generally accepted conclusion that Diomedes depends at least partly on Charisius, and partly on common source(s), which includes material from Palaemon, the first-century author of the first *Ars grammatica* (now lost). The fundamental work of Karl Barwick (1922) described in detail the mutual links among the so-called Charisian group, including Dositheus, Diomedes, and the *Anonymus Bobiensis*.[12] While Charisius composed his treatise in five books, Diomedes has chosen a three-book structure, as in the *Ars maior* of Donatus.[13] The *artes grammaticae* written for Greek-speaking audience do not differ much in grammatical theory from those addressed to a Roman audience. They deal with the same topics in a similar order. Diomedes starts with a discussion of *oratio* and continues with a treatment of the *partes orationis*. The first book (300–419), the longest of the three (120 pages in Keil's edition), deals with the parts of speech after comments about *genera nominum* (301.4–17), *numeri* (301.18–22), *figurae* (300.23–30), and *casus* (301.31–320.9), with much material also found in Charisius' first book. In the section *de casibus* (301.31–320.9), there are several excursus, including the section titled *de consensu verborum cum casibus* (310.31–320.9), which deals with syntactic *idiomata*, in other words case constructions in which Latin diverges from Greek.[14] By contrast, Charisius' section *de idiomatibus* is placed at the beginning of book 5. The

---

[12] Some details of this reconstruction remain under dispute and cannot be resolved here. In particular, Barwick posited the existence of a *Charisius plenior* partly to explain cases where Diomedes seems to have known a lengthier version of Charisius' text. But these expansions can be explained if Diomedes also had access to Charisius' main source, as Dammer (2001, 43–7) argues; so too Schenkeveld (2007, 17–22), siding with Tolkiehn, Schmidt, and Bonnet. Conversely, a *Diomedes plenior* has sometimes been posited to explain material that surfaces in some early medieval *artes* (esp. the *Anonymus ad Cuimnanum*); see e. g. Garcea (2019, 58–9, 71 n. 86). On Barwick's thesis and its reception see *CCC* 187–9.

[13] In addition to his remarks in the preface, Diomedes discusses the structure of his manual at 299.14–18, 420.2–7, and 473.2–14. Holtz (1981, 428) well describes Diomedes' method of combining sources: "Diomède ... a soigneusement juxtaposé ses deux sources principales, Charisius et Donat et il est facile de distinguer ce qu'il a emprunté à l'un et ce qu'il a emprunté à l'autre." On the framework of Diomedes' *Ars* compared to that of other *artes*, see Baratin (1994, 144).

[14] On *idiomata* as a genre see Gitner (2019).

THE USE OF GREEK IN DIOMEDES' *ARS GRAMMATICA* 77

inclusion of a section *de idiomatibus* immediately before the *de nomine* shows that Diomedes aims to help his Greek audience by comparing the Greek and Latin language systems. In the second book, Diomedes speaks about several basic notions (*ars, vox, littera,* etc.), the letters of the alphabet, syllables, accents, punctuation, and the qualities and defects of speech. The third book is devoted to poetic topics, with a very developed account of meter (*de arte metrica*). As in other manuals, such as Charisius, pseudo-Probus' *Instituta artium,* and even Priscian, Diomedes presents a combination of material taken from the "Schulgrammatik" and the *regulae* types of grammar that was intended to benefit a non-native speaker of Latin.[15] Morphology is an important element of Diomedes' grammar.

Whereas Charisius addresses his son who is described as making progress in Latin, Diomedes does not assume his readers have limited competence in Latin, nor does he present it as a foreign language.[16] To study the role of Greek in both grammarians it is important to take into account this difference of proficiency. Diomedes addresses readers who are more proficient in Latin.[17] Furthermore, he is aware of differences between the languages, as shown in the section *de litteris* when he discusses the letter *z*: here he implicitly contrasts, on one side, Greek and Latin together (*utraque lingua*) against *barbara nomina,* on the other side.[18] Inside this Greco-Latin unity, Latin is similar to Greek but not identical.[19]

3. The Role of Greek in Diomedes' *Ars grammatica*

In her study of the role of Greek in Charisius' *Ars grammatica,* Karen Stoppie has distinguished eight categories: (1) Greek grammatical terminology,

---

[15] This distinction was made by Law (2003, 65). The "Schulgrammatik" type, whose model is Donatus' *Ars grammatica,* defines the parts of speech and indicates their properties without providing many examples. The *regulae* type are shorter manuals that provide more extensive paradigms and examples.

[16] Uría (2006, 117).

[17] Schenkeveld (2007, 187): " I think that Diomedes aims at a somewhat higher level of readership than Charisius does, for Diomedes offers a large amount of Greek grammatical terminology, whereas Charisius excels in giving translations and explanations in Greek for Latin examples."

[18] Diom. 426.8–11 *z consonans semivocalis duplex Graeca, quae propter Graeca vel barbara nomina admittitur, ut Zenon Zacynthus Mezentius gaza. pro hac veteres duabus s utebantur, ut Messentius et pitisso tablisso et cetera* ("The consonant *z* is a Greek semi-vowel double which is adopted because of Greek or foreign words, like *Zenon Zacynthus Mezentius gaza.* In its place the ancients used two *s*'s like *Messentius et pitisso tablisso* and so on.").

[19] A point made by Desbordes (1988, 16).

78 PROFESSIONAL GRAMMARIANS

(2) Greek expressions, (3) Greek quotations, (4) Greek etymologies, (5) bilingual references to Latin literature, (6) bilingual examples, (7) passages where explicit knowledge of Greek grammaticography is transmitted, and (8) passages where the Latin language is taught by referring to the corresponding Greek. In the case of Diomedes, we can simplify this framework by concentrating on four categories: (1) direct quotations of Greek, (2) Greek or Greco-Latin grammatical terminology, (3) comparison between Greek and Latin as an explicative strategy, and (4) intra-sentential code-switching. The differences among these categories will become clearer in the examples that follow.

3.1 Direct Quotations of Greek

This category, in which Diomedes directly quotes or uses Greek, falls under three subheadings: Greek literary citations (3.1.1), examples in Greek (3.1.2), and etymologies in Greek (3.1.3). In these examples, the use of Greek typically come at the sentence or phrase boundary, unlike the examples in category 4, where Greek is integrated syntactically into a predominately Latin sentence.

3.1.1 Greek Literary Citations

There are nineteen direct quotations from Greek literature, including fifteen from Homer[20] and, in chronological order, from Arctinus of Miletus (477.9–13 = *Iliou Persis* frg. 7 Bernabé [1987] = Arctini spuria frg. 1 Davies [1988] = *Aethiopis* frg. 5 West [2003]), Aristophanes (475.24–5 = *Ra.* 153), Demosthenes (469.4–5 = *De corona* 1), and Theophrastus (487.11–12 = text no. 708 in Fortenbaugh [2005]).[21] Many more Greek authors are mentioned by name, including Alcaeus, Callimachus, Empedocles, Euripides, Sappho, and Stesichorus (see Keil's *Index scriptorum*). All these sources fall between the seventh or eighth and the fourth centuries BCE, in other words in the archaic and classical periods. If we compare with Charisius, who directly quotes

[20] The Homeric quotations include ten from the *Iliad*: 1.334 (= 335.5–6), 2.824 (= 420.12), 3.164 (= 429.16), 3.182 (= 499.17), 12.208 (= 500.16), 13.807 (= 475.18), 14.1 (= 429.27), 22.128 (= 300.22), 23.2 (= 500.10), 23.221 (= 495.25). A further five come from the *Odyssey*: 1.1 (= 429.18), 5.237 (= 430.4), 9.24 (= 430.10), 9.347 (= 495.18), 10.60 (= 500.13).

[21] Furthermore, a sequence of Greek mythological names at 323.24–9 appears to be cited from the Greek lyric poet Ibycus (323.29 *sicut Ibycus Graecus retulit*; cf. 321.30 = Ibyc. frg. 305 *PMG*), probably taken from an intermediate grammatical source (Rodríguez-Noriega Guillén and Uría 2017).

THE USE OF GREEK IN DIOMEDES' *ARS GRAMMATICA* 79

perhaps only one Greek literary source, we can conclude that Diomedes relies very strongly on the authority of Greek authors, especially Homer.[22] It is not surprising, however, that he cites Latin authors much more often—almost five times more often—than Greek authors: for example, Virgil is quoted more than eighty times. The function of such quotations is clear: a Latin or a Greek author confers literary authority on a grammatical rule.

I give only one example on the more sophisticated side, taken from the section *de oratione*, at the beginning of the work. Here Diomedes gives an etymological explanation of the term *oratio* in Latin (decomposed into two elements: *oris* + *ratio*) and in Greek with Latin translation, supporting it with a Homeric quotation. The citation of Homer helps to bolster the proposed etymology and links the prestige of Greek, both its language and literature, to Latin grammar.

(1) Diom. 300.20–2: "oratio" . . . videtur dicta quasi "oris ratio," vel a Graeca origine, ἀπὸ τοῦ ὀαρίζειν, hoc est sermocinari. unde Homerus ὀαρίζετον ἀλλήλοισιν (*Il.* 22.128).[23]

Oratio ["speech"] seems to be said as if it were *oris ratio* ["reason/method of the mouth"] or from a Greek origin ἀπὸ τοῦ ὀαρίζειν, that is "to converse." Whence Homer [says] ὀαρίζετον ἀλλήλοισιν [*Il.* 22.128, "hold dalliance one with the other"].

3.1.2 Examples in Greek

This category is more difficult to characterize, but the Greek citations can be described as "examples" since they are used to illustrate or exemplify features of Latin and they are usually introduced with Latin particles, such as *ut* or *quasi*.

(2a) Diom. 407.10–15: in nominibus Latinis propriis quae "o" littera casu ablativo terminantur . . . mutata "o" littera in "a" accedente syllaba "ne"

---

[22] It depends on whether one regards Charisius' quotation in Greek of Hermes Trismegistus' Κρύφιος λόγος (p. 312.5–7) as "literary"; in any case it was taken over verbatim from Romanus. Charisius also translates a passage of Demosthenes' *Philippics* (p. 365.3–7 = *Phil.* 3.12), and he paraphrases Aristophanes of Byzantium on ἀναλογία (p. 149.30 = Ar. Byz. frg. 375 Slater; see Uría 2007, 139–41). Stoppie (2005, 132) mentions Charisius' quotation of a Greek remark by Statilius Maximus in a second-century CE rhetorical handbook (p. 313.2–3, on an expression in Cato), which I do not count as a literary source (likewise directly from Romanus).

[23] About the etymology of *oratio*, see Dammer (2001, 71 n. 215).

80 PROFESSIONAL GRAMMARIANS

adverbia faciunt, ut a "Vergilio" "Vergiliane," <a> "Tullio" "Tulliane."
et **quae apud Graecos adverbia κως terminantur**, ea apud nos iuxta
Latinum sermonem in "e" littera finiuntur, ut Ὁμηρικῶς "**Homerice.**"

Among Latin proper nouns that end with *o* in the ablative case, ... they
form adverbs by changing the letter *o* into *a* and adding one more syllable
ne, as from *Vergilio Vergiliane*, from *Tullio Tulliane*. **And those adverbs
that among the Greeks end in -κως, are terminated among us with the**
letter *e* in accordance with Latin usage, **for example** Ὁμηρικῶς *Homerice*.

(2b)   Diom. 406.26–34: sed in hoc [sensu] distinctio sensum mutat, ut sit "**humane**" ἀνθρωπίνως, ut est apud Terentium "tamen vix humane patitur"
(= *Ad*. 145); et "**humanitus**" φιλανθρώπως, ut idem Terentius ait "coepi
non humanitus / neque ut animum decuit aegrotum adulescentuli
/ tractare" (= *Haut.* 99–101). <sunt> quaedam nomina in "us" litteris
terminata quae ex se bina adverbia faciunt, ut est veterum auctoritas.

However, in this matter a distinction changes the sense, for example
humane ἀνθρωπίνως, as in Terence *tamen vix humane patitur* (*Ad.*
145); and *humanitus* φιλανθρώπως, as Terence likewise says *coepi non
humanitus / neque ut animum decuit aegrotum adulescentuli / tractare*
(*Haut.* 99–101). There are nouns ending with the letters -*us* that produce two adverbs, according to the authority of the ancients.

(3)   Diom. 333.21–2: hoc pronomen quod est "qualis," item quod sequitur
"talis," communia sunt masculino et feminino generi. "**qualis**" ποταπός,
οἷος, ὁποῖος.

This pronoun, that is *qualis* ["of what sort"], and likewise what follows,
talis ["of such a sort"] are common to both male and female gender.
Qualis: ποταπός, οἷος, ὁποῖος.

(4)   Diom. 405.35–7: sed tamen lectum invenimus "**in primo,**" quod est ἐν
πρώτοις, et quae dixerunt veteres, "a mane" et "ab hinc annos decem
natus est," quod est "ante decem annos natus."

However, we have found *in primo* ["at first"] written, which is [in
Greek] ἐν πρώτοις ["at first"], *a mane* ["from the morning"] and *ab hinc*

THE USE OF GREEK IN DIOMEDES' *ARS GRAMMATICA* 81

annos decem natus est ["he was born ten years ago"] which is *ante decem annos natus* ["he was born ten years ago"].

(5) Diom. 397.15–20: non numquam et ipsa verba inpersonalia numero plurali funguntur, quotiens in rem sane intenduntur quasi possessiva significatione, ut cum dicimus: "decet me penula," item "decent nos penulae," et similia. quae tali significatione et primam admittunt personam, cum dicimus et "ego te deceo" et "tu me deces," quasi πρέπω σοι πρέπεις μοι.

Sometimes even impersonal verbs are used in the plural, whenever they are used of a thing with a possessive sense, as when we say *decet me penula* ["the cloak suits me"] also *decent nos penulae* ["the cloaks suit us"] and so on. And they also admit the first person in that sense, when we say *ego te deceo* ["I suit you"] and *tu me deces* ["you suit me"], like πρέπω σοι πρέπεις μοι.

(6) Diom. 316.32–5: nam ut Graeci dicunt χρείαν ἔχω χρείαν εἶχον, nos non dicimus "opus habeo" "opus habebam," sed "opus est mihi" "opus erat mihi"; et quod illi dicunt χρείαν σου ἔχει ὁ πατήρ, nos dicimus "pater vult te," "praeceptor volebat te" et similia.

Indeed, just as the Greeks say χρείαν ἔχω χρείαν εἶχον ["I need, I needed"], we don't say *opus habeo opus habebam* ["I have need, I had need"], but *opus est mihi, opus erat mihi* ["the need exists for me, the need existed for me"], and what they express as χρείαν σου ἔχει ὁ πατήρ ["your father needs you"], we say *pater vult te, praeceptor volebat te* ["your father wants you, the master wanted you"], and so on.

In these passages Diomedes gives the Greek equivalent of a Latin word or construction. Latin is the target language being taught by reference to Greek. Diomedes clearly presupposes his students have knowledge of Greek. In examples 2a–b, in order to explain the ending -*e* with adverbial function derived from the ablative case, he says that Latin adverbs ending with -*e* correspond to Greek adverbs ending in -κως. Greek adverbs in -κως similarly occur in the grammars of Charisius and Dositheus, as well as in other Latin literature, for example the correspondence of Cicero, as Adams has pointed out (2003, 323–9).[24] Diomedes uses Greek as a linguistic and terminological

---

[24] On these adverbs in Charisius see Stoppie (2005, 132); for Dositheus: Bonnet (2007, 198).

82 PROFESSIONAL GRAMMARIANS

point of reference. In example 3, he makes a parallel between *qualis* and three Greek equivalents (ποταπός, οἷος, ὁποῖος) without explanation. In example 4, the prepositional group ἐν πρώτοις is presented as an equivalent of *in primo* (preposition and adverb), illustrating an equivalence between a Latin singular and a Greek plural (the Greek is presented as the translation of the Latin: *quod est . . .*). In example 5, the impersonal construction is presented as an aid for understanding the Latin one. The example is very interesting because the Greek is not a literal translation of the Latin: there is a difference of construction between both languages (*decere* governs the accusative, whereas πρέπειν the dative). In example 6, we find an explicit opposition—very widespread in the Latin grammars—between Greeks (*Graeci/illi dicunt*) and Latins (*nos dicimus*). Such an opposition becomes very frequent in Priscian, who among all Roman grammarians is the most attached to Greek models.[25] In these examples, the didactic nature of the Greek is clear and requires no special explanation. Such references to Greek language and grammar are usually very general: the basic equivalence of the two languages is taken for granted.

3.1.3 Greek Etymologies

Etymologies that derive Latin words from Greek origins are common in Latin literature. The etymologies in Diomedes mostly concern technical terms. In the definition of *syllaba* (no. 7) we find a Greek etymology that is also found in a nearly identical passage in Charisius (p. 8.10–13).[26] The opposition *Graece/Latine* is clearly emphasized in this example:

(7) Diom. 427.7–9: syllabae autem dicuntur **Graece** παρὰ τὸ συλλαμβάνειν τὰ γράμματα; **Latine** conexiones vel conceptiones dici possunt, quod litteras concipiant atque conectant.

Syllables are called **in Greek** παρὰ τὸ συλλαμβάνειν τὰ γράμματα ["from the expression 'to gather the letters' "]. **In Latin** they can be called *conexiones* ["connections"] or *conceptiones* ["combinations"] because the syllables combine the letters and connect them.

---

[25] Biville (2008, 45–9) refers to him and his approach as a "tertium ex utroque" because Priscian tends to assimilate Latin to Greek and to reduce the borders between the two languages.

[26] Mentioned by Stoppie (2005, 133). The same etymology is attested in the metrical treatises of Apthonius (Ps. Mar. Victorin. *gramm.* VI 35.25) and Fortunatianus (*gramm.* VI 279.24–5), as well as in Servius' commentary on Donatus (*gramm.* IV 423.11–12) and in Sergius/Servius' *De littera* (*gramm.* IV 478.10–11). Only Apthonius agrees with Diomedes in the odd use of παρά, while the others have ἀπό.

THE USE OF GREEK IN DIOMEDES' *ARS GRAMMATICA*   83

This example is somewhat strange. It is introduced by the preposition παρά after the Latin verb *dicuntur*: typically Latin would use the preposition *ab* here (*dicere ab*), whose Greek equivalent is ἀπό, as found in Charisius (p. 134.9–11 *alii... schidam ex Graeco* ἀπὸ τοῦ σχίζειν *dictam putant*). Why παρά? We seem to have a Greco-Latin hybrid in this example, a *tertium ex utroque*, to use an expression of Priscian (*gramm.* II 2.29). The preposition παρά fits only in the framework of a Greek sentence. Here the Greek syntagm is embedded in a Latin clause with a preposition that is not adapted to the Latin structure. Accordingly, this example arguably also counts as an intra-sentential code-switch, of the kind discussed under category four (section 3.4).

Nevertheless, although Diomedes expresses the etymology in Greek, he does not provide the standard etymology of συλλαβή found in the Greek grammarians, which emphasizes that it is a "joining together" of consonants with one or more vowels (e.g., Dionys. Thrax 7 συλλαβή ἐστι κυρίως σύλληψις συμφώνων μετὰ φωνήεντος ἢ φωνηέντων).[27] This may be significant for understanding the Greek sources Diomedes used, especially since Dammer (2001; 30–1, 112) has drawn attention to some possible points of contact with Dionysius Thrax's grammar.

3.2 Use of Greek or Greco-Latin Grammatical Terminology

Latin grammar is heavily indebted to Greek terminology. The Romans created many grammatical terms by translating Greek terms literally, so-called calques (e.g., *casus* "case" for πτῶσις, which both mean "falling").[28] For other grammatical phenomena, they simply borrowed the Greek word into Latin. I give only one example (no. 8). In the section about *schemata lexeos*, we find a long list of Greek terms transliterated and written in Latin alphabet:

(8)   Diom. 443.15–20: huius species sunt multae, sed necessariae traduntur, per quas similes colligentur, **prolepsis zeugma hypozeuxis syllepsis asyndeton anadiplosis anaphora, alia anaphora, epanalepsis epizeuxis**

---

[27] The scholia (*GG* I.3 23–5) attribute some part of this definition to Aristotle; see also Lallot (1998, 107–8). This Dionysian definition of *syllaba* is also found in the second-century Terentianus Maurus 1314–16 *una vocalis iugata consonanti aut pluribus / syllabam reddat necesse est. "syllabam" Graeci vocant / ore quod simul profectae copulant unum sonum.*

[28] Stoppie (2005, 130–2) discusses such Greek grammatical terminology in Charisius.

84 PROFESSIONAL GRAMMARIANS

> paronomasia, schesis onomaton, paromoeon homoeoteleuton homoeoptoton polyptoton hirmos polysyndeton dialyton climax.

> There are many kinds of this [i.e., *schema lexeos*, figure of speech], but the following are considered necessary by which similarities can be joined: *prolepsis zeugma hypozeuxis syllepsis asyndeton anadiplosis anaphora, alia anaphora, epanalepsis epizeuxis paronomasia, schesis onomaton, paromoeon homoeoteleuton homoeoptoton polyptoton hirmos polysyndeton dialyton climax.*

In this passage we have twenty Greek technical terms written in the Latin alphabet, representing distinct types of *schemata lexeos*. Similarly, the discussion of metaplasm (440.27–31) names fifteen species with Greek technical terms, not counting the name of the genus itself. This represents only a small fraction of all the Greek loanwords (or transliterations) present in the *Ars*, in addition to the roughly sixty-five Greek words written in the Greek alphabet. The choice of alphabet is significant, as this passage shows, where all the terms are presented in the Latin alphabet. Deciding whether Greek words were originally written in Greek or Latin script can be a difficult matter, especially since the Greek alphabet was sometimes transliterated into Latin over the course of transmission. Therefore, it is possible in some cases that Latin script was not the original reading.[29] In an important contribution by Louis Holtz (2007) about the transformation and deformation of Greek grammatical terminology, he shows that late Latin *artes* (of both western and eastern production) typically distinguish between Greek technical terms, which were written in Latin script, and Greek citations and isolated words, which were usually written in Greek script.[30] In the case of Diomedes, the lost Carolingian archetype presumed to be the ancestor of all surviving manuscripts seems to have distinguished between Latin transliteration and Greek script. For my part, I will follow Keil's editorial choices, which also

---

[29] On the alphabet used to write the Greek words in Latin texts, see Vottero (1974, 313–15) and Schironi (2007, 325 with n. 8). See also the recent discussion about the manuscripts of Cicero's works by O'Sullivan (2018).

[30] Holtz (2007, 42–6), and in particular his words on 45: "Charisius, Diomède et l'*Anonymus Bobiensis* se conformaient aux traditions de la pédagogie latine en reprenant sans la remettre en cause la terminologie grecque latinisée qu'ils trouvaient dans leurs sources. Si d'aventure il leur arrive de mentionner une catégorie grammaticale en grec sans la translittérer, c'est ordinairement en l'accompagnant d'une traduction latine qui ne s'est pas encore pleinement imposée." See also Holtz (1981, 525–6). By contrast, Pelttari (2011, esp. 480) argues that late antique literary authors were more inclined to use Latin script for Greek than is generally supposed.

THE USE OF GREEK IN DIOMEDES' *ARS GRAMMATICA* 85

involves assessing the degree to which a term has become naturalized or a part of Latin.[31]

The following examples illustrate Diomedes' use of Greek technical words in more detail:

(9a) Diom. 482.14–17: poematos genera sunt tria. aut enim activum est vel imitativum, **quod Graeci dramaticon vel mimeticon,** aut enarrativum vel enuntiativum, **quod Graeci exegeticon vel apangelticon dicunt,** aut commune vel mixtum, **quod Graeci κοινόν vel μικτόν appellant.**

There are three genres of poetry. For either the poem is active or imitative, what the Greeks call *dramaticon* ["dramatic"] or *mimeticon* ["mimetic"], or it is narrative or explanatory, what the Greeks call *exegeticon* ["exegetic"] or *apangelticon* ["informative"], or it is common or mixed, what the Greeks call κοινόν ["common"] or μικτόν ["mixed"].

(9b) Diom. 426.15–18: grammaticae partes sunt duae: altera, quae vocatur **"exegetice,"** altera **"horistice." "exegetice"** est enarrativa, quae pertinent ad officia lectionis, **"horistice"** est finitiva, quae praecepta demonstrat.

There are two parts of grammar: the first one is called *exegetice* ["exegetic"] the second *horistice* ["definitional"]. *Exegetice* is explanatory, which concerns the tasks of reading, *horistice* is concerned with definition, which gives an account of rules.

(10) Diom. 501.30–2: modi metrici sunt sex: κατὰ στίχον definitivus vel principalis, συστηματικός conpositus, ἀσυνάρτητος inconpositus, συγκεχυμένος confusus, συνεζευγμένος coniunctus, παραγωγός derivativus.

There are six modes of meter: κατὰ στίχον "definite" or "principal," συστηματικός "composed," ἀσυνάρτητος "decomposed," συγκεχυμένος "mixed," συνεζευγμένος "connected," παραγωγός "derived."

(11) Diom. 423.3–5: "s" littera suae cuiusdam potestatis est ideoque apud Graecos μοναδικόν appellatur, quae in metro plerumque vim consonantis amittit.

---

[31] See the criteria proposed by Vottero (1974, 314–15) for Seneca's philosophical works.

86   PROFESSIONAL GRAMMARIANS

The letter *s* has its own value and **is called by the Greeks μοναδικόν** because in meter it often loses the value of a consonant.

(12)   Diom. 453.21–8:[32] (*1*) soloecismus est contra rationem Romani sermonis disturbans orationem et vitium in contextu partium orationis contra regulam artis grammaticae factum, id est non conveniens rationi sermonis iunctura verborum. (*2*) **soloecismus dicitur Graece λόγου σώου αἰκισμός, id est integri sermonis corruptio:** (*3*) vel a civitate Ciliciae quae Soloe olim dicebatur, nunc Pompeiopolis vocatur, cuius incolae quia sermone corrupto loquebantur, similiter vitiose loquentes apud Athenienses σολοικίζειν dicebantur, unde id vitium soloecismus dictum est; **Latine** a quibusdam "stribiligo" appellatur.

(*1*) Solecism is something that disrupts speech contrary to the system of the Latin language and it is a fault in the structure of the parts of speech formed contrary to the rule of the grammatical handbook, that is, a connection between words that is not in accordance with the language's system. (*2*) **Solecism is so called from the Greek expression λόγου σώου αἰκισμός, this is, corruption of pure language:** (*3*) or from the city in Cilicia that was formerly called Soloi and now Pompeiopolis. Because its inhabitants spoke with corrupt speech, they were said by the Athenians σολοικίζειν ["to speak as the inhabitants of Soloi"]. Hence this defect was called *soloecismus*; **in Latin** it is termed *stribiligo* ["incorrectness"] by some people.

(13)   Diom. 364.29–31: proprie . . . est **quod Graeci dicunt μασσῶμαι,** hoc est identidem mando, ideoque Probus negat recte dici piscem vel aliud tenerum quid manduco, sed potius edo, **quod significat ἐσθίω.**

It is properly **what the Greeks call μασσῶμαι,** that is, "I repeatedly *mando* ["I chew"]," and on that account Probus says it is not correct to say *manduco* ["I chew"] a fish or something tender, but rather *edo*, **which means ἐσθίω** ["I eat"].

In example 9a Diomedes explains the three main poetic genres and gives a definition of each by using the Greek equivalent of the Latin words in the traditional form *quod Graeci . . . dicunt/appellant*: the Greek term in a relative clause. A range of similar constructions for this is very widespread in

---

[32] This passage about *soloecismus* was analysed by Dammer (2001, 247–9).

THE USE OF GREEK IN DIOMEDES' *ARS GRAMMATICA*   87

Latin technical prose: X (Latin word) *quod Graeci* Y (Greek word) *vocant*; or Y (Greek word) *quod nostri* X (Latin word) *vocant*; or Y (Greek word) *quod Latine* X (Latin word) *dicitur*.[33] We find also an attenuated expression such as X *non absurde* Y *dicimus* (Diom. 324.10–11 ῥηματικά ... *non absurde verbalia dixerimus*). In example 9a, we have the Latin alphabet twice and the Greek alphabet once. Of the six Greek terms, four are in Latin characters and two in Greek. I am not sure if the use of the Latin alphabet can be justified in this case because, as shown in Saalfeld's *Tensaurus Italograecus* (1884), Diomedes is the first to use these Greek words.[34] They have not yet been integrated into the Latin vocabulary, as shown by the relative clause beginning *quod Graeci*. Example 9b shows that the Latin equivalent of a Greek technical word can be extended by an explanation of its meaning.

In the last book of his grammar, where he explains metrical principles, Diomedes gives Latin translations of Greek technical terms. The Greek comes first and the Latin translation follows (G/L, G/L ...), as we can see in example 10. As example 11 shows, Diomedes sometimes gives a Greek technical term with the expression *apud Graecos* followed by an explanation in Latin.[35] The Greek is not the translation of a Latin expression here, but a technical description found in Greek sources.

Another interesting phenomenon is the explanation of terminology using Greek. We have some examples where Diomedes gives a Greek technical term with its Latin equivalent. He uses expression such as: *quod Graece ... dicitur, Latini ... vocant* (e.g., 301.12–13) or *(quem) ... Graeci ... vocant, ... dicimus* (e.g., 302.3–4) or *quod Graeci vocant ... et apud nos est ...* (e.g., 317.13).

More interesting and complex is example 12, studied by Raphael Dammer (2001, 248–9). In this long definition of *soloecismus*, we can distinguish three parts. The word is first explained by an etymology and followed by the translation into Latin of the Greek expression. The third part contains an alternate Greek etymology from the name of the town of Soli.

By contrast, the use of Greek equivalents to ordinary non-technical words is rare, as noted by Schenkeveld (2007, 185). In example 13, Diomedes discusses the difference between two Latin verbs, *manducare* and *edere*, by

---

[33] See examples from medical Latin in Langslow (2000, 80–91).
[34] Reifferscheid includes Diomedes' passage 9a as a fragment of Suetonius' *De poetis* (no. 3), but the identification may not be correct. By contrast, Kaibel prints the text in *Comicorum Graecorum fragmenta* (1899, 53) using Greek script.
[35] Schenkeveld (2007, 184) shows, following Desbordes (1988), how the expression *apud Graecos* is used by Priscian, who, pointing out that Latin is like Greek, repeatedly introduces his remarks by the expression *nec mirum ... cum apud Graecos quoque. ...*

88 PROFESSIONAL GRAMMARIANS

giving Greek equivalents, in the first case with an explicit indication *quod Graeci dicunt*, in the second one without such an expression.

While Diomedes uses Greek grammatical terms throughout his three books, Charisius is much more sparing with Greek technical terms, which he uses only a few times, mainly in book 2, section VI *de nomine* (p. 195.14–16).[36] In Diomedes' first book, the Greek technical terms are especially important and serve to explain the Latin words. Diomedes clearly wishes to help his reader understand the Latin terminology or to show that Latin grammar has much in common with Greek.

I shall now examine some characteristic phenomena that reflect Diomedes' bilingualism (and that of his readers), turning to the two last categories of my framework.

3.3 Comparison between Greek and Latin

This category involves passages where Diomedes explicitly compares or contrasts Greek and Latin as languages, typically with pedagogical or explanatory intent. Let us consider the following examples:

(14a) Diom. 421.32–422.3: litterae quibus utimur XXIII hae sunt, a b c d e f g h i k l m n o p q r s t u x y z. harum differentiae sunt tres. prima differentia <in> litteris qualitates habet duas, **quod aut Latinae sunt aut Graecae**. **Latinae** sunt una et viginti, **Graecae** duae, y et z, quae in usum nostrum propter nomina Graeca venerunt. ex his vocalis est y (nam et in ea observare debemus quaecumque in vocalibus observantur), semivocalis z.

The letters we use are these twenty-three: *a b c d e f g h i k l m n o p q r s t u x y z.* Their distinguishing features are three. The first distinguishing feature is that the letters have two qualities: **they are either Latin or Greek.** The **Latin** letters are twenty-one, the **Greek** letters are two, *y* and *z*, which came into our usage because of Greek words. Between them *y* is vowel (for in its use we have to follow all the rules that are followed in the case of vowels) and *z* a semi-vowel.

(14b) Diom. 422.9–13: sunt . . . numero quidem quinque, a e i o u, potestate autem septem, si quidem e pro η et pro ε [et pro ει] **Graecis** ponitur.

[36] So Schenkeveld (2007, 186–7).

THE USE OF GREEK IN DIOMEDES' *ARS GRAMMATICA*   89

namque e brevis est scriptura, pronuntiatione longa, ut conticuere [et moenia]. et o pro o et ω **Graecis** similiter ponitur, ut "rapti Ganymedis honores."

The vowels are five in number, *a e i o u*, but seven in value, if *e* is used for the **Greek** η and ε. Indeed *e* is short in writing, but long in pronunciation, as in *conticuere*. And *o* is used in the same way for **Greek** o and ω, as in *rapti Ganymedis honores*.

(15)   Diom. 427.12–16: longae aut natura sunt aut positione fiunt. natura, cum aut vocalis producitur, ut "a" "o," aut duae vocales iunguntur, ut "ae" "oe" "au" "eu" "ei" "ui." ex his diphthongis "ei," cum apud veteres frequentaretur, usu posteritatis explosa est. **item "ui" Graeca potius quam Latina est in Graecis sumenda dictionibus.**

The vowels either are long by nature or become long by position. By nature, when a vowel is lengthened, like *a o*, or when two vowels are attached, as in *ae oe au ei ui*. Among these diphthongs *ei*, although it was frequent among the ancients, was excluded from the usage of posterity. **Similarly, the diphthong *ui*, more Greek than Latin, has to be included among the Greek expressions.**

(16)   Diom. 433.4–7: **sane Graeca verba Graecis accentibus efferimus,** si isdem litteris pronuntiaverimus. **in Latinis** neque acutus accentus in ultima syllaba potest poni nisi discretionis causa, ut in adverbio "pone," ideo ne verbum putetur, et in quibusdam praepositionibus.

Certainly we produce Greek words with Greek accents, if we have pronounced them with the same letters/sounds [as in Greek]. **In the case of Latin** words, an acute accent cannot be placed on the last syllable, except for the sake of distinction, as in the adverb *pone* ["behind"] in order not to be considered a verb, and in some prepositions.

As these examples show, Diomedes' use of Greek and Latin elements sometimes leads to reflections about the similarities and differences between the languages more generally. In the first example (14a–b), he makes a clear comparison between the Greek and Latin alphabet, emphasizing the bilingual character of the latter, which has twenty-one Greco-Latin letters and two purely Greek letters. In example 15, Diomedes divides syllables into two categories: long and short, and he mentions a typically Greek diphthong.

90 PROFESSIONAL GRAMMARIANS

Speaking about accents (no. 16), Diomedes starts with Greek words and their different accentuation.

I would like to discuss the following passages in more detail:

(17a) Diom. 300.26–301.2: partes orationis sunt octo, nomen pronomen verbum participium adverbium coniunctio praepositio interiectio; Scauro videtur et appellatio. ex his primae quattuor declinabiles sunt, sequentes indeclinabiles. **Latini articulum, Graeci interiectionem non adnumerant.**

There are eight parts of speech: noun, pronoun, verb, participle, adverb, conjunction, preposition, interjection. Scaurus adds *appellatio* ["common noun"]. Among these the first four are declinable, those that follow are non-declinable. **The Latins do not count the article, the Greeks the interjection.**

(17b) Don. *gramm. mai.* 2.1 p. 613.5 Holtz: **Latini** articulum non adnumerant, **Graeci** interiectionem.

The **Latins** do not count the article, the **Greeks** the interjection.

(17c) Pomp. *gramm.* V 135.20–2: non dixit aut **Latinos** non habere articulos aut **Graecos** non habere interiectionem, non, sed non computare. ita enim dixit "**Latini** articulos non adnumerant," non dixit "non habent."

He did not say that the **Latins** do not have the articles or the **Greeks** do not have the interjection, no, but rather that they do not count them. Indeed, he said, "the **Latins** do not count the articles"; he did not say, "they do not have them."

(17d) Char. *gramm.* p. 246.26–247.3: quam partem orationis **nostri**, non ut numerum octo partium articulo, id est τῷ ἄρθρῳ, deficiente supplerent, sed quia videbant adverbium esse non posse, segregaverunt.

Our grammarians set aside this part of speech, not in order to complete the number eight of the parts [of speech] on the ground that the article, that is τῷ ἄρθρῳ, was missing, but because they saw that [the interjection] could not be an adverb.

THE USE OF GREEK IN DIOMEDES' *ARS GRAMMATICA*   91

Example 17a, which appears in the section *de partibus orationis*, concerns the presence of the article in Latin and the lack of *interiectio* in Greek. Diomedes makes a clear parallel between the two languages. Especially notable is his use of the verb *adnumerare* ("to count"): he says not simply that Latin has no article, but that the article is not "counted" in the description of Latin. The standard number of *partes orationis* was eight, though the actual *partes* are not the same in the two languages. Diomedes clearly wants the number to be the same because he aims to establish a close parallel between Greek and Latin.

We can compare the descriptions in Donatus (no. 17b) and in Pompeius (no. 17c), who take a different approach. A passage in Charisius (no. 17d) implies that some grammarians added the interjection to the Greek parts of speech in order to make up for the Latin lack of article.[37]

In the following passage at the end of book 1, Diomedes uses a similar strategy, making the same opposition between *Graeci* and *Latini*, but in the opposite order:

(18) Diom. 419.19–21: interiectionem **Graeci** inter adverbia posuerunt; **Latini** ideo separarunt, ...

The **Greeks** placed the interjection among the adverbs, the **Latins** set it apart for this reason ...

We find this text in the section *de personis verborum*, where Diomedes discusses the verb (*de verbo*). We see here how Diomedes has a unified or universal conception of the functions of the eight categories of words in both languages. The verb *adnumerant* is very important: the apparent difference regarding the article is only a question of classification. Accordingly the grammarian tries to find an equivalent in Latin for the Greek article.[38]

A similar strategy is apparent in Diomedes' discussion of the dual in his section *de personis verborum*, also discussed in more detail by Denecker (Chapter 8, §2) in this volume:

(19)   Diom. 334.25–30: numerus praeterea accidit verbis prorsus uterque, singularis et pluralis. **dualis enim apud Graecos dumtaxat valet**, a nobis excluditur, eodem modo quo et in nominibus. nequaquam enim

---

[37] This passage is discussed by Lacerda Faria Rocha and Fortes (2016, 239) and by Rodríguez-Noriega Guillén and Uría (2017, 455).
[38] See Desbordes (1988, 23).

92 PROFESSIONAL GRAMMARIANS

> reperiri potest **Latino sermone** ulla dictio quae dualem exprimat numerum. antiquitatis enim **Romani** memores dualem numerum posteritatis usu receptum quasi novellum usurpare noluerunt.

> Furthermore, both numbers straightforwardly apply to verbs: the singular and the plural. **For the dual is only valid among the Greeks**, while it is excluded by us, in the same way as it is in nouns. For nowhere in **the Latin language** can a single utterance be found that expresses the dual number. For those **Romans** who were aware of ancient usage refused to make use of the dual, which had been accepted in later usage, on the grounds that it was an innovation.

Diomedes says that the difference between the two languages has its origin in the fact that the Romans preserved an archaic state of the language while the Greeks innovated. The dual was originally present but not morphologically marked. The Romans refused to adopt the innovation because it was unnecessary for them. Diomedes implies the superiority of Latin over Greek by emphasizing its faithfulness to ancient tradition (*antiquitatis . . . memores*).

The same strategy is also apparent in Diomedes' discussion of the ablative case:[39]

(20)   Diom. 302.3–7: **quem nominativum Graeci non** πτῶσιν **sed** ὀρθήν **vel** εὐθεῖαν **vocant.** καταχρηστικῶς tamen nominativum casum dicimus. **ablativum Graeci non habent.** hunc tamen Varro sextum, interdum Latinum appellat, quia Latinae linguae proprius est, cuius vis **apud Graecos** per genetivum explicabitur.

> The nominative the Greeks call not πτῶσιν ["case"] **but** ὀρθήν ["upright"] **or** εὐθεῖαν ["direct"]. However, we call the nominative a case καταχρηστικῶς ["erroneously"]. **The Greeks do not have an ablative case.** However, Varro calls this case "the sixth case," sometimes "the Latin case" (cf. *ling.* 10.62) because it is peculiar to the Latin language, a case whose value will be expressed **among the Greeks** by the genitive.

---

[39] As Dammer (2001, 113) notes, Diomedes' view differs from Dionysius Thrax's, who counts the nominative as a case.

THE USE OF GREEK IN DIOMEDES' *ARS GRAMMATICA*   93

After using the traditional Greek terminology drawn from Chrysippus to classify the nominative, Diomedes says that Greek has no ablative case and he associates the Latin ablative with the Greek genitive.[40] He uses the same strategy, but reversed, to explain the preterite participle, such as the Greek φιλήσας (402.3–4 *participia in activis praeteriti temporis non sunt, ut Graece dicimus* φιλήσας ποιήσας).[41] The Latin language does not have a preterite active participle like the Greek. This view is summarized at 311.3–7 (see below 22).

Diomedes begins his presentation of the irregular verbs by saying he neglects the *ambages* of the Greeks, implying the greater simplicity of Latin:[42]

(21)   Diom. 384.15–6: analogia apud nos, id est proportio, **praetermissis Graecorum ambagibus** simplici modo tam in verbis quam in nominibus observatur.

Analogy among us, namely *proportio* ["proportion"], **leaving aside the complexities of the Greeks**, is observed in a simple way both in verbs and in nouns.

This passage is also interesting for its translation of *analogia* by *proportio*.[43] Similarly Varro, Quintilian, and Gellius all use *proportio* only when introducing the concept of analogy for the first time, as do other grammarians (Terentius Scaurus, Servius, Pompeius, Consentius, and Isidore of Seville).[44] Like these other authors, Diomedes typically uses *analogia* elsewhere, such as when discussing nominal declension (e.g., 377.21).

About the link between Latin and Greek, there is a very interesting passage, which is paralleled in Charisius (p. 380.20–5 Barwick):[45]

(22)   Diom. 311.3–6: verba diversis casibus apud Romanos hoc modo iunguntur. **nam cum ab omni sermone Graeco Latina loquella**

---

[40] Diomedes' explanation that the nominative can only be called a case καταχρηστικῶς is also attributed to Heliodorus (*Scholia in Dion. Thr.* in *GG* I.3 546.6). Zanker in this volume (Chapter 4, §4) discusses Varro's metaphorical understanding of *casus*.

[41] Mentioned by Schenkeveld (2007, 185).

[42] Desbordes (1988, 25) discusses this attitudes more generally. Schironi (2007, 330 with n. 32) compares Greek and Latin definitions of *analogia*. The same definition is found at Char. *gramm.* p. 150.2.

[43] According to Seneca (*epist.* 120.4–5), the Latin grammarians had already given the *civitas* to the Greek loanword *analogia*. The metaphor is discussed in more detail by Gitner (Chapter 10); see also Vottero (1974, 318); Schironi (2007, 336 n. 51).

[44] See references in Schironi (2007, 327).

[45] Mentioned by Rodríguez-Noriega Guillén and Uría (2017, 455). Diomedes uses *loquella* where Charisius has *lingua*.

94 PROFESSIONAL GRAMMARIANS

> pendere videatur, quaedam inveniuntur vel licentia ab antiquis vel proprietate Latinae linguae dicta praeter consuetudinem Graecorum, quae idiomata appellantur.

> Among Romans verbs are connected with various cases in the following way. **For although Latin speech seems to be wholly dependent on the Greek language,** some [combinations] are found that are used by the ancient Romans with either as a form of license **or because of the peculiar nature of the Latin language and are different from Greek usage. They are called** *idiomata*.[46]

This passage discusses *idiomata*, words or constructions where Latin differs from Greek.[47] The emphasis falls on the peculiarities of Latin since it was regarded as deriving from or being dependent on Greek. From the first century BCE the idea that Latin was a variety of Greek, especially related to Aeolic, was widespread among Greek and Latin grammarians, including Philoxenus and Varro.[48] As Bonnet (2011, 365) points out with reference to this passage, "in front of a bilingual audience, contrast is an efficient pedagogical device."

3.4 Intra-Sentential Code-Switching

Code-switching is a general term for the juxtaposition within the same utterance of words or phrases belonging to two different languages or sub-systems of a language.[49] According to this broad definition, many of the previous examples that contain a mixture of Greek and Latin exhibit code-switching. Here I would like to focus on three cases of intra-sentential code-switching, where a Greek expression is adapted to the syntax of the Latin clause (another possible example is no. 7 above). Intra-sentential switching is significant because it implies a greater fluency with Greek than the uninflected quotation

---

[46] Transl. Schenkeveld (2007, 185).

[47] This passage is mentioned by Baratin (1988, 192–3) and Bonnet (2011, 365). Incidentally, the passage contains three words for "language" (*sermo, loquella, lingua*). *Lingua* perhaps represents "language" in the Saussurian sense, and there does not seem to be much practical difference between *sermo* and *loquella* (which are rarer), which apply to oral speech; see Rochette (2009, 46).

[48] On Aeolism see Gabba (1963), Stevens (2007), and Gitner (2015). The first grammarian to explain Latin words with the help of Greek was Hypsicrates of Amisos in the Sullan period (Collart 1954, 207–8).

[49] Adams (2003, 19–29) is an essential point of orientation for code-switching in Latin sources.

THE USE OF GREEK IN DIOMEDES' *ARS GRAMMATICA* 95

of Greek words or phrases (typically at sentence or phrase boundaries, hence "inter-sentential switching" or "tag switching"), which can be accomplished without much in-depth knowledge of Greek.

(23) Diom. 430.30–431.3: nam ut nulla vox sine vocali est, ita sine accentu nulla est; et est accentus, ut quidam recte putaverunt, velut anima vocis. accentus est dictus ab accinendo, quod sit quasi quidam cuiusque syllabae cantus. apud Graecos quoque ideo προσῳδία dicitur, quia προσᾴδεται ταῖς συλλαβαῖς.

Indeed, just as there is no word without a vowel, there is no word without an accent; and the accent, as some have correctly thought, is like the soul of the word. The accent is designated from *accinere* ["to sing"] because it is like the song of each syllable. Among the Greeks too, προσῳδία ["prosody"] is so called because προσᾴδεται ταῖς συλλαβαῖς ["one chimes in with the syllables"].

(24) Diom. 360.24–7: futuri (*sc. infinivitum*) non habet: instantis "posse," praeteriti "potuisse." participia instantis tantum; futuri non habet: instantis hic et haec et hoc potens. sed quidam dicunt participia ne instantis quidem temporis habere. nam potens nomen est, ὁ δυνατός, οὐχ ὁ δυνάμενος.

[The verb *possum*] has no future [infinitive], its present infinitive is *posse*, its past infinitive is *potuisse*. There is only the present participle. There is no future participle: the present participle is *hic et haec et hoc potens*, but some say that there is no present participle either. Indeed *potens* is a noun ὁ δυνατός, οὐχ ὁ δυνάμενος ["the strong (one)," not "the (one) being able"].

(25) Diom. 336.8–10: id enim Graeci ὑπερσυντελικόν appellant, quasi ὑπὲρ τὸν συντελοῦντα χρόνον, quod nos praeteritum plusquamperfectum dicimus. at vero tempus perfectum apud nos pro ἀορίστῳ καὶ παρακειμένῳ valet.

For the Greeks call it ὑπερσυντελικόν ["the pluperfect tense"], as if it were ὑπὲρ τὸν συντελοῦντα χρόνον ["going beyond the completed time"], which we call *praeteritum plusquamperfectum*

96   PROFESSIONAL GRAMMARIANS

["the more-than-complete past"]. But among us the *tempus perfectum* ["perfect tense"] has the value of ἀόριστος ["the aorist tense"] and παρακειμένος ["the perfect tense"].

In example 23 the Greek sentence is embedded in the Latin clause. Diomedes wants to explain the Latin accent. He gives the Greek term for *accentus* and, after the conjunction *quia*, continues in Greek without translation. He obviously expects his reader to be able to understand the Greek sentence.

Examples 24 and 25 present the same pattern. In example 24, a passage about *verba temporibus confusa*, Diomedes suggests that the verb *posse* has no participle.[50] Even *potens* cannot be considered as the participle present of *posse* but rather as a noun, an *appellatio*. He compares *potens* with its Greek equivalents and uses Greek negation rather than Latin (*nec* or *neque*) between the two Greek forms. The same phenomenon can be observed in another passage (25) with καί instead of *et* or *atque* between ἀορίστῳ and παρακειμένῳ.

4. Conclusions

The *artes grammaticae* addressed to a Greek audience have specific features that reveal their orientation. This is especially evident in the case of Dositheus, whose bilingual grammar was composed in both Greek and Latin simultaneously, as Eleanor Dickey (2016a) has shown based on its internal organization.[51] The importance and the role of the Greek elements in Charisius and Diomedes are more difficult to judge. Studying the Greek elements in Diomedes helps to show the grammarian's knowledge of Greek as well as that of his imagined audience and to illustrate his didactic strategy.

Is the Greek in Diomedes' *Ars* a byproduct of the indebtedness of Latin grammar to its Greek models (τέχνη γραμματική) or is it a deliberate strategy, a conscious choice to add Greek, in order to make Latin more intelligible to a Greek-speaking audience? For Françoise Desbordes (1988), the first descriptions of Latin were made by Greeks with reference to Greek and even composed in Greek. Gradually grammatical texts were produced in

---

[50] Schenkeveld (2007, 185) points out that "these explanatory notes are few and rare."
[51] Lenoble, Swiggers, and Wouters (2000, 14–19) also highlight the relationship between Greek and Latin in Dositheus' *Ars*.

THE USE OF GREEK IN DIOMEDES' *ARS GRAMMATICA*   97

Latin with Greek elements until the "réinjection massive" (Desbordes 1988, 18) of Greek by Priscian, whose theoretical discourse presupposes the synthesis of both languages and aims to produce a symbolic reconciliation between the Greek-speaking east and the Latin-speaking west.[52] He professedly translated Apollonius and Herodian in large swathes of his *Institutiones*. In the case of Diomedes, both these elements play a role: the tradition of Greek artigraphy and his specific pedagogical objective.

Furthermore, Diomedes deliberately includes the comparison between the Greek and Latin languages as part of his didactic project. The inclusion of a section *de idiomatibus* (entitled *de consensu verborum cum casibus*) in the last position among the introductory chapters before the chapter *de nomine* reveals Diomedes' intentions clearly. The chapter *de nomine* itself includes comparisons between Greek and Latin. Diomedes follows an old tradition of Greek scholars, such as Claudius Didymus (80–10 BCE), who aimed to establish a link between both languages.[53] This tradition was not exclusively Greek. Aelius Stilo, Varro's master, attempted to link Greek and Latin, and Varro himself emphasized similarities between Latin and Aeolic.[54] The political intention that inspired this theory is evident: it was a means for Greek intellectuals to flatter the desire of many Romans to integrate both Greeks and Romans into a Greco-Roman empire. Diomedes understood that such parallelisms between Greek and Latin were also appropriate for his didactic aims. His Greek audience could better understand the complex Latin linguistic system by realizing that it was not completely alien to Greek. I would like to quote again Françoise Desbordes (1988, 15): "les grammairiens latins ont . . . conservé longtemps le sentiment que cette description (i.e., of Latin grammar by means of Greek grammar) avait été rendue possible par le fait que les deux langues étaient en quelque façon comparables." Later, Macrobius would explore the resemblances between Greek and Latin more systematically and theorize them in his treatise written by a Roman for Romans, the *De verborum Graeci et Latini differentiis vel societatibus excerpta*, whose motive is scholarly and not pedagogic.[55]

Finally, it is worth noting some similarities and differences with Charisius, the grammarian with whom Diomedes has most in common. As the

---

[52] Fortes (2014) discusses this strategy in Priscian.

[53] See the five fragments of his Περὶ τῆς παρὰ Ῥωμαίοις ἀναλογίας *sive de latinitate* (*GRF* pp. 447–50); discussed by Della Corte (1937, 114 n. 1).

[54] On Stilo: Collart (1954, 209, 228); on Varro: Collart (ibid., 215, 219).

[55] On the similarities between Greek and Latin noted by Latin grammarians, see Desbordes (1988, 15–16) and De Paolis (1990, xxviii–xxx).

98　PROFESSIONAL GRAMMARIANS

framework adopted here suggests in comparison with Stoppie's (2005) categories for Charisius, the biggest differences are to be found in two areas: Diomedes' use of Greek expressions and his quotations of Greek literary sources. As Schenkeveld also noted (2007, 187–8), Diomedes has far fewer Greek glosses of Latin vocabulary, but he also uses standard Greek terminology more regularly and assumes his audience is familiar with it. This might be a sign of Diomedes seeking to address a more advanced Greek-speaking audience, for whom such glosses were not necessary, but it might also result from Diomedes' attempting to give his grammar a more integrated and polished appearance (perhaps by eliminating glosses that were present in their common source(s)). Diomedes' quotation of Greek literary sources, especially Homer, is one area where the difference between the grammarians really stands out, and it suggests Diomedes cared about the display of Greek literary culture or that he imagined his audience would care.

An open question remains about the extent to which Diomedes made firsthand use of Greek grammatical sources, as Priscian certainly did about a century later in Constantinople. As we have seen, Diomedes does not give the standard etymology of συλλαβή found in Dionysius Thrax (example 7), and he does not mention any Greek grammarians by name. Nevertheless, despite many ostensible differences with the Dionysian τέχνη in its surviving form, Dammer (2001, 112–14) has noted at least one striking parallel between Diomedes and Dionysius Thrax, which is not found in other Latin grammarians (his discussion of the seven types of nominal derivation, 323.21–3). It remains unclear where this could have come from, but it is possibly suggestive of Diomedes' Greek milieu, and it deserves more investigation. In any case, while Diomedes is keen to show his knowledge of Greek as a language and Greek literary sources, he is less keen to show off his knowledge of Greek grammarians, of whose *ambages* (example 21) he is rather dismissive. Instead his reference to Greek is motivated by two characteristics: his desire to establish a close parallel between the two languages, and his aim to facilitate understanding of Latin grammatical peculiarities among his Greek-speaking audience.

6

The Grammarian Consentius on Language Change and Variation

Tommaso Mari

Consentius has earned a special place in ancient grammar because his *De barbarismis et metaplasmis* provides more information about "vulgar" and regional Latin than any other grammatical work.[1] In a volume dedicated to the grammarians as "guardians of language," it seems fitting to look at Consentius' views on language change and variation, including language contact and borrowing. The focus on the grammarian's place and function in society that is central in Kaster's *Guardians of Language* also encourages consideration of how Consentius' views fit in his socio-cultural context. There emerges the figure of a member of the provincial elites who, while being aware of language change, strove to preserve the Latin of his educated contemporaries from what he perceived as forces of corruption introduced by the uneducated and especially those speaking provincial and low varieties.

1. Consentius' Work and Identity

Consentius was the author of two grammatical works transmitted independently in medieval manuscripts: *De nomine et verbo* and *De barbarismis et metaplasmis*.[2] The former discusses noun and verb, the main parts of speech; the latter discusses errors arising in one word (barbarisms) and poetic licenses consisting of one word (metaplasms), with an appendix on verse

---

[1] Abbott (1909) and Maltby (2012) focus on "vulgar" Latin in Consentius; Kohlstedt (1917) on Romance reflexes; Mari (2017a) on the regional diversification of Latin.

[2] For *De nomine et verbo*, I refer to the text established by Keil in *Grammatici latini* V. For *De barbarismis et metaplasmis*, the text is that of my own edition (Mari 2021), in which I have kept the page and line numbers of Niedermann (1937).

Tommaso Mari, *The Grammarian Consentius on Language Change and Variation* In: *Roman Perspectives on Linguistic Diversity*. Edited by Adam Gitner, Oxford University Press. © Oxford University Press 2023.
DOI: 10.1093/oso/9780197611975.003.0006

100 PROFESSIONAL GRAMMARIANS

scansion (*De scandendis versibus*). There is evidence that Consentius wrote more on grammar than we have, and it has been argued that *De nomine et verbo* and *De barbarismis et metaplasmis* originally belonged together.[3]

But who was Consentius? As is the case with many ancient writers of grammar, little is certain and much is conjectural about him. The manuscripts style him as *vir clarissimus*, so he must have been a member of the senatorial class. As he cites many Gallic towns when discussing toponyms in his *De nomine et verbo*, it has been suggested that he was the same as, or related to, either of the *Consentii* of Narbonne (father and son) mentioned by Sidonius Apollinaris in his poem 23 and letters 8.4 and 9.15 (see *Guardians* 396–7).[4] If that is the case, he must have lived between the fourth and the fifth century or in the fifth century; that is in keeping with the fact that Consentius cites Lucan a few times, if Wessner (1929) was right to assume that citations from Lucan are common in grammarians only starting with Servius (see *Guardians* 396).

It is important to remember that the fifth century was a time of profound change in the western part of the Roman Empire, and in some contemporaries' perception change also affected the language. Sidonius Apollinaris himself voiced concerns about the decadence of Latin: in a rhetorically exaggerated account addressed to the grammarian or rhetorician Hesperius, he presented Latin as so infested by barbarisms that he feared it could become extinct (*epist.* 2.10.1). It seems fitting that the most extensive work on barbarisms was written in a context such as that depicted by Sidonius.

We shall see in section 4 that Consentius makes remarks about the Latin spoken by Greeks, Africans, Gauls, and Roman plebeians. This too is possibly compatible with the biography of Sidonius' Consentius, not only because he came from Gaul but also because he traveled for his job. Consentius was a *tribunus et notarius* under the emperor Valentinian III in 437–50 and had the *cura palatii* under Avitus in 455–56. Thanks to his knowledge of Greek, he was sent by Valentinian III on diplomatic missions to Theodosius II at Constantinople (Sidon. *carm.* 23.228–32). If the author of *De barbarismis et metaplasmis* was Sidonius' Consentius, his four remarks on the Greeks' pronunciation of Latin may well have derived from direct observation during his missions at Constantinople. It would be surprising if Sidonius' Consentius,

---

[3] See Fögen (1997–98, 165–7) for a discussion of the evidence.
[4] On Consentius father and son, see *PLRE* II Consentius I and II (308–9).

GRAMMARIAN CONSENTIUS 101

during his work at court, did not have chances to meet Africans or spend time in Rome, which could explain his remarks on the Latin of the Africans and of the Roman *plebs*.[5]

We shall return to the question of Consentius' identity in the conclusions, when addressing the question as to how Consentius' views reflect his socio-cultural milieu.

2. Consentius on Language Change

By language change I mean the alteration of language over time. In his extant work Consentius does not address language change per se; observations to this effect are incidental to his discussion of the main subjects of his work. For example, Consentius is bound to confront language change when discussing nominal and verbal morphology in *De nomine et verbo*; as he comes across forms that have gone out of use but have a place in the literary tradition and, unlike barbarisms or metaplasms, cannot be explained away as errors or poetic licenses, he offers some reflections on diachronic change.

The concept of language change is connected to that of linguistic correctness. According to some grammarians, correct Latinity was based on *ratio* (the "rational" system of the language), *auctoritas* (literary authority), and *consuetudo* (usage);[6] according to others, following Varro, it was based on *natura, analogia, consuetudo*, and *auctoritas*.[7] Consentius never defines *latinitas* and its parts, but he does employ the concepts of *ratio, auctoritas*, and *consuetudo*. It is evident that *auctoritas* and *consuetudo* are inherently dynamic principles, or at least they are historically determined: literary authority is based on authorial choices that were made at some point in time, and language use has also been formed over time. For many grammarians, *consuetudo* was the key principle of *latinitas*. As De Nonno (2017, 220–4) points out, it was clear at least since Varro that there had been a *consuetudo vetus* diachronically distinct from *consuetudo nostra*, and at least since Quintilian that there was a *consuetudo eruditorum* "diastratically" distinct from a *consuetudo vulgaris*—the one to follow was obviously the *consuetudo eruditorum*.

---

[5] Even when Ravenna was the capital of the eastern part of the Roman Empire, fifth-century emperors spent time in Rome, and their staff with them (see Jones 1964, 366–7).

[6] Ps. Mar. Victorin. *gramm.* VI 189.3–4; Audax *gramm.* VII 322.22–323.1; Aug. *gramm.* 1.1.

[7] Char. p. 62.14–15; Diom. *gramm.* I 439.15–17.

102 PROFESSIONAL GRAMMARIANS

Consentius understands that there are differences between the Latin of writers who lived long before him and the Latin of his times, and so he is aware that language changes over time. It is in the interplay between *ratio*, on the one hand, and *auctoritas* and *consuetudo*, on the other hand, that he seems to identify change: the regularity of *ratio*, with its *regulae* and *analogia*, is undermined by *auctoritas* and *consuetudo*. In discussing the number of nouns, he says that by way of *ratio* nouns like *sordes* are always plural, while some uncountable nouns (like *aurum*, *oleum*, and *ferrum*) are always singular; yet he has to admit that "authority has changed many words contrary to the system (*pleraque auctoritas contra rationem inmutavit*); for Cicero said *sordem* in the singular, and Virgil used *vina* and *hordea* in the plural" (*gramm.* V 348.11–13).[8] When it comes to the question as to whether the ablative of the third declension should end with -*i* or -*e*, Consentius formulates a rule (completely unfounded): if the diminutive of a noun ends in -*ĭcula*, the noun has the ablative in -*i* (he thinks of *turris*, but he is wrong to assume that *turricula* has long *i*); if it ends in -*ĭcula*, it has the ablative in -*e* (like *securis*). Yet he has to admit that "usage and authority battle in various ways against this (*consuetudo et auctoritas varie contra hoc pugnat*), so that many have said that the ablative in this part is doubtful" (*gramm.* V 355.14–15).

In Consentius as well as in other grammarians, a powerful principle that sometimes opposes and prevails over *ratio* is euphony (*euphonia*).[9] Consentius does not clarify precisely what this is and how it works, but he invokes it when he is unable to explain a form that does not follow the *regula*. Sometimes he also prescribes that it be followed as a criterion of linguistic correctness, especially when one has to make a choice among forms established by recourse to *analogia*.[10] *Auctoritas* and *euphonia* can work in combination so as to produce a change to the rule. For example, Consentius has to explain why the dative and ablative plural of *domus* and *iugerum* are *domibus* and *iugeribus* instead of *domis* and *iugeris*, as is the case with all other nouns whose ablative singular ends with -*o*. The alleged reason is that the *veteres*, who are repositories of *auctoritas*, used *domu* and *iugere* as the ablative singular of *domus* and *iugerum*. According to the inherent system of the language (*ratio*), it followed that the dative and ablative plural

---

[8] Cf. Don. *mai.* 2.1 p. 623.1–6. For *hordea* and *pluralia/singularia tantum* as used by the grammarians see Zetzel (Chapter 1).

[9] On *euphonia* see Siebenborn (1976, 154–5) and Schad (2007, 153–4); *euphonia* is defined by Aug. *gramm.* p. 107.21 M. and Cledon. *gramm.* V 47.16.

[10] Consent. *gramm.* V 356.14–20; 363.24–38; 365.17–18.

GRAMMARIAN CONSENTIUS   103

ended with -*ibus* (*gramm*. V 354.14–17 *quae tamen varietas declinationis ex auctoritate veterum exorta est. illi enim ablativum et "ab hac domu" et "ab hoc iugere" declinabant, quam declinationem secuta est ratio, ut dativus et ablativus pluralis in "bus" terminentur*). Subsequently, the principle of euphony changed *domu* and *iugere* to *domo* and *iugero*, while sticking to the ancient rule in the plural by maintaining -*ibus* (*gramm*. V 354.17–19 *sed euphonia, quae plus in vocibus valet <quam regula, in> plurali numero antiquam rationem retinet, cum declinationem ablativi singularis abiecerit*); hence these two words have a mixed inflection in Latin (cf. Don. *mai*. 2.10 p. 627.7–13).

A similar case is that of the inflection of *vas* according to the second declension in the genitive plural *vasorum* and dative/ablative plural *vasis*, as opposed to the ablative singular *vase*, which follows the third declension. The *veteres* used *vaso* in the singular, hence *vasorum* and *vasis* in the plural; euphony did the rest by selecting *vasorum* and *vasis* in the plural but changing *vaso* to *vase* in the singular (*gramm*. V 354.24–30).

Euphonia also has a link to *consuetudo*. For nouns of the third declension that have the genitive plural in -*ium*, euphony plays a role in the selection of the accusative plural, whether it should be in -*is* according to the rule or in -*es*; for Consentius is aware that many such nouns have changed in the usage (*pleraque enim ex omnibus istis regulis consuetudine cernimus inmutata*), as the principles regulating them are not immutable (*gramm*. V 356.25–357.4).

Consentius' reflection on the topic of language change reaches back to the very origins of the Latin language, with the imposition of names and the application of gender. Consentius writes that the masculine and feminine genders were first applied to the nouns of animate beings (whereby it was clear "by nature" which were masculine and which were feminine), then this practice was extended by custom (*extenta res est consuetudine*), so that also nouns indicating entities that lacked sex, such as air, port, earth, and house, were classed as being of masculine or feminine gender (*gramm*. V 343.20–4; cf. Corbeill 2015, 30–1).

The discussion of nominal gender also prompts observations on language change in progress. That is the case of the gender of *Narbo*, which normally was masculine but, according to Consentius, then began to be used as a feminine: "*hic Narbo*" *et, sicut nunc praesumi coepit,* "*haec Narbo*" (*gramm*. V 346.5–6). This remark might seem especially relevant because Consentius was a Gaul, possibly from Narbonne, and it would be tempting to think that that was one reason why Consentius knew about this usage. As a matter of

104 PROFESSIONAL GRAMMARIANS

fact, however, *Narbo* had been used as a feminine long before Consentius' time (e.g., Mart. 8.72.4 *pulcherrima . . . Narbo*).

3. Barbarisms as a Force of Language Change

Consentius' observation on language change in progress brings us to his discussion of barbarisms, for which he is best known. Barbarisms were a traditional topic in Latin grammar; many texts of the so-called *Schulgrammatik* type discuss this kind of change in the section on the *vitia et virtutes orationis*. Barbarism is variously defined, but all definitions make clear that it involves a single incorrect word in ordinary speech, not in poetry (e.g., Consent. *barb.* 1.10–11 *barbarismus est, ut quidam volunt, una pars orationis vitiosa in communi sermone*). As such, barbarism is different from solecism, which consists of the defective connection between several words in ordinary speech (i.e., a syntactic error), and from metaplasm, which is defined as a single incorrect word in poetry (i.e., a poetic license). It is commonly held among grammarians that the error known as barbarism consists of the addition, removal, substitution, or transposition of a letter, syllable, accent, quantity, or aspiration (e.g., Consent. *barb.* 1.18–2.1); in other words, a barbarism is a phonological or phonetic change. For lack of better categorization, Consentius includes semantic errors among the barbarisms, as for example if someone were to say *tyrannicidae* for *tyranni* (*barb.* 22.2–18).

In the previous section we have seen Consentius dealing with language change from the viewpoint of the end of the process. He is aware that some forms have changed over time; such innovations were grounded in the literary authority of the ancients (*auctoritas*), and, by Consentius' time, they have long become part of current usage (*consuetudo*). Consentius is not a promoter of the language of old; he does not want to bring back forms that belong in the past if they are contrary to current usage, which is the key principle of good Latinity. For example, he disapproves of the use of *fluctubus* instead of *fluctibus* on the part of those who believe they are following antiquity, because usage has rejected this (*gramm.* V 354.33–355.2 *plerique antiquitatem sequi aestimantes "u" litteram retinent, ut "fluctubus" potius quam "fluctibus" dicant. sed id consuetudo inprobavit*; cf. Don. *gramm. mai.* 2.10 p. 627.14–628.2).[11] However, although archaic forms should be avoided when alternatives are established in current usage, they are not barbarisms.

---

[11] Another form that Consentius finds in the *veteres* but does not recommend is the imperfect of the fourth conjugation in -*ibam* instead of -*iebam*, as for example *nutribant* (*gramm.* V 384.6–9).

GRAMMARIAN CONSENTIUS   105

Barbarisms are neither established in current usage nor grounded in literary authority; this is seen quite clearly in Consentius' explanation of the differences between barbarism and metaplasm (*barb.* 3.7–13):[12]

> barbarismus citra auctoritatem lectionis inperite nunc a quibusdam praesumitur, metaplasmus autem ille est qui ex veterum scriptorum auctoritate vel praeiudicatae consuetudinis ratione profertur; item quod metaplasmus ob similitudinem lectionis aut veteris consuetudinis a doctis fit scienter, barbarismus vero ab inprudentibus nulla aut veterum aut consuetudinis auctoritate perspecta adsumitur.

> Barbarism is committed now by some people without the authority of literature and in an ignorant manner, while metaplasm is produced in conformity with the authority of ancient writers or by reason of an accepted usage; also, metaplasm is consciously made by learned people on account of the analogy with literature or ancient usage, while barbarism is committed by ignorant people, without looking at the authority of either the ancients or usage.

Here Consentius stresses that unawareness and/or ignorance (note *inperite*, *ab inprudentibus*) are among the reasons why mistakes are made—a point that was traditional in ancient grammar. From a passage like this it might seem that, in Consentius' view, barbarisms are but occasional mistakes of the sort that have no long-term consequences on the language. As a matter of fact, several of the examples that Consentius claims to have found in everyday speech (*barb.* 10.24–11.1 *in usu cotidie loquentium*) are not only attested in other sources, which means that they were not one-off errors, but reflected more general tendencies of "vulgar" Latin and have reflexes in the Romance languages.[13]

4. Barbarisms as a Force of Language Variation

This brings about the topic of language variation. While discussing barbarisms arising by means of the four categories of change, Consentius

---

[12] For Consentius' extensive discussion of metaplasms, see Mari (2016).

[13] The remarks on errors concerning aspirates, vowel and consonant length, the accentuation of *triginta*, to mention only a few especially interesting ones, all have reflexes in the Romance languages (see Kohlstedt 1917, 20, 39–45, 70–9).

106 PROFESSIONAL GRAMMARIANS

makes some remarks concerning the geographic and social variation of Latin: errors concerning vowel length, like lengthening a short vowel or shortening a long vowel, are typical of the Africans (*barb.* 11.8–9 *vitium Afrorum familiare est*; *barb.* 11.18–19 *et ipsum vitium Afrorum speciale est*); errors consisting of the substitution of one letter are typical of the Roman *plebs* (*barb.* 11.23–6 *quod vitium plebem Romanam quadam deliciosa novitatis affectatione corrumpit*).[14]

Consentius does not explicitly make a connection between language change and variation, but he seems to understand geographic and social variation as a consequence of change, and quite inevitably as corruption of good Latin: the Africans' confusion with vowel length derives from their adding or removing a unit of length, and the Roman plebeians substitute one letter for another; in both cases, change is not occasional but has spread and has become to some extent entrenched in the speakers of that community. In the latter case, one of the very few truly sociolinguistic remarks made by a Roman grammarian, Consentius expresses a negative value judgment that seems to reflect the attitude of the senatorial class toward lower classes: Consentius thinks that the diffusion of this sound change among the Roman *plebs* is due to their indulgent desire for novelty, thus implicitly connecting linguistic and moral vices (see Adams 2007, 205–6; Mari 2017a, 118). In so doing, Consentius attributes to the Roman plebeians an active role in bringing about language change, for they select the innovations that they like.[15]

Consentius brings up geographic variation again as he tries to go beyond the limits of traditional grammar in the discussion of barbarisms. He laments that previous grammarians have considered only barbarisms arising from the four categories of change but have left out errors concerning syllabification. In order to find examples of these, he announces that he will look at errors which belong generally to some nations, not only errors of individuals (*barb.* 12.22–13.1 *per vitia non solum specialia hominum, sed generalia quarundam nationum*). Unfortunately, he fails to make it clear which of the errors discussed in this section belong to which nations.[16]

---

[14] Such substitutions are *bobis* for *vobis*, *peres* for *pedes*, *stetim* for *statim*. In Mari (2017a,113, 118; 2021, 217–19) I explain why I choose *affectatione* instead of *affectione* and why Consentius ascribes all three of these errors, not just the last one, to the Roman *plebs*.

[15] This might be compared to the role that Varro assigns the *populus* in linguistic innovation: see Varro *ling.* 9.6, discussed by Gitner (Chapter 10, n. 23).

[16] The examples provided are trisyllabic instead of disyllabic *solvit*, *vam* instead of *uvam*, and trisyllabic *indurvit* for quadrisyllabic *induruit* (*barb.* 13.2–8).

GRAMMARIAN CONSENTIUS   107

4.1. Geographic Variation in the Pronunciation of Specific Latin Sounds

Consentius does a better job of discussing geographic variation as he moves on to consider the faulty pronunciation of specific Latin sounds (which he calls "letters"). Already Quintilian noted that some peoples pronounced certain sounds in peculiar ways (*inst.* 1.5.33); Latin grammarians traditionally focused on the errors concerning *i*, *l*, and *m*, which had each a specific name: iotacism, labdacism, and mytacism.[17] Consentius once again criticizes grammarians for not acknowledging that other letters as well are pronounced incorrectly, and establishes a general principle: barbarisms also arise whenever a letter sounds "richer" or "thinner" than the rule of the Latin language requires (*barb.* 15.2–4 *cum aut pinguius aliquid aut exilius sonabit quam ratio Romani sermonis exposcit*). There is a clear contrast here between a normative principle, the prescribed pronunciation of Latin sounds, and any deviations from it; as will become clear soon, deviations often fall under the category of regionalisms.

That is the case of Latin *i*. Consentius first describes the different errors made by Gauls and Greeks in pronouncing it: Gauls pronounce a sound in between *e* and *i*, while Greeks pronounce semivocalic *i* as vocalic (*barb.* 15.15–19). Secondly, he provides two different sets of rules for pronouncing it correctly (*barb.* 15.20 *Romanae linguae . . . moderatio*), depending on its position within a word or depending on its quantity (*barb.* 15.20–16.5).

That is also the case of Latin *l*, about which Consentius says that both a "thinner" and a "richer" pronunciation of it are innate in some peoples (*barb.* 16.7 *insitum alterutrum vitium quibusdam gentibus est*). As a matter of fact, labdacism is presented as a regional vice by other grammarians as well: Pompeius, for example, ascribes errors in the pronunciation of *l* to the Africans, who have issues pronouncing double *l* (see Zago 2017a). Consentius mentions the Greeks as pronouncing double *l* "thinly" and other unspecified speakers as pronouncing it too "richly" (*barb.* 16.8–13 *Graeci subtiliter . . . alii . . . pinguissimae prolationis*).[18] After that, he outlines the correct pronunciation of *l* in Latin according to its phonological context, a passage that has many similarities with the discussion of *l* of Pliny the Elder

---

[17] On these, see Zago (2016, 2017a, and 2018).

[18] I take Consentius to mean that the Greeks pronounce double *l* as single, while others pronounce it as "dark" (velar) when it should be "light" (alveolar) (see Mari 2019, 129–31 and Mari 2021, 248–51).

108 PROFESSIONAL GRAMMARIANS

as reported by Priscian and of Martianus Capella (Plin. *dub. serm.* frg. 8 Della Casa = 2 M., in Prisc. *gramm.* II 29.8–12; Mart. Cap. 3.241).

After talking about the incorrect pronunciation of the three letters traditionally discussed by the grammarians, Consentius moves on to explain those that the grammarians have left out, pointing out that "inherited" vices affect these too, apparently meaning that such errors are passed down generationally within a linguistic community (*barb.* 17.1–2 *sed et in aliis litteris sunt genitalia quaedam quorundam vitia*).[19] That is the case of *t*: some unspecified speakers (*aliqui*) pronounce it as a stop where it should be an affricate, as in *etiam*, and the Greeks pronounce it as an affricate where it should be a stop, as in *optimus* (*barb.* 17.2–6).[20] Consentius also mentions errors in pronouncing *c*, but he vaguely refers to the perpetrators as *quidam* and *alii* (*barb.* 17.6–14). He then refers to the Greeks again as he condemns their simplification of double *s*, as in *iussit* (*barb.* 17.14–16). Some pronounce semivocalic *u* (*v*) as vocalic, as for example in *ŭeni* (*barb.* 17.16–17); although Consentius vaguely talks of *aliqui*, it has been plausibly suggested that the Greeks are the perpetrators of this error as well (e.g., Adams 2003, 434; 2013, 185). Finally, Consentius does not rule out that other errors too might be native to some peoples (*barb.* 17.18–19 *fortasse sint etiam alia genitalia quorundam vitia*); he suggests that those aiming for language purity should watch out for them with diligence.

We have seen that in many a case Consentius explicitly contrasts the errors of peoples of the provinces (Greeks and Gauls, and we could probably add the Africans) with the *Romanus sermo* or *Romana lingua*. To be sure, in Consentius as well as in other grammatical authors these expressions do not identify the Latin spoken in Rome, but correct Latin as the language of the Roman empire (Adams 2007, 247). That is worth pointing out because still in Consentius' time the Latin of Rome enjoyed considerable prestige, as is attested by several provincial writers. Sidonius Apollinaris, for one, went out of his way to praise the Latin spoken by his provincial friends, which was just as good as that spoken in Rome: of his friend Consentius (our Consentius?) he said that he spoke Latin like one born in the Roman Subura (*carm.* 23.235–6 *seu Latialiter sonantem / tamquam Romulea satum Subura*); of Arbogastes, governor of Augusta Treverorum, he said that although he dwelt by the

[19] On the reading *genitalia* see Mari (2021, 254–5).
[20] It has been suggested that in the former case Consentius refers to the Italians and the text should read *Itali*, not *aliqui* (so Niedermann); in Mari (2017a,114–5; 2021, 255) I explain why I think that *aliqui* is correct and Consentius is not talking about Italians.

GRAMMARIAN CONSENTIUS   109

Moselle, he spoke the Latin of the Tiber (*epist.* 4.17.1 *potor Mosellae Tiberim ructas*).[21] It may be that Consentius too attached particular prestige to the Latin of Rome; however, as we have seen, he did not hesitate to condemn the linguistic innovations of the lower orders of the Roman people, the *plebs*. In other words, all was not gold that was Roman.

5. Language Contact and Borrowing

After discussing language variation, it seems fitting to address the topic of language contact. Roman grammarians had to confront language contact when discussing lexical borrowing. Consentius looks at borrowings from different perspectives. One is that of the *vitia et virtutes orationis*, for in this section Consentius refers to a borrowing as *barbarolexis* (literally, "barbarian word"): one has a *barbarolexis* when a foreign word is introduced into Latin from a foreign language (*barb.* 2.7–8 *cum ex aliena lingua in nostrum usum pars aliqua orationis inducitur*).[22] Unsurprisingly, Greek is not a source of Consentius' examples of *barbarolexis*, which include instead words designating objects of the Gauls (*cateia*, a sort of dart), Sardinians (*mastruca*, a leather coat), Africans (*magalia*, huts), and Medes (*acinacis*, a sword).[23]

The other perspective is that of the inflection of loanwords in Latin, which is traditional in the discussion of nouns. According to Consentius, foreign words (*peregrina*) should be inflected in the Latin way whenever possible. That is the case of Gaulish *mannus* (a horse), Mede *acinacis* (a sword) and *gaza* ("treasure"), and Punic *tubur* (an exotic fruit, probably the azarole): one should inflect them following the declension of the Latin noun that is most similar to them (*gramm.* V 364.8–11 *omne peregrinum nomen . . . dirigi ad eius Latini sermonis similitudinem debet cui proximum est*).

The situation is more complicated with Greek nouns, which are used more frequently; Consentius is aware that Greek nouns can be more or less assimilated, for some keep their Greek nominative and therefore are inflected in the Greek way, like *Pan, paean*; the ones whose nominative has been Latinized, on the other hand, are inflected in the Latin way, like *Helena*,

---

[21] Sources of the fourth century, especially Aug. *ord.* 2.17.45, show that the idea of the superiority of Italian Latin was not only a literary topos (see Adams 2007, 188–203).

[22] Other grammarians had a different idea of *barbarolexis*; for a history of the term and concept of *barbarolexis*, see Vainio (1994).

[23] *Cateia, mastruca*, and *magalia* are Donatus' examples of *barbarolexis* (*mai.* 3.1 p. 653.4); *acinacis* features in many of Donatus' manuscripts, but neither Keil nor Holtz have accepted it into the text.

110   PROFESSIONAL GRAMMARIANS

Achilles, and so on (*gramm.* V 364.18–23). There are also some nouns that keep the Greek nominative but are inflected in the Latin way, such as *Aeneas* and *Paris*. Where the nominative has not been Latinized, it all comes down to whether the form is similar to a Latin nominative or not; if it is similar, it is inflected like a Latin noun (e.g., *Paris Paridis*, not *Paridos*), for Consentius' general rule is that whenever the morphology of a foreign noun is similar to that of a Latin noun, one has to follow the Latin rule and not the foreign one (*gramm.* V 365.12–13 *ubi enim similitudo est nostrae regulae, nostra sequi potius quam peregrina debemus*). Consentius acknowledges that poets have some freedom to choose Latin or Greek forms based on euphony, which emerges again as a decisive criterion of morphological selection; yet when euphony allows it, Latin forms are to be preferred (*gramm.* V 365.27 *ubi decora datur occasio, nostris uti debemus, non aliena sectari*). That is why Desbordes (1991, 47) speaks of Consentius' "nationalism": for Consentius, Latin is no less prestigious than Greek and should not be too influenced by it.

6. Consentius: Guardian of What Language?

We are used to referring to Latin grammarians as guardians of language; but what language did Consentius aim to guard exactly? As much as it would be tempting to answer the Latin of classical authors, that would not be altogether correct. Consentius' language itself has several features that are rather typical of late Latin texts. Whenever he can, Consentius constructs the future perfect passive with the perfect participle and the future perfect, instead of the simple future, of *esse* (*barb.* 3.4–5 *fuerit intimata*; *barb.* 14.16 *exsecuti fuerimus*; *barb.* 18.15 *prolatum fuerit*).[24] Although this construction is not unparalleled in Early and Classical Latin, it becomes much more common in Late Latin, and Consentius lists it as a type of *futurum ulterius* (*gramm.* V 375.11–13). He sometimes uses *de* with the ablative where one would expect the genitive in Classical Latin, although only depending on *exemplum* and *modus* (*barb.* 3.2–3 *de singulis exempla accommodemus*; *barb.* 3.19 *exempla de metaplasmo prius dabimus*; *barb.* 12.19 *aliquos modos de metaplasmis*; *barb.* 16.23 *exempla de his tribus litteris*). A couple of times he also uses a *quod*-clause instead of the accusative with the infinitive after a verb of saying or knowing, although

---

[24] *Transformata fuerit* at *barb.* 5.15–17 is rather a perfect subjunctive (*ubicumque locorum transformata fuerit qualitas dictionis, eodem nomine censentur*).

GRAMMARIAN CONSENTIUS 111

he uses the latter construction as well (*gramm.* V 340.13–15 *scire debemus quod . . . sunt derivativa; barb.* 30.25–31.1 *adnotari etiam hoc loco potest quod interdum duae "m" pereunt*). In indirect questions, he mostly uses the "classical" subjunctive, but sometimes the indicative, as was quite common in Late Latin (e.g., *gramm.* V 347.13–14 *quae genera efficiuntur inveniet; barb.* 23.16–17 *quot modis excusatio euenit . . . conprehendisse me scio*).[25] If the text is correct, *duos metaplasmos habet* "there are two metaplasms" at *barb.* 20.19–20 may be a very rare case of impersonal *habet*, which is also late (cf. *TLL* VI.3 2461.78–2462.11). Some idioms are also common mostly in Late Latin, as for example *fraudem facit* with the dative ("damages something") at *barb.* 14.10 (cf. *TLL* VI.1 1268.64–76).

In these cases, there is no discrepancy between Consentius' own language use and his prescriptions, because he does not discuss these topics. One such discrepancy can be observed, however, between his prescription of how to use *prior* and the way he actually uses it; for Consentius teaches, according to the classical usage, that *primus* indicates the first of many, *prior* the first of two (*gramm.* V 340.3–5), yet he often uses *prior* to indicate the first element in a series of more than two (e.g., *barb.* 11.18–19 *"orator" correpta priore syllaba; barb.* 11.10 *"triginta" . . . priorem syllabam acuat; barb.* 11.20–1; *barb.* 15.18–19; *barb.* 20.4–5). This usage can be observed in other late authors (see *TLL* X.2 1337.12–38).

As we have seen, Consentius' (and other grammarians') fight against language change is especially evident in the realm of phonology. When it comes to his observations on errors that, in hindsight, reflect long-lasting tendencies of Latin, we see that Consentius aims to preserve a language that is "classical" in that it has vowel length distinction, consonant length distinction, aspirates, accents in the right places, distinction between *b* and *v*, and so on.[26] There might even be one instance in which the spelling pronunciation—that is, the attempt to pronounce Latin exactly how it was written—possibly underlying Consentius' (and others') discussion was already outdated in Classical Latin: that would be the case of final *m*, if Consentius actually meant that in expressions like *dixeram illis* one cannot tell whether *m* belongs to the preceding or following word (*barb.* 15.6–9). We know that already in Classical Latin final *m* was not really pronounced

---

[25] The grammarian Diomedes noted that many, because of ignorance, did not observe the rule of the subjunctive in indirect questions (*gramm.* I 395.15–24); a grammarian who often used the indicative in indirect questions was Pompeius (see Adams 2013, 766–9, and 747–73 more generally).

[26] See the collection of examples in Abbott (1909) and Maltby (2012).

112 PROFESSIONAL GRAMMARIANS

as such, but represented nasalization of the preceding vowel (see Quint. *inst.* 9.4.40). But we also know from Cornutus that in the first century CE some *eruditi* pronounced final *m* (Cassiod. *gramm.* VII 147.24–148.2), so it might be that some later grammarians too were keen on pronouncing final *m* (see Encuentra Ortega 2004).

Contemporary authors, especially Augustine, famously protested against the pedantic conservatism of grammarians and showed that even among certain educated speakers, let alone uneducated ones, some of the grammarians' precepts were not observed anymore or were even laughed off (see Adams 2013, 191–4). It has been pointed out, however, that in some respects grammarians were rather more receptive of changes and did not always prescribe outdated pronunciations (Wright 1982, 54–61). Consentius, for one, is the only grammarian to describe and prescribe as correct Latin what appears to be the proto-Romance situation of the *i*-sound: long *i* is closed, short *i* is open (*barb.* 15.20–16.5 *Romanae linguae in hoc haec erit moderatio . . . quando producta est, vel acutior vel plenior esse; quando autem brevis est, medium sonum exhibere*).[27] Like several other grammarians, Consentius also thinks that the correct pronunciation of *ti* followed by a vowel is the assibilated one, which will become the norm in Romance, and finds fault with those who pronounce *t* as a stop in words like *etiam* (*barb.* 17.2–6).[28]

In sum, as far as we can tell, the language Consentius is trying to preserve must be by and large the Latin of his educated contemporaries, including some features that were definitely innovative compared to Classical Latin, but also a few features that were rather outdated if not altogether anachronistic.

7. Conclusions: Consentius' Views in His Socio-Cultural Context

If, as seems most likely, the grammarian Consentius really was either of the *Consentii* mentioned by Sidonius Apollinaris or related to them, he

---

[27] Another account of the sounds of *i*, less clear than Consentius', is provided by the second-century grammarian Velius Longus (*gramm.* VII 49.16–20); on this, see Lindsay (1894, 26–7). Other grammarians describe the quality of *e* and *o* as depending on their quantity (e.g., Serv. *gramm.* IV 421.16–21; Serg. *gramm.* IV 520.27–31; Pomp. *gramm.* V 102.4–18; ps. Mar. Victorin. *gramm.* VI 33.3–8).

[28] The assibilated pronunciation of *ti* followed by a vowel is also recommended by Servius (*gramm.* V 445.9–10), Pompeius (*gramm.* V 104.6–7 and 286.7–17), Papirius or Papirianus (*gramm.* VII 216.8–9), and Isidore (*Orig.* 1.27.28).

GRAMMARIAN CONSENTIUS 113

must have been active in Gaul between the fourth and fifth century or in the fifth century. In a context of profound change on many levels, it was all too natural for some educated individuals to fear a corruption of Latin. Consentius' work, especially his *De barbarismis et metaplasmis*, fits well in this context and can be seen as a reaction to this fear of linguistic corruption.

Consentius, as an educated provincial, cultivated and prescribed "standard" Latin, ideally identified as *Romanus sermo*, and condemned provincialisms, including those of his fellow countrypeople, the Gauls. How come Consentius was acquainted with features of the Latin spoken by Greeks, Africans, and the Roman *plebs*? Surely multiple explanations are possible that do not require Consentius' direct observation, as for example his use of lost written sources. However, if for the author of *De barbarismis et metaplasmis* we can follow the path leading to Sidonius' friend Consentius, who worked at the imperial court and traveled to Constantinople, we can hypothesize direct experience. At any rate one has to take into account that in the fourth or fifth century there obviously existed trade and other kinds of exchange between Gaul and the rest of the Mediterranean (see, e.g., Hitchner 2005), so even a Gaul who never traveled may well have been exposed to other accents.

When it comes to social variation, Consentius' remark on the linguistic habits of the Roman *plebs* is rather derogatory. Consentius' attitude fits in well with his senatorial status and the prejudices that the upper classes of the Roman Empire held toward lower classes.

On the grounds of Consentius' originality in content and style and his polemical attitude toward other grammarians, it has been argued that he was not a professional *grammaticus* but rather a learned amateur (see *Guardians* 396). This is plausible, although one cannot exclude that a professional grammarian would try to distinguish himself from other grammarians as a self-promoting strategy.[29] At any rate, a pedagogical concern is visible in Consentius' work, and in one passage he explicitly refers to teaching children how to avoid mistakes (*barb.* 21.21 *ad ostendenda aut declaranda pueris vitia*). His target, however, was not limited to school children; in one passage, Consentius discusses extralinguistic elements of oratorical delivery and

---

[29] On grammarians criticizing other grammarians see Zetzel (Chapter 1).

114 PROFESSIONAL GRAMMARIANS

states that instruction in this area would be beneficial to those engaged in politics (*barb.* 18.4 *qui civilem scientiam professi*). Consentius may or may not have been a professional grammarian; at a time of momentous change, any educated person who took the fate of Latin to heart could join the ranks of the "guardians of language."[30]

---

[30] If one were to situate Consentius in relationship to the distinction that Zetzel makes in this volume between the *grammaticus*, who "guards against future decline" and the Latinist, who "laments past losses," he would certainly be closer to the former.

7

Antiquus = squalidus? Pompeius' Attitude toward Antiquity

Anna Zago

1. "Professor Pompey"

According to Wallace M. Lindsay, there is no better way to imagine an ancient classroom than by opening up Pompeius' *Commentum* (1916, 35): "If anyone wishes to transport himself in imagination to an ancient lecture-room, let him read *G[rammatici] L[atini]* V.95 sqq. . . . The formal title is 'Pompei Commentum Artis Donati', but what these pages give us is apparently a verbatim, short-hand report of the lectures of . . . 'Professor Pompey' to a dunces' class in some University of his own country. The class must have been a 'soft option'; no student could fail to pass with the help of so vivacious and painstaking a teacher." This description highlights the main features of Pompeius' style, a grammarian and schoolteacher active in North Africa in the fifth or sixth century CE.[1] His *Commentum* is a very long—sometimes verbose—exposition of Donatus' *Ars maior*, which also takes into account similar work by Servius. Pompeius' style is a peculiar mix of didacticism and vividness, and his work preserves for us perhaps the most realistic picture of a late antique lecture course in a peripheral area of the Roman Empire.

2. Pompeius' Prologue

However, the real opening of Pompeius' work is not the one we read in the fifth volume of Keil's *Grammatici Latini*, since the *incipit* of the *Commentum*

---

[1] Zago (2017b, I:xciii–xciv). The characteristics of Pompeius as a lecturer are described in more detail in *Guardians*, Chapter 4 "Pompeius."

116 PROFESSIONAL GRAMMARIANS

was missing in the manuscripts used by Keil for his edition.[2] The real prologue of Pompeius' commentary was discovered and edited by "the late" Louis Holtz (1971, esp. 59–60), in a fundamental study on the manuscript tradition of Pompeius. Holtz published the missing portion of the prologue on the basis of two manuscript witnesses, and his discovery was of the utmost importance for two main reasons: first of all, the "new" prologue yielded very interesting information about Pompeius' choice to bypass Donatus' *Ars minor* and to comment only on the major *Ars*; secondly, the loss of the prologue in most of the extant manuscripts led Holtz to hypothesize some form of material damage in their common ancestor, which is the main piece of evidence supporting a twofold *stemma* for the whole manuscript tradition of Pompeius.[3]

While doing my research on the ancient and medieval traditions of the *Commentum*, I chanced on another, previously unknown, manuscript containing the missing portion of the prologue, so that we now have three witnesses for the prologue of Pompeius. On the basis of these manuscripts and an in-depth investigation into the indirect tradition (which is very significant for this specific part of the *Commentum*), I have recently offered a new critical edition of the prologue, with a small but substantial number of textual improvements.

For reasons of space, I will not present the new prologue in its entirety here,[4] but rather focus my attention on a short passage in which Pompeius is dealing with Donatus' choice to write two different *artes*. In doing so, the grammarian underlines the didactic purpose of the so-called *Ars minor* (text 1):

(1)   Pomp. *gramm*. prol. p. 158.14–20: primam ergo partem scimus scriptam esse institutorie, id est ut instrueret infantes ad artem: non plene, non perfecte scripsit hanc partem. alii autem scripserunt artem, sed illos alios non potes intellegere, nisi hinc sumpseris principium. nam ecce

---

[2] I will cite Pompeius' work from Keil's edition for the first two books (Pomp. *gramm*. V 95–282) and from my critical editions for the third book, including the so-called *barbarismus* (Zago 2017b, I:1–82 = *gramm*. V 283–312), and the prologue (Zago 2019, 157–62). The texts on their own, including the new prologue, are available online in the *Digital Library of Late-Antique Latin Texts* (https://digiliblt.uniupo.it/). Essential information and an up-to-date bibliography on Pompeius are to be found in *CCC* 308–9.

[3] On Pompeius' *stemma codicum* see Holtz (1971 and 2005); for the sole third part of the *Commentum*, I sketched a new *stemma* in Zago (2017b, I:ci–cxlv, esp. cxlv); a separate *stemma codicum* for the prologue is in Zago (2019, 150–5).

[4] For a full presentation of the text, see Zago (2019).

ANTIQUUS = SQUALIDUS? 117

scripsit Probus bene et plene, sed per multum circuitum tam verbosus quam superfluus ‹non›nusquam invenitur. scripsit etiam Caesar artem bene quidem, sed squalidas regulas posuit antiquas, quae hodie non sunt in usu.

Therefore, we know that the first part [*sc.* the *Ars minor*] was written with a didactic purpose, that is, to instruct pupils in the *ars grammatica*: he did not provide all information in this section, nor did he write it exhaustively. Of course, other authors wrote *artes*, but with all those people, you cannot understand their work unless you start from here. For example, Probus wrote with care and thoroughness, but sometimes we find him verbose and superfluous through much circumlocution. Caesar too wrote an *ars*, certainly a good one, but the rules he devised are rude in style and old-fashioned, and really outdated today. (transl. Zago 2019 with modifications)

This passage is a very interesting sample of Pompeius' easy-going attitude toward the earlier grammatical tradition. Even if he shows proper consideration and respect for Probus' care in writing his *ars bene et plene* and for Caesar's proficiency in the grammatical field, he cannot restrain himself from cutting them down to size: the former is long-winded and gives too much information, the latter too old-fashioned to be of use to Pompeius' pupils, and this is because of his ancient and rough-and-ready way of teaching.

3. "Squalid" in Rhetoric and Stylistics

This last remark is the one I would like to take as the starting point for this paper, as it raises, I think, an interesting question about the real meaning of the adjective *squalidus*: what does it mean in reference to the word *regula*? In order to answer this question, it will be useful to take a look at the figurative use of *squalidus*, in rhetorical or stylistic contexts.

Two very interesting passages come from Cicero (texts 2 and 3), who employs the adjective just once in his surviving *oeuvre*,[5] concerning the

---

[5] But we count twenty-six occurrences for *squalor* and two for the verb *squaleo*.

118 PROFESSIONAL GRAMMARIANS

educational background an accomplished orator is expected to possess. In the first of these passages (text 2), Cicero is referring to the teaching of ancient Stoics logicians, "the compact deductive modes of dialectic" (Freudenburg 1993, 154), labelled as rather harsh and thus unfitting for the ideal orator:

(2) Cic. *orat*. 115: ergo eum censeo, qui eloquentiae laude ducatur, non esse earum rerum omnino rudem, sed vel illa antiqua vel hac Chrysippi disciplina institutum. noverit primum vim naturam genera verborum et simplicium et copulatorum; deinde quot modis quidque dicatur; qua ratione verum falsumne iudicetur; quid efficiatur e quoque, quid cuique consequens sit quidque contrarium; cumque ambigue multa dicantur, quo modo quidque eorum dividi explanarique oporteat. haec tenenda sunt oratori (saepe enim occurrunt), sed quia sua sponte squalidiora sunt, adhibendus erit in iis explicandis quidam orationis nitor.

I believe, therefore, that a speaker eager for praise ought not be entirely ignorant of these matters [i.e., dialectic] but should be trained either in the old form of the discipline or in that of Chrysippus. He should first know the meaning, nature, and varieties of words, both by themselves and in combination with others; then all forms of predication; how statements are judged true or false; what emerges from each statement— what follows from it or contradicts it; and since many statements are am- biguous, how ambiguities should be resolved and clarified. The orator should understand these principles, since they are frequently relevant, but use a certain rhetorical polish in presenting them, because they are rather unattractive in themselves. (transl. Kaster 2020)

Another interesting passage from Cicero (3) shows us a figurative meaning of the adverb derived from *squalidus*, when Cicero again gives an account on the shortcomings of the Stoics opposed to the "neat and polished manner" of the early Peripatetics and Academics:

(3) Cic. *fin*. 4.5: quam multa illi de re publica scripserunt, quam multa de legibus! quam multa non solum praecepta in artibus sed etiam exempla in orationibus bene dicendi reliquerunt! primum enim ipsa illa quae subtiliter disserenda erant polite apteque dixerunt, tum definientes, tum partientes, ut vestri etiam; sed vos squalidius; illorum vides quam niteat oratio.

ANTIQUUS = SQUALIDUS? 119

What a vast amount they have written on politics and on jurisprudence! How many precepts of oratory they have left us in their treatises, and how many examples in their discourses! In the first place, even the topics that required close reasoning they handled in a neat and polished manner, employing now definition, now division; as indeed your school does also, but your style is rather out-at-elbows, while theirs is noticeably elegant. (transl. Rackham 1914)

In both passages, Cicero opposes an elegant and graceful style to a slovenly (and thus unattractive) style. It is worthwhile pointing out here that, in the passage taken from the treatise *On Ends*, the chronological perspective is quite the opposite of Pompeius'. While the refined and elegant writers belong to the past, the orators of the contemporary age are accused of writing *squalidius*.

If we were to judge only from the passages we have analyzed so far, Pompeius' remark about the *squalor* of Caesar's grammatical work could simply refer to the style of his treatise. Even if the hypothesis cannot be completely dismissed, I think it to be quite unattractive, because ancient sources all agree that the chief quality of Caesar's eloquence consists in *elegantia*, as shown in great detail by Alessandro Garcea in his recent edition of Caesar's *De analogia*.[6]

4. "Squalid" and "Ancient" at the Same Time

In order to gain a better understanding of the problematic reference to Caesar in Pompeius' prologue, we must address a second issue, which is the connection between *squalor* and *antiquitas*, because Pompeius sets up a clear relationship between the two when he says that Caesar *squalidas regulas posuit antiquas*.

To test the diffusion and the possible meaning of these words, I decided to restrict my research to the combination of *squalor*, *squaleo*, or *squalidus* (including the adverb *squalide*) with words from the semantic field of "antiquity": the most suitable ones were of course *antiquitas* and *antiquus*, together with *vetustas* and *vetus*, in all possible forms.

The combination of these semantic fields appears to be well attested in Latin, and in most cases refers to the description of places (especially of cities

[6] Garcea (2012, 49–113). A very useful survey about Caesar as a linguist is by Pezzini (2018).

120   PROFESSIONAL GRAMMARIANS

and villages).[7] Among the texts where the concept of antiquity is linked to the idea of *squalor*, two passages deserve particular attention, as they employ the metaphor of squalid places which need to be cleaned to regain their original splendour.

The first passage (4) is taken from the second book of Quintilian's *Institutio oratoria*, where the rhetorician discusses reading suitable for advanced students:

(4)   Quint. *inst.* 2.5.23–4: firmis autem iudiciis iamque extra periculum positis suaserim et antiquos legere (ex quibus si adsumatur solida ac virilis ingenii vis deterso rudis saeculi squalore, tum noster hic cultus clarius enitescet) et novos, quibus et ipsis multa virtus adest: neque enim nos tarditatis natura damnavit, sed dicendi mutavimus genus et ultra nobis quam oportebat indulsimus: ita non tam ingenio illi nos superarunt quam proposito.

Once tastes have been formed and are secure from danger, I should recommend reading both the older orators (because, if the solid, masculine force of their genius can be acquired, but without the layer of uncouthness incident to that primitive age, our own more polished product will shine with extra brilliance) and the moderns, who also have many good qualities. Nature has not condemned us to be slow-witted, but we have changed our style and indulged ourselves more than we ought; it is not in natural talent that the ancients are better than we are, but in their aims. (transl. Russell 2001, with minor modifications)

The general meaning of this passage is very clear: the prose of ancient writers is solid and, so to speak, "masculine" (Quintilian says *virilis*), but—maybe for this very reason—also quite uncouth, as if there were a layer of roughness we would have to remove in order to appreciate it. The context is not so different from Pompeius' passage: both scholars say that ancient orators

---

[7] As we can see in Cassiodorus (*var.* 4.24.1), when King Theoderic writes to his friend (and doctor), the deacon Helpidius, who had previously asked him to contribute actively to the restoration of the city of Spoleto: *petitionis tuae proinde tenore comperimus loca in Spoletina civitate, quae iam longo situ squalor vetustatis obnuberat, splendorem reparationis expetere, ut rebus antiquitate confusis novitatis facies adulta reddatur et beneficio tuo rediviva consurgant, quae annositate inclinata corruerant* ("From the content of your request we learned that in the city of Spoleto some places, abandoned for a long time and covered with the squalor of age, call out loud to be restored to their splendour, so that the works spoiled by age regain their youthful looks, and thanks to you all things rise to new life divesting themselves of the burden of time").

ANTIQUUS = SQUALIDUS?   121

or grammarians are to be considered very good per se, provided that the modern readers are able to wipe off the dirt of time.[8]

A second passage, this time from Tertullian's *Apologeticum*, displays a worse opinion of ancient texts, even if it refers to a very specific field, that of legislation:

(5) Tert. *apol.* 4.6–7: miramini hominem aut errare potuisse in lege condenda, aut resipuisse in reprobanda? . . . nonne et vos cottidie, experimentis inluminantibus tenebras antiquitatis, totam illam veterem et squalentem silvam legum novis principalium rescriptorum et edictorum securibus ruspatis et caeditis?

Do you wonder that a man may have made a mistake in framing a law, or returned to sense in disallowing his law? . . . Yes, and you yourselves, as experiment every day lightens the darkness of antiquity, do you not lop and fell all that old and squalid jungle of laws with the new axes of imperial rescripts and edicts? (transl. Glover and Rendall 1931)

I believe that Tertullian is here using *squalentem* to convey two different meanings: the first one is "lying waste" (out of neglect), a usage of the verb *squaleo* that is well attested with *silva* and similar words (with *arva* in Vergil's *Georgics* and Lucan's *Bellum Civile*, and with *campi* in Silius' *Punica*);[9] the second one is "dark," "murky," as suggested by the reference to the "darkness of antiquity" (*tenebras antiquitatis*). Tertullian is juxtaposing the jungle of confused, arid, and obscure laws of ancient times with the new rescripts and edicts, metaphorical axes poised to fell the forest of squalid shrubs.

Turning now to grammatical texts, we can find three additional passages testifying to a critical approach to either *regulae* or *vetustas*. The first one (6) is taken from Gellius, who describes the scorn of Valerius Probus for grammatical *finitiones*:[10]

(6) Gell. 13.21.1: interrogatus est Probus Valerius, quod ex familiari eius quodam conperi, "has"ne "urbis" an "has urbes" et "hanc turrim"

---

[8] On this passage, see Reinhardt and Winterbottom (2006, 139–40); see also Calcante (2007, esp. 119–21).

[9] For a complete survey of the semantics of *squaleo* in imperial epic poetry see Sacerdoti (2007), whose starting point is Verg. *Aen.* 10.314 (*tunicam squalentem auro*) as analyzed by Gell. 2.6.4.

[10] See Holford-Strevens (2003, 163–65), and in this volume (Chapter 11).

122 PROFESSIONAL GRAMMARIANS

an "hanc turrem" dici oporteret. "Si aut versum," inquit, "pangis aut orationem solutam struis atque ea verba tibi dicenda sunt, non finitiones illas praerancidas neque foetutinas grammaticas spectaveris, sed aurem tuam interroga, quo quid loco conveniat dicere; quod illa suaserit, id profecto erit rectissimum."

Valerius Probus was once asked, as I learned from one of his friends, whether one ought to say *has urbis* or *has urbes* and *hanc turrim* or *hanc turrim*. "If," he replied, "you are either composing verse or writing prose and have to use those words, pay no attention to the musty, fusty rules of the grammarians, but consult your own ear as to what is to be said in any given place. What it favours will surely be the best." (transl. Rolfe 1927, with minor modifications)

Even though there is no explicit mention of oldness, the meaning of *praerancidae* and *foetutinae* is suggestive of obsolete rules, too strict and out-dated to be useful to a modern reader (and writer), who instead should consult his own taste.[11] The "musty, fusty rules of the grammarians" are compared to a rotting corpse, dead and unburied, whose rancidity must be regarded as a health hazard to anyone who wants to write anything in verse or prose.[12]

The reference to rancidness in Gellius' passage brings us to another inter-esting passage (text 7),[13] this time from Julius Romanus, cited in Charisius' *Ars*: the object of the discussion is an alleged nominative *haec suppellectilis*, which is not recommended by the grammarian.[14]

(7)   Char. *gramm.* p. 183.2–4: sed necdum nobis idoneum proin loquentis occurrit exemplum, velut "ancipes" et "praecipes," quod vetustas cum ratione rancidum protulit.

We have not yet found a suitable example of such kinds of expression, and the same applies to *ancipes* and *praecipes*: these forms have been transmitted by antiquity for the sake of *ratio*, but they smell foul.

---

[11] A stimulating discussion on the different attitude shown by *grammatici* and "Latinists" towards linguistic changes is found in Zetzel's contribution in this volume (Chapter 1).

[12] A complete survey of the use of *rancidus* in Latin critics, commentators, and grammarians has recently been made by Rosellini (2021; the Gellius passage is cited at 156–7).

[13] On this passage and the following one see De Nonno (2017, esp. 217–19).

[14] The example of *suppellectilis* is also discussed by Zetzel in this volume.

A similar comment is found in Charisius and Diomedes (text 8), whose common source speaks of *inculta vetustas* in relation to the long final -*o* in the first person of the present indicative:

(8)   Char. *gramm.* p. 13.29–32 = Diom. *gramm.* I 435.24–6: adeo ut Vergilius quoque idem servaverit, in aliis autem refugerit incultae vetustatis horrorem et carmen contra morem veterum levigaverit.

> So that Vergil too preserved this quantity; in other cases, however, he shunned the roughness of uncouth obsolescence and he polished his poem contrary to the manner of the ancients.

A last passage (text 9) can be added, taken from the *praefatio* of Cassiodorus' *De orthographia*.[15] Here the author explains the story behind his choice to write an orthographical treatise, leaving aside other demanding obligations he was working on at the time (i.e., the *De complexionibus apostolorum*): his fellow monks, tired of studying ancient (and difficult) writings they were not even able to read aloud nor copy down, needed a clear set of rules on spelling and orthography.

(9)   Cassiod. *orth.* praef. 6 (= *gramm.* VII 143.9-12): ideo duodecim auctorum opuscula deducimus in medium, quae ab illis breviter et copiosa dicta sunt, ut et nos ea compendiosius dicamus et a priscis auctoribus sine varietatis studio dicta recolantur.

> That is why we selected for common use the short treatises of twelve ancient authors, written either very briefly or at length, so that we could both abridge them and polish up what the ancient authors said without any care for variety.

Cassiodorus' remarks concerning the style of ancient grammarians are suggestive rather than an in-depth assessment; nevertheless, it is worth noticing the double meaning of *recolere* that I think applies here: Cassiodorus feels the need both to "recultivate" ancient orthographical doctrine and to "polish" it at the same time. According to Cassiodorus, the *prisci auctores* were either

---

[15] I am grateful to Tim Denecker for pointing out this passage to me. The text is cited from Stoppacci (2010); on the genesis and composition of Cassiodorus' orthographical treatise cf. Stoppacci (2010, xxxvii–l, esp. xliv–xlviii).

124 PROFESSIONAL GRAMMARIANS

long-winded (whence the need of an abridged version: *compendiosius*) or too flat, as they lacked variety (*sine varietatis studio*). To some extent, this pair of flaws recalls the double remark Pompeius makes in his prologue, where Probus is accused of being *verbosus*, "wordy," and thus full of unnecessary information, while Caesar's grammatical writings are labelled as "rough-and-ready in style" and "old-fashioned." In both cases, the point of view is that of a late grammarian, concerned as much with didactic aims as with stylistic care. Cassiodorus and Pompeius thus try to balance the (basic) needs of their public and a taste for good writing.

5. Surveying Pompeius

Having analyzed the relevant passages for the "rhetorical" usage of *squaleo* and similar words, let us turn to Pompeius again. At a superficial level, his short comment about Caesar looks more like a quip—the first of a long series—than a deeply considered opinion about the style of Caesar's grammatical work, or even the style of a text written according to Caesar's grammatical rules. But to contextualize and draw out the implications of this allusion, which is very clear, despite its rapidity, it will be useful to consider all the references to *antiqui* and *antiquitas* in Pompeius' commentary.

I shall now present a selection of passages that are representative of Pompeius' view of ancient tradition, in order to identify its role within the teaching activity of the *magister*.

5.1. A Positive (?) Attitude

When considering Pompeius' views on grammatical and linguistic topics, it should be borne in mind that he often takes the *current* usage as both the starting point and the goal of his reflection about the Latin language.[16]

Thus, it is not rare for Pompeius first to present the ancient tradition as nonsensical and far from modern (and functional) usage, and then proceed, sometimes in a histrionic manner, to reveal the real reasons that lie behind

---

[16] This attitude is evident, for instance, in the long and often confused treatment of the *vitium* called *iotacismus* (Pomp. *gramm.* p. 13.1–14, 12). As I have shown in Zago (2016, esp. 298–99 and 308), Pompeius presents the assibilation of *ti* before a vowel as both normal (as it would have been at his period) and correct, and in doing so he dismisses the "classical" pronunciation as erroneous.

ANTIQUUS = SQUALIDUS? 125

the ancients' choices. One of the most interesting examples (10) is a passage about the alleged existence of the dual verb in Latin, a topic discussed in more detail by Denecker in this volume:[17]

> (10) Pomp. *gramm.* V 234.17–33: singularis "lego," pluralis "legimus." temptaverunt non nulli dicere accidere verbo etiam dualem illum numerum graecum. Graeci, quando de uno loquuntur, ita dicunt "unus homo legit"; quando de multis, ita dicunt, "multi homines legunt"; quando de duobus, nec "legit" dicunt nec "legunt," sed "legēre." ... et quid est "legēre"? nihil aliud, nisi quod et "legerunt," quia hoc significat "legēre" quod "legerunt." quare maluerunt maiores nostri duplicem regulam dare? metrorum causa. . . . ideo duplicem regulam fecerunt. tamen quantum ad sensum pertinet, hoc significat "legerunt" quod "legēre."

> The singular form is *lego*, the plural is *legimus*. Some people ventured to say that the dual, the Greek number, applies also to Latin verbs. The Greeks, when they speak of a single person, say *unus homo legit* (one man reads); when they speak of several persons, they say *multi homines legunt* (several men read); when they speak of two persons, they say neither *legit* nor *legunt*, but rather *legēre*. . . . And what does *legēre* mean? Nothing else but *legerunt*, as *legēre* and *legerunt* have the same meaning. Why did the ancients choose to give a double rule? For the sake of metre. . . . That is why they established a double rule. At any rate, with respect to the meaning, *legerunt* and *legēre* mean the same thing.

Another passage (11) clearly demonstrates Pompeius' effort to find a balance between consideration and respect for classical, canonical authors, which is the standard attitude of a good teacher, and his natural pragmatism. Pompeius tries to defend *idonei auctores*, the "suitable authors,"[18] against the accusation of disrupting the *necessitas artis*, "normative grammar": therefore, it is not surprising that he chooses a famous ancient grammarian, Asper, to play the role of Sallust's defence lawyer.

> (11)   Pomp. *gramm.* V 273.9–23 interim nos hodie hoc teneamus, ut "ad" semper "ad locum" sit, "apud" semper "in loco" sit. legimus quidem

---

[17] Denecker (2019, 117–8) also gives a full account of this passage and reasonably concludes that in Pompeius' view "the alternation between *legēre* and *legerunt* is a *duplex regula* created by the *maiores* to fulfill the varying needs for short or long syllables (viz. the final short -*ĕ* or long -*ūnt*) in the practice of verse composition."

[18] On the concept and definition of *idonei auctores* see Kaster (1978).

126   PROFESSIONAL GRAMMARIANS

apud Sallustium, in historiis (*hist.* frg. 1.119 = 1.102 Ramsey) habemus "ille Conisturgim apud legiones venit": mutavit praepositionem. Asper defendit et ita dixit, "'Conisturgim venit.' ad quam Conisturgim venit? ubi fuerant legiones, quo venit. convertas ordinem: iste enim dixit 'Conisturgim apud legiones venit,' id est apud Conisturgim fuerant legiones, quo iste venit. mutavit ordinem." ergo "apud" "in loco" esse debet, ut "apud amicum ‹sum›." "ad" vero cum artis necessitate "ad locum" significet, id est "ad amicum vado," tamen omnes antiqui et idonei et firmi auctores iunxerunt quasi "in loco": "prima quod ad Troiam pro caris gesserat Argis" (Verg. *Aen.* 1.24); in Cicerone "decem fiscos ad senatorem illum relictos" (*Verr.* I 22), "ad Marcum Lecam te habitare dixisti" (*cf. Catil.* 1.19). ergo licet nobis "ad" et in loco ponere et ad locum ponere.

Now, at present time we must follow this general rule, that *ad* always means "to a place," *apud* always means "in a place." And yet, in Sallust's *Historiae* we read *ille Conisturgim apud legiones venit* [*hist.* frg. 1.119 = 1.102 Ramsey "he came to Conisturgis, where the legions were"]: he chose a different preposition. Asper defends him and objects: "*Venit Conisturgim* ["he came to Conisturgis"]. Which Conisturgis? The one where the legions were waiting, that is where he came to. Change the order of the words: as a matter of fact, he said *Conisturgim apud legiones venit*, that is the legions were in Conisturgis, and there he came. It is just a different word order." So *apud* means "in a place," such as "I am at my friend's house," while *ad*, if we look at the rules of grammar, means "to a place," as in "I am going to my friend's house." However, all the ancient and suitable authors used *ad* to mean "in a place": *prima quod ad Troiam pro caris gesserat Argis* [Verg. *Aen.* 1.24 "[the war] which erstwhile she had fought at Troy for her beloved Argos"]; in Cicero: *decem fiscos ad senatorem illum relictos* [*Verr.* I 22 "ten baskets left at this senator's house"], *ad Marcum Lecam te habitare dixisti* ["you said that you lived at the home of Marcus Leca"; cf. *Catil.* 1.19]. It is therefore permitted to use *ad* to mean both "in a place" and "to a place."

Pompeius discusses a passage of Sallust that apparently violates the standard grammatical precept (*artis necessitas*) regarding the use of the preposition *apud*, which should indicate place in which (*in loco*), as opposed to *ad*, which should indicate motion towards (*ad locum*). First Pompeius introduces Asper's defense of the passage, who paraphrases in an attempt to show that *apud* has its standard meaning of place in which (i.e., *Conisturgim apud legiones venit* should be interpreted as *apud Conisturgim fuerant legiones, quo iste venit*). This seems to reaffirm the general rule, which Pompeius restates. Nevertheless, he immediately adds an observation of his own that the *antiqui et idonei et firmi auctores*—the most laudatory way of referring to classical authors—frequently used *ad* in a way that violates the precept. Thus balancing authority against *necessitas artis*, Pompeius concludes that it is permitted to use *ad* to mean either "in a place" or "to a place."

5.2. A Negative Attitude

As we have seen from the previous passages, the ancients seemed to have freedom and ability to choose among different forms, declensions, prepositions, cases, and so on. The other side of the coin is a sort of unpredictability in their choices, which makes their usage almost non-applicable (and as a result irrelevant) at the period when Pompeius was writing.[19]

One of the most significant passages on the licence of ancient writers is taken from the chapter *de praepositione*, where Pompeius discusses the double construction of some prepositions, namely *in*, *sub*, *super*, and *subter*:

> (12) Pomp. *gramm.* V 275.17–25: sunt etiam aliquae praepositiones quae communes vocantur, eo quod nunc accusativo serviunt, nunc ablativo. sunt autem istae, "in" "sub" "super" et "subter." hae apud maiores nostros sine aliqua ratione ponebantur: quando placebat, dicebant "eo in foro," dicebant "eo in forum" pro arbitrio suo. huius rei extant exempla innumerabilia, quod quadam licentia utentes, quando volebant ad locum, quando volebant in loco, ponebant easdem praepositiones . . . hodie non possumus dicere.

> Some prepositions are called *communes* because they take nouns in either the accusative or ablative case. These are *in*, *sub*, *super*, and *subter*. Our forefathers used them without any kind of rule: when they liked it, they said *eo in foro*, or they said *eo in forum* as the whim took them. We have plenty of examples of this usage, because they made use of a certain license, and they used the same prepositions to signify motion to a place or rest in a place . . . Now we cannot speak this way.

[19] On the concept of *licentia antiquitatis* see De Nonno (2017, esp. 18 n. 12).

128 PROFESSIONAL GRAMMARIANS

Even though Pompeius is sometimes dismissive of antiquity in his discussions of what is correct and what is not, of course he cannot forget the proper respect owed to the ancient "guardians of language." The following passage (13) may not be the best example of rigorous teaching, but it is pure Pompeius:[20]

(13)   Pomp. *gramm.* V 277.3–11: et hodie si vis dicere "super tecto" et "super tectum," dabitur tibi facultas. sed non loqueris secundum praesentem usum, sed secundum antiquum. nam si maiores nostri utebantur nunc accusativo, nunc ablativo, sic et tu habes uti? nam habes apud Vergilium exemplum, "ferre iuvat subter densa testudine" (Verg. *Aen.* 9.514). *subter testudinem* non dixit, sed *subter testudine.* vides ergo quid habet antiquitas. usus praesens hoc habet, ut istae praepositiones *in* et *sub* varie ponantur; illae vero *super* et *subter* accusativo iunguntur, sive euntis sive permanentis habeant significationem.

These days, if you want to say *super tecto* and *super tectum*, you are entitled to do so. But you are not speaking according to present usage but according to old-fashioned usage. For if our forefathers sometimes used the accusative, sometimes the ablative, will you do the same? You have a relevant example in Vergil, *ferre iuvat subter densa testudine* [*Aen.* 9.514 "but beneath their compact shield, [the enemy] delight to endure"]: he did not say *subter testudinem*, but *subter testudine.* That's the way it is with antiquity. The present usage is that these prepositions *in* and *sub* take various cases, whereas *super* and *subter* take the accusative, whether they express a movement or a state.

The balanced solution he offers ("do as you want, provided that you know you are speaking/writing according to old-fashioned usage") does not apply to every grammatical issue: sometimes antiquity is outdated no matter what, as demonstrated by the figure of *schesis onomaton*, that is a sentence constructed only of nouns, adjectives, or participles, and so on:

(14)   Pomp. *gramm.* p. 59.13–60.4: schesis onomaton est: habebant hanc consuetudinem antiqui, modo nemo facit hoc. schesis onomaton est coacervatio nominum. difficile est ut aut nomina sint omnia aut pronomina

---

[20] I made a slight but significant change in the punctuation of this passage, reading *sic et tu habes uti* as a direct question (very common in Pompeius).

ANTIQUUS = SQUALIDUS? 129

sint omnia aut participia omnia; hoc pro ingenti adfectatione faciebant maiores nostri.

This is the definition of *schesis onomaton*: the ancients had this habit, now no one does it. *Schesis onomaton* is an accumulation of nouns. It is difficult [to make it so] that all [words] are nouns, or all pronouns, or all participles; ancient writers used this trope as a great affectation.

Times are changing, Pompeius says, and the very principle of *imitatio*, a real foundation of ancient literature, becomes a double-edged sword, so that a bravura passage taken from Cicero risks sounding ridiculous when performed in modern times:

(15)   Pomp. *gramm.* p. 62.1–4: puta habemus apud Ciceronem apertissime positum: "itaque in illum non animadvertisti, sed hospitem reliquisti" (*cf. Deiot.* 10): paene unus est exitus rerum omnium. antiquum est hoc totum, hodie nemo facit; siqui fecerit, ridetur.

You know, we can find it on display in Cicero: *itaque in illum non animadvertisti, sed hospitem reliquisti* ["so you did not chastise him, but left him as your host"; cf. *Deiot.* 10]: almost every single word ends with the same letters. This is an ancient usage, it is out of date now; if one tries to do it, he makes a fool of himself.

6. Conclusion

The passages we have seen so far show that Pompeius' attitude toward ancient tradition cannot be easily described by an all-purpose definition. Pompeius is not the greatest admirer of antiquity nor does he recommend ancient usage over the modern trends of language.

His relationship with the previous tradition is inspired by practical thinking and pragmatism, and this is true also for the whole *Commentum*: in this way, antiquity can either be a mine of classical examples to learn and imitate or a distant world full of complicated (and random) rules, with differing tastes and differing usage.

This tendency in Pompeius was already envisaged by Kaster (*Guardians* 164), who offers one of the best portrayals of the African grammarian: "When

130 PROFESSIONAL GRAMMARIANS

the received doctrine works, his pleasure is audible: . . . And he is plainly satisfied when the *maiores*—the ancients, the classical authors—can be thought to have followed *ratio*. He is satisfied, that is, when the *maiores* seem to behave as he and his colleagues behave. But when their *auctoritas* goes against the *regulae firmissimae* he has inherited, his satisfaction gives way to a strong warning against literary blandishments. The shift is only to be expected, since the past practitioners who built up the tradition of firm rules piece by piece have an *auctoritas* of their own, a match for the *auctoritas* of antiquity."

Ultimately, our grammarian never hesitates to dismiss antiquity and argue in favor of a more up-to-date doctrine: in this sense, the reference to the *squalidae regulae antiquae* at the beginning of the work is a sort of manifesto, to warn the pupils about the difficulty—both in form and in content—of a long tradition of scholarly work, whose burden seems too heavy to bear without the help of such a painstaking a teacher.

8

T(w)o Be or Not T(w)o Be?

The *dualis numerus* according to Latin Grammarians Up to the Early Middle Ages

Tim Denecker*

1. Introduction

As is commonly acknowledged, ancient Greek grammar provided the conceptual and terminological framework for the description of the Latin language (see, e.g., Barwick 1922; Desbordes 1988 and 1995; Swiggers and Wouters 2007). Although this transfer was generally speaking quite successful, some structural differences between both languages gave rise to categorial "frictions," which in turn triggered metalinguistic or "metagrammatical" observations of a specifically contrastive nature (Schöpsdau 1992). As with the "optative," the "article" (Denecker and Swiggers 2018), the "aorist," and (in the other direction) the "ablative" (Uría 2017), this was also the case with the "dual number." Greek inherited this morphological marker for "two distinct real world entities" (Corbett 2000, 20) from Proto-Indo-European, and could apply it to nouns, pronouns, and verbs (Meier-Brügger 1992, II:68–9), designating it by means of the collocation δυϊκὸς ἀριθμός (this is for instance the case in Dionysius Thrax). Latin, by contrast, never knew the dual number as a morphological "category" in its own right, although it contained "formal relics" of it, namely the numerals *duo* and *ambo* (Fritz 2011, 192). It should be noted that in the Latin grammatical tradition, these forms were categorized

---

* Thanks are due to Adam Gitner, Wolfgang de Melo, Pierre Swiggers, and the anonymous referees, all of whom formulated valuable comments on earlier drafts of this contribution. I also deal with the question of the "dual number" in Latin grammaticography in Denecker (2019). Whereas in the latter account, I have tried to be as detailed and exhaustive as possible, in the present contribution my aim was to follow a number of main threads throughout the Latin grammatical tradition, and to formulate some methodological observations, based on the peculiar case of the "dual number" in Latin grammaticography but pertaining to the historiography of (Latin) grammaticography in general.

132 PROFESSIONAL GRAMMARIANS

either as "nouns" or as "pronouns," not as "numerals." Apart from these obvious candidates for being labelled "duals," the same frequently happened to those verb forms in -ēre which are often referred to as "contracted" or "syncopated" alternatives for the third person plural past perfect forms in -ērunt (think of legēre versus legērunt), although the "short forms" are actually the original ones from a historical point of view (Meiser 1998, 217–18 §141). In this contribution, I want to explore the different ways in which Latin grammarians tried to identify a nominal and/or a verbal dual in their language, for the simple reason that it existed in Greek. Since the relevant material is quite extensive,[1] I will first try to deal comprehensively with antiquity and Late Antiquity, and subsequently focus on one particular "microtradition" that runs into the early Middle Ages.

2. Antiquity and Late Antiquity: A Nominal and/or a Verbal Dual in Latin?

The question is taken up explicitly and extensively for the first time only in the first century CE, by the Roman professor of rhetoric Quintilian, who refers to the grammatical category of number, "in which we have the singular and the plural, and the Greeks also the dual."[2] Interestingly, Quintilian's reference to a certain Antonius Rufus—who can perhaps be identified with a playwright mentioned by the commentator pseudo-Acro (*GRF* pp. 508–9)—strongly suggests that the issue had been a matter of discussion in Latin language scholarship before Quintilian (Ax 2011, 198–9). In any case, it seems possible to gather from the reference that this Antonius Rufus defended the existence of a dual in Latin, at least for verb forms such as *dixēre*. Quintilian, however, denies this point of view, explaining the forms in -ēre as simple

---

[1] For a collection and schematic classification of the relevant material, cf. Schad (2007, 141) as well as *TLL* s.v. *dualis*, V.1 2071.82–2072.18.

[2] Quint. *inst.* 1.5.42–4 *praeterea numeros, in quibus nos singularem ac pluralem habemus, Graeci et* δυϊκόν. *quamquam fuerunt qui nobis quoque adicerent dualem "scripsere legere": quod evitandae asperitatis gratia mollitum est, ut apud veteres pro "male mereris" "male merere," ideoque quod vocant duale in illo solo genere consistit, cum apud Graecos et verbi tota fere ratione et in nominibus deprendatur et sic quoque rarissimus sit eius usus, apud nostrorum vero neminem haec observatio reperiatur, quin e contrario "devenere locos" (Verg. Aen. 1.365) et "conticuere omnes" (Verg. Aen. 2.1) et "consedere duces" (Ovid. met. 13.1) aperte nos doceant nihil horum ad duos pertinere, "dixere" quoque, quamquam id Antonius Rufus ex diverso ponit exemplum, de pluribus patronis praeco pronuntiet. quid? non Livius circa initia statim primi libri "tenuere," inquit, "arcem Sabini" et mox "in adversum Romani subiere" (1.12.1)? sed quem potius ego quam M. Tullium sequar? qui in Oratore (157) "non reprendo," inquit, "scripsere: scripserunt esse verius sentio."*

T(W)O BE OR NOT T(W)O BE?   133

stylistic variants of those in *-ērunt*, allegedly the result of what would nowadays be called "euphonic apocope." Since Quintilian does not even bring up the possibility of a dual for Latin nouns, we can conclude that he entirely denied the existence of a Latin dual.

In the late third century, the grammarian Sacerdos (*Guardians* no. 132; *CCC* §12.38) counts two numbers in Latin, singular and plural, both for nouns and verbs. Possibly relying on Quintilian and his reference to Antonius Rufus, but without mentioning their names, Sacerdos specifies that for verbs, "some believe . . . that there also exists a dual number, namely when we say *dixēre scribsēre* instead of *scribserunt dixerunt.*" This is a belief that he, as Donatus will do, simply reports without explicitly refuting or accepting it.[3] By contrast, plainly "negative" comments are made by two Latin grammarians who wrote for a Greek audience. The first of these two is Charisius (*Guardians* no. 200; *CCC* §12.13), who was active sometime in the fourth century and who claimed that Latin as a language "depends" from Greek.[4] Devoting extensive attention to those aspects in which Latin differs from Greek, Charisius points out with respect to both pronouns and nouns (no mention is made of verbs) that there are two numbers, singular and plural, "for there is no dual among the Romans."[5] The second of these grammarians writing for a Greek audience is Diomedes, who was active in the second half of the fourth or in the fifth century (*Guardians* no. 47; *CCC* §14.18; see Rochette in this volume, Chapter 5). Diomedes, too, notes with regard to both nouns and verbs that "the dual is only valid among the Greeks," and that it is "excluded by us," that is, by the Romans.[6] In the case of the verb, Diomedes adds an elaborate and challenging exposition, which is here quoted in full, followed by my own tentative translation and interpretation (on this passage, see also Rochette, Chapter 5, example 19):

> Diom. *gramm*. I 334.25–335.7 numerus praeterea accidit verbis prorsus uterque, singularis et pluralis. dualis enim apud Graecos dumtaxat valet,

---

[3] Sacerd. *gramm*. VI 432.7–9 *numeri in verbis tot sunt quot et in nominibus, singularis, ut "amo," pluralis, ut "amamus." numerum vero dualem etiam quidam putant esse, cum dicimus "dixere" "scribsere," quod est pro "scribserunt" "dixerunt."*

[4] Char. *gramm*. p. 380.21–2 *cum ab omni sermone Graeco Latina lingua pendere videatur*; also discussed by Rochette in this volume (Chapter 5, example 22).

[5] Char. *gramm*. p. 15.22–3 *numeri sunt duo, singularis et pluralis. dualis enim apud Romanos non est.* And at p. 195.1–2 *numeri sunt duo, singularis, ut "hic praeceptor," pluralis, ut "hi praeceptores." dualis enim apud Romanos non est.*

[6] Diom. *gramm*. I 301.21–2 *dualis enim dumtaxat apud Graecos valet, a nobis excluditur; de quo etiam mox referemus.*

134   PROFESSIONAL GRAMMARIANS

a nobis excluditur, eodem modo quo et in nominibus. nequaquam enim reperiri potest Latino sermone ulla dictio quae dualem exprimat numerum. antiquitatis enim Romani memores dualem numerum posteritatis usu receptum quasi novellum usurpare noluerunt. is namque, sicut a primordio adseritur sermonis a natura proditi, in obscuro habitus ignorabatur et diutius incertus inter utrumque numerum, tam singularem quam pluralem, latebat. sero autem supervenientibus saeculis scrupulosae curiositatis observationibus captus quasi intercalaris inrepsit, et hac de causa apud veteres raro reperitur, quoniam erroribus inlaqueatus multiplicatur. adeo per huius modi omnes usus Graecorum linguae nesciae declarantur. apud Atticos vero dumtaxat plurimum valet, et maxime apud Homerum, qui cum sit Atticae linguae cultor, utpote patrii sermonis adsertor, ut quidam putant, tamen non erat nescius antiquitatis, sicut versus ille testatur. cum enim duo fuissent, ipse vetustatis memor pluraliter salutationem protulit hoc modo, χαίρετε κήρυκες ἄγγελοι (Il. 1.334). praeterea superfluus antiquis visus est, si quidem ex numeri pluralis imagine dualis declinatio formata normabatur.

Furthermore, both numbers straightforwardly apply to verbs: the singular and the plural. For the dual is only valid among the Greeks, while it is excluded by us, in the same way as it is in nouns. For nowhere in the Latin language can a single utterance be found that expresses the dual number. For those Romans who were aware of ancient usage refused to make use of the dual, which had been accepted in later usage, on the grounds that it was an innovation. For it [viz. the dual number], as it is revealed by the origin of speech coming forth from nature, was held in low esteem and ignored, and for a rather long time it remained hidden, wavering between both numbers, the singular on the one hand and the plural on the other. Later, however, as ages went by, it was captured by the observations of careful study, and it stole in as it were in an "intercalary" [i.e., intermediate] position, and for this reason it is rarely found among the ancients, since in many cases it is entangled in mistakes. Through all uses of this kind, the languages of the Greeks [i.e., the Greek dialects other than Attic] are shown to be ignorant [viz. in their use of the dual or of number in general]. By contrast, it [viz. the dual number] holds a prominent place only among the Athenians, and most of all in Homer, who, although he cultivated the Attic language—in doing so, as some believe, propagating his mother tongue—nevertheless was not unfamiliar with ancient usage, as the following verse testifies. For although

T(W)O BE OR NOT T(W)O BE? 135

it concerned a pair, aware of old usage he formulated the salutation in the plural, in the following way: χαίρετε κήρυκες ἄγγελοι [*Il.* 1.334]. Apart from these [viz. from Attic and Homer] it [viz. the dual number] appeared superfluous to the ancients, since indeed the dual declension was shaped after the model of the plural number and subsequently squared away.

What Diomedes seems to be saying is that the dual number originally existed both in Greek and in Latin (apparently even as a universal, "natural" category), but that it gradually began to "flourish" (i.e., became grammaticalized) only in the Attic variety and—allegedly on the basis of Attic—in Homeric usage too.[7] In the other varieties of Greek and in Latin, the dual also existed from the very beginning, but lay dormant as a superfluous form in between the singular and the plural, morphologically largely modelled on the plural, and difficult to use correctly (in any case in Latin). Only in a later historical stage did it come in vogue in these other varieties of Greek and in Latin too, when it was "revived" as a learned innovation on the model of Attic usage— and then still with a limited number of possible applications, and to the disapproval of those Romans who were mindful of ancient usage. Diomedes thus adds interesting historical, sociolinguistic, and metagrammatical dimensions to his exposition.[8]

A rather independent voice—dating to around the year 400—is that of the versatile scholar Macrobius, at least insofar as can be gathered from the extant collections of excerpts from his explicitly contrastive work entitled *De verborum Graeci Latinique differentiis vel societatibus* (edited by De Paolis 1990). In one preserved passage, Macrobius singles out the difference between Latin and Greek number, consisting in the fact that "no usage in Latin has admitted the dual." His reference to *usus* seems to imply a historical selection process of Latin forms or, alternatively, a gradual decision-making

---

[7] In the Greek tradition, an interesting precedent for this view is offered by the grammarian and Homeric commentator Aristarchus (third–second century BCE), who claims that Homer's excellent mastery of the dual is proof to his alleged Attic origins, since the dual is really "proper to" (idiomatic in) the speech of Athens; see Schironi (2018a, 171–2).

[8] This interpretation differs from the more concise one which I offer in Denecker (2019, 108), where I follow more closely the explanation given by Desbordes (1988, 23): "Quant à l'identité d'origine, c'est le moyen de réduction le plus commun, le plus accommodant aussi, vu le brouillard dont il était question plus haut. On nous dit ainsi que la différence est due au fait que les Latins sont restés fidèles à un très ancien passé, alors que les Grecs évoluaient: voir par exemple un magnifique texte de Diomède sur la chasse au duel, qui se cachait soigneusement aux origines, s'abritant dans l'ombre tantôt du singulier et tantôt du pluriel, et qui ne fut capturé qu'après des siècles de patiente observation, pour se révéler, du reste, inutile."

136   PROFESSIONAL GRAMMARIANS

process (and elimination process) in grammatical categorization. In both cases, the presentation with reference to *usus* involves some degree of arbitrariness and conventionality. Quoting verse parts from Vergil, Macrobius furthermore claims that the verb forms in *-ēre* are used not as duals, but in order to "gather a collectivity." Remarkably, the notion that perfect verb forms in *-ēre* signify a "collective" plural rather than a dual or a "normal" plural appears to be unique to Macrobius.[9] In a second preserved passage, Macrobius acknowledges to have omitted from his discussion "the dual number, the aorist tense and the manifold system of tenses, because speakers of Latin lack all of these . . ., by which Greece alone is more widely scattered."[10] This statement seems to suggest that in Macrobius' opinion, Greek is characterized by a greater "richness" or "refinement" in grammatical means of expression as compared to Latin.

Having dealt with Macrobius, we need to go a little back in time for the two brief but highly influential comments that were made in the mid-fourth century by the famous *grammaticus urbis Romae*, Aelius Donatus (Holtz 1981; *Guardians* no. 52; *CCC* §14.20), twice in his *Ars maior*. With regard to the noun, Donatus notes that apart from the singular and the plural, "there is also a dual number, which cannot be inflected in the singular, as in *hi ambo, hi duo.*"[11] Second, with regard to the verb, he observes that in addition to a singular and a plural, "according to some there is also a dual, as in *legēre.*"[12] Although these statements are characterized by a certain didactic simplification, their phrasing does raise some questions, in particular in the case of *ambo* and *duo*. If these are dual forms "because they cannot be inflected in the singular," and if they can be combined with *hi*—which serves as the didactic equivalent for the Greek article in the masculine plural nominative (see Denecker and Swiggers 2018)—then should the nominal dual be considered (a) a fully fledged number category, (b) a subcategory of the plural, or (c) merely a "lexical" dual instantiated only by *duo* and

---

[9] Macr. *verb.* De Paolis p. 11.7–13.3 *at in numeris haec una dissensio est, quod* δυϊκόν *usus in Latinitate nullus admisit. nam qui putant "fecere" "dixere" dualis esse numeri, subinepti sunt arguente Vergilio, qui verbis talibus universitatem vult continere, ut "conticuere omnes" et "una omnes fecere pedem."*

[10] Macr. *verb.* De Paolis p. 93.21–95.2 *ideo autem praetermisimus disputare de duali numero et de tempore aoristo et de multiplici ratione temporum, quia his omnibus carent Latini, id est* περὶ δευτέρων καὶ μέσων ἢ παρακειμένων ἢ ὑπερσυντελίκων ἢ μελλόντων, *quibus latius Graecia sola diffunditur.*

[11] Don. *gramm. mai.* 2.7 p. 622.10–12 *numeri sunt duo, singularis et pluralis: singularis, ut "hic sapiens," pluralis, ut "hi sapientes." est et dualis numerus, qui singulariter enuntiari non potest, ut "hi ambo," "hi duo."*

[12] Don. *gramm. mai.* 2.12 p. 637.3–4 *numeri verbis accidunt duo, singularis et pluralis: singularis, ut "lego," pluralis, ut "legimus"; item secundum quosdam dualis, ut "legere."*

T(W)O BE OR NOT T(W)O BE?   137

ambo? Whereas he leaves this implied question unanswered, by means of his statements Donatus plainly recognizes the existence of a dual number for Latin nouns, while for verbs he reports the possibility without explicitly confirming or denying it.

As we will see, Donatus' comments have been highly consequential in two different ways. On the one hand, Donatus' mention of the dual legitimated extensive and detailed discussions of this rather peripheral issue in Latin grammaticography of subsequent ages. On the other, because Donatus dealt with the dual number exclusively in his *Ars maior* and not in his *Ars minor*,[13] one finds no trace of this category in the "propaedeutic," didactic grammars of subsequent ages (most importantly, those of Cassiodorus, Isidore of Seville, Julian of Toledo, the Venerable Bede, Alcuin of York, and Rabanus Maurus). In other words, as a result of Donatus' decision not to discuss the dual in his *Ars minor*, the category would remain a matter of discussion only in the more advanced grammatical analyses contained in commentaries on Donatus' *Ars maior*.

Another influential position with a somewhat higher degree of linguistic acuity was taken in the fifth century by the Gaulish scholar Consentius (*Guardians* no. 203; Fögen 1997–98; *CCC* §12.15; see Mari in this volume). Consentius reports the opinion that dual "nouns" exist in Latin, namely *duo* and *ambo*, but also *uterque*. In Keil's edition of Consentius' grammar, *uterque* has been deleted from this series of forms, but since this form is frequently incorporated alongside *duo* and *ambo* in later grammatical commentaries, it may well have been the present passage in this version that inspired later grammarians to include this morphologically heterogeneous instance in their discussion. For the classification of these forms as "duals," Consentius reports a justification proposed by others: since these forms can neither be considered singulars nor plurals, they should be considered duals. However, he objects to this that in Latin, the "correct account" or "right system" (*recta ratio*) "has obtained that there are" only a singular and a plural.[14] Consentius' observation on the dual in verbs runs along similar lines. The grammarian

---

[13] Don. *gramm. min.* 2 p. 586.9–10 *numeri nominum quot sunt? duo. qui? singularis, ut "hic magister"; pluralis, ut "hi magistri."* And *gramm. min.* 4 p. 593.4 *numeri verborum quot sunt? duo. qui? singularis, ut "lego"; pluralis, ut "legimus."*

[14] Consent. *gramm.* V 347.32–348.4 *numeri nominum sunt duo, singularis et pluralis, quamvis quidam etiam dualem dixerint, qui "duo" et "ambo" [uterque], quoniam neque singularis neque pluralis numeri dicere possumus, dualis esse dixerunt. sed recta ratio obtinuit apud Latinos duos esse, singularem, ut "hic magister" "haec Musa" "hoc scamnum," et pluralem, ut "hi magistri" "hae Musae" "haec scamna."*

138   PROFESSIONAL GRAMMARIANS

reports the distinction others make between the alleged dual *legēre* and the plural *legerunt*, but objects that usage (*usus*) "has disapproved of this assertion," and that "on the basis of usage" both should be considered plurals. Unlike Donatus, Consentius is thus explicit in his rejection of the dual, both for nouns and for verbs. However, when Consentius writes that *recta ratio* "has obtained" and that *usus* "has disapproved," he may be implying that in an earlier stage, the Latin language used to contain certain dual forms, or at least that in an earlier stage, grammarians used to classify certain Latin forms as duals. In doing so, Consentius adds a language-historical or discipline-historiographical perspective that is absent from Donatus' plain and didactically oriented observation.[15]

3. Late Antiquity and the Early Middle Ages: The *dualis numerus* as a *numerus communis* in Verbs?

As mentioned above, I will now move on to tracing a particular "micro-tradition" in grammatical doctrine, starting in what one could term the "first generation" of grammatical commentaries on Donatus and running into the early Middle Ages. I will largely leave out the "mainstream" tradition in general, and the commentaries by Servius and Pompeius in particular, although these two—central members of the aforementioned "first generation" of grammatical commentaries on Donatus (*Guardians* 139–97)—dealt rather extensively with the dual and functioned as important "filters" through which later grammarians read Donatus in this connection. For my present purpose, I will instead concentrate on the relevant treatment in the pseudo-Cassiodorean *Commentarium de oratione et de octo partibus orationis*, which has been attributed—besides Cassiodorus—to the elusive grammarian known as "Sergius," and which is probably to be situated roughly in the fifth or sixth century (*CCC* §12.40.11). In the passage at issue, the grammarian— I will call him "Sergius"—states that apart from the singular and the plural number for nouns, "the third place is claimed by the dual number, which only occurs in two nouns, namely in *duo* and *ambo*." He corroborates this

---

[15] Consent. *gramm.* V 379.3–9 *numeri verbis accidunt duo, singularis et pluralis: singularis, ut "lego," pluralis, ut "legimus." quamvis quidam dicant tempore praeterito perfecto personae tertiae esse dualem numerum: ut ecce "legimus" "legistis" "legerunt" praeteritum perfectum est numeri pluralis; "legere" autem dualem esse dicunt, ut hoc de duobus recte dici videatur, "legerunt" autem de pluribus. sed hanc adsertionem usus inprobavit. itaque ex consuetudine pluralem utrumque dicimus.*

claim by pointing out that these forms can neither be considered singulars nor plurals, in the latter case because they cannot be combined with *omnes*. This is a "collocational" argument, which I should note is also present in Pompeius.[16] "Sergius" thus plainly recognizes the existence of the dual number for the noun in these two cases, but he appraises the verb differently. He notes that "some say a dual, that is, a common number exists for verbs, such as *legere*, but wrongly so; for no one says *ego lego, nos legere*." In his dense paraphrase of the opinion to which he opposes, and in which it is actually unclear whether one should read *legĕre* or *legĕre*, the grammarian seems to interpret "dual" as "common." In doing so, he adopts or transposes a concept and its designation—*numerus communis*—from discussions of nominal declension.[17] Subsequently, he seems to interpret "common" not as "both singular and plural"—which it means in the case of nouns—but as the first person plural, specifically understood as the "sum" of second and first person singular: "we, i.e., you and I." Moreover, the form is analyzed as a present rather than a perfect indicative, hence the example of "I read (now), we (i.e., you and I) read (now)." This is a remarkable explanation, but it should be repeated that it is an interpretation that "Sergius" ascribes to *quidam* and that he himself denies. We are thus possibly confronted with a deliberate distortion of a divergent position, meant to facilitate its subsequent refutation. In any case, according to this grammarian, the existence of an "actual" dual number is restricted to the nominal (and "lexical") duals *duo* and *ambo*.[18]

For the next step in this chain of elaboration in grammatical doctrine, we move on to the *Ars Ambrosiana*, which is presumably a product of the monastery of Bobbio in seventh-century Northern Italy (Holtz 1992; Visser 2011; CCC §13.35). When dealing with the possibility that the noun has a dual number in addition to the singular and the plural, the anonymous commentator explains that Donatus here "thinks of this number, which is frequent among the Greeks, although among the Latins, according to the correct account (*recta ratio*), it has not obtained a prominent place, because of the paucity of nouns in which it is found." Note that in the reference to

---

[16] Ps. Cassiod. *de orat.* p. 65.2–6 St. (= p. 1227^A Migne) *numeri nominum duo sunt: singularis et pluralis; usurpatur etiam tertium dualis numerus, qui invenitur in duobus tantum nominibus, in "duo" et "ambo." nam neque unum significo, cum dico "duo venerunt" neque plures; non enim de duobus loquens possum dicere "omnes venerunt."* See at greater length Pomp. *gramm.* V 165.20–166.20.

[17] This opinion may go back to pseudo-Probus, *Instituta artium* (*gramm.* IV 156.5–7): *numeri verborum sunt tres, singularis pluralis communis. nunc hi, quem ad modum verbis deserviant, in declinatione probantur.*

[18] Ps. Cassiod. *de orat.* p. 94.10–12 St. (= p. 1236^B Migne) *in verbis quidam dualem numerum esse dicunt, id est communem, ut "legere," sed falsum est; nemo enim dicit "ego lego," "nos legere."*

140 PROFESSIONAL GRAMMARIANS

recta ratio, we recognize the influence of Consentius rather than Donatus. The commentator specifies that the dual is only found in two nouns, *duo* and *ambo*, which—as both "Sergius" and Pompeius had argued—can neither be considered singulars nor plurals, since it is allegedly impossible to combine these forms with *omnes*.[19] Further on, in its discussion of the verb, the *Ars Ambrosiana* signals the possibility that *legēre* is a dual form, but adopts Consentius' position in objecting that Donatus' statement is not confirmed by usage. What follows next is a somewhat confused interpretation of the already idiosyncratic exposition given by "Sergius." According to this interpretation, the dual number in verbs indicates the "common number," which is exemplified by *legere*, presumably understood by the commentator as the infinitive form *legĕre*—a confusion easy to make since vowel quantity was no longer contrastive and quantity marks were absent from the manuscripts. However, drawing on "Sergius," the *Ars Ambrosiana* rejects this interpretation by pointing out that no one says *ego legĕre* or *vos legĕre*. It is important to recall that "Sergius" had the readings *ego lego* and *nos legēre* (or possibly *legĕre*). This adjustment seems to suggest that whereas "Sergius" presented the "dual" *legēre* (or *legĕre*) as "common" in the sense of "we, i.e., you and I," the *Ars Ambrosiana* interpreted it as being "undifferentiated," in other words, "common to" all three persons of a verb, singular and plural. It should be repeated, however, that both "Sergius" and the *Ars Ambrosiana* themselves object to these interpretations.[20]

The next and final step in this chain of elaboration takes us to the so-called Carolingian renaissance, here represented in the work of Smaragdus, a monk at Saint-Mihiel (where he would later become abbot) who died in 825 (*CCC* §13.26). Whereas Smaragdus says nothing about the dual when dealing with

---

[19] *Ars Ambrosiana*, section *De nomine*, p. 49.16–28 (ed. Löfstedt 1982): *sequitur:* ETIAM EST ET DUALIS NUMERUS [= *gramm. mai.* 2.6 p. 622.11]. *commentarium de oratione, qui frequens est apud Grecos, licet apud Latinos recta ratione non optinuerit principatum ob paucitatem nominum, in quibus invenitur: in* II *tantum nominibus invenitur,* UT DUO ET AMBO. *haec enim nomina neque singularis neque pluralis numeri sunt. nam si dicas "duo," neque unum potest significare neque plures. nam de duobus loquens, non possum dicere "omnes venerunt," et idcirco "dualis" dicitur. nonnulli haec ipsa numeri pluralis esse temptaverunt hac definitione: singularis numerus est, qui unum significat; quicquid non unum significat, iam videtur esse plurale. sed hoc falsum est. quid enim necesse est, ut qui unus non est decem sint aut qui decem sunt centum sint? non est hoc verum. mala diffinitio.*

[20] *Ars Ambrosiana*, section *De verbo*, p. 114.756–768 (ed. Löfstedt 1982): *haec sunt numeri nomina:* SINGULARIS ET PLURALIS, *quae de actuum qualitate procedunt.* ET SECUNDUM QUOSDAM DUALIS NUMERUS EST, UT LEGERE [= *gramm. mai.* 2.12 p. 637.3]. *"legere" autem dualem esse dicunt, ut hoc de duobus recte dici videatur, legerunt autem de pluribus. sed hanc adsertionem usus inprobavit. itaque ex consuetudine pluralem utrumque dicimus. sed Sergius aliter dicit. ait enim: quidam dualem numerum in verbis esse dicunt, id est communem, ut legere. sed falsum est. nemo enim dicit "ego legere," "vos legere." et hoc metrici per auctoritatem ac sensus discretionis causa. Donatus autem non negat, sed pro tertio non accipit numero; non enim per omnes modos et tempora et personas et numeros currit.*

T(W)O BE OR NOT T(W)O BE?   141

nouns, he does comment on Donatus' reference to *legĕre* as possibly being a dual verb form. Smaragdus, too, reads this form as the infinitive *legĕre*, and he seems to interpret the term *dualis* as meaning "both singular and plural." On this basis, he argues that "the infinitive verb *legĕre* shows itself to possess persons as well as numbers, albeit not plainly and overtly but rather in a 'confused' way; thus, in the singular [and this is important!]: *legĕre volo, vis, vult*, and in the plural: *legĕre volumus, vultis, volunt.*" Like its predecessors "Sergius" and the *Ars Ambrosiana*, this peculiar account seems to have been triggered by a misinterpretation of Donatus' *legĕre*. However, Smaragdus manages to go beyond his predecessors by developing what is actually a sensible and consistent model, in which infinitives, by virtue of being combined with an auxiliary verb, can indeed be said to be "of either number."[21] Of course, this interpretation is quite far removed from the original conceptual load of *dualis numerus* in Latin grammaticography.

4. Concluding Observations

To conclude, I would like to extrapolate from my analyses some general observations regarding the development of Latin grammar and the methodology of writing its history. Two evident main threads are (1) the role of Greek as a so-called super-standard in the grammatical description of Latin (see Joseph 1987, *passim*), and (2) the importance of intellectual authority in the elaboration of grammatical doctrine. One can also draw attention to (3) the influence of the grammarians' linguistic and social environments upon their elaboration of grammatical doctrine (see Zetzel and Holford-Strevens in this volume)—think for instance of the gradual loss of vowel quantity in Latin, or of the grammarians' varying command of Greek and their varying need to boast their knowledge of it, possibly in relation to their own (desired) social status and that of their intended audience. Furthermore (4), the fact that some rather far-fetched constructions originated in a simple

---

[21] Smaragdus, *Liber in partibus Donati*, section *De verbo*, *textus* 9T, p. 134 l.701–135 l.712 (ed. Löfstedt, Holtz and Kibre 1986): [*xx. De numero verbi*] NUMERI verbo, ut Donatus ait, ACCIDUNT DUO: SINGULARIS, UT LEGO; PLURALIS, UT LEGIMUS; *et* SECUNDUM *aliquos, ait,* DUALIS, UT LEGERE [= *gramm. mai.* 2.12 p. 637.3]. *"legere" enim verbum infinitivum, quamvis non nude et aperte, tamen confuse, et personas et numeros se habere demonstrat, ut singulariter: legere volo vis vult, et pluraliter: legere volumus vultis volunt. similiter et inpersonalia verba faciunt cum pronominibus iuncta, ut: legitur a me a te ab illo a nobis a vobis ab illis. et gerundia similiter faciunt, ut lectum est a me a te ab illo a nobis a vobis ab illis. unde apparet, quod verbum et singularem per omnia et pluralem continet numerum.*

142   PROFESSIONAL GRAMMARIANS

misreading may remind us of the "material" factor in the development of grammatical doctrine. Undoubtedly, both genuine misunderstanding and intentional misrepresentation are issues that have been hard to avoid in the history of scholarship (and science) until the present day. Nevertheless, it is entirely conceivable that the less advanced state of the media and "encoding" of linguistic information, such as vowel quantity, in pre-modern or at least pre-renaissance scholarship gave rise to a higher degree of unintentional confusion than is nowadays the case. Lastly (5), I would like to cite Quintilian's reference to Antonius Rufus, who allegedly defended the existence of a Latin verbal dual, as a reminder of the fragmentary and lacunose state of Latin language scholarship as it has come down to us. Combined with the doubtful identification and dating of many grammarians (think for instance of "Sergius"), this reality often makes it a highly challenging task to contextualize and interpret specific points of grammatical doctrine, and to trace lines of influence and interaction between grammarians. Fortunately for historians of ancient grammar, during the past half century or so, some highly valuable instruments have become available which render this task considerably more feasible. An indispensable reference work for anyone active in the field, Robert Kaster's 1988 *Guardians of Language* undoubtedly ranks among the foremost of these.

9

Anonymous Grammatical Scholarship

Insights from an Annotated Juvenal Codex from Egypt

Alessandro Garcea and Maria Chiara Scappaticcio*

1. Introduction

Information about Roman linguistic thought comes not just from the theoretical treatises that grammarians and scholars left behind, but also from their direct engagement with literary texts as recorded in scholia and the margins of ancient manuscripts. Direct witnesses to Roman scholarly and pedagogic activity up to late antiquity are rare, and some have been found over the last century from excavation.[1] Annotated texts reveal, in particular, what linguistic features attracted the interest of the annotator and, if the context is pedagogical, what kind of help students might have needed while struggling through a literary work, typically produced in a time and place remote from its later audience. Such annotations thus engage implicitly with the problems of language change and language diversity: emphasizing differences between earlier and later Latin, between literary and ordinary registers of speech, and even sometimes regional differences, between the imperial center and periphery.

---

* The research leading to this paper has received funding from the European Research Council (ERC) under the European Union's Horizon 2020 research and innovation program (Grant agreement no. 636983); ERC project PLATINUM (Papyri and LAtin Texts: INsights and Updated Methodologies), University of Naples "Federico II." The present work is based on direct examination of the manuscript (conducted in Oxford, July 2019), a new edition of which will be published in the forthcoming *Corpus of Latin Texts on Papyrus* (*CLTP*). We are very grateful to Adam Gitner for his help with the final version of this paper.

[1] Among surviving late antique annotated manuscripts of literary works are: the *Scholia Bembina* on Terence (Vatican, Lat. 3226, perhaps fifth-century text with sixth-century annotations); the Bobbio palimpsest of Juvenal (Vatican, Lat. 5750, fifth century?); the *Scholia Veronensia* on Virgil (Verona, Biblioteca Capitolare XL (38), fifth century); the *scholia Bobiensia* on Cicero also survive as a separate, continuous commentary (Milan, Ambros. E 147 sup. + Vatican, Lat. 5750, fifth century?). There are several annotated manuscripts of Virgil: *P.Ant.* I 29 with the end of *Georgics* 2 and start of 3 (LDAB 4148; late fourth/early fifth century, on which see Scappaticcio 2020b); the codex Mediceus (Florence, Laur. Plut. 39.1, fifth century); in general, see *CCC* 253–77.

Alessandro Garcea and Maria Chiara Scappaticcio, *Anonymous Grammatical Scholarship* In: *Roman Perspectives on Linguistic Diversity*. Edited by Adam Gitner, Oxford University Press. © Oxford University Press 2023. DOI: 10.1093/oso/9780197611975.003.0009

144 PROFESSIONAL GRAMMARIANS

One such source is a remarkable fragment of a Juvenal codex of eastern provenance from the sixth century, which on its surviving parchment folium contains the text of *Satires* 7.149–98 with extensive annotations.[2] By sheer luck, this section includes Juvenal's caustic remarks on school instruction (150–4). Several of the annotations discuss ancient classroom practice, including remarks on the payment of grammarians and their attitude toward students. Thus it also sheds light on the social environment of ancient education, a field of research where Robert Kaster's *Guardians of Language* has made a significant contribution. Since the publication of Kaster's volume in 1988, the discovery and re-evaluation of fragmentary grammatical texts, such as the Antinoöpolis codex as well as texts on papyrus and ostraca, has played a noteworthy role in advancing our knowledge of ancient grammarians and their pedagogical context.[3]

As we will show, the annotations on this document reveal a complex linguistic engagement with the text of Juvenal on the part of several different readers, who explain different features of the text in both Latin and Greek. Many of the annotations indicate features of Latin vocabulary or syntax that students were likely to struggle with. This makes the document a unique record of ancient scholarship in action, of particular relevance to the late antique classroom and to contact between Latin and Greek.

In what follows, we introduce this multifaceted document and identify the contributions of three different annotators, as well as the nature of their comments and relationship to one another.

---

[2] Oxford, Sackler Library, Papyrology Rooms, Ant. inv. *s.n.*: Leuven Database of Ancient Books no. 2559; Mertens–Pack[3] no. 2925; *Codices Latini Antiquiores*, Suppl. no. 1710; Cavenaile 1958, no. 37; Seider (1972–81, II.1 no. 53). The extant fragment consists of an entire page from a bifolium of a codex of 22.3x16 cm. The upper and lower margins measure 3 cm each, the side ones 2.6 cm, and the written space of 16.7x12 cm contains 25 lines. The original codex has been assigned to the fifth group within Turner's classification (see Turner 1977, 27 no. 450), together with an almost contemporary manuscript, Milan, Biblioteca Ambrosiana, L 120 *sup., foll.* 113–20 (*scriptio inferior*). The lines of script coincide systematically with poetic verses. The script is a kind of BR-uncial recently defined as "juridical" (Ammirati 2015, 56). It was first published by Roberts (1935b), who gave a briefer account in (1935a). The Juvenal text as transmitted by this folium is given in the Appendix together with a palaeographical apparatus (recording signs of palaeographic interest) and with a critical apparatus (reporting both the readings of the previous editors and of Juvenal manuscripts). On the seventh *Satire* see Bellandi (2008); we follow the Teubner critical edition by Willis (1997) and the English translation by Braund (2004) with some modifications.

[3] These sources comprise Latin grammatical treatises—including proper *artes grammaticae* such as one known from a second- or third-century roll from Karanis, recently discussed by Scappaticcio (2020a)—as well as grammatical tools, such as alphabets and inflectional tables. These are known thanks to fragmentary rolls, codices and ostraca mainly from Egypt. They are collected, edited, and discussed by Scappaticcio (2015).

ANONYMOUS GRAMMATICAL SCHOLARSHIP 145

2. Juvenal and His Commentators in Late Antiquity

The Juvenal fragment from Antinoöpolis is the only preserved manuscript of this author of eastern provenance, and probably also production.[4] It thus attests to the circulation of Juvenal's challenging poetry in the well-educated milieu of late antique Egypt. Juvenal's influence in Late Antiquity is not astonishing in itself: the importance of this *ethicus poeta*, already acknowledged by Lactantius, is documented by Ammianus, who compared the alleged decadence of contemporary society with an idealized image of the Roman past.[5] In the grammatical tradition, Juvenal, among other *iuniores* such as Lucan and Statius, became more prominent starting from around the time of Servius' commentary on Virgil.[6] By contrast, Donatus in his commentary on Terence, like Servius *auctus* and the theoretical works by Servius himself on grammar and metrics, showed no interest in Juvenal as an *auctoritas*.[7] There is also evidence that *Servius magister* included Juvenal in the school syllabus: a subscription preserved in several Juvenal manuscripts records a certain Nicaeus, possibly of non-Roman origin, engaged in *emendatio* under the direction of Servius in Rome, presumably while preparing for a career in the imperial bureaucracy.[8] Juvenal is also found in the anonymous *Scholia Bembina* on Terence's comedies,[9] and is quoted by Cledonius[10] and even later by Priscian[11] and John the Lydian.[12] The latter three authors attest to the circulation of the *Satires* in the learned milieu of Constantinople at least from the mid-fifth century onward. Moreover, Juvenal's peculiar vocabulary stimulated the

---

[4] The parchment folium was found during the Egypt Exploration Society excavations in Antinoöpolis (also called Antinoë) in spring 1914. Its discovery in Antinoöpolis does not necessarily mean that the original codex from which the fragment comes was produced there, as it could have been imported from elsewhere. Palaeographic reasons have been adduced to locate its production in Constantinople or certainly somewhere in the east (Ammirati 2015, 56, 70).

[5] See Lact. *inst.* 3.29.17 (quoting Juv. 10.365–6) and Amm. 28.4.4, as well as Highet (1954); Pecere (1986, 77–8); Sogno (2012).

[6] However, Cameron (2011, 452–4) argues strongly against a rediscovery of Juvenal.

[7] See already Thomson (1928) and Wessner (1929); more recently Monno (2009).

[8] The subscription is found in Florence, Biblioteca Medicea Laurenziana Plut. 34.42, fol. 20r–v (saec. XI^ex); Cambridge, King's College, 52, fol. 27r (saec. IX^2); and Leiden, Bibliotheek der Rijksuniversiteit BPL 82, fol. 45r (saec. XI); see Pecere (2016, 234–9).

[9] See Mountford (1934, 116). The above-mentioned scholia come from the so-called *codex Bembinus* of Terence, Vatican, Biblioteca Apostolica Vaticana, Lat. 3226 (saec. IX).

[10] See for instance Cled. *gramm.* V 64.14.

[11] See Dierschke (1913, 85–91); Wessner (1929); Nocchi Macedo (2016b, 223–4), with bibliography.

[12] John the Lydian *mag.* 1.20.2, paraphrasing Juv. 5.110–11. See also *mag.* 1.41.4 with Dubuisson and Schamp (2006, I:1, 28; 51); Nocchi Macedo (2016b, 224–6) with bibliography.

146 PROFESSIONAL GRAMMARIANS

compilation of author-specific glossaries.[13] Although the bulk of the surviving material dates to the ninth century, two important manuscripts confirm that exegetical activity already began at least four centuries earlier: Bobbio's palimpsested manuscript Vatican, Biblioteca Apostolica Vaticana, Lat. 5750 (fifth century) is representative of the western Roman Empire; the codex from Antinoöpolis (sixth century) of the eastern empire.[14]

In this paper we will not deal with the transmission of Juvenal's text itself[15] since the Antinoöpolis fragment gives "on the whole, a sound and trustworthy text."[16] We limit ourselves to the remark that it preserves the correct reading *crambe* at 7.154,[17] against the wrong *crambre* and *cambr(a)e* of the branches ε and Φ. *Crambe* is only known through later manuscripts (*G*: Paris, Bibliothèque Nationale, Lat. 7900A, tenth century, and Vatican, Biblioteca Apostolica Vaticana, Urb. 342[2], eleventh or twelfth century) and in a conjecture by Angelo Poliziano, who recognized in this form an allusion to the Greek saying found in *Suda* Δ 1272 δὶς κράμβη θάνατος. This detail shows the textual quality of the exemplar of our fragmentary codex, which was likely produced in an eastern scriptorium, where scribes were capable of preserving an abstruse Greek word such as *crambe* from error.[18] The presence of lines 191 and 192 in the original codex is also significant. Whereas they are transmitted by the manuscripts of the *Satires* without exception, several editors have proposed deleting either part of 191–2 or all of 192 as an explanatory gloss.[19] The fact that our fragment has two forked *paragraphoi*—one above and one below line 192—has been considered ancient evidence for its deletion.[20] Nevertheless, there are no occurrences of *diplai obelismenai* such as this for indicating spurious lines,[21] and it is uncertain on what basis the commentator isolated this verse.[22] Moreover, this double sign was added not by the scribe who copied Juvenal's text, but by a later hand (*m*[2]) together with several lectional signs and glosses almost certainly not belonging to the original exemplar of the codex.

---

[13] E.g., *CGL* V 652–6 with Latin monolingual glosses; for other glossaries, see *CCC* 277.

[14] See *CCC* 275–7, with bibliography; the *scholia Bobiensia* from the Vatican manuscript are discussed by Wessner 1931, v–vi.

[15] See Willis (1997, vii–lii); Parker (2012, 144–58).

[16] Roberts (1935b, 203–6; esp. 203).

[17] Oxford, Sackler Library, Papyrology Rooms, Ant. inv. *s.n.*, recto l. 6: *[cr]ạmbe* (Juv. 7.154: *occidit miseros crambe repetita magistros*); see Roberts (1935b, 205); Courtney (1980, 369). Willis (1997, *app. crit. ad loc.*) is wrong in attributing the reading *crambe* only to *G*.

[18] Among classical authors besides Juvenal, only Plin. *nat.* 20.79 used *crambe* (*TLL* IV 1097.25–30).

[19] See Reeve (1971, 328).

[20] Suggested at least since Prinz (1867, 91); Jahn (1868); see now Willis (1997, 105).

[21] See Nocchi Macedo (2016a, 175–6), with bibliography.

[22] See Stramaglia (2008, 208).

ANONYMOUS GRAMMATICAL SCHOLARSHIP   147

The existence of this annotated text of Juvenal—with commentaries and critical signs—shows that scholarly and editorial work on the text of Juvenal certainly occurred in antiquity, perhaps even in the archetype of the manuscript tradition, as has been hypothesized.[23] Thus the Antinoöpolis folium makes an important contribution to addressing this difficult and still open philological question, throwing light not only on the history of Juvenal's text but also the way ancient readers engaged with it.

3. A Multifaceted Bilingual Commentary

Since the edition of Juvenal's *Scholia vetustiora* by Paul Wessner in 1931, several attempts have been made to identify the sources and chronology of an ancient, lost commentary on the *Satires*, the latest datable parts of which might have been written in the mid-fifth century,[24] although there is no reason to think that it was the only one circulating in late antiquity.[25] On the contrary, the Antinoöpolis fragment suggests that scholarly engagement with the text of Juvenal was widespread and could appear in multiple different forms, even within the same document. Although there is no identifiable connection to Nicaeus' work in our fragment,[26] it bears annotations by three readers,[27] both in Latin and in Greek, revealing that the *Satires* met both Latin-speaking and bilingual audiences. Differently from other glosses on Latin literary authors coming from the Greek east, it would be inappropriate to separate Latin from Greek materials, since two (m^2 and m^4) of the three annotators wrote in both languages. Whether these hands belong to scribes copying from one or more exemplars or to reader-annotators who produced their own commentaries cannot be stated with certainty; studying

[23] See Roberts (1935b, 203), supporting the theory of Ulrich Knoche (see Knoche 1934, 596, 599, 601).

[24] A general overview is offered by R. J. Tarrant in Reynolds (1983, 200): "by the last decade of the (*scil.* fifth) century the vogue of Juvenal was at its height, and the poems had been equipped with an ample commentary, large parts of which survive," referring to the standard edition of the *Scholia vetustiora* by Wessner (1931). See Townend (1972), systematically examined and criticised by Cameron (2010), with further bibliographical references; for Carolingian commentaries: Grazzini (2011–18); see also the overview by Zetzel in *CCC* 275–7.

[25] See already Roberts (1935b, 301).

[26] See Cameron (2011, 454), but his assertion that "the ignorance and lack of understanding the scholia reveal are enough to prove that the papyrus was no scholar's copy" is weakened by the analysis given below.

[27] Although five different hands were previously recognised by Roberts (1935b) in the dense annotations and thick quantity of lectional signs, our direct examination of the parchment suggests that it is more plausible to distinguish three hands. See also Nocchi Macedo (2016a, 171–3).

148   PROFESSIONAL GRAMMARIANS

the forms and functions of the different annotations will give us the opportunity to put forward some hypotheses. The three annotators (m^2, m^3, m^4)
are discussed in the following sections, each of which begins with a full list of
annotations and is followed by analysis.[28]

3.1 The Annotations by m^2

The annotations include lectional signs, such as accents, horizontal strokes,
diaereses, high, medial and low dots, as well as with dotted *obeli*, "Z" (possibly standing for ζήτει or ζήτησον "look up"), and *diplai obelismenai*
("forked paragraphos").[29] All these signs were marked by the same reader
(m^2), who also emended some scribal mistakes.[30] He also added the bulk of
the annotations in Greek and Latin between the lines and in the margins.
Although it is possible that m^2 came up with some of these interventions on
his own, their nature suggests that he had one or more exemplars at his dis-
posal (which could have included a codex *emendatus*, *distinctus*, and possibly *adnotatus*).

In two cases m^2 puts in the margins a kind of short Latin title, summarizing
the topic of the relevant sections of the seventh *Satire*. Thus Juvenal's
lines 149–50 are labeled "on teaching students" (recto ll. 2–3: *de docendis
discipulis*) and 174–5 "on the dole ticket" (verso l. 1: *de tessera*). More analytical summaries, found both in Latin and in Greek, reveal an effort to
understand the text in greater depth: they introduce the rhetorical *exemplum* of Hannibal (in Greek: recto ll. 14–16); explain the choice of unskilled
teachers to leave their classroom (in Greek: recto ll. 23–4) and quit their
duties (in Latin: recto, in the lower margin); develop Juvenal's remark that

---

[28] Each annotation is followed by the indication of its position in the extant fragment and the reference to the lines of the Juvenal text (see Appendix). The text of the annotations is given as a continuous text without respecting its original layout; papyrological details are found in the edition of both
Juvenal's text and its annotations in *CLTP*. Where our readings differ from those of former editors—
namely C. H. Roberts and K. McNamee (whose consensus is indicated with "edd.")—we report their
previous textual proposals as well. The annotations marked "supralinear" are typically written above
the relevant words of Juvenal.

[29] Given that they are of no value for the present discussion, these signs are not reported here. They
can be found in the forthcoming *CLTP* edition; on these signs see Roberts (1935b, 201–2); Nocchi
Macedo (2016a, 173–7), with further bibliographical references.

[30] In the extant fragment m^2 corrects *versib* to *versibus* (recto l. 5; Juv. 7.153), *adiat* to *audiat* (recto
l. 18; Juv. 7.166) and *munde* to *mundae* (verso l. 8; Juv. 7.181). These corrections were probably
produced *ope ingenii*, because of their self-evident character for someone having a sufficient command of Latin.

ANONYMOUS GRAMMATICAL SCHOLARSHIP   149

Table 9.1 Annotations by m^2

Juvenal	m^2
149–50 (title)	*de docendis discipulis* recto ll. 2–3, left margin
150 *ferrea* (?)	ἀφυκ. δ[....].... recto l. 2, supralinear: ουκ.. δ[....].... edd.
152 *quaecumque*	ἅτ.. α (*i.e.,* ἅτινα) recto l. 4, supralinear: α.. α *edd.:* ἅττα or ἅτινα McNamee (comm.)
?	]χυρη ειατ. τος [.]αρ[recto l. 6, right margin:]χορπ().. ατατος |]αρ[*Roberts:* χορτ. ατ. |]αρ[(from χόρτος McNamee comm.)
155–6 *ubi summa /* *quaestio*	πο.. εστι........-λίγου recto l. 8, right margin
156 *fronte* (?)	υοσιουι recto l. 8, supralinear
158–9 *culpa docentis /* *scilicet arguitur*	ἐκείνου ἀφυοῦς ὄντος ὡς ῥάθυμος κρίνεται κἂν σπουδαῖος ᾖ recto ll. 10–11, right margin
159 *laevae parte mamillae*	*sine corde* recto l. 11, supralinear: ạnnẹ *corde* edd.
160 *salit*	*mobetur*.. recto l. 12, supralinear
160–1	ὡς ἀπὸ τοῦ ποιητοῦ recto l. 12, right margin
161 (?)	κατὰ σα-. ϊον recto l. 13, left margin: κατα σα[β]βατον edd.
161 *miserum* (?)	ὠγ...... recto l. 13, supralinear: not identified by previous editors
161 *dirus*	sạevus recto l. 13, supralinear
162–4 (summary)	τὸ διήγημα τὸ κατὰ Ἀννιβάλ recto ll. 14–16, right margin
162 *deliberat* (?)	a... sạṭ (or a... ṭaṭ) recto l. 14, supralinear:. ọs. ẹṭạṭ edd.
162 *petat*	*o Annibal* recto l. 14, supralinear: o αννιβαλ edd.
?	.... ω recto l. 15, left margin: υ Roberts
166 *haec*	*dicunt* [.......]n recto l. 18, supralinear
168 *agitant lites*	*discipulis* [...... l]iṭẹṣ recto l. 20, supralinear

(*continued*)

150 PROFESSIONAL GRAMMARIANS

Table 9.1 Continued

Juvenal	m^2
169 *fusa . . . ingratusque*	̦eu̦ṣ̦ . [. . . . . . .]. . . ̦et necetur recto l. 21, supralinear: ε̦ ̦ ̦ε̦υ̦ [ ]. . . ̦et ̦necetur edd.
170 *mortaria*	*seniles veneni* recto l. 22, supralinear: *senum* edd.
171–2 (summary?)	εἴ τις ἀφυὴς εἰα̦ ̦ ̦ τω[. .]ς παιδευτήριον καὶ ἀφελείας recto ll. 23–4, right margin: ει τις αφυη(ς) | εργατητω[. .]ς | παιδευτη υιον | και αφελη̦ ̦ ς Roberts: εἴ τις ἀφυὴ(ς) | παισὶ ἀφίει τ(ὸ) | παιδευτήριον | καὶ ἀφορμᾷ McNamee
172 *ingredietur*	ἐπι[β]αίνει recto l. 24, supralinear: επι βαινει edd.
171–2	[ ]e̦r̦e̦ quod d̦e̦-. . . qui fit r῾h´etor u̦t em̦ ̦ ̦ et (perhaps emigret) ex officio̦ summary? recto, right bottom margin:]e̦n̦d̦o̦ ̦ ̦ o̦b̦ and *antiquï fit r῾h´etor ut em̦i̦gret ex officio* (two annotations) Roberts:]e̦n̦d̦o̦ ̦ ̦ o̦b̦ and *antique fit rhetor ut emigret ex officio* McNamee
174–5	ὅτι ἀπέλαβε χοράγιον σίτου̦ [.]πεκ̦ ̦ α̦ [. ̦]. σύνταξις ὃ ἀνεκβλήθη πρὸς τῷ μη̦ ̦ α̦ ̦ ̦ ο[. . . ̦]π̦ον [ ] ἐπ᾽ οἴκτρῳ ὡς ὑπόθεσιν οἴκοθεν ἀπο[. . . .]̦ νογ̦ ̦ χοράγιον σίτου ἐν ε̦ι̦ ̦ ̦ ̦ τρ[ο]ις verso, upper margin: εντ( )ε[ ]̦ τρο̦ις edd.
174–5 (title)	*[d]e̦ ̦tess[era]* verso l. 1, left margin
174 *venit* (?)	̦te̦ ̦ ̦t verso l. 1, supralinear: not identified by previous editors
176 *Chrysogonus* (?)	*[si]y̦e grammati̦ç῾u̦´s* verso l. 3, left margin: [. ̦]vis r̦a̦ ̦ i̦ | ma̦d̦is edd.
176 *quanti*	̦ ι επιτοκ̦ ̦ verso l. 3, supralinear: ο̦ι επιτοκ( ) edd.
176 *Pollio* (?)	̦și̦ ve verso l. 3, supralinear
177 *lautorum*	*divitum* verso l. 4, left margin
177 *pueros* (?)	[ ]. . . verso l. 4, supralinear:̦ ̦vo[edd.
177 *scindens*	*sep[ar]ans* verso l. 4, supralinear: *dividens* edd.
178 *balnea*	. . . τορα̦ verso l. 5, left margin
178 *porticus* (?)	̦στο[. . . . .] (perhaps στοά) verso l. 5, supralinear: το[ ] Roberts
179 *gestetur*	̦po̦rtetur verso l. 6, supralinear

ANONYMOUS GRAMMATICAL SCHOLARSHIP   151

Table 9.1 Continued

Juvenal	m^2
179 *dominus*	κατὰ ἔλλειψιν· παρὰ τῶν δούλων verso l. 6, left margin
180	*ille dives* verso l. 7, left margin
179–80 *anne . . . expectet spargatque*	*anne* verso l. 7, supralinear
181 *hic*	ἐν τῷ μεσαυλίῳ· ἐν τῇ στόᾳ γυμνάζει verso ll. 8–9, left margin
182–3 (summary)	*in alia parte porticus cenatio fulta erat columnis Numidarum ant- honestis* verso ll. 10–12, left margin: *columnis* McNamee: *colimnis* Roberts: *ant(iquis)* edd.
183 *surgat*	*aedificatur* verso l. 10, supralinear
183 *algentem*	ψυχροποιόγ verso l. 10, supralinear
183 *rapiat*	*çapiąt* verso l. 10, supralinear: we identified this Latin annotation where previous editors only read one longer Greek note. ψυχροποιος στοα edd.
183 *cenatio*	ἀριστητήριον verso l. 10, supralinear
184 *quanticumque*	*dives* verso l. 11, supralinear
184 *quanticumque*	ὅσου ἀγοράζει verso l. 11, infralinear
184 *veniet*	*emit* verso l. 11, supralinear
184 *fercula*	δίσκους verso l. 11, supralinear
184 *docte*	εὐφυῶς verso l. 11, infralinear
184–5 *qui . . . conponit*	παραρ. .θειτης verso l. 12, supralinear *cocuṣ* verso l. 12, supralinear: *cocum* edd.
185 *pulmentaria*	φάγια verso l. 12, supralinear
185 *condit*	ἀρτύει verso l. 12, supralinear
187 *ut*	πῶς verso l. 14, left margin

(continued)

152 PROFESSIONAL GRAMMARIANS

Table 9.1 Continued

Juvenal	m^2
187 *multum*	*r.......... es* verso l. 14, supralinear: .... [....]es Roberts
187–8 *res . . . filius*	*nullum est humile et minor videtur patri ut filius* verso ll. 14–15, left margin (*patri* added by m^4)
188–9 *unde . . . saltus* (?)	*ex parentibus habet* verso ll. 15–16, left margin
187–8 *res nulla minoris . . .* *patri quam filius* (?)	ὡς ἀπὸ ἀντιθέσεως verso ll. 15–16, right margin
189 *novorum*	τῶν νέων verso l. 16, infralinear
190 *transi*	*... ie* verso l. 17, supralinear
190–4	*eruditus est solus qui pauper est.. c bestias i.. et.... enium* *est divesexeuntem tion eius.... spit* verso l. 18–21, left margin: *eruditus est	solus quï pau-|-per* *est [ne]c	[m]olestias t[i-]|-met	quï enim	est dives	[e]x eo* *atem	n. tion et ᾽c᾽u-|. s. tespit* edd.
192 *nigrae . . . alutae*	ὅστις φορεῖ δέρμα ἐκ τῆς πενίας............. verso l. 19, supralinear: δερμα εκ της πενιας ελαβε τοστ. π.. υ Roberts: δέρμα ἐν τῷ ὑποδήματι McNamee
193 *quoque* (?)	σῆς verso l. 20, infralinear
194 *perfrisit*	*algerit* verso l. 21, supralinear
194 *si* (?)	εἰ verso l. 21, supralinear
195 *modo* (?)	*]. [* verso l. 22, supralinear:]ρ( ) Roberts
196 *edere*	ἀποδοῦναι verso l. 23, supralinear
196 *adhuc a matre* (?)	[.......] απ.. [verso l. 23, supralinear

with his meagre salary (*summula*) a rhetor could hardly afford more than the
dole ticket (*tessera*; in Greek: verso, in the upper margin); describe the rich
man's sumptuous porticos decorated with columns in Numidian marble (in
Latin: verso ll. 10–12);[31] state how his son's education would be inexpensive

---

[31] The abbreviated form *ant*(?) cannot be easily understood, since it does not seem to be otherwise
attested, although it has been read as *ant*(*iquis*) by both Roberts (1935b) and McNamee (2007, 486).
For *honestus* "having fine appearance, handsome," see OLD *s.v. honestus* 4.

ANONYMOUS GRAMMATICAL SCHOLARSHIP   153

for a wealthy father (in Latin: verso ll. 14–15);[32] and sketch a definition of a lucky man (in Latin: verso ll. 18–21).[33]

Some glosses are of remarkable exegetical value. One of them, in Greek, sketches the portrait of a student who refuses to pay his teacher: "that boy being stupid, (the teacher) is judged to be negligent even if he is conscientious" (Juv. 7.158–9: recto ll. 10–12).[34] The genitive absolute ἀφυοῦς ὄντος is particularly apt to show pupil's flaws, since ἀφυής is understood in bilingual glossaries as "lacking *ingenium*."[35] The same word is applied to unskilled teachers who leave their classroom at 7.171–2 (recto ll. 23–4). The explanation of the dole ticket is particularly extensive. Although fragmentary, it is meant like other Greek glosses not to be a mere translation but to give complementary information endowed with its own syntactic and semantic autonomy. Two occurrences of the rare Doric form χοράγιον "revenue," which the glossaries translate with *inpensa*,[36] always combined with the genitive σίτου "(allowance of) grain" (see *frumenti* at Juv. 7.175), seem motivated by the necessity of rendering the Latin technical term *tessera frumentaria* and as an equivalent to *frumenti . . . merces* (175); moreover, the third-person aorist subjunctive ἀνεκβληθῇ could have been chosen to parallel *pereat* (174). An annotation on a much-debated line explaining how a lucky man could sew on to his black shoe the senatorial crescent (Juv. 7.192 *alutae*: verso l. 19) seems to include traces of the glossographic explanation δέρμα στυπτηριακόν "alum leather"[37] and proves that the annotator was working on a text where the disputed line 192 was present. Finally, against the allusion to astral determinism made by Juvenal to justify some exceptional cases of wealthy rhetors, m^2 answers the question "from where do such vast domains come to Quintilian?" (188–9) by the witty response *ex parentibus habet* (verso ll. 15–16).

Another significant group of Latin and Greek annotations aims to clarify the locutionary context of the seventh *Satire* and to supply syntactic elements only left implicit. For example, it is clarified that the interrogative sentences *mercedem appellas? quid enim scio?* "pay indeed? why, what have I learnt?" (Juv. 7.158) are addressed by a student to his teacher (recto ll. 10–11), and that they are elicited by a request made by the latter to his pupils (recto

---

[32] *patri* is a later addition by m^4.
[33] The commentator dryly replaces the *felix* ("successful" man) of Juvenal with *eruditus* ("learned").
[34] For another interpretation see McNamee (2007, 481).
[35] See *CGL* II 56.29 *dubingeniosus*; 254.6 *sine genio* (*bargus*); III 334.5 *duri ingenii*.
[36] *CGL* II 84.56.
[37] *CGL* II 439.30 and 496.19.

154 PROFESSIONAL GRAMMARIANS

l. 10).[38] Remarkably, when this teacher complains that he must listen again and again to the same tale about Hannibal, the first-person pronoun in *mihi . . . caput . . . implet* (Juv. 7.160–1) is taken as a quotation from the poet himself: ὡς ἀπὸ τοῦ ποιητοῦ (recto l. 12).[39] Implied components in elliptical sentences are often made explicit and equivalent forms are repeated, even to the point of redundancy, to clarify complex structures: thus *Annibal* supplies the subject of *petat* (162: recto l. 14);[40] *dicunt*, added to the resumptive *haec* of line 166, anticipates the verb *conclamant* that appears only at 167 (recto l. 18); similarly, after *anne . . . / expectet* at 179–80, another *anne* is added before *spargatq(ue)* at 180, in order to clarify the syntactical dependence of this verb (verso l. 7); the implicit subject of the action is also given by the marginal annotation *ille dives* at 180 (verso l. 7). The deictic *hic* at the beginning of line 181 is a brachilogic expression for *in porticu potius gestetur*: m^2 fills the gap adding ἐν τῇ στοᾷ γυμνάζει in the margin (verso ll. 8–9), with the equivalence γυμνάζω ~ *gesto* found in the bilingual glossaries,[41] preceded by the non-classical form ἐν τῷ μεσαυλίῳ "in the inner court," also frequently attested in the bilingual glossaries.[42] Finally, the gloss *cocus* identifies the profession implied by Juvenal's phrase "the man who makes up tasty dishes" (Juv. 7.185: verso l. 12), an identification also found in the *Scholia vetustiora* and the *Colloquia* of the *Hermeneumata Pseudodositheana*.[43]

The recourse to specific Greek grammatical labels is a clear sign of the school environment in which the glosses (or the manuscript's annotated exemplar) were produced. The annotation to Juv. 7.178–9 *porticus in qua / gestetur dominus* "colonnade where the master is driven" describes the agentless passive expression as an ἔλλειψις of "by his slaves" (verso ll. 6–7); the grammatical notion of ἀντίθεσις is applied to the comparative phrase *res nulla minoris / constabit patri quam filius* "no item will cost a father less than his son" at Juv. 7.187–8 (verso ll. 15–16).[44] In the first case, m^2

---

[38] It has been previously stated that the annotation is based on a misunderstanding, since the question is put by the students to their teacher (see McNamee 2007, 480), but in fact it must be seen as a reaction to the requests made by teacher.

[39] A different explanation is given by McNamee (2007, 481).

[40] Should we interpret *o* as the Greek article? This would be compatible with the fact that the scribe identified with m^2 was fluent in Greek.

[41] See *CGL* II 33.42, 44, 48, 49.

[42] See the equivalences for *atrium* (*CGL* II 22.30; 368.2; III 267.54; μέσαυλον II 250.56; III 19.27), *compluvium* (III 20.1; 91.52; 442.77; 484.44; μέσαυλον II 368.2; III 191.7; 267.54; 313.38; 365.24; 500.20; 530.27), and *contila* (II 521.53 = *cortina, cortile?*).

[43] See *schol. vet.* Juv. 7.184 "*qui fercula docte (componit)*": *id est structor. aut cocus.* For the *Colloquia*, see below, note 72.

[44] See Scappaticcio (2015, 491–7).

ANONYMOUS GRAMMATICAL SCHOLARSHIP 155

paraphrased *gestetur* by *portetur* (verso l. 6),[45] an equivalence also found in the glossaries.[46]

Other annotations by *m²* reformulate allusive or poetical terms with straightforward expressions. In Latin, *sine corde* explains *laevae parte mamillae / nil salit* at 159–60 (recto l. 11),[47] and *seniles veneni* is meant to interpret *veteres sanant mortaria* at 170—with a remarkable masculine *venenus* (recto l. 22).[48] Several synonymic reformulations keep the same morphological class as Juvenal's forms: *mobetur* (i.e., *movetur*) for *salit* (recto l. 12), *saevus* for *dirus* (recto l. 13), *divitum* for *lautorum* (verso l. 4), *separans* for *scindens* (verso l. 4), *aedificatur* for *surgat* (verso l. 10), *capiat* for *rapiat* (verso l. 10), and *emit* for *veniet* (verso l. 11), which is here understood as a form of *veneo* (on which, see below). In the case of the perfect *perfrisit* (i.e., *perfrixit*, verso l. 21), designating the lucky man who is an excellent singer even when he has a cold, the equivalence *algerit* (a "vulgar" coinage *algero, -ere*?, modeled on *frigero, -are*) ~ *perfrisit* is indirectly found in Juvenal's scholia:[49] the perfect of *perfrige(sc)o* is explained by *infrigdatus* (*sic!*) *fuit*, and the form *infrigidat* is in turn glossed by *alget* in the glossaries.[50]

The same criteria are also followed in Greek: the *sagittae* ("arrows") of Juv. 7.156 are explained as "refutations" (ἀντιρρήσεις, rhetorical "arrows"!, recto l. 8);[51] the temporal phrase *sexta / quaque die* ("every sixth day of the week," at 160–1: recto l. 13) is reformulated by ἐπιχρόνιον "everlastingly"; the winter sun qualified as "becoming cold" (183 *algentem*: verso l. 10) is interpreted as ψυχροποιόν "making cold";[52] the adverb *docte* is paraphrased by εὐφυῶς (verso l. 11); *edere* is explained as ἀποδοῦναι "to give out" (verso l. 23). At Juv. 7.183, *cenatio* is correctly rendered by ἀριστητήριον "refectory" (verso l. 10)—a post-classical word, frequently attested in the *De ceremoniis aulae*

---

[45] The reading *gestatura* given by Willis (1997, *ad* Juv. 7.179) is an error: see Astbury (2000, 310).

[46] See *CGL* IV 82.26 and 30; 241.29; 346.51; 522.2; 588.14; 597.15–16; 604.15.

[47] Roberts (1935b) and McNamee (2007, 481) read *anne corde*. The *Scholia vetustiora* read: *si tu cor non habes*.

[48] For masculine *venenus* compare ps. Cypr. *aleat.* 5 *venenum . . . letalem*.

[49] Also the interlinear annotation to *transi* (190) must have been a synonym, but only . . . . *iẹ* can be read (verso l. 17); given that traces are very scanty and damaged, it is impossible to say if the almost illegible word was similar to the *tace* or *omitte* attested as synonymous to *transi* in the Carolingian commentaries.

[50] *CGL* IV 14.10; 475.11; V 165.21; 264.18.

[51] The parchment is highly damaged here: the "rhetorical arrows" are qualified by a possible adjective, now illegible.

[52] In the bilingual glossaries *algeo* is generally translated by ῥιγῶ; see *CGL* II 14.29; 428.6; III 6.16 (= Flammini 2004, 8.234); 78.69; 157.30–2; 343.8; 399.67–70; 439.18; 503.15; ψυχίζομαι is also attested (*CGL* II 481.27); see also *algidum* ~ ψυχρόν at *CGL* II 481.34.

156　PROFESSIONAL GRAMMARIANS

Byzantinae, recalling the Constantinopolitan court and its administrative environment.[53]

Another group of Greek annotations has significant parallels in the bilingual glossaries, reminiscent of the mechanical, word-for-word translation technique found in eastern manuscripts of Terence, Cicero, Sallust, and Vergil. The scanty ατ. . α (for ἅτινα) translates *quaecumque* (recto l. 4) and is probably motivated by the possibility that this pronominal form could stand for a feminine;[54] ἐπιβαίνει renders *ingredietur* (recto l. 24), an equivalence also given by the Greek-Latin glosses of Pseudo-Cyril;[55] στοά *porticus* (verso l. 5), also in the bilingual glossaries and the *Hermeneumata Pseudodositheana*.[56] The translations of *condio* ~ ἀρτύω (verso l. 12),[57] *novus* ~ νέος (verso l. 16),[58] and *vagitus* ~ κλαυθμυρισμός (verso l. 23)[59] also belong to this type of textual tradition. No occurrences of *ut* ~ πῶς (verso l. 14)[60] are known from the bilingual glossaries, and *ut* might just introduce a rhetorical question meant to convey doubt. Whether this gloss corresponds to a mere translation of *ut* or to an exegetical paraphrase of Juv. 7.187 *ut multum* "at most" is uncertain.

Other Greek annotations introduce more complicated equivalences. The gloss δίσκους on *fercula* (verso l. 11) does not have any parallel in the Greek-Latin glossaries, where δίσκος is mostly rendered with the loanword *discus*[61] or translated as *lanx*,[62] and *ferculum* is found as περιφόρημα[63] or προσφάγιον.[64] Nevertheless, it is significant that *ferculum* is found in monolingual Latin glossaries, where it is glossed as *vasculum*[65] and *discum* (or *discus*).[66] In the following line, when complaining that rich people do not refrain from having a cook to spice their food (*veniet qui pulmentaria*

---

[53] See *caer. Byz.* 2.4 (529.6 Reiske), 2.15 (581.1–2, 597.17 Reiske), 2.18 (602.4, 603.2, 604.15 Reiske). Roberts (1935b, 206) suggests that this word belongs to ecclesiastical language.

[54] On *quicumque* ~ ὅστις in bilingual glossaries see, for instance, *CGL* II 167.7; 325.64; 383.5; 388.23.

[55] *CGL* II 307.8. *Ingredior* is also translated with βαίνω (*CGL* II 255.26; III 73.50), ἐμβατεύω (II 295.49), εἴσειμι (II 287.6), εἰσπορεύομαι (II 287.28), and εἰσέρχομαι (II 286.61).

[56] See for instance *CGL* II 154.6; 438.10; III 20.5; 91.56; 267.49; 305.65; 353.40; 365.34; 503.80.

[57] See for instance *CGL* II 246.23; III 254.71; 401.22–8; 443.12.

[58] See *CGL* II 375.49; III 255.32. Note the presence of the article in the Greek translation.

[59] See *CGL* II 350.20.

[60] In the bilingual glossaries πῶς is generally paralleled by *quam, quatenus, quomodo*.

[61] See *CGL* II 278.53; III 379.8.

[62] See *CGL* II 121.8; 278.53; 519.19.

[63] *CGL* III 379.7; the *Hermeneumata Stephani* distinguish *ferculum* ~ περιφόρημα from *discum* ~ δίσκος (379.7–9).

[64] *CGL* III 254.38.

[65] See *CGL* V 294.31; 360.26; 361.56.

[66] See *CGL* IV 75.14; 341.29; 342.13; 518.37; V 199.32; 294.41; 542.26.

ANONYMOUS GRAMMATICAL SCHOLARSHIP 157

condit), Juvenal uses the word *pulmentaria*, which m^2 translates as φάγιον (verso l. 12). Similarly this word is never found in the bilingual glossaries as a translation of *pulmentum*, which is instead usually rendered by ἔδερμα.[67] However, προσφάγιον[68] is indeed attested as an equivalent to *pulmentum*[69] and as a synonym of *pulmentarium*.[70] More interestingly, the parallel *pulmentaria* ~ προσφάγια appears in the *Colloquia* of the *Hermeneumata Pseudodositheana*:[71] the cooking scene sketched in the *Colloquium Montepessulanum* contains the term *cocus* and the equivalence *condio* ~ ἀρτύω already mentioned, giving the impression that it follows Juvenal's text, with the same syntagm *pulmentaria condire*. A thematic list of *escae* in the *Hermeneumata Pseudodositheana Einsidlensia* also gives the equivalence προσφάγιον *pulmentum, ferculum*,[72] presenting the simultaneous occurrence of the Latin words, taken as synonyms and translated by the same Greek equivalent. Some annotations to Juvenal's text seem to have undergone a circular path, starting from a commentary to the *Satires* that was dismembered in multiples and autonomous generic bilingual glossaries, which were used in turn as glosses on Juvenal's vocabulary.[73] The perfect of the technical verb *perfrige(sc)o* is also found in the bilingual glossaries.[74]

The richness of the annotations by m^2 sometimes results in double glosses in both Latin and Greek for the same passage. The portrait of the rhetor who can buy at most the dole ticket (Juv. 7.174–5) is both summarized by the Latin title *de tessera* and explained by a long Greek gloss on the Roman concept of *tessera frumentaria* (verso l. 1). The commentary on the tale about Hannibal introduced at line 161 takes the forms of a Greek label "on the story of Hannibal" and of a syntactic clarification from the point of view of the Latin grammar (recto ll. 14–16). As we have already seen, the image of the rich porticos and luxurious banquet (181–5) has similarly provoked multiple annotations, with translations, synonymic interpretations and explanations in both languages. Moreover, the two occurrences of *veniet* (184–5: verso l. 11),

---

[67] *CGL* II 220.15.

[68] *CGL* II 164.45; III 183.51; 215.3 = 230.54 = 650.9; 285.63 = 656.11; 314.12.

[69] *CGL* II 423.21.

[70] *CGL* IV 377.38; V 477.32.

[71] *Hermen. Monac.* coll. 9b ἆρον ἔψησον ἐπιμελῶς τὰ προσφάγια *tolle, coque diligenter pulmentaria*; *Montepess.* coll. 11b καὶ τῷ μαγείρῳ εἰπὲ ἵνα τὰ προσφάγια καλῶς ἀρτύσῃ *et coquo dic ut pulmentaria bene condiat*; *Celtis* coll. 44b <καὶ> ἔνεγκε ἄρτον καὶ προσφάγιον *et affer panem et pulmentarium*. See Dickey (2012–15, II:228).

[72] *CGL* III 254.38.

[73] See Friedländer (1895, 106–12).

[74] *CGL* II 146.42 *perfrixit* περιεψύγη.

158 PROFESSIONAL GRAMMARIANS

preceded by *quanticumque domum*, are mistakenly taken as forms of *veneo* and explained in the first case by *emit* and in the second by ὅσου ἀγοράζει "at whatever price it comes to market" (with the gloss *veneo* ~ ἀγοράζω found in the glossaries).[75] The presence of the nominative *dives* as a gloss on *quanticumque* (verso l. 11) can be explained either as describing the subject of this phrase or as connected with *domus*, which is the correct reading in contrast to the variant *domum* that our codex shares with several other manuscripts (P^1FG^1HZ, with the exponent 1 standing for *ante correctionem* in both Knoche's and Willis' editions). In the latter case, then the exemplar of m^2 had a different text than our fragment.

3.2 The Annotations by m^3

The writing of m^3 appears both in the margins and in the interlinear space, but is undoubtedly less substantial than that of m^2. His annotations are exclusively in Latin, which is per se a remarkable feature in the eastern Roman Empire; again, their purpose is to explain Juvenal's difficult text.

A striking feature of this commentary is the use of the second person designating the teacher, which is first found in the correct explanation of the impersonal *si placuit mercedem ponere linguae* "if the decision has been made to make a living with eloquence" at Juv. 7.149 as "if you want to make money from your teaching" (recto l. 1). This second person is then continued in the gloss at 151 *perimit* (*peremit* Ant.) *saevos classis numerosa tyrannos* "the crowded class slays the cruel tyrants," where Juvenal mentions the class of a teacher named Vettius. For his part, m^3 creates a direct dialogue with the *magister*, addressing him in these terms: "your students make recitations aloud about dead tyrants" (recto ll. 3–4). The third person is used to refer to the *auctor*, namely, Juvenal. Accordingly *post nimbos et fulmina* "after the rain and thunder" at 163 is taken as if Juvenal would have meant (*vocabit*, i.e., *vocavit*) "after the winter" (*post hiemem*: recto l. 15).[76] In the following section, m^3 comments upon the expression *accipe quid do* "take it on the spot" at 165, indicating that the teacher

---

[75] *DGE* gives ἀγοράζω only the active sense "comprar," but the equivalence given in the glossaries suggests that in late or vulgar contexts it might have had a middle or inverted sense "be on sale."

[76] We give this new reading for the first time; both Roberts (1935b) and McNamee (2007, 482) read *post pietatem vocabit*, which was not confirmed by direct examination of the fragment and is hardly explicable in the context of Juvenal.

ANONYMOUS GRAMMATICAL SCHOLARSHIP 159

Table 9.2 Annotations by m^3

Juvenal	m^3
149 *si placuit mercedem ponere linguae*	*et[ ]e si vis ex doctrina tua lucrum habere* recto l. 1, right margin
150 *o ferrea pectora Vetti*	*[eti]amsi admi[r]atio[ni]s* recto l. 2, right margin: .. *ra mirantia* edd.
151 *peremit saevos classis numerosa tyrannos*	*voce [r]ecitant de mortu[i]s tyrann[is] tui discipuli* recto l. 3–4, right margin
163 *post nimbos et fulmina*	*post hiemem vocabit* (lege *vocavit*) recto l. 15, right margin: *pïetatem* (in place of *post hiemem*) edd.
165 *quantum vis*	*qu‹o›dvis hoc* recto l. 17, right margin: *[? h]oc* edd.
165–6 *accipe quid do / ut totiens*	*[accip]ẹ tu quid do ut totiens multi sofistae dicunt* recto ll. 17–18, right margin: το *qud dō* | *ut totiens et multis cu-|-ris taedi sunt* (two annotations) edd.
168–9 (summary/ explanation)	*de latrone non consultant. de venefic[is,] de maritis non consultant.* recto ll. 20–2, right margin
169 *malus ingratusque maritus*	*moechus* recto l. 21, supralinear
186 *Quintiliano*	*magister filii divitis* verso l. 13, right margin (inked over by m^4)

of the *Satire* would be ready to pay every possible price to let the parents of his pupils listen to their declamations. His gloss *multi sofistae dicunt* "many sophists say that" (recto ll. 17–18) is remarkably similar to *scholia vetera* on this passage: *omnes scilicet professores conqueruntur*.

Other glosses aim at defining the characters of the seventh *Satire*. The "wicked and ungrateful husband" (*malus ingratusque maritus*) at 169 (recto l. 21) is an "adulterer," an equivalence found in the glossographic tradition.[77] Quintilian, mentioned at 186, is qualified as "the teacher of the son of the rich man" (verso l. 13).[78] Another gloss reformulates in a clearer and more synthetic manner Juvenal's lines about rhetors entering upon real lawsuits and leaving rhetorical topics aside (168–70): "they do not deliberate about the thief, they do not deliberate about poisonings, about husbands" (recto ll. 20–2). An example of a grammatical gloss is found at *quantum vis* "any sum

---

[77] See *CGL* IV 365.51 (*adulter cum maritata*); V 466.7.
[78] This gloss by m^3 has been inked over by m^4: this detail proves that m^3 wrote before m^4.

160   PROFESSIONAL GRAMMARIANS

you please" at 165, which is explained by *quodvis hoc* (recto l. 17). The *scholia vetera* also explain this expression: *pro: roga quantum tibi dem*. Similarly, the grammatical form of *o ferrea pectora Vetti* "Vettius must have a heart of steel!" at 150 probably gave the commentator the opportunity to specify this as an expression of admiration in Latin (recto l. 2).

3.3 The Annotations by m^4

If the hypothesis that both m^2 and m^3 cannot be identified with the original authors of several glosses holds, one must postulate in both cases the existence of one or more annotated exemplars. In the case of m^4, on the contrary, there is certainty that his glosses are the product of a fresh analysis of the seventh *Satire*. A striking feature of m^4 is that he inks over previous annotations by m^2 and m^3 and he also translates them. Was m^4 the original author of these glosses in both Greek and Latin or was he copying the Latin annotations while creating the Greek ones? Whatever the case may be, he might have been relying on the help of a bilingual Greek-Latin reference work, as the frequent parallels with the bilingual glossaries show.

The short school scene, where each pupil in turn "will repeat standing up what he has just read sitting down" at Juv. 7.152–3 (*quaecunque sedens modo legerat, haec eadem stans / perferet . . .*), is explained, in Greek, as ". . . whatever the student said standing and sitting." This involves the addition of μαθητής, a subject only implicit in Juvenal's lines (recto l. 4), the use of two participles from κάθημαι and ἵστημι, which are usual correspondences found in the bilingual glossaries for *sedeo* and *sto*.[79] The genitive *mamillae* at 159 is translated as τοῦ μαστοῦ ("of the breast": recto l. 11), a common equivalence in the bilingual glossaries.[80] Here m^4 does not pick up (*sine*) *corde* from m^2, but finds a morpholexical equivalent for Juvenal's wording. The case of ἀναχωροῦν (verso l. 10) is ambiguous, since this form could either render Juvenal's *rapiat* at 183 or render the gloss *capiat* provided by m^2. The same holds for πονεῖται (verso l. 21), depending on either Juvenal's *perfrisit* at 194 or the annotation by m^2, *algerit*. By contrast, there is no doubt that the description by m^4 of Quintilian at 186 as "teacher of his (*scil.* the rich men) son"

---

[79] On *sedeo* ~ κάθημαι see *CGL* II 335.9; *Hermen. Ampl.* 76.10; *Hermen. Monac.* 148.5; *Hermen. Leid.* coll. 4a; on *sto* ~ ἵστημι see *CGL* II 333.28. McNamee (2007, 480) suggests that part of the gloss misses the poet's point, but this is probably an over-interpretation of this short paraphrase.

[80] See *CGL* II 126.44; III 569.11.

ANONYMOUS GRAMMATICAL SCHOLARSHIP   161

Table 9.3 Annotations by m^4

Juvenal	m^4
152–3 *quaecumque sedens modo legerat haec eadem stans / perferet*	ἐντ ἅτινα ὁ μαθητὴς εἶπεν ἱστάμενος καὶ καθήμενος recto l. 4, supralinear: εντ edd. (perhaps ἔν τ(ισι) McNamee comm.)
159 *laevae parte mamillae*	τοῦ μαστοῦ recto l. 11, supralinear
162 *quidquid id est de quo deliberat*	ὄντινα ἔλαβες recto l. 14, supralinear: perhaps ελαβε McNamee
175 *tempta*	*provata* (lege *probata*) verso l. 2, supralinear: *provata()* Roberts: *pro vaṭịc(in-)* McNamee
180 *spargatque*	γυμνάζῃ verso l. 7, supralinear: γυμναζει edd.
183 *rapiat*	ἀναχωροῦν to explain *rapiat* at 183, or better to translate *capiat* annotated by m^2; verso l. 10, supralinear: χωρουν edd.
183 *algentem rapiat cenatio solem*	ὅτε τοῦ χειμ[ῶνος] ψῦξις γίνεται verso ll. 10–11, right margin
186 *Quintiliano*	παιδευτὴς τοῦ υἱοῦ αὐτοῦ translating m^3; verso l. 13, supralinear
187–8 *res . . . filius*	*nullum est humile et minor videtur patri ut filius* verso ll. 14–15, left margin (only *patri* by m^4, added to further explain the annotation by m^2)
194 *perfrisit* (?)	πονεῖται verso l. 21, supralinear
194 *bene*	ạ. ω (perhaps καλῶς) verso l. 21, supralinear: [ε]ι εχει τ[ο] ψ[υ]χọς. ω.. [edd.
196 *vagitus*	κλαυθμυρισμούς verso l. 23, supralinear
193 *iaculator* (?)	*e* or ε or *s* or σ verso, right bottom margin (preceded by the sign //)

is an almost literal translation of the annotation by m^3 (verso l. 13), which m^4 also inked over. As for *spargat(que)* at 180, explained by γυμνάζῃ (verso l. 7), the bilingual glossaries generally translate *spargo* by ῥαίνω[81] and γυμνάζω by *exerceo*.[82] The correspondence with *gesto* was used by m^2 for his annotation

---

[81] See *CGL* II 427.22–9; III 6.17; 157.14–18; 186.38; 417.44–9; 464.22; 503.12. Also *spargo* ~ πάσσω (*CGL* II 399.35) and ~ σκορπίζω (II 433.57) are known.
[82] See *CGL* II 64.34; 265.31–4; III 132.24–6; 352.18.

162   PROFESSIONAL GRAMMARIANS

to line 179 (verso ll. 8–9: ἐν τῷ μεσαυλίῳ ἐν τῇ στοᾷ γυμνάζει). It is therefore possible that m^4 took this verb from the margin and put it in the subjunctive to explain not *gestetur* but *spargat(que)*. Other Greek explanatory glosses are: "whomever you got (to declaim about)" (recto l. 14) for Juvenal's *quidquid id est de quo deliberat* "whatever be the question which he (*scil.* the student) is pondering" at 162; "when a chill develops in the winter" (verso ll. 10–11),[83] that partially develops the description of a dining room well placed to catch the winter sunshine at 183.

Interestingly enough, m^4 follows the same principles in his Latin glosses. *Provata* (for *probata*) glossing *tempta* at 175 (verso l. 2) is a synonymic gloss, but no equivalence between *probo* and *tempto* appears in the monolingual glossaries; one might also consider it to be a scribal corruption of *proba*, if m^4 is drawing on an earlier source. We do not know whether m^4 was copying this gloss from somewhere else, such as a monolingual Latin commentary, or whether he was resorting to his own knowledge of the Latin language. An original intervention by m^4 in Latin can be seen with certainty in the addition of an explicative dative to the paraphrase by m^2 of Juv. 7.187-8 *res nulla minoris / constabit patri quam filius* "no item will cost a father less than his son": m^4 picked up Juvenal's *patri* and added it to the *videtur* written by m^2 (verso ll. 14–15).

4. Conclusion

Some striking characteristics of this triple commentary from Antinoöpolis demonstrate that the work is related to a context of bilingual education, showing many parallels with the school tradition of the *Hermeneumata*, and more specifically to the *Colloquia*. It also reveals an interest in bureaucratic matters, as the explanations of *tessera frumentaria*, senatorial ceremonial dress, and *cenatio* show. Historical exegesis, by contrast, is not taken into account, since nothing is offered on Hannibal and Cannae, nothing on Roman defeats and marching on Rome.

Juvenal's text itself contained many references to the pedagogical practices of rhetors (Juv. 7.150–214) and grammarians (215–43), and the three commentators were probably in the situation of explaining a poem that gave details of their own activities. Juvenal's description of the pupil memorizing

---

[83] English translation and interpretation by McNamee (2007, 486).

ANONYMOUS GRAMMATICAL SCHOLARSHIP 163

a text that he received from his teacher first sitting and then standing is commented on in Greek by m^4 in a way that recalls a specific scene of the *Colloquia*.[84] The dialogue opposing teacher and pupil on the definition of the former's salary is also a scene found in these texts.[85] Moreover, the allusion in Juvenal to the *suasoriae* on Hannibal corresponds to the presence of the Carthaginian general in many paraliterary genres, as shown for example by the letter of Hannibal to the Athenians in *P.Hamb.* II 129 (second century, coll. VI–VII ll. 106–37) or by the example of the sub-type κατὰ μετάστασιν of the *qualitas iuridicialis adsumptiva* given by the rhetor Julius Victor (13.2214.1 Giomini-Celentano). This lively rhetorical context perfectly matches the general features already described.

Furthermore, the comments illustrate some of the difficulties a late antique reader or student faced when reading Juvenal, and therefore show awareness of the linguistic differences between poetic and ordinary registers of Latin, as well as between Latin and Greek. For example, rare or poetic words are glossed with more familiar equivalents or to emphasize some nuance: *dirus* as *saevus* (m^2 on 161), *lautorum* as *divitum* (m^2 on 177), *scindens* as *separans* (m^2 on 177). Contemporary Greek equivalences are given for some Latin words that may have been difficult or ambiguous: ἀριστήριον for *cenatio* (m^2 on 183), ἀποδοῦναι for *edere* (m^2 on 195), τοῦ μαστοῦ for *mamillae* (m^4 on 159). One unusual and and possibly late Latin form is m^2 *algerit* as a gloss on *perfrisit* "catch cold."

However, as we have shown, the annotations go far beyond offering simple lexical glosses and also respond to and explicate the syntactic, rhetorical, and cultural dimensions of Juvenal's text. Moreover, m^2 seems to give alternative hypotheses about the identities of certain names, since the word *sive* survives at 176 *Chrysogonus* (?) and *Pollio* (?); both interest in names and the presentation

---

[84] See *Hermen. Monac.* coll. 2m κελεύσαντος καθηγητοῦ ἐγείρονται οἱ μικροὶ πρὸς τὰ στοιχεῖα *iubente magistro surgunt pusilli ad elementa*; 2n ἔπειτα ὡς ἐκαθίσαμεν, διέρχομαι ὑπομνήματα *deinde ut sedimus, pertranseo commentarium*; *Celtis comm.* 39a τότε ἐπανέρχεται ἕκαστος, ἐν τῷ ἰδίῳ τόπῳ καθέζουσιν *tunc revertitur quisque, in suo loco consident*; 40a κελεύοντος καθηγητοῦ ἀνιστάνται οἱ μικρότατοι πρὸς <συλλαβάς>, καὶ ἡμεῖς ἀνηγορεύκαμεν ἄμιλλαν καὶ στίχους *iubente praeceptore surgunt minores ad syllabas, et nos recitamus dictatum et versus*. See Clarke (1968); Dickey (2012–15, I:50–1; II:224–6).

[85] *Hermen. Harl.* coll. 6a-b <τὸν μισθὸν> οὐκ ἤνεγκας; ᾔτησα τὸν πατέρα καὶ εἶπεν ἐγὼ αὐτὸς ἐλεύσομαι ἐκεῖ ἅμα *mercedem non attulisti? petivi patrem et dixit: ego ipse veniam ibi noviter* (see Dickey 2012–15, II:53–4). More generally, on questions and answers in Latin grammarians, see De Nonno (2010).

164 PROFESSIONAL GRAMMARIANS

of alternative explanations are very suggestive of the *personae "Iuvenalianae"* tradition. It would therefore be a mistake to think that our commentary is a simple work of mechanical translation, made with general tools conceived for every author and text. Bilingual glossaries are one of the sources of this commentary, but traces of an exegetical tradition on unusual expressions (e.g., *pulmentaria, perfrisit*) found in Juvenal are also present in this multi-layered commentary from Antinoöpolis, as well as a more general effort to understand the content of the satire, its structure, and dialogic features—characteristics that are not explicable without a thorough study of the entire work and without an audience that goes beyond a single scholar on his own.

Appendix
Juvenal's Text in Oxford, Sackler Library, Papyrology Rooms, Ant. inv. *s.n.*

recto (Iuv. 7.149–73)
|¹ Africa, si p`l´acuit mercedem inponere linguae.
|² Declamare doces? o ferrea pectora Vetti,   [7.150]
|³ cum peremit saevos classis numerosa tyrannos!
|⁴ nam quaecumque sedens modo legerat, haec eadem stans
|⁵ [perferet a]tque eadem ca[nt]abit versib`us´ isdem.
|⁶ [Occidit miseros cr]ambe repetita magistros.
|⁷ [Quis color et quo]d sit causae genus atque ubi summa   [155]
|⁸ [quae]stio, quae [ve]niant diversa fronte sagittae,
|⁹ nosse volunt omnes, mercedem solvere nemo.
|¹⁰ 'Mercedem appellas? Quid enim scio?' 'Culpa docentis
|¹¹ scilicet arguitur, quod la[evae] parte mamillae
|¹² nil salit Arcadico iuveni, cuius mihi sexta   [160]
|¹³ quaque di [[c]] `e´i miserum dirus caput Hannubal implet,
|¹⁴ quidquid id est de quo deliberat, an petat urbem
|¹⁵ a Cannis; an post nimbos et fulmina cautus
|¹⁶ circumagat madidas a tempestate cohortes.
|¹⁷ [Quan]tum vis [stipula]re e[t] protinus accipe: quid do   [165]
|¹⁸ [ut toti]ens illum pater a`u´diat?' Haec alii [sex]
|¹⁹ [vel plure]s uno co[n]clam[ant] ore sophistae
|²⁰ [et veras agi]tan[t] l[i]tes raptore relicto;
|²¹ [fusa venen]a silen[t], m[a]lus ingratusque maritus
|²² [et quae iam vet]eres sanant mortaria caecos.   [170]
|²³ [Ergo sibi dabit] ipse rudem, si nostra movebunt
|²⁴ [consilia, et vi]tae diversum iter ingredietur
|²⁵ [ad pugnam qui] rhetorica descendit ab umbra,

verso (Iuv. 7.174–98)
|¹ summula ne pereat qua vilis tessera venit
|² frumenti: quippe haec merces lautissima. Tempta   [7.175]

ANONYMOUS GRAMMATICAL SCHOLARSHIP   165

|³ Chrysogonus quanti doceat vel Pollio quanti
|⁴ lautorum pueros, arte scindens Theodori.
|⁵ Balnea sescentis et pluris portic[us in qua]
|⁶ gestetur dominus quotien[s pluit. Anne serenum]
|⁷ expectet spargatque luto ium[enta recenti?]   [180]
|⁸ Hic potius, namque hic mund`a´e n[ite]t ung[ula mulae.]
|⁹ Parte alia longis Numidarum fulta colu[mnis]
|¹⁰ surgat et algentem rapiat cenatio solem.
|¹¹ Quanticumque d[omu]m, veniet qui fercula docte
|¹² conponit, veniet qui pulmentaria condit.   [185]
|¹³ Hos inter sumptus sestertia Quintiliano,
|¹⁴ ut multum, [[s]] duo sufficiunt: res nulla minoris
|¹⁵ constavit patri quam filius. 'Unde igitur tot
|¹⁶ Quintilianus `habet´ saltus? Exempla novorum
|¹⁷ fatorum transi. Felix et pulcher `et´ acer;   [190]
|¹⁸ fel[ix e]t sapiens et nobilis et gener[osus]
|¹⁹ adpositam nigrae lunam subtexi[t alutae;]
|²⁰ felix orator quoque maximus e[t iaculator]
|²¹ et, si perfrisit, cantat bene. D[istat enim quae]
|²² sidera te excipiant modo p[rimos incipientem]   [195]
|²³ edere vagitus et adhuc a m[atre rubentem.]
|²⁴ Si Fortuna volet, fies de r`h´et[ore consul;]
|²⁵ si volet haec eadem, fies de [consule rhetor.]

recto (Iuv. 7.149–73): 1 *sì* | upper addition by the scribe || 2 ·I· on *declamare* | *doces.* ||
3 *tyránnōs* || 4 *quaecumq(ue)* | *légerat* | *stàns* || 5 *a]tq(ue) eadém* | upper addition by
m² || 6 *magistrōs* || 7 *caúsae génus atq(ue)* || 8 ·I· on *fronte* || 9 *sólvere némó* | Z in the
right margin by *m²* || 10 *scio·* | *docéntīs* || 11 *scilicet arguïtur·* || 12 Z in the left margin
by *m²* | *nil sálit arcadicō ïuveni·cuïus* || 13 *quaq(ue);* I· on *quaq(ue)* | deletion and ad-
dition by the scribe | *dírus* | *hánnubal ímplet;* ·I· on *Hannubal* || 14 *deliberat an petat
urbe(m)* || 15 *cannis . an* || 16 *circumágat* | *cohórtes.* || 17 *vìs* | *áccipe* | *dō* || 18 upper
addition by *m²* | ·I· on *haec* | *alïi* || 19 *sophistae.* || 20 *relictō* | 21 *ingratusq(ue) marítus;*
·I· on *maritus* || 22 *mortária caecōs* || 23 *movébunt* || 24 *ingrediétur* || 25 *rhetórica
descéndit*

verso (Iuv. 7.174–98): 1 *uïlis téssera* || 2 *haèc mérces lautíssima·témpta* || 3 *chrysógonus*
| ·I· on *doceat* | *polliō* || 4 *lautōrum púeros;* ·I· on *pueros* || 5 *bálnea* | *pórtic[us]* || 7
expéctet; ·I· on *expéctet* | *spargátq(ue)* || 8 *hic pótius·namq(ue) hic mund`a´e;* upper ad-
dition by *m²* || 9 *párte ália lóngis.;* ·I· on *lóngis* | *fúlta* | ·I· on *fulta columnis* || 10 *súrgat
et algéntem rápiat cenātiō sólem;* ·I· on *cenatio* || 11 *quánticúmq(ue)* | *véniet quï fércula
dócte* || 12 *conpónit . véniet quï pulmentária* | Z in the right margin by *m²* || 13 *hōs
ïnter súmptus sestértia quintiliánō* || 14 *múltum* [[s]] *dúo sufficiunt· rēs núlla minóris;*
·I· on *duo* || 15 *constávit* | ·I· on *patri* | *fílius . unde ïgitur* || 16 `*habet´*: addition by the
scribe | *saltus · exémpla novórum;* ·I· on *saltus* || 17 *fatōrum transi·* | upper addition by
the scribe | *ácer* || 18 *fĕl[ix e]t sápiens* || 19 the line is between two *diplai obelismenai*
by *m²*; *nígrae* || 20 *fēlix orátōr quōq(ue) máximus* | double oblique stroke on *et: m⁴* ||
21 oblique stroke after *et* | *pérfrisit* | *cāntat béne* || 22 *sídera te excípiant modó* | ·I· on
primos || 23 *édere vagítus* || 24 *sì fórtúna vólet · fíes* | upper addition by the scribe || 25 *sì
vólet* | *éadem fíes* || double oblique stroke by *m⁴* in the bottom margin

recto (Iuv. 7.149–73): 1 inponere Φ: ponere *P¹Arov.*: poscere *Bücheler Markland
Willis* || 2 Vetti *P¹Arov.FGU Willis*: vecti Φ || 3 cum *codd.*: cui *Jahn Willis* | peremit

166 PROFESSIONAL GRAMMARIANS

P^1*Arov.FGU*[1]: perimit *cett. Willis* || **5** *versum om. F* | cantabit *Willis*: cantavit P^1*Arov. schol.* | idem *Willis* || **6** crambe *G Willis*: crambre *Arov.*: grambe *FH*: cambre *cett.* || **8** diversa e *PArov.FHKTZ Willis* | fronte *Markland*: parte Φ *Willis*: forte *PArov.*[1]: aperte *Arov.*[2] || **9** volunt Φ *Willis*: velunt P^1*Arov.*: velint *Pithou* | ponere *codd. Willis* || **13** die *codd. Willis* | Hannibal *codd. Willis* || **14** quicquid *codd. Willis* || **15** fulmina *Willis*: flumina *Arov.A*: fulgura *GU* || **17** accipe *Willis*: accipere P^1*Arov.* | quid do P^1*Arov. FGKTUZ Prisc. gramm. 8.21 (GL II 387.21) Willis*: quod do *cett.*: quiddam *cod.Vallae Merry* || **18** toties *codd. Willis* | haec *PGUArov. Willis*: ast haec *FH*: ast *cett.* || **19** vel P^1*Arov. Willis*: et Φ: aut *recc.* || **22** mortaria *Willis*: mortalia *GUZ*[1]

verso (Iuv. 7.174–98): **2** tempta Φ *Willis*: temptat *PT*[1] || **3** Pollio *Willis*: Polio *P* || **4** artem *codd. Willis* | scindens *codd.*: scindes *recc. Jahn Willis* || **6** quoties *codd. Willis* || **7** exspectet *codd. Willis* | spargatque *codd.*: spargatve *Heinrich Markland Willis* || **8** *versum mulinum Heinrich del.* || **11** quanticunque *codd. Willis* | domum P^1*FG*[1]*HZ*: domus *cett. Willis* || **12** componit *GT Willis*: componat *cett.* | condit *Willis*: condat *LOU*: condet *H* || **14** sufficient *codd. Willis* || **15** constabit *codd. Willis* || **18–19** sapiens ... appositam *damn. Reeve* || **19** *versum damn. Jahn Scholte* | appositam *codd. Willis* || **20** iaculator *Willis*: ioculator *A*[1]*KO* || **21** perfrixit *codd. Willis* || **24–5** *versum damn. Scholte* || **24** fies Φ*P*[2] *Willis*: fiet *P*

PART III
SCHOLARS AND INTELLECTUALS

10

Civic Metaphors for Lexical Borrowing from Seneca to Gellius

Adam Gitner

In his *Lives of the Grammarians* (22.2), Suetonius describes a tense showdown between the grammarian Pomponius Porcellus, "an extraordinarily obnoxious overseer of the Latin language" (22.1 *sermonis Latini exactor molestissimus*), and the emperor Tiberius.[1] Porcellus had reprimanded the emperor for using a foreign word in one of his speeches. The scholar Ateius Capito retorts that even if the word were not acceptable Latin, the emperor could certainly make it so. But Pomponius has the last word: "Capito's lying," he says, "for you, Caesar, are able to give citizenship to people, but not to words" (*tu enim, Caesar, civitatem dare potes hominibus, verbis [verba* trad.] *non potes*).

I would like to start with this anecdote for several reasons. First, it illustrates the fraught relationship between professional grammarian and the *princeps*, two rising stars of the first-century cultural scene.[2] While the two often supported each other, exchanging cultural capital for financial patronage, here the grammarian is anxious to defend his linguistic *imperium* from political encroachment. In Kaster's words (*Guardians* 53), the episode "mark[s] out the period when the grammarian became identified in his own mind and in others' eyes as the agent of linguistic control." The episode also gives me the opportunity to mention another element of Bob Kaster's contribution to the study of the ancient grammarians: namely, his edition and commentary on the *Lives of the Grammarians* (1995, 222–7), which supplies

---

[1] The kernel of this paper originated many years ago in a seminar on the age of Tiberius, co-taught by Bob and Ted Champlin (my attempt to collect the fragments of the grammarians active under Tiberius did not go very far). I am grateful to Bob for his inspiration, to an anonymous reader for helpful comments, and to audiences in Cologne and at the SCS Annual Meeting in 2018.

[2] On the rise of the grammarian, see *Guardians* 51–60 and Wallace-Hadrill (2008, 70).

Adam Gitner, *Civic Metaphors for Lexical Borrowing from Seneca to Gellius* In: *Roman Perspectives on Linguistic Diversity*. Edited by Adam Gitner, Oxford University Press. © Oxford University Press 2023.
DOI: 10.1093/oso/9780197611975.003.0010

170   SCHOLARS AND INTELLECTUALS

all the essential comparanda for this anecdote. Exploring these comparanda in their full social and linguistic complexity is, I hope, a fitting tribute to a teacher to who has done so much to breathe life into ancient scholars and make their work relevant and accessible.

Just as importantly, the episode introduces the central focus of my paper, not the ancient grammarian per se, but rather the striking metaphor Porcellus deploys to make his point: the comparison of words to citizens. The metaphor raises intriguing questions about the relationship between conceptions of language and political community. As we will see, it occurs with different emphases at least five times in Latin literature, including in Seneca the Younger, Quintilian, Suetonius, and Aulus Gellius. Although the metaphor is attributed to a grammarian in the case of Porcellus, the actual sources themselves are not professional grammarians at all but members of a broader, scholarly public. These sources sometimes provide a valuable contrast to the attitudes and conceptions found in more specialized sources. In particular, these passages demonstrate a powerful connection between Roman civic ideology and imperialism, on the one hand, and Roman conceptualizations of language contact, on the other.

1. Lexical Borrowing

Without insisting on the episode's historicity, there is good reason to think that the anecdote addresses what we would now call lexical borrowing, when a word from one language enters another (e.g., "chef" or "cuisine" as borrowed into English from French).[3] Unfortunately, the offending word at issue is not quoted by Suetonius or by Cassius Dio, who preserves a slightly different version of this episode (57.17.1–2).[4] Nevertheless, ancient historians do mention Greek words in similar anecdotes about Tiberius' aversion to foreign vocabulary. These anecdotes might well be related to the Porcellus episode, either as reminiscences or creative reworkings of the same motif. In his biography of Tiberius (*Tib.* 71), Suetonius gives two examples of the emperor's careful linguistic habits: he once apologized before saying *monopolium* in the

---

[3] On loanwords in general see Matras (2009, 166–92) and Haspelmath (2009); on the contrast between integrated loanwords and code-switches in Latin see Adams (2003, esp. 26).

[4] In Dio's version the offending word occurs in a decree (γράμμα), promulgated in 17 CE, rather than a speech; and it is the emperor, racked by post-publication anxiety, who initiates the proceedings by requesting advice from the grammarians.

CIVIC METAPHORS FOR LEXICAL BORROWING   171

Senate and went so far as to change the word ἔμβλημα "inlay" (transmitted in Greek script) in a senatorial decree.[5]

It has often been remarked that "borrowing" (and the related "<u>loan</u>word") is an imperfect metaphor to describe this phenomenon since the borrowing language is not obliged to give anything back nor has the lending language become impoverished in any way as a result of the exchange. The action can only be described as "borrowing" in an attenuated sense of the word, according to which something is acquired without the obligation to give anything back.[6] To avoid the misleading implications of this metaphor, some linguists prefer to talk about linguistic "transfer" or "replication."

Strikingly, this use of "borrowing" to describe loanwords is almost completely alien to antiquity, even though *mutuor* "borrow" had a similar attenuated sense (cf. *TLL* VIII 1731.61–1732.17 "latius vel in imagine [vi mutua fere detersa]"). The only possible example known to me occurs in Quintilian's *Institutio oratoria* (1.5.58): *confessis quoque Graecis utimur verbis, ubi nostra desunt, sicut illi a nobis nonnumquam mutuantur* ("we also openly use Greek words where we have none of our own, just as they sometimes borrow from us"). Quintilian's vague reference to Greeks "borrowing" from Latin might describe either spontaneous code-switching or integrated lexical borrowing. Typically, however, *verbum mutuatum* describes a different kind of lexical innovation: the use of a word in an extended or figurative sense.[7] Perhaps the negative moral and social implications of indebtedness and usury made the idea of lexical "borrowing" unsavory. In this connection it is striking that in Quintilian's phrasing it is the Greeks who "borrow" Latin vocabulary rather than the other way around. Though the Romans sometimes took pride in the frugal poverty of Latin, perhaps an "indebted" language was a less attractive proposition.[8]

More typically, Roman writers called loanwords *verba peregrina* (also *adventicia, aliena, externa*) to distinguish them from native vocabulary

---

[5] Dio discusses the ἔμβλημα incident under the year 16 CE (57.15.1–2) as distinct from the Porcellus episode. The precise relationship between these episodes historically and in the historical imagination is not my concern.

[6] This is the sense of "borrow" when a student asks to "borrow" a piece of paper from a classmate, knowing full well that it will not be returned. Cf. *OED* s.v. "borrow" I2a: "To render oneself indebted for; to make temporary use of (something not one's own; . . . more usually of immaterial things: as, to adopt (thoughts, expressions, modes of conduct) from another person, or (words, idioms, customs, etc.) from a foreign language or people; to obtain (a temporary favour) by request."

[7] In this sense, a *verbum mutuatum* is equivalent to a *verbum translatum* ("figurative usage"), e.g., Cic. *orat.* 80, 211; Fest. p. 136; Sen. *benef.* 2.34.2; Quint *inst.* 10.1.13; Mart. Cap. 5.109.

[8] Fögen (2000) discusses the topos of *patrii sermonis egestas.*

172   SCHOLARS AND INTELLECTUALS

(*verba* or *vocabula nostra*, *vernacula*, *Latina*). The distinction is already found in Cicero (*Arch.* 26; *de orat.* 3.44) and becomes central to Varro (e.g., *ling.* 5.10 *verba*, *quae sunt aut nostra aut aliena aut oblivia*), Quintilian (*inst.* 1.5.55 *verba aut Latina aut peregrina sunt*), and the Roman grammarians.[9] The terminology originates in juridical status: a *peregrinus* is a "resident alien," a foreigner residing in Roman territory, whose legal disputes were overseen by the *praetor peregrinus*.[10] More distantly, *peregrinus* may conceal a fossilized spatial metaphor, if the adverb *peregre/-i* "abroad," from which *peregrinus* derives, itself reflects an earlier adjective **per-agro-* "going across the fields."[11]

The phrase *verba peregrina* superficially resembles the typical Greek expression ὀνόματα βαρβαρικά (or βάρβαρα).[12] However, the difference is telling: the adjective βάρβαρον or βαρβαρικόν implies purist disapproval, expressed also by the use of βαρβαρισμός to describe a linguistic fault.[13] By contrast, *peregrinus* suggests a more neutral attitude to foreign interaction: *verba peregrina* may be distinct from native *verba vernacula*, but they are nevertheless tolerated interlopers.

The metaphor of words "acquiring citizenship" takes the juristic conception implicit in the word *peregrinus* one step further. It not only gives a more precise and culturally specific way to talk about linguistic belonging, but also opens up the possibility to describe finer gradations of linguistic assimilation than *verba peregrina* on its own. Such a distinction is found

---

[9] See also Varro *ling.* 5.100, 5.103–4, 6.77, and Müller (2005, 371 n. 1). Garcea and Lomanto (2004) emphasize the threeway distinction between *Latinus*, *Graecus*, and *barbarus*, in which *Latinus* and *Graecus* were closely aligned. For later usage, see Schad (2007) s.v. *peregrina*. Some later grammarians, such as Diomedes (e.g., *gramm.* I 433.32), distinguish between *verba peregrina* (Greek) and *verba barbara* (non-Greek). In general see *TLL* s.v. *peregrinus* X.1 1311.26–42. Later grammarians also include: *barbara locutio* (Fronto *gramm.* 7.526.19–20), *barbaros lexis* (Charis. *gramm.* citing Cominianus), and *barbarolexis* (first attested in this sense at Don. *gramm. mai.* 3.1 p. 653.2). On these categories see Vainio (1999, 23–7) and more generally Rochette (1996).

[10] See Kübler, *RE* XIX.1 639–43; and *TLL* X.1 1309.46–1310.12.

[11] Certainly for Varro, the adjective *peregrinus* implies motion. He derives it from *pergendo* "going ahead," and believes it was coined when the Romans first "advanced" out of the *ager Romanus* (*ling.* 5.33). De Vaan (2008, 29) includes *peregre* among the derivatives of *ager* without explaining the precise development; cf. *TLL* X.1 1298.39–44.

[12] The phrase ὀνόματα βαρβαρικά goes back to Herodotus (3.115 βάρβαρον [βαρβαρικόν var. l.] ὄνομα) and seems to become standard among professional grammarians, for example in Herodian (e.g., *GG* III.3 351.24; III.2 920.16–17). The expression ξενικὰ ὀνόματα also occurs about a half dozen times, mainly of borrowings from non-Attic dialects (e.g., Pl. *Crat.* 401c). The adjective ξενικός comes closer to *peregrinus* in implying a more neutral attitude to foreign interaction.

[13] Found already among the early Stoics (D. L. 7.59 attributed to Zeno). The *scholia Londinensia* to Dionysius Thrax, explaining the concept of βαρβαρισμός, make clear that foreign words are meant to be avoided (*GG* I.3 447.26–7 περὶ λέξιν ξένην, ὡς εἴ τις τὸν κλάδον τοῦ φοίνικος βαΐον ὀνομάζει, δέον λέγεσθαι ὁμωνύμως τῷ φυτῷ).

CIVIC METAPHORS FOR LEXICAL BORROWING   173

in German, which distinguishes between assimilated borrowings, called *Lehnwörter*, and borrowings that remain perceptibly foreign, *Fremdwörter*.[14] In English the former are sometimes called "integrated borrowings" to distinguish them from unintegrated borrowings and code-switches (admittedly the boundary line between these last two categories is somewhat fuzzy). By contrast, ancient vocabulary in this domain appears to have been relatively impoverished: I have not found any Greek or Latin terminology that marks this distinction. The metaphor of lexical citizenship therefore makes an innovative contribution to ancient linguistic thought by filling this apparent gap in the technical vocabulary, and it draws attention to the phenomenon of lexical assimilation, not otherwise much discussed in antiquity.

2. Expanding the Lexical Franchise

The striking thing about this metaphor is not only its originality but also that it rests on a particularly Roman conception of citizenship.[15] Fundamental is the idea of extending the citizenship, whether to resident aliens, favored allies, or conquered enemies, as expressed by the legend of Romulus' asylum.[16] Though honorary grants of citizenship were known in the Greek world, the Romans elevated this to an instrument of foreign policy and regarded it as an outstanding feature of their commonwealth.[17] This view is well represented by Dionysius of Halicarnassus, who writes (*Ant.* 1.9.4):

ἔθνος τε μέγιστον ἐξ ἐλαχίστου γενέσθαι σὺν χρόνῳ παρεσκεύασαν καὶ περιφανέστατον ἐξ ἀδηλοτάτου, τῶν τε δεομένων οἰκήσεως παρὰ σφίσι

---

[14] See Eisenberg (2012, 29–34).

[15] The metaphor of citizenship was also exploited in other domains besides language. For example, Cicero claimed that Cato "gave citizenship" to philosophy by expressing it in Latin (*fin.* 3.40 *itaque mihi videris Latine docere philosophiam et ei **quasi civitatem dare**; quae quidem adhuc peregrinari Romae videbatur nec efferre sese nostris sermonibus . . .*). Also used of domesticating agriculture as a science: Colum. 1.1.12 *et ut agricolationem **Romana tandem civitate donemus** (nam adhuc istis auctoribus Graecae gentis fuit), iam nunc M. Catonem memoremus, qui eam Latine loqui primus instituit, post hunc duos Sasernas, patrem et filiem, eqs.* Of eloquence: Fronto p. 131.2–6 *sed etiam omnes universos, quicumque post Romam conditam oratores exstiterunt, illos etiam quos in Oratore Cicero eloquentiae **civitate gregatim donavit**, si numerare velis, vix trecentorum numerum conplexebis . . .*

[16] See Dench (2005).

[17] The Romans' generous extension of the franchise was already portrayed positively by Philip V of Macedon in in 215 BCE (*SIG* 543.27–40). Compare Dionysius of Halicarnassus's remarks in the preface to his history (1.3.4–5, esp. 1.9.4), his comparison between Roman and Greek policy (2.16–17) and discussion of Servius' manumitting slaves (4.22.3–4); cf. Libanius *Or.* 30.5. For this material see Sherwin-White (1973, 397–444) and Ando (2016, 12–13).

174   SCHOLARS AND INTELLECTUALS

φιλανθρώπῳ ὑποδοχῇ καὶ πολιτείας μεταδόσει τοῖς μετὰ τοῦ γενναίου ἐν πολέμῳ κρατηθεῖσι, δούλων τε ὅσοι παρ' αὐτοῖς ἐλευθερωθεῖεν ἀστοῖς εἶναι συγχωρήσει, τύχης τε ἀνθρώπων οὐδεμιᾶς εἰ μέλλοι τὸ κοινὸν ὠφελεῖν ἀπαξιώσει.

And in the course of time they [the Romans] contrived to raise themselves from the smallest nation to the greatest and from the most obscure to the most illustrious, not only by their humane reception of those who sought a home among them, but also by sharing the rights of citizenship with all who had been conquered by them in war after a brave resistance, by permitting all the slaves, too, who were manumitted among them to become citizens, and by disdaining no condition of men from whom the commonwealth might reap an advantage. (trans. Cary 1937)

It has sometimes been said that the Greek conception of citizenship was basically ethnic and cultural—a status typically inherited from both parents—whereas the Roman conception was more civic and juridical. This is overly schematic, since Romans could also view their nationality in ethnic terms, but the formulation captures something important. In the Roman system, citizenship and ethnicity were often uncoupled, since non-Romans could more easily become Romans. Analogously it was perhaps easy to imagine that the same was true of words: although some words may have originated elsewhere, they could still gain full acceptance as part of a new language. The peculiar nature of Roman citizenship seems to have provided a helpful model for describing and understanding the linguistic phenomenon of lexical contact.

Just as they celebrated the creation of a multi-ethnic empire, the Romans could also celebrate the resulting linguistic diversity. Perhaps the best example comes from Quintilian's *Institutio oratoria* (1.5.55–8):

verba aut Latina aut peregrina sunt. peregrina porro ex omnibus prope dixerim gentibus ut homines, ut instituta etiam multa venerunt. taceo de Tuscis et Sabinis et Praenestinis quoque (nam ut eorum sermone utentem Vettium Lucilius insectatur, quem ad modum Pollio reprendit in Livio Patavinitatem): licet omnia Italica pro Romanis habeam. Plurima Gallica evaluerunt, ut "raeda" ac "petorritum," quorum altero tamen Cicero, altero Horatius utitur. et "mappam" circo quoque usitatum nomen Poeni sibi vindicant, et "gurdos" quos pro stolidis accipit vulgus, ex Hispania duxisse originem audivi.

CIVIC METAPHORS FOR LEXICAL BORROWING   175

Words are either Latin or foreign. Foreign words, just like people and indeed many institutions, have come to us from almost every nation. I say nothing of Tuscan, Sabine, and even Praenestine elements (Lucilius [frg. 1322 Marx = 1138–41 W.] attacks Vettius for using Praenestine words, as Pollio criticizes "Patavinity" in Livy); I can surely treat all Italian words as Roman. Many Gaulish words have become established (*raeda*, *petorritum* one used by Cicero [*Mil.* 54; *Phil.* 2.58], the other by Horace [*sat.* 1.6.104]. *Mappa* (familiar in the circus) is claimed as Punic; and I have heard that *gurdus*, the vulgar word for "fool," comes from Spain. (transl. Russell 2001)

Even though the metaphor of lexical citizenship is not explicit here, the Latin language is clearly a mirror of Roman society: just as institutions come to Rome from around the Mediterranean world, so too do words.[18] Quintilian's description captures an important linguistic reality, insofar as Latin does appear to have been more open to lexical transfer than Greek, or at least classical, literary Greek. Yet it also reflects implicit political views about the diversity of Roman society. Provincial Roman citizens, such as Quintilian who came from Hispania Tarraconensis, would have found it congenial to emphasize the diverse, regional contributions to the richness of the Latin vocabulary. Furthermore, many of the foreign languages Quintilian explicitly names, such as Punic and Gaulish, belonged to peoples who were conspicuously vanquished and subjugated to Rome. To the extent that such names evoke Rome's military glory, the passage should not be understood anachronistically as a celebration of multiculturalism, but rather of Roman imperialism.

However, not all Romans shared this positive view of the expanding franchise. Tacitus provides a glimpse of such dissent in his account of the senatorial resistance to Claudius' proposal allowing Gallic aristocrats into the

---

[18] On this passage see Fögen (2000, 149). There are striking antecedents to Quintilian's claim in what can be reconstructed of Varro's views on the origin and development of Latin. In particular, Lydus preserves a revealing claim about the mixed nature of Latin: *Mag.* 2.13.6 ὅτι δὲ οὐ Ῥωμαικὸν τουτὶ τὸ ῥημάτιον (i. e. *balteus*), μάρτυς ὁ Ῥωμαῖος Βάρρων ἐν βιβλίῳ †πέμπτῳ Περὶ Ῥωμαικῆς διαλέκτου, ἐν ᾧ διαρθροῦται ποία μέν τις λέξις ἐστὶν Αἰολική, ποία δὲ Γαλλική· καὶ ὅτι ἑτέρα μὲν ἡ †Θούσκων, ἄλλη δὲ Ἐτρούσκων, ὧν συγχυθεισῶν ἡ νῦν κρατοῦσα τῶν Ῥωμαίων ἀπετελέσθη φωνή ("That this peculiar word [*balteus*] is not Roman, the Roman Varro attests in Book 5 of his *De lingua Latina* [?] in which it is precisely defined what sort of word is Aeolic and what sort is Gallic; and that one is Tuscan and another Etruscan; after these had mixed together, the now prevailing language of the Romans was formed.")

176   SCHOLARS AND INTELLECTUALS

Senate (*Annales* 11.23–4).[19] Though the Gauls had been Roman citizens for generations, their opponents claimed that ancestral ties of kinship and geographic rootedness—in other words, blood and soil—counted more than judicial status. Similar criticism, also directed against Claudius, surfaces in the *Apocolocyntosis* (3.3):

> sed Clotho "ego mehercules," inquit "pusillum temporis adicere illi volebam, dum hos pauculos qui supersunt civitate donaret—constituerat enim omnes Graecos, Gallos, Hispanos, Britannos togatos videre—sed quoniam placet aliquos peregrinos in semen relinqui ut tu ita iubes fieri, fiat."

> But Clotho said, "By George, I was wanting to give him a fraction of time more, until he had endowed with citizenship those tiny few who are left over—for he had resolved to see all Greeks, Gauls, Spaniards and Britons wearing the toga—but since it is your pleasure that some foreigners should be left for propagation, and since you command it to be so, so be it."
> (adapted from Eden 2008)

The increasing number of new citizens, especially during the early empire, clearly made some established citizens nervous about the decreasing value of their privilege. It was also an uncomfortable sign of the expanding power of the emperor, who was usurping a power that originally depended exclusively on laws passed by the Roman people.[20]

3. The Metaphor Elaborated

This contested political context informs, sometimes subtly and sometimes more overtly, the metaphor of lexical citizenship in its surviving instances. To return to the initial anecdote about Tiberius, the political context suggests that Porcellus' *bon mot* in fact rests on a controversial premise: that it was within the emperor's power and in the interest of the Roman commonwealth

---

[19] On this episode see esp. Sherwin-White (1973, 237–50) and Malloch's commentary (2013, 338–80).
[20] Sherwin-White (1973, 237–51).

CIVIC METAPHORS FOR LEXICAL BORROWING   177

to extend the franchise at all.[21] It was this constitutional innovation that caused alarm among Claudius' contemporaries. While Porcellus does not contest the emperor's juridical power to make new citizens, simply to mention it draws attention to the constitutionally unprecedented and, at least to some members of the Roman aristocracy, alarming position of the *princeps*.

The anecdote also raises an implicit question: if the emperor does not have the power to confer lexical citizenship on words, who does? One tempting answer is, the grammarian. On this view, the grammarian would play the same role in the lexical domain as the emperor does in the civic one. This might be described as an imperial view of the grammarian's power, and it certainly fits with Porcellus' cheeky attitude as *Latini sermonis exactor molestissimus*. However, in this context there is another and possibly more subversive answer.[22] Grammarians could not have simply declared a word to be Latin by personal fiat any more than an emperor could. Even though they may have been the final arbiters of language—*custodes* in Seneca's description (*epist.* 95.65)—they were still themselves at the mercy of other linguistic forces, such as *consuetudo*, *natura*, and *vetustas*, whose competing claims they merely helped to adjudicate. On this conception, the grammarian would have been less like a lexical *princeps* and perhaps more like a *censor*, whose job was to review the citizen rolls and censure bad behavior. Much real power would have rested with other linguistic forces, notably usage (*consuetudo* or *usus*), that is to say the majority of competent language users. To translate this into political terms, we are talking about the *populus*, a word Varro in fact uses to describe the collective power of the language community to determine usage.[23] In answer to an imperial view of language, and the emperor

---

[21] The emperor's ability to extend the franchise was based on earlier war-time powers given to *imperatores* to recognize military valor (Lavan 2019, 27–31). The innovation lay in concentrating this power in a single individual.

[22] Poets are another possibility, who are frequently mentioned as name-givers: e.g., Varro *ling.* 5.7 *grammatica . . . ostendit, quemadmodum quodque poeta finxerit verbum* and Horace *ars* 50–1 *fingere . . . non exaudita* (sc. verba) *. . . continget dabiturque licentia sumpta pudenter*. In practice Latin poets were certainly a main channel by which elevated Grecisms entered Latin, but I leave this possibility aside since the anecdote focuses on the relationship between *imperator* and *grammaticus*.

[23] Varro *ling.* 9.6 *populus . . . in sua potestate, singuli in illius. itaque ut suam quisque consuetudinem, si mala est, corrigere debet, sic populus suam. ego populi consuetudinis non sum ut dominus, at ille meae est* (cf. 10.74). The legal or political implications of *potestas* are made more explicit in the previous chapter, where Varro distinguishes the "rights" (*ius*) of the average language user from those of the *orator* and *poeta* (9.5 *alia . . . populi universi, alia singulorum, et de ieis non eadem oratoris et poetae, quod eorum non idem ius*). An echo of this republican conception of the *populus* is found much later in Macrobius' *Saturnalia* (1.5.10), where he uses the metaphor of "verbal elections" (*in verborum comitiis*) to describe the power of *auctores* to determine *usus: hisne tam doctis viris* (sc. Quadrigario, Lucilio), *quorum M. Cicero et Varro imitatores se gloriantur, adimere vis in verborum comitiis ius suffragandi et tamquam sexagenarios maiores de ponte deicies?*

178   SCHOLARS AND INTELLECTUALS

or grammarian's unique power within it, this advocates a kind of linguistic republicanism. Read along these lines, Porcellus' retort is not just a rebuke of Tiberius' word choice, but an implicit critique of monarchical power in both the linguistic and political domains.

4. Seneca

The Porcellus anecdote is the oldest occurrence of the metaphor of lexical citizenship in terms of its narrative setting, but it reaches us via Suetonius, writing about a century after the event described. By contrast, the oldest direct attestations of the metaphor are in the works of the Younger Seneca, who uses the metaphor twice.

The more straightforward instance occurs in the *Naturales quaestiones* within a discussion of the names for the winds (5.16.4):[24]

> (*sc. ventus*) qui surgit ab oriente aequinoctiali, Subsolanus apud nos dicitur, Graeci illum Ἀφηλιώτην vocant. ab oriente hiberno Eurus exit, quem nostri vocavere Volturnum. T. Livius hoc illum nomine appellat in illa pugna Romanis parum prospera, in qua Hannibal et contra solem orientem exercitum nostrum et contra ventum constitutum venti adiutorio ac fulgoris praestringentis oculos hostium vicit. Varro quoque hoc nomen usurpat, sed et **Eurus iam civitate donatus est, et nostro sermoni non tamquam alienus intervenit.** ab oriente solstitiali excitatum Καικίαν Graeci appellant, apud nos sine nomine est. aequinoctialis occidens Favonium mittit, quem Zephyrum esse dicent tibi etiam qui Graece nesciunt loqui.

> The wind which rises from the equinoctial sunrise [i.e., east] is called by us Subsolanus; the Greeks call it the *Apheliotes*. Eurus comes from the winter sunrise [i.e., southeast], a wind which our people call Vulturnus. T. Livy [22.43.10] calls it by this name in connection with that famous battle which was disastrous for the Romans when Hannibal defeated our army which was drawn up facing the rising sun and wind. He had the help of the wind and the glare that dazzled the eyes of his enemy. Varro also uses the name Vulturnus. But **Eurus has already been granted citizenship and does not come into our speech as though it were a foreign word.** The wind which is

---

[24] On this passage in general see Williams (2005, 417–50, esp. 433–5).

CIVIC METAPHORS FOR LEXICAL BORROWING   179

aroused from the summer-solstitial sunrise [i.e., northeast] the Greeks call *Caecias*; it has no name in our language. The equinoctial sunset [i.e., west] sends Favonius, which even those who do not know how to speak Greek will tell you is Zephyr. (adapted from Corcoran 1972)

The passage subtly discriminates different ways that Greek and Latin vocabulary relate to one another and different degrees of lexical integration. In the case of the first wind-pair (Subsolanus–Ἀφηλιώτης), Latin and Greek simply possess different names for the same wind: Subsolanus is equivalent to Ἀφηλιώτης. In the second case, the Greek name *Eurus* (Εὖρος) is equivalent to Latin *Volturnus*, supported by the authority of Livy and Varro. Yet Seneca adds an important qualification: Eurus has "already been granted Roman citizenship" (*iam civitate donatus est*), even though a native alternative exists. The Latin form *Eurus* is found as early as Furius Antias (*poet.* 5) and the pseudo-Caesarian *Bellum Alexandrinum* (9.4). Indeed, Livy appears to use both *Eurus* (25.27.11) and *Volturnus* (22.43.10) with no apparent difference.

Seneca adds a gloss that helps explain the metaphor: *non tamquam alienus intervenit*. The operative verb *intervenio* emphasizes the arrival of something inopportunely or by way of interruption: "the break in on" or "interrupt" (*OLD* s.v. 1b, 5). Unlike an integrated borrowing, a foreign word draws aesthetic attention to itself; it shows up where it does not quite belong.

In the final wind pair (Favonius–Zephyr), Seneca describes a subtly different situation. *Zephyrus* falls short of full Roman citizenship; Seneca only asserts that it is familiar even to Greek-less speakers of Latin. This is not merely a case of rhetorical variation. Rather, the word *Zephyrus* preserves overt traces of its Greek origin both orthographically and phonetically: namely, the *Graecae litterae* zeta and upsilon, as well as the aspirated phi. It is precisely the word *Zephyrus* that Quintilian uses in order to illustrate the pleasant aesthetic effect of Greek vocabulary (*inst.* 12.10.28): *velut hilarior protinus renidet oratio, ut in "zephyris."* Perhaps these foreign elements were an impediment to its full integration, but they did not prevent it from being more familiar to Latin speakers than Ἀφηλιώτης or Καικίας.

Seneca deployed the same metaphor in a more sophisticated way in his *Epistulae ad Lucilium*, composed shortly before his suicide in 65, with reference to the loanword *analogia* "analogy" (120.4):

nobis videtur observatio collegisse et rerum saepe factarum inter se conlatio; per analogian nostri intellectum et honestum et bonum iudicant.

180   SCHOLARS AND INTELLECTUALS

hoc verbum cum Latini grammatici civitate donaverint, ego damnandum non puto, <puto> in civitatem suam redigendum (<puto> *inseruit Buech.*; <immo> *Mueck, Reynolds*; damnandum *ut glossema sustulit Haase*; civitatem <autem> *Beltrami*). utar ergo illo non tantum tamquam recepto sed tamquam usitato.

Our own view is that the honorable and the good are inferred through observation and comparison of repeated actions; in the judgment of our school, they are understood "by analogy." Since this term "analogy" has been naturalized by Latin scholars, rather than rejecting it, I think it should be fully accepted into the Roman community. So I will use it not only as legitimate but as fully established. (Graver and Long 2015)

The passage requires more elucidation. Seneca is suggesting that people acquire their conception of the good through inferential reasoning. To describe this kind of reasoning, he introduces the Stoic technical term *analogia* (ἀναλογία), which had previously been borrowed into Latin to denote linguistic analogy.[25] The appearance of this Greek word with its foreign inflection, the accusative ending *-an*, prompts an excursus or apology, whose meaning is at first glance not entirely clear. Seneca describes three possible kinds of linguistic status for the word: full lexical citizenship (*hoc verbum cum Latini grammatici civitate donaverint*); some kind of censure, which he appears to reject (*damnandum non puto*); and a third possibility, which he appears to favor: *in civitatem suam redigendum.*[26] The consensus view, represented here by the translation of Graver and Long (2015), takes this as full acceptance into Latin citizenship. But on this interpretation, what is the significance of such "acceptance," and how does it differ juridically from the grant of citizenship that has apparently already taken place?

Much turns on the meaning of the ambivalent verb *redigendum*. Does it mean "fully accept," as it is usually understood, or the opposite, "return to its prior state" (e.g., *OLD* s.v. 2a) or "reduce (in status)"? Furthermore, what is the significance of the reflexive adjective *suam* "its own," modifying *civitatem*? If the point is full acceptance into the previously mentioned citizenship of the

---

[25] An excellent survey of the word *analogia* in Latin grammatical texts, as well as various native alternatives (e.g., *proportio, ratio, similitudo*), is found in Schironi (2007). It is earliest attested in Varro's *De lingua Latina* in both Greek script (8.23 ἀναλογίας [*analogiias* F]; 10.39 ἀναλογίᾳ) and as a Latin loanword (e.g., 8.32 *analogia*; 9.33 *analogian*).

[26] For *condemnare* of citizen status compare Cic. *Balb.* 52 *audebo etiam hoc contendere, numquam esse condemnatum quem constaret ab imperatore nostro civitate donatum.*

CIVIC METAPHORS FOR LEXICAL BORROWING   181

Latin language, no possessive adjective is strictly necessary; if one is supplied for emphasis, *nostram* seems like a more natural choice. Lastly, if Seneca is claiming that the word should be fully domesticated, why has he used it with a Greek accusative ending (unless this is a scribal corruption)?

There is an important historical analogy that suggests *redigere* here means "send back" rather than "accept." The controversial Lex Licinia Mucia of 95 BCE, which helped spark the Social War, appears to have been titled *de civibus redigundis* "about withdrawing citizen rights" (Cic. or. frg. A 7.21).[27] The expression occurs several times with this meaning, specifically in relation to this notorious law (Schol. Cic. Bob. p. 129.10 *leges . . . de civibus redigendis*; cf. Cic. *de orat.* 2.257 [addressing Licinia Mucia] *tuam legem de civitate*). Asconius elaborates on this law in a way that makes its relevance to Seneca clear (*Corn.* p. 54.16–18 = p. 67.22–68.4 Clarke):

> hi . . . legem eam de qua loquitur **de redigendis in suas civitates sociis** in consulatu tulerunt. nam cum summa cupiditate civitatis Romanae Italici populi tenerentur et ob id magna pars eorum pro civibus Romanis se gereret, necessaria lex visa est ut **in suae quisque civitatis** ius redigeretur.

> These two in their consulship passed the law of which he speaks on restoring the allies to their own local citizenships. For at a time when the Italic peoples were gripped by extreme eagerness for the Roman citizenship, and on that account a large portion of them was behaving as if they were Roman citizens, legislation appeared to be a necessity so that each man should be restored to his proper legal rights. (transl. Lewis 2006)

The legislators feared that too many Italians were passing themselves off as full Roman citizens; their solution was *redigere in civitates suas*. These allies were apparently reduced to a previously held, lesser municipal status, such as *ius Latium* or *civitas sine suffragio*, nevertheless without receiving the judicial penalty for impersonating a Roman citizen.

Redigere thus appears to be terminological for "returning" fake Roman citizens to their municipal status. If this is correct, Seneca sketches a middle ground between outright condemnation (*damnare*) and total acceptance (*civitate donare*). This historical context lends additional point to the phrase

---

[27] See Mommsen (1871–88, III:639 n. 2).

182 SCHOLARS AND INTELLECTUALS

Latini grammatici, perhaps implying a contrast in social status with fully Roman grammarians, such as the *eques Romanus* L. Aelius Stilo (Suet. *gramm.* 3.1). A sneering reference to the low social status of many grammarians might fit in with Seneca's somewhat dim view of the profession.[28]

This view also requires reinterpreting Seneca's last sentence: *utar non tantum tamquam recepto sed tamquam usitato* "I will use it not so much as a word that has been fully accepted (*recepto*) but rather as an ordinary one."[29] Like *redigere*, the verb *recipere* also has a terminological meaning in connection with Roman citizens, of being "formally acknowledged."[30] Here it stands in contrast to the linguistic term *usitatus* "ordinary." This formulation only sounds paradoxical in the context of a modern nation state, where citizenship is typically assumed to be an ordinary status. By contrast, despite Rome's willingness to incorporate conquered elites, full citizenship was still a mark of distinction that was not shared by most urban inhabitants, many of whom were slaves and resident aliens.

On this view, Seneca appears to be proposing limited toleration of the word *analogia* as a word with Latin municipal status (*ius Latium*) without accepting it as a full Roman citizen. This explains why he preserves the Greek inflection (-*an*) and supplies a native Latin alternative (*conlatio*). He uses the word only once more before dropping it entirely (*epist.* 120.5 *quae sit haec analogia dicam . . .*). The philosophical context is also relevant. As mentioned, Seneca is taking *analogia* from the Stoic theory of mind to describe a process of inferential reasoning about virtue, whereas previous Latin writers had apparently confined their use of *analogia* to grammatical description.[31] Seneca

---

[28] Compare Seneca's attitude to the loanword *aetiologian* (*epist.* 95.65): *his adicit causarum inquisitionem, aetiologian quam quare nos dicere non audeamus, cum grammatici, custodes Latini sermonis, suo iure ita appellent, non video.* He expresses disdain for grammarians, e.g., *epist.* 48.11 *ad grammaticorum elementa descenditis*; 58.5 *ut ostendam, quantum tempus apud grammaticum perdiderim*; cf. *epist.* 27.7 and 108.30. This dismissive attitude toward the grammarian resembles that of Gellius as described by Holford-Strevens (2003, 172): "Gellius, purveyor of much grammatical information, despises professional *grammatici* both intellectually and socially. He prides himself on not providing elementary instruction. . . ." See further in Chapter 11.

[29] Deleting *tantum* (a mistake in anticipation of *tamquam*?) provides an even smoother sense. I have translated here as "so much," but it *non tantum . . . sed* could also be "not only . . . but (also)." In that case, *recepto* would mean "accepted" with respect to *ius Latium*.

[30] E.g., Cic. *Arch.* 22 (Ennius) *maiores nostri in civitatem receperunt*; *dom.* 78 *quidam non prius hanc civitatem amittebant, quam erant in eam recepti, quo . . . mutandi soli causa venerant*; *Balb.* 32 *ne quem populus Romanus Gaditanum recipiat civitate*; *rep.* 2.35.

[31] I am grateful to an anonymous reader for emphasizing this point. The letter is perhaps in dialogue with Cic. *fin.* 3.33 (= *SVF* III 72), where Cicero uses the phrase *collatio rationis* to describe this kind of reasoning: *cumque rerum notiones in animis fiant, si aut usu aliquid cognitum sit aut coniunctione aut similitudine aut collatione rationis, hoc quarto, quod extremum posui, boni notitia*

CIVIC METAPHORS FOR LEXICAL BORROWING   183

would then be saying: since the word has been adopted by Latin-speaking grammarians, let us send it back to their domain (i.e., grammar), but let us try to avoid it in general conversation or philosophical discussion.[32]

5. Quintilian

Despite being favorably disposed to the lexical diversity of Latin, Quintilian provides an unexpected negative twist on the citizenship metaphor (8.1.2–3):

> sed ea quae de ratione Latine atque emendate loquendi fuerunt dicenda in libro primo, cum de grammatice loqueremur, executi sumus. verum illic tantum ne vitiosa essent praecepimus: hic non alienum est admonere ut sint quam minime peregrina et externa. multos enim, quibus loquendi ratio non desit, invenias quos curiose potius loqui dixeris quam Latine . . . quare, si fieri potest, et verba omnia et vox huius alumnum urbis oleant, ut oratio Romana plane videatur, non civitate donata.

> I have already, in discussing *grammatice* in Book One [*inst.* 1.5], said what was necessary about the principles of speaking pure and correct Latin. But there, my advice bore only on avoiding faults; here it is relevant to warn that there should be as few non-Roman or foreign words as possible. One can find many speakers, not lacking in linguistic understanding, whose style may be said to be pedantic rather than Latin. . . . If possible, then, let all our words and our pronunciation have a whiff of city breeding, so that our speech seems to be native Roman, not simply naturalized. (transl. Russell 2001)

Summing up his advice to avoid an excessively foreign or convoluted style, Quintilian contrasts language that "smells like a nursling of the City" with

---

facta est. Seneca's toleration of the loanword *analogia*, which Cicero avoids, would be an implicit correction of the earlier author. The role of *analogia* in the Stoic theory of mind is discussed by Merry (2016, 205–7), e.g., *SVF* III 471 (Chrysippus cited by Galen).

[32] Other interpretations of this passage are possible, but *redigendum* as "return/reduce" seems necessary. One attractive alternative is to defend the transmitted text (without a second *puto*): *hoc verbum cum Latini grammatici civitate donaverint, ego damnandum non puto in civitatem suam redigendum. utar ergo illo non tantum tamquam recepto sed tamquam usitato.* In this version, Seneca simply acknowledges *analogia* as fully Latin and Roman and proposes that he will use it in its accepted and most common sense (but why then *analogian* with a Greek morpheme?).

184   SCHOLARS AND INTELLECTUALS

language that has merely "been granted citizenship." As usual, the metaphor describes a situation where the geographic origin of a word and its juridical status do not coincide, but uniquely Quintilian emphasizes the inferiority of naturalized words to their native counterparts. The vocabulary of nursing and rearing (*alumnus*) is significant: it implies a quasi-biological relationship between territory and inhabitant.[33] Quintilian also relies on a synesthetic metaphor, imputing an urban smell to specific kinds of language. As Benjamin Stevens has emphasized (2008), the sense of smell is closely tied to social cognition and the portrayal of class difference in antiquity.[34]

The verb *donare* itself also has darker connotations, capable of expressing not just generosity but also sometimes superiority and condescension (e.g., *OLD* s.v. 5 "to condone, excuse [faults in]"). This is a feature of gift exchange generally: a gift can sometimes be a form of aggression or a demonstration of social superiority, a way of "flattening" one's rivals, to use the language of the Tlingit potlatch.[35] This ambivalence is found in the changing significance of citizenship grants over the course of Roman imperialism. The earliest grants of Roman citizenships seem to have been punitive measures, intended to deprive neighboring rivals of their civic status and identity and forcibly assimilate them to the Roman commonwealth. As Clifford Ando notes (2016, 11), "Long after this practice had ceased, the language and symbolism of the forcible imposition of citizenship remained available, even into the late Republic, when the Romans described the concession of citizenship as a grant to those who had surrendered."[36] The negative connotation of *civitate donare* is perhaps sometimes perceptible in non-metaphoric contexts.[37]

It is perhaps surprising that Quintilian, an author well disposed to linguistic assimilation, as we have seen, nevertheless exploits the citizenship metaphor disparagingly, in order to emphasize the difference between native and assimilated vocabulary. This suggests that the metaphor itself is not consistently ideological, but that its ambivalence can be harnessed to emphasize

---

[33] See *OLD* s.v. *alumnus* 2a, e.g.: Cic. *Verr.* 2.5.169 *ut . . . Italia . . . alumnum suum servitutuis extremo . . . supplicio adfixum videret*; Verg. *Aen.* 6.877 *nec Romula quondam ullo se tantum tellus iactabit alumno*; Prop. 4.3.67 *Parthae telluris alumnis*.

[34] Stevens (2008, 164) also helpfully compares this passage of Quintilian to Cicero's *De oratore* (3.44), where he describes language smelling foreign: *quare cum sit quaedam certa vox Romani generis urbisque propria, in qua nihil offendi, nihil disiplicere, nihil animadverti possit, nihil sonare aut olere peregrinum, hanc sequamur* eqs.

[35] Mauss (1990, 41).

[36] Cicero also calls them *duo nequissimi Graeculi*. Ando cites Gran. Lic. 35.34 *dediticiis omnibus civita<s> data*. On early, forcible grants of citizenship see Lavan (2019, 2–3).

[37] For example, note the scorn in Cic. *Phil.* 13.33: *securi percussos Petraeum et Menedemum, civitate donatos et hospites Caesaris, laudastis* and compare Sen. *apocol.* 3.3, quoted above.

CIVIC METAPHORS FOR LEXICAL BORROWING   185

different nuances in different contexts. This ambivalence is rooted in turn in the contested history of Roman citizenship.

6. Gellius

Aulus Gellius provides the last and most elaborate instance of the metaphor. He relates a literary vignette from his youth under the Antonine emperors, whose context needs to be quoted in full (19.13.1–3):

> stabant forte una in vestibulo Palatii fabulantes Fronto Cornelius et Festus Postumius et Apollinaris Sulpicius, atque ego ibi adsistens cum quibusdam aliis sermones eorum quos de litterarum disciplinis habebant, curiosius captabam. (2) tum Fronto Apollinari "fac me," inquit, "oro, magister, ut sim certus, an recte supersederim 'nanos' dicere parva nimis statura homines maluerimque eos 'pumiliones' appellare, quoniam hoc scriptum esse in libris veterum memineram, 'nanos' autem sordidum essse verbum et barbarum credebam." (3) "est quidem" inquit "hoc" Apollinaris "in consuetudine inperiti vulgi frequens, sed barbarum non est censeturque linguae Graecae origine; νάνους enim Graeci vocaverunt brevi atque humili corpore homines paulum supra terram exstantes idque ita dixerunt adhibita quadam ratione etymologiae cum sententia vocabuli competente, et si memoria" inquit "mihi non labat, scriptum hoc est in comoedia Aristophanis, cui nomen est Ὁλκάδες (frg. 441 Kassel–Austin). **fuisset autem verbum hoc a te civitate donatum aut in Latinam coloniam deductum, si tu eo uti dignatus fores,** essetque id inpendio probabilius quam quae a Laberio ignobilia nimis et sordentia in usum linguae Latinae intromissa sunt."

> Cornelius Fronto, Festus Postumius, and Sulpicius Apollinaris chanced to be standing and talking together in the vestibule of the Palace; and I, being near by with some companions, eagerly listened to their conversations on literary subjects. Then said Fronto to Apollinaris: "I pray you, Sir, inform me whether I was right in forbearing to call men of excessively small stature *nani* and in preferring the term *pumiliones*; for I remembered that the latter word appears in the books of early writers, while I thought that *nani* was vulgar and barbarous." "It is true," replied Apollinaris, "that the word *nani* is frequent in the language of the ignorant vulgar; yet it is not barbarous, but is thought to be of Greek origin; for the Greeks called men of short and

186 SCHOLARS AND INTELLECTUALS

low stature, rising but little above the ground, νάνοι, or 'dwarfs,' using that word by the application of a certain etymological principle corresponding with its meaning,[38] and if my memory is not at fault," said he, "it occurs in the comedy of Aristophanes entitled Ὁλκάδες, or *The Cargo Boats* [frg. 441 Kassel–Austin]. **But this word would have been given citizenship by you, or established in a Latin colony, if you had deigned to use it,** and it would be very much more acceptable than the low and vulgar words which Laberius introduced into the Latin language." (transl. Rolfe 1927)

It is significant that this learned exchange takes place in the vestibule of the imperial palace on the Palatine, a location that recalls the encounter between Tiberius and Porcellus.[39] Indeed, the scholar Sulpicius Apollinaris, Gellius' own teacher and a skilled ironist, almost self-consciously plays the role of Ateius Capito as flatterer.[40] Standing in for the emperor is the emperor's close confidant, Cornelius Fronto. Discussing the status of the Greek loanword *nanus* "dwarf," Apollinaris claims that Fronto's usage of the word would be sufficient to grant it either citizenship or Latin status (*civitate donatum aut in Latinam coloniam deductum*). In this re-enactment, however, there is no outspoken Porcellus to contest this claim, and Fronto silently accepts the apparent compliment.

Given Apollinaris' ironic demolition of pseudo-scholars elsewhere in Gellius (the episode at 18.4 is especially relevant), one should not accept his extravagant praise of Fronto at face value. It would be extraordinary for Fronto to have the power to naturalize foreign vocabulary that was denied to emperors. Apollinaris is partly teasing Fronto for his excessive fastidiousness in avoiding *nanus*, without descending to outright mockery of a well-respected rhetor.[41] As Gellius' narrative continues, Apollinaris' lexical instinct

---

[38] Orion's *Etymologicum* (p. 108.18 Sturz) offers a native Greek etymology to which Apollinaris might be referring: ἄνω "up" with a prefixed nu privative ν- yields νάνος, ὁ μὴ αὐξανόμενος ("a dwarf, the one does not grow").

[39] This entire exchange has been well discussed by Alessandro Garcea and Valeria Lomanto (2004) in the context of Gellius' view of loanwords and of Laberius, the usage of *nanus*, and Roman grammatical theory more generally.

[40] On the grammarian Apollinaris (not to be confused with the fifth-century Sidonius, discussed by Mari in Chapter 6) and his portrayal by Gellius see Holford-Strevens (2003, 83–6). In another episode (18.4), Gellius ascribes to him "that kind of witty irony which Socrates used against the sophists" (18.4.1 *genere illo facetissimae dissimulationis, qua Socrates ad sophistas utebatur*).

[41] On Fronto see Holford-Strevens (2003, 131–9). On the use of *nanus* and *pumilio* in Latin see especially Garcea and Lomanto (2004, 41–4, 50–2) and Panayotakis (2010, 121–2; commenting on Laberius frg. 2). The *Suda* associates dwarves with large genitalia (ν 26 καὶ ὁ Θεόφραστος ὡς νᾶνον καὶ αἰδοῖον ἔχοντα μέγα. οἱ γοῦν νᾶνοι μέγα αἰδοῖον ἔχουσιν, quoted by Kassel–Austin), which might have contributed to the word's disrepute.

CIVIC METAPHORS FOR LEXICAL BORROWING   187

is partly confirmed as it turns out that the borrowing is attested in Helvius Cinna, at least with reference to animals (frg. 9 Blänsdorf *bigis . . . nanis* "with dwarf steeds"). Gellius elsewhere notes that *nanus* occurred in Laberius' mimes (16.7.10 = frg. 2 Panayotakis), but clearly such a source known for vulgar coinages would not have allayed Fronto's puristic concern.

Though the elaborate discrimination of Apollinaris' reply is part of its humor (*est quidem . . . in consuetudine inperiti vulgi frequens, sed barbarum non est . . .*), it nevertheless speaks to the literary and lexical sensitivity that educated Romans were encouraged to cultivate, especially in distinguishing fine gradations of style and semantic nuances. In particular, Apollinaris provides a twist on the familiar citizenship metaphor by distinguishing between a grant of full Roman citizenship and the less prestigious acquisition of the Latin right (*ius Latium, ius Latii,* or *Latinitas*).[42] If my reading of Seneca is correct, he is alluding to the same distinction in his discussion of the loanword *analogia. Ius Latium* was a kind of second-tier citizenship, which developed out of the bundle of reciprocal rights held by Rome's Latin allies and was later used in Roman colonial ventures. Besides providing marital and commercial rights, it also automatically enrolled local magistrates as Roman citizens, thus providing a mechanism for enfranchising provincial notables. Starting with Augustus, emperors granted numerous communities Latin rights as a compromise short of full citizenship status.[43]

The distinction between "Latin right" loanwords and "full citizen" loanwords may sound deliberately far-fetched, but it shows how the complexity of Roman civic status could be exploited to describe subtle gradations of lexical foreignness. In Apollinaris' implicit lexical hierarchy, *barbarum* is the lowest rung, describing words not fit to be used. *Nanus* belongs to a somewhat higher level, as a word that is foreign word but acceptable, associated with the *vulgus imperitum*.[44] Above this are two higher rungs of dignity that

---

[42] On *ius Latium* see the summary by Lavan (2019, 7–9).

[43] It may be relevant that at some point in the middle of the second century, an enhanced form of Latin right, the *Latium maius*, was introduced, which granted citizenship to a community's entire senate, rather than just the chief magistrates (Lavan 2019, 37–8). Did this give renewed prominence to the Latin right in the period when Gellius was writing? The only two known or inferred cases of *Latium maius* belong to Africa Proconsularis (Gigthis and Thisiduo). Fronto was born in nearby Numidia, and an African origin has sometimes been suspected for Gellius.

[44] It is difficult to confirm or deny this stylistic evaluation based on the sparse attestations of *nanus* in relation to *pumilio*. Both words are found in post-classical prose (e.g., Suet. *Tib.* 61.6, Arnob. *nat.* 3.14 p. 172.22) and relatively informal verse (e.g., Iuv. 8.32, Laber. *mim.* frg. 3 Panayotakis, Anth. 209.2). However, it is surely significant that *nanus* survives in multiple Romance languages (e.g., Sardian *nano*, French *nain*, Spanish *enano*, and so on), whereas *pumilio* does not.

188   SCHOLARS AND INTELLECTUALS

nanus could attain if it were used by the right *auctoritas*, namely *ius Latium* and ultimately full *civitas Romana*.

7. Conclusions

The highly reticulated system of Roman citizenship provided Roman writers with a valuable tool for imagining and understanding the Latin language, especially its relationship to foreign languages. At the same time, by projecting Roman institutions onto Latin vocabulary, Roman authors reveal something about how they viewed their own society and themselves. The different instances of the metaphor do not illustrate a straightforward linear progression of some kind; instead we find different authors exploiting and developing different possibilities of expression inherent to a single metaphor. Nevertheless, a few common features can be identified. All authors operate with the assumption that Latin should behave like Roman society in its handling of foreign elements. At the same time, the metaphor reveals some of the fault lines and points of contestation inherent to Roman identity. *Civitate donatus* could be turned into an insult or positioned as the less desirable alternative in contrast to other forms of identity, based on class and geography.

There are perhaps historical reasons why this metaphor clusters within a relatively narrow, hundred-year period, from Seneca to Gellius. This was a period of civic experimentation and change. Emperors energetically granted individuals and communities different bundles of rights, ranging from different kinds of Latin status to full citizenship. Nevertheless, citizenship still remained a minority right within the geographic expanse of the empire, leaving a gap between the conquerors and the conquered, which was not erased until the Edict of Caracalla (*Constitutio Antoniniana*) in 212. Before the edict, the political pressures that this situation generated may have lent greater prominence and potency to the metaphor of lexical citizenship. After the situation was considerably simplified in 212, the metaphor simply vanishes among the sources.[45] Presumably the cognitive salience of citizenship decreased as it became more widespread. Other forms of identity correspondingly assumed greater importance, such as the distinction

---

[45] A distant echo of this metaphor in Macrobius' *Saturnalia*, where he mentions the *ius suffragii* of literary authors to shape correct usage, is discussed in n. 23. A reference in the early fifth century to popular elections seems wistfully antiquarian; in any case, it is not used to describe loanwords, but the preservation of archaic constructions in contemporary usage.

CIVIC METAPHORS FOR LEXICAL BORROWING 189

between *honestiores* and *humiliores*. The Roman grammarians active between the fourth and sixth centuries, who were professionally concerned with patrolling the boundaries of Latinity, apparently show no interest in the metaphor of citizenship.

This metaphor also promotes a certain view of Latin, and of language in general, as a society based on consensual or contractarian ties.[46] This is of course only one way of viewing or conceptualizing language; it can also understood in relation to other elements, such as natural kinship (*patrius sermo*), divine revelation (especially prominent in descriptions of Hebrew as a *lingua divina* or *sacra*), or natural-biological development (which characterizes nineteenth-century linguistics). All these viewpoints jostle against one another in antiquity, sometimes in the same author. Nevertheless, this juridical conception of language, if it can be called that, seems to be especially prominent among Roman authors, and it can be opposed to a shallow linguistic naturalism, according to which language is a natural force entirely outside the control of human agency. Instead, Romans were keen to emphasize the constructed and inter-subjective nature of language, making it into a collective project, much like their own commonwealth.

This juridical slant is apparent in other ways that Romans spoke about language: for example, in terms of *societas* "partnership" and in the juridical terminology Horace used to discuss the *licentia* of "coining" new words (*ars* 51, 59).[47] It is also apparent, for instance, in Quintilian's portrayal of linguistic analogy as something (*inst.* 1.6.16) "not sent down from heaven to frame the rules of language when men were first created, but (rather) was discovered only when they were already using language." This viewpoint is also given memorable expression in a text preserved by Charisius, but which has been plausibly attributed to Pliny the Elder or another first-century author (Char. *gramm.* p. 61.16, 62.2–10):

> ne ipsa quidem rerum natura tam finita est ut nobis . . . (ca. 8 letters missing) . . . Latinus vero sermo cum ipso homine civitatis suae natus significandis intellegundisque quae diceret praesto fuit (praestitit *trad.*). postquam plane supervenientibus saeculis accepit artifices et solertiae

---

[46] See Ando (2015, 13).

[47] E.g., Cic. *de orat.* 3.223 *verba enim neminem movent nisi eum, qui eiusdem linguae societate coniunctus est, sententiae que saepe acutae non acutorum hominum sensus praetervolant*; Varro *ling.* 6.5.40 *quod neque his fere societas cum Graeca lingua*; Ps.-Prob. *gramm.* IV 49.29 *nullius vocalium egeant societate*; Cassiod. *gramm.* VI p. 182.12 *nomina cum verbis habent societatem*. On Horace's hesitation between naturalist and artificial conceptions of language, see Dufallo (2005).

190 SCHOLARS AND INTELLECTUALS

> nostrae observationibus captus est, paucis admodum partibus orationis normae suae dissentientibus, regendum se regulae tradidit et illam loquendi licentiam servituti rationis addixit. quae ratio adeo cum ipsa loquella generata est ut hodie nihil de suo analogia inferat.

> Not even nature is finished in such a way that it. . . As to the Latin language, it was born at the same time as the people of its state and so was at hand in order to express and understand what they said. As time went by, it drew the attention of the writers of handbooks and was tied down by what we cleverly noted; though a very few words still conflicted with the system, it handed itself over to be governed by rule and subjected the old laxity of speech to the straitjacket of a system. This system came into existence so closely together with speech itself that nowadays analogy does not introduce anything from and by itself. (transl. Schenkeveld 1998)

This text, probably a preface to a grammatical treatise, makes the birth of the Latin language coincide with the birth of the Roman commonwealth. In language that is strikingly personified, it describes the creation and evolution of linguistic rules as a give-and-take or compact between grammarians and the language, which is both "captured" (*captus est*) but also willingly "handed itself over to be governed" (*regendum se . . . tradidit*). This ambivalence evokes the ambivalent position of the Roman imperial subject, who was supposed to be thoroughly conquered, on the one hand, but also a willing participant in Roman civic institutions, on the other—Virgil's *parcere subiectis et debellare superbos* (*Aen.* 6.853).

It also brings us full-circle back to Porcellus' vision of the linguistic commonwealth. Unlike in many ancient visions of glottogenesis, here there is no king or philosophical name-giver dictating terms, as we find in Plato's *Cratylus* and hinted at in Varro's *De lingua Latina* (e.g., 5.8). Instead the Latin language is closely identified with the citizenry itself (*cum ipso homine civitatis*), what Varro calls the *populus* (see n. 23). In this linguistic republic, there is no obvious place for an emperor to enfranchise either words or people.

11

Grammar and Grammarians, Linguistic and Social Change from Gellius to Macrobius

Leofranc Holford-Strevens*

In his grammatical discussions, almost all on Latin matters, Gellius frequently expresses scorn for normative grammarians whose rules are not supported by the pre-Ciceronian authors whom they have not read. He asserts that there is no reason why *opus est* must be constructed with the ablative *nisi qui grammaticorum nova instituta ut θεμένων ἱερά observant* ("unless people observe the new rules of the grammarians as if they had laid down sacred laws," 17.2.15);[1] a *semidoctus* grammarian, unaware that *frons* used to be masculine, has to take Gellius' examples on trust, demanding instead a justification, which he supposes him not to have (15.9.6): *at ille semidoctus grammaticus "missas," inquit, "auctoritates facias, quas quidem ut habeas posse fieri puto, sed rationem dic, quam non habes"* ("but that half-educated grammarian said, 'Never mind your authorities, which I suppose it's possible that you have, but state the principle, which you have not.'"). Gellius, who despises artificial rules not based on authoritative usage, retorts by inventing an explicitly unsound justification (15.9.7 *"audi," inquam, "mi magister, rationem falsam quidem, sed quam redarguere falsam esse tu non queas"*; "'Hear,' said I, 'my good schoolmaster, a principle, false to be sure, but one

---

* It is at once a great honour and a great pleasure to participate in the tricennalia of that admirable book, *Guardians of Language*, yet at the same time a cause of embarrassment, in that it is hard to tell its author something on the subject of grammarians that he does not already know, and smacks a mite of impudence to tell him what he does. *Sed tamen*, as Cicero said in a far worse cause, *qui semel verecundiae finis transierit, eum bene et naviter oportet esse impudentem (fam.* 5.12.3).

[1] So the manuscripts; editors who printed τεμενῶν failed to recognize the aorist participle middle of τίθημι. Claudius Quadrigarius, Gellius' favourite historian, many of whose linguistic oddities and archaisms are listed in this chapter, had written *nil sibi divitias opus esse*, not *divitiis*.

Leofranc Holford-Strevens, *Grammar and Grammarians, Linguistic and Social Change from Gellius to Macrobius*
In: *Roman Perspectives on Linguistic Diversity.* Edited by Adam Gitner, Oxford University Press.
© Oxford University Press 2023. DOI: 10.1093/oso/9780197611975.003.0011

192   SCHOLARS AND INTELLECTUALS

you cannot prove false' "), which sure enough the grammarian proves unable to refute.[2]

The average schoolmaster with his simplistic rules of thumb has not caught up with the revival of early Latin. But simplistic rules of thumb have their place in teaching children before they are old enough to put the exceptions in context, especially when, as in Gellius' time, there is an increasing divergence between the literary language and the spoken *consuetudo*.[3] Inclusion of the pre-classical authors would merely have brought confusion.

Nevertheless, there was, once one had grown out of the schoolroom, a vogue for linguistic renewal by reviving usages that had gone out of fashion in the time of Cicero or even before; this archaism was not confined to the emperor Hadrian and the triad of Fronto, Gellius, and Apuleius, for there are traces of it in Suetonius (Holford-Strevens 2003, 51, 355), who has been commonly believed immune to it. However, it did not take the same form in all authors: while Gellius, like Hadrian as it seems, seeks to expel from the literary language usages not attested before the time of Augustus, there is no sign of this in either Apuleius or Fronto, once we have separated the real Fronto from the character "Fronto" in Gellius' dialogues (Holford-Strevens 2017, 202–4). It is of course no surprise that, like Britons who inveigh against Americanisms in modern English, he picks on a few while others slip by unnoticed, nor that he sometimes overlooks examples in approved authors: *profligare*, for instance, is used in the disallowed sense of "nearly finish" more than once by Cicero.[4] Moreover, his practice does not always match his theory, as when at 16.11.7 he uses the plural *harenae* for which an unnamed poet is rebuked at 19.8.3 because Caesar had maintained it did not exist.[5]

Sometimes Gellius is content to note that usage has changed: the invariable future infinitive in -*urum* is no longer recognized (1.7); the oblique cases

---

[2] The false rule is that substantives in -*ons -ontis* are masculine, refuted by **spons spontis* feminine, which escaped the grammarian because the nominative was not in use.

[3] The pedagogic context is discussed in more detail by James Zetzel (Chapter 1). To be sure, simplistic rules will also have a place in teaching Latin to native Greek speakers, especially after the establishment of a Latinate capital in Constantinople; see, for example, Rochette on Diomedes (Chapter 5) and Garcea and Scappaticcio (Chapter 9) on teaching Juvenal in the sixth century.

[4] Gellius classes this usage with the changes of sense created *ignoratione et inscitia improbe dicentium quae non intelligant* (15.5.1); the correct verb, in his opinion, is *adficere*. However, "nearly finish" is the sense at Cic. *Prov.* 35, *Tusc.* 5.15 (cited by Non. p. 237 Lindsay [= p. 161 M.]), cf. Lentulus at Cic. *fam.* 12.14.2; see *TLL* X.2.1725.1–31.

[5] See Caes. *anal.* frgg. 11A–B Garcea; Fronto, the speaker in the dialogue, is Gellius' mouthpiece, expressing a restrictive purism alien to his real self, who in fact uses the plural at *M. Caes.* 1.6.5 (= p. 11.30 van den Hout 1988).

of *Hannibal* no longer have a long third syllable (4.7); "twenty-second" is no longer *duovicesimus* (5.4), nor is the reduplicating syllable in perfects formed with *e* (6.9); fifth-declension dative and genitive endings are no longer monosyllabic (9.14); *elegans* had ceased to be pejorative by Cicero's day (11.2); the vocative of *Valerius* is no longer accented *Váleri* (13.26);[6] but on other occasions there is censure: those who criticize Vergil's use of *vexo*, *inlaudatus*, and *squaleo* do so *inprobe* (2.6 cap.), it was a man of insufficient education who failed to understand that *deprecor* might be said, as by Catullus, of cursing or averting (7.16), the meaning "quickly" bestowed on *mature* is contrary to its proper sense (10.11), it is modern ignorance that has restricted *facies* to the human countenance (13.30), changed the meaning of *profligare* (15.5), and transferred *vestibulum* from the access to the atrium (16.5).

Whereas Gellius is willing to use the term *grammaticus* of the unassailable Probus and Terentius Scaurus, reportedly a teacher of Hadrian and perhaps related to a governor of Dacia, he does not apply it to his own teacher Sulpicius Apollinaris, never writing *Sulpicius grammaticus* as he does time and again *Favorinus philosophus*; the nearest he comes to it is by association (7.6.12 *adulescens ego Romae, cum etiamtum ad grammaticos itarem, audivi Apollinarem Sulpicium, quem imprimis sectabar* . . . ; "as a young man at Rome, when I still frequented the grammarians, I heard Sulpicius Apollinaris, whose lessons I especially attended"). Although Sulpicius was a *grammaticus*, he clearly prefers to treat him as a scholar on a par with himself, to whom even in disagreement (2.16.10, 12.13.21) he shows the respect he does not to others. Evidently Gellius wished to present him as intellectually superior to the common-or-garden *grammaticus*; but since he also presents him as engaging with such eminent men as Sex. Erucius Clarus, twice consul and prefect of the city (7.6.12; 13.8.2–3), and the consular orators M. Cornelius Fronto and M. Postumius Festus (19.13), one may surmise that Sulpicius of Carthage, like Galen of Pergamum though without his preening bumptiousness, despite keeping a school,[7] enjoyed a higher social status than his run-of-the-mill competitors and therefore was not to be represented as of their company.[8]

However that may be, Gellius speaks from a position not only of gentlemanly but of Platonic superiority to those who taught for money, Sulpicius

[6] On this passage see Probert (2019, 269–74).
[7] Subsequently taken over by his former pupil Helvius Pertinax (hist. Aug. *Pert.* 1.4).
[8] On the social status of *grammatici* in this period, Gellius's attitude toward them, and the exceptional place of Sulpicius see *Guardians* 50–60, 65; Holford-Strevens (2003, 84–6, 172–3).

194   SCHOLARS AND INTELLECTUALS

excepted: a grammarian defeated by the expression *caninum prandium* covers his retreat with the words *talia gratis ego non doceo* (13.31.12–13), echoing Thrasymachus in the *Republic* (1.337D);[9] others are exposed by Socratic interrogations explicitly so described (4.1 cap., 18.4.1). One of them admits to a Trimalchionic non-interest in philosophy (4.1.13; cf. Petron. *sat.* 71.12); this puts him on a par with those other specialists, the lawyer who knows nothing of grammar or even of legal antiquities (16.10)[10] and the grammarian who knows nothing of law (20.10). Yet we may observe a difference: the lawyer, a *familiaris* of Gellius, being a jurisconsult who provides knowledge of the law rather than a teacher or a draftsman who makes his living by it,[11] escapes censure; the grammarians are treated with scorn.

There was no need to state openly that this scorn was social as well as intellectual; Gellius' readers, clearly envisaged as belonging to what passed at Rome for the leisured class (praef. 16, 19), would surely have shared it, as their counterparts in other times and places have done, but might have thought that Gellius himself was not grand enough for such airs. Certainly there were grammarians who could not pass for members of polite society: Porphyrio indeed, a man not devoid of merit as an instructor of schoolboys but neither a man of the people nor a gentleman, was ignorant alike of the amphitheatre and the triclinium,[12] as if a modern schoolmaster should have never attended either a football match or a black-tie dinner. Others were more presentable: Sulpicius, as we have seen, engaged both professionally and socially with men of consular rank; Cornelianus rose to be *ab epistulis Graecis* to Marcus, and Atticized official documents (Phrynichus, Ἐκλογή 231, 357). But although Juvenal's picture of the ill-paid schoolmaster who has to sue for his salary (*sat.* 7.215–53, esp. 228–9)[13] may exhibit his familiar exaggeration, the standing of the profession was not particularly high.

---

[9] However, Thrasymachus speaks once paid, whereas Gellius' charlatans make good their escape (13.31.13, 18.4.9, 19.10.14).

[10] On jurists' attitude to legal history see Mantovani (2018, 120–83); on their linguistic attitudes see Ferri in this volume (Chapter 12).

[11] Although by this time senatorial jurists had largely given way to equestrian, the ethos of the calling had not changed (Kunkel 1967, 291, 335–6).

[12] Diederich (1999, 76 with nn. 389–90). At Hor. *epist.* 1.18.66 *fautor utroque tuum laudabit pollice ludum* he comments VTROQVE POLLICE *utraque manu. tropos synecdoche: a parte totum*, not knowing how spectators signalled that the defeated gladiator should be killed or spared; at *serm.* 1. 4. 88, glossing *praeter eum qui praebet aquam* with *id est qui pascit*, he does not know that the host would provide water for his guests to wash their hands.

[13] For fifth-century marginalia on these lines, see Garcea and Scappaticcio in this volume (Chapter 9).

GRAMMAR AND GRAMMARIANS 195

Neither Fronto nor Gellius had any permanent influence on Latin style; Apuleius had a Christian successor in Tertullian, and license to write oddly was arrogated by the Lucretianizing Arnobius and the remorselessly perverse Julius Valerius; but for the most part even adherents of the new faith like Minucius Felix and Lactantius obeyed the by then thoroughly time-hallowed dictates of the grammarians, as did exponents of the late antique floridity that left imperial constitutions in need of plain-language *interpretationes*[14] and rendered Sidonius' prose more opaque than his verse. These dictates became all the more necessary as ordinary speech departed more and more from the written norm; with this increase in grammarians' importance came an increase in their social status, if not in their wealth (*Guardians* 99–134, 201–30). Whereas Suetonius had written about grammarians just as he had written in the same book about rhetors and in another about whores, but nowhere in his imperial biographies named the *grammatici* who taught the Caesars, the *Historia Augusta* readily imparts the corresponding information, even if not all of it is genuine. Already grammarians had at least risen far enough in public esteem for Ausonius—who himself rose the highest of all—to celebrate the Bordelais grammarians in verse along with the rhetors; they ranged in origin from the sons of freedmen to a scion of the Republican *nobilitas*,[15] but these appear to be exceptional. Those who (like Ausonius) entered the imperial service did so only after becoming rhetors; to the rhetor, who had the opportunity to flaunt his skills, belonged prestige (*Guardians* 104–5, 204–5), but the grammarian enjoyed the respect accruing to those who imparted the élite acquisitions of correct Latin and literary culture, provided that they possessed the moral qualities valued by the upper class. These included knowing how to conduct a friendship with one's social superior (Libanius, *Epistulae* 1256.3 τὸν δὲ ὁμώνυμόν σοι γραμματιστὴν ἄνδρα τε ἀγαθὸν ἡγοῦ καὶ λόγων ἔμπειρον ὅτι πλείστων καὶ ἐν τοῖς φιλεῖν ἐπισταμένοις γράφου; "consider your schoolmaster namesake a good man practiced in as many topics as can be and register him amongst those who understand how to be a friend"), a lesson Gellius had already discerned in Ennius' verses on Servilius' good companion (Gell. 12.4.1); but while Stilo

---

[14] Examples abound in the Codex Theodosianus; the worst excesses are purged in Justinian's Code, but the Latin text of Constitutio *Tanta*/Δέδωκεν ratifying the Digest (*dig.* praef. 3; cf. *cod. Iust.* 1.17.2) is considerably more extravagant than the Greek.

[15] Respectively Crispus and Urbicus, *liberti ambo genus* (*Comm. prof.* 21.27 Green = 211.27 Souchay), and Acilius Glabrio, *stemmate nobilium deductum nomen avorum* (*Comm. prof.* 24.3 Green = 214.3 Souchay), whose line had been ennobled by the consul of 191 BCE and continued to provide consuls down to 256 CE or even 438.

196 SCHOLARS AND INTELLECTUALS

had allegedly thought them the poet's self-portrait (ibid. §5), and Gellius perhaps had in mind his own position as the guest but never the host of great men, not even Sulpicius is represented in that light.

A few generations after Ausonius, when grammarians were continuing to rise, Macrobius can include Servius in the company at his *Saturnalia*,[16] grander than that at either Plutarch's or Athenaeus' banquets, which are also (unlike any dinner described by Gellius) attended by grammarians. He is represented as no ordinary schoolmaster (such a person would never have been invited) and as surpassing the *grammatici* of old, even though he is still an *adulescens* (*Sat.* 7.11.2). The shyness that makes him attempt to creep in unnoticed (1.2.15) is therefore the product not merely of his youth (it is quite alien to that other *adulescens* Avienus before he taught his manners by Praetextatus), nor of his having only just begun to teach; he is by no means sure that intellectually or socially he belongs in this exalted company. The former doubts are dissipated when Symmachus invites him to defend Caecina's Latinity against Avienus (1.4.4), the latter by Praetextatus' support in the ensuing altercation about the value of expertise in obsolete usage (1.5.4); when the parts in the forthcoming discussion of Vergil are assigned, it is Avienus who makes the gesture of insisting that Servius be consulted about obscurities (1.24.20). That does not mean he will speak about Vergil's knowledge of learned disciplines other than grammar, despite Symmachus' complaint that grammarians leave such things alone (1.14.21–4); the others present are capable of expounding them themselves, but Servius is the expert at explaining words. He is still reluctant to speak outside his brief when it is his turn to tell a joke; this brings upon his head the insulting address *grammatice* from the boorish Evangelus (2.2.12), an echo like much else of Athenaeus, whose boorish Cynulcus addresses Myrtilos ὦ γραμματικέ (*Deip.* 13.610c). This allows Athenaeus, in Myrtilos' reply, to discharge another fusillade against philosophers, and in particular Cynics (610D–612F); in Macrobius (as opposed to others in his day and afterwards) there is no such battle of the professions, but Evangelus' speech, for all its discourtesy (and its utter unfairness to Dysarius and Horus, who are not yet due to speak), jolts Servius out of his reticence with the assertion that Servius means to tax everyone else with *impudentia*, a monstrous representation but a warning, no less useful now than then, that in the wrong circumstances *verecundia* may

[16] For social commentary see Kaster (1980b).

GRAMMAR AND GRAMMARIANS 197

be mistaken for arrogance.[17] Having been admitted as an equal, he needs to behave like one.

Of course Servius' presence, even as an *adulescens*, is one of the anachronisms that Macrobius has justified by Platonic precedent (*Sat.* 1.1.5–6); but that underlines his insistence on having him there, grammarian that he is, and rather than any other grammarian; so far ahead is he of the common schoolmaster that it would be an insult to make him answer Evangelus' village-atheist quibbles against Vergil (*Sat.* 1.24.8). He was the outstanding grammarian of Macrobius' lifetime; by the dramatic date Donatus was no doubt already dead, and no one of the right age seemed up to scratch.

But how ought one to address a grammarian? Here we must bear in mind the general difference pointed out by Eleanor Dickey between Greek and Roman forms of address, that whereas in Greek address by name remained the norm amongst free men at least in the written language, except of course to kings, in Latin it gave way to titles in the early empire (Dickey 2002, 45, 239). In Gellius grammarians are freely called *magister*, from the most respectful context (19.13.2) to the least (4.1.4)[18] or in Socratic irony (18.4.2), be they anonymous *Scheingelehrte* or named persons; Favorinus so addresses Domitius Insanus, as Fronto does Sulpicius Apollinaris; the same term had already been used by Trimalchio to the rhetor Agamemnon (Petron. *sat.* 55.5) and is Marcus Aurelius' constant address to Fronto. By contrast, *grammatice* is used in Gellius only by one grammarian to another, and that only as a prop for the disputed vocative of *egregius* in a sardonic riposte with the implication that the other man is not really an outstanding grammarian at all (14.5.3). In Greek, διδάσκαλε is almost confined to the Gospels, where it represents *rabbī* or *rabbōnī*,[19] and the innumerable quotations therefrom, though in Lucian it is addressed to a philosopher (*Gallus* 10) and playfully to Palaistra (*Asinus* 10) as instructress in wrestling, or rather in *clinopale*; however, it is found once in Athenaeus, amongst the additions to the vocative Μυρτίλε (9.386E). Whether in a reversion to Ciceronian usage, or in Hellenizing imitation of Athenaeus, Macrobius lets Servius be addressed as

---

[17] Observe Plato's use of θρύπτεσθαι and καλλωπίζεσθαι for both pride (*Lg.* 777E6, *Phdr.* 252A5) and inappropriate silence (*Phdr.* 228C2, *Prot.* 333D1).

[18] Although "whoever you are" and "what's your name" are not in themselves insulting in Latin as they are in English (Dickey 2002, 252–3), *quidquid est nomen tibi*, an exact quotation (Plaut. *Pseud.* 639) from the prolonged skirmish between Pseudolus and Harpax, carries with it a context of disrespect.

[19] For the latter see John 20:16, whereas at Mark 10:51 the Greek text (ῥαββουνί) indicates an ō > ū shift also found in Phoenician.

198   SCHOLARS AND INTELLECTUALS

Servi (3.18.1, 7.11.2), on a par with the other participants; both Cynulcus' and Evangelus' rudeness consists in using the specific term, which as a vocative was evidently still degrading.

It is of course well known that this Servius bears no more resemblance to the real Servius than Gellius' Fronto to the real Fronto.[20] Whereas the Macrobian Servius plays his part in the parade of antique learning, not a little of it from Gellius, and introduces one such Gellian item in the best Gellian spirit (*Sat.* 6.9.9), complaining that the present age is puzzled by many things because it no longer reads Ennius and the other ancients, the real Servius eliminated from his commentary on Vergil most of the Republican examples he found in Donatus (Lloyd 1961). All that remains of Gellius is a reference to his exposition of the civil day (the discussion of *maturare* is found only in the expanded version); an author who by both precept and example commended the Latin of a time already bygone when Cicero wrote had little to offer a schoolmaster constantly engaged in telling the boys that a usage does not become acceptable in their writing just because it is in Vergil, whether because it is no longer current or because it constitutes a *figura*; reference to Ennius or Lucretius can serve only to spare the poet, not the pupil, censure, and when Servius on *Aen.* 7.289 warns that *abusque* is improperly formed because prepositions like *ab* must not be combined with other prepositions or with adverbs, one or other of which *usque* is, the last thing he needed was a justification from ancient authority of *praeterpropter* (Gell. 19.10). The battle against linguistic change could not be fought with museum-piece weapons.

[20] See Kaster (1980a, 219–21; 1980b, 255–8).

12

Language Variation and Grammatical Theory in Roman Legal Texts

*Rolando Ferri**

1. *Jurists and Grammarians*

In this contribution I intend to discuss passages by Roman jurists in which the language of a specific text is an object of legal controversy (typically wills, but also trusts, legacies, contracts, and legal texts, such as the Urban Praetor's Edict, which was fixed in the imperial period and the foundation of civil law), and in which jurists deploy linguistic and grammatical language to analyze that document.[1] My purpose is to chart common ground with or influence from ancient scholarship—primarily grammatical writers and commentators—at various levels of language analysis, from the study of the structure of the lexicon, language register and variation, and etymology, as well as morphosyntactic analysis and pragmatics.[2]

Jurists were consulted by judges, or local administrators, on points of law, but also on the interpretation of written evidence produced in court, such as contracts and wills, when a dispute arose among prospective and disappointed inheritors. Their opinions are therefore on record on very precise details of interpretation and were based on realistic cases, even if the names on the deeds have been anonymized to the fictional *Maevius, Titius*, and so

---

* My thanks to the editor, Adam Gitner, for his comments and help throughout, and to Dario Mantovani (*Collège de France*), for important corrections on many points.

[1] Much of the evidence for this chapter comes from book 50 of the Digest, which includes a section (or *titulus*) *De verborum significatione*, "The meaning of words"; the same title occurs also in the *Codex*, and earlier compilations may have included similar rubrics concerned with language definitions and ambiguities. Most of the other extracts I discuss here come from books 32–34 devoted to wills. All English translations from the Digest come from Watson (1985).

[2] Some references to discussions of grammar in jurisprudents' responses are in Wieacker (1989, 658, esp. n. 108); Horak (1969, 194–211); Stein (1971, 757–69). Contacts with grammatical thought and writers are the topic of Pavese (2013); connections with philosophical and linguistic discourse are also discussed in Mantovani (2018).

Rolando Ferri, *Language Variation and Grammatical Theory in Roman Legal Texts* In: *Roman Perspectives on Linguistic Diversity*. Edited by Adam Gitner, Oxford University Press. © Oxford University Press 2023. DOI: 10.1093/oso/9780197611975.003.0012

200 SCHOLARS AND INTELLECTUALS

on. Their language in casting their views on these matters shows affinities with not only the teaching of grammarians, but also with the language of commentators on the *auctores*, school authors, and other classics. *Iuris prudentes* and school grammarians and commentators deal with different types of textuality (the wills of common men and women versus the lofty epics and the artful comedies of the great poets), but both engage in close readings of written documents using similar rhetorical and grammatical tools. One of the main sources for legal reflection on language cited here is the Digest, a compilation promulgated by emperor Justinian in 533, drawing on a vast range of earlier legal texts dating back to the Late Republic.[3]

2. The Analysis of Lexical Meaning

Jurists were confronted with conflicts between the lexical and inferred meanings of a written text and tried to reconstruct the communicative intentions behind it. Expressions such as *voluntas scriptoris* as well as *voluntas* (or *mens*) *legis* are common.[4] Often reference is made to the accepted lexical meaning or a word, and to the sub-meanings that are contextually or situationally appropriate. The study of the "true" or proper meaning and of contextual, evolved, and figurative meanings were taught at the school of the grammarian, whose primary task was the teaching of correct language with the purpose of understanding, explaining, and preserving the text of the classical poets. Authors of *artes grammaticae* did not necessarily discuss "usage," since they were primarily concerned with "rules" of language, and in general their primary concern was morphology and morphological correctness, or the evolution of spelling diachronically. However, commentators on literary texts, such as Donatus or Servius, often discussed usage and meaning in context, so their work provides a convenient parallel for much of what legal sources say on *usus*.

The first area in which jurists and grammarians share common ground is that of the selection of the lexicon, and above all the definition of the proper

---

[3] Occasionally the compilers of the Digest made minor changes and additions to the sources they cited; the precise nature of these changes has been the subject of long and inconclusive debate (Lenel 1889 provides one attempted reconstruction of the original form of some of these sources). The dates of the jurists given in this essay come from Kunkel (1967).

[4] For a fuller discussion of this topic see Meyer (2004, 265–75), with bibliographical references. An important discussion can be found in Cicero, *Pro Caecina* 51–2, with the commentary of Frier (1985, 122).

LANGUAGE VARIATION AND GRAMMATICAL THEORY 201

meaning of words. For grammarians, words have a primary meaning, usually explained by their etymology (*propria significatio*), and extended and metaphorical meanings (*tralaticia,* or *abusive, usurpative*), as well as meanings assigned as sheer malapropisms or by mistake (*aliena, falsa significatio*).[5] Who determines the proper meaning of words? Grammatical writers tend to use arguments *ex auctoritate*, sometimes backed up by etymological explanations. As Quintilian sums up, the evaluation of language is based on "reason, antiquity, authority, and usage" (*inst.* 1.7.1 *sermo constat ratione, vetustate, auctoritate, consuetudine*). They also call upon *usus* as a supporting argument, preferably the usage of the classical writers, the *auctores.*

Jurists too are interested in the definition of the "proper" meaning, which they view as determined by *usus* or *consuetudo*, although etymology also plays a part in describing and explaining the primary meaning.[6] Meaning is not arbitrary, they argue, but some latitude is admissible when a testator was known to use words in an idiosyncratic way during his or her lifetime.[7] In the Digest there are no references to *auctoritas* to define the primary or appropriate meaning of a word against other extended meanings or ad hoc coinages; *usus* and *consuetudo* are the supporting arguments for a decision based on the meaning of an expression.

For example, in a fragment preserved by Ulpian, the Tiberian jurist Nerva thus outlines the literal and extended meanings of the word *bibliotheca*:

(1)   *Dig.* 32.52.7 (Ulpianus): eleganter Nerva ait interesse id quod testator
      senserit: nam et locum significari "bibliothecam eo": alias armarium,

---

[5] For an important survey of the ancient philosophical and linguistic theories about "proper" and "metaphorical" meanings of words see Zanker (2016, 164–90).

[6] An exhaustive study of etymologies produced by Roman jurists can be found in Ceci (1892); more recently, see Babusiaux (2014). Here I limit myself to an etymology in Ulpian for which a grammatical source can now be identified. Ulpian's etymology of *miles* in a *rubrica* devoted to hereditary prerogatives of the military closely resembles a passages in Festus-Paulus in which a similar etymology is assigned to "Aelius." Cf. *Dig.* 29.1.1.1 (Ulpianus) *miles autem appellatur vel a militia* (*malitia* Mommsen in app.), *id est duritia, quam pro nobis sustinent* ("The term 'soldier' is understood to have been derived from *militia*, that is to say *duritia*, the hardships which soldiers endure for us") = Paul. Fest. p. 122 (= 109.22–3 Lindsay) *militem Aelius a mollitia* κατὰ ἀντίφρασιν *dictum putat, eo, quod nihil molle, sed potius asperum quid gerat.* If this parallel is accepted, Ulpian must have written *mollitia*, and the banalization to *militia* must have occurred at an early date. The thought goes back to Stilo, even if another Aelius quoted by Festus was Aelius Gallus, a jurist who discussed the meaning of words used in civil law. However, as D. Mantovani pointed out to me, this type of etymology by antiphrasis, common in the grammatical tradition, is counterintuitive and not the expected procedure for a jurist.

[7] There was a philosophical tradition describing language as represented by various different and sometimes diverging linguistic "usages," as described at length by Sextus Empiricus *Adv. Math.* 228–35.

202   SCHOLARS AND INTELLECTUALS

sicuti dicimus "eboream bibliothecam emit": alias libros, sicuti dicimus "bibliothecam emisse."

Nerva elegantly says that what makes the difference is what the testator had in mind. For *bibliotheca* can mean a place as when we say, "I am going to the *bibliotheca*." At other times it can mean a cupboard, as when we say, "He bought an ivory *bibliotheca*." At other times it can mean books, as when we say, "He bought a *bibliotheca*."

Nerva here adopts a lexicographer's synchronic perspective and presents various senses of the lemma: first an extended meaning, "the place where books and their shelves are housed," then the etymological meaning, and finally a metonymical subsense, "a collection of books," not necessarily fitting a bookshelf. In several cases jurists point out the distinction between the proper and figurative or extended meaning of a word, also adding an indication of where this extended usage can be found and in what contexts of communication, typically "common speech," or the "current usage," as in (2):

(2)   *Dig.* 32.52.4 (Ulpianus): nam et in usu plerique libros chartas appellant.

In common usage most people call books "papyri." [That is they use the word *chartae* also signifying "white sheets," "sheets used for writing."]

Aelius Gallus was the author of a study of words used in civil law, and from his fragments—significantly transmitted by a Republican lexicographer, Verrius Flaccus, and his epitomator Pompeius Festus—comes (3), concerned with the proper meaning or correct usage (*recte dici*) of the word *flumen*, which can be used also in reference to water flowing in *torrentes* "brooks" in common speech:

(3)   Fest. p. 352 (= 482.34–484.4 Lindsay): quius (*lege* cuius, *sc.* torrentis) aquam ipsam, quae fluit, flumen recte dici ait Aelius Gallus lib. II. quae ad ius pertinent; ceterum volgi consuetudine utrumque iam dici flumen, et perennem fluvium et torrentem.

Aelius Gallus, in the second book of his *Words of Interest in the Study of the Law* says that "river" is the correct denomination for the water flowing in it, but in the common speech of the people both ever-flowing rivers and brooks are called "rivers."

LANGUAGE VARIATION AND GRAMMATICAL THEORY   203

(4)   *Dig.* 50.16.235 pr. idem (*sc.* Gaius): libro tertio ad legem duodecim tabularum. "ferri" proprie dicimus, quae quis suo corpore baiulat: "portari" ea, quae quis iumento secum ducit: "agi" ea, quae animalia sunt.

Gaius, XII Tables, book 3: Properly speaking we use "to be carried" of those things which someone transports with his body; "to be conveyed" of those things which someone takes with him on a beast of burden; "to be driven" of those things which are animals.

We do not know in what context Gaius asserted the distinction between *ferre* and *portare* (4),[8] but we find it mentioned in other sources, since confusion and overlapping of the two was common in informal and spoken language (*consuetudo*, see below), as we see in (5), an entry in the dictionary of the imperial lexicographer Nonius Marcellus:

(5)   Non. p. 302.18: "ferre" consuetudine "portare" dicimus.

By custom for *ferre* ["to carry"] we say *portare* ["to convey"].

This opposition between the "correct" or "proper" meaning of a word and the meaning assumed by the same word in ordinary speech is a leitmotif of Roman scholarship from Varro onward, in which a distinction is often drawn between the "archaic" and the "modern" sense of a word:

(6)   Gell. 9.1.8: animadvertendum est usum esse eum (*sc.* Quadrigarium) verbo "defendebant," non ex vulgari consuetudine, sed admodum proprie et Latine.

It should be noticed that he [i.e., Quadrigarius] used the word *defendebant*, not in the sense which it commonly has, but yet quite properly and in accordance with good Latin usage.

(7)   Ascon. *Corn.* p. 56.24–7 (= 71 Clark): iubet eum (*sc.* populum) is qui fert legem discedere: quod verbum non hoc significat quod in communi consuetudine, <ut ab>eant de eo loco ubi lex feratur, sed in suam quisque tribum discedat in qua est suffragium laturus.

---

[8] According to Humbert (2018, 352), Gaius was discussing *leg. XII tab. 7.7 qua volet, iumenta agito.*

204   SCHOLARS AND INTELLECTUALS

[The legislator] bids it [i.e., the people] "disperse," but this term does not
bear the meaning that it does in common usage—that they depart from the
location in which the law is being carried—but that each man should make
his separate way into his tribal bloc in which he is to cast his vote. (transl.
Lewis 2006, 143).

References to the proper or primary meaning of a word are not adduced
per se, but are viewed in the context of the debate between intention and
expression, or the so-called *scriptum/voluntas* debate, which often arose in
connection with the opening of wills, when certain expressions taken literally were seemingly at odds with the general gist of a document or with
what an interested party argued had been the custom of the testator. Thus
some jurisprudential sources argued for making greater allowance for not
only an individual's manner of expression, for example use of metaphors and
metonymies, but even more idiosyncratic choices:

(8)   *Dig.* 32.69.1 (Marcellus): Titius codicillis suis ita cavit: "Publio Maevio
      omnes iuvenes, quos in ministerio habeo, dari volo": quaero, a qua aetate
      iuvenes et in quam intellegi debeant. Marcellus respondit . . . non . . . in
      causa testamentorum ad definitionem utique descendendum est, cum
      plerumque abusive loquantur nec propriis nominibus ac vocabulis
      semper utantur.

      Titius provided in his codicil as follows: "To Publius Maevius I wish to
      be given all the young men in my service." Question: By what upper and
      lower limit of age are young men to be defined? Marcellus replied that it
      was for the person taking *cognitio* of the matter to decide whom the tes-
      tator wished to indicate by the words stated. For in the case of wills, one
      surely must not stoop to definitions, since most people speak carelessly
      and do not employ the right names and words.

The careless or improper manner of speaking referred to in (8) with the
phrase *abusive loquantur* is exemplified in (9), by a hypothetical testator who
included silver dining vessels and clothes under the label of *supellex* "furniture." Linguistic idiosyncrasies should be considered but always within restricted limits:

(9)   *Dig.* 33.10.7.2 (Celsus): Servius fatetur sententiam eius qui legaverit aspici
      oportere, in quam rationem ea solitus sit referre: verum si ea, de quibus

LANGUAGE VARIATION AND GRAMMATICAL THEORY   205

non ambigeretur, quin in alieno genere essent, ut puta escarium argentum aut paenulas et togas, supellectili quis adscribere solitus sit, non idcirco existimari oportere supellectili legata ea quoque contineri: non enim ex opinionibus singulorum, sed ex communi usu nomina exaudiri debere.

Servius admits that the opinion of the testator should be considered, that is, the category in which he was accustomed to place the objects. But if anyone was accustomed to ascribe to furniture those things concerning which there is no doubt that they belong to another category, as, for instance, silver dining vessels or cloaks and togas, it should not on that account be held that if furniture is legated, those things too are included; for words should not be interpreted according to the opinions of individuals but by common usage.

3. Linguistic Variation

The diastratic label found in (3) occurs in very similar form in (10), *vulgi sermone* "in common speech" in the second-century jurist Pomponius:

(10)   *Dig.* 50.16.162.1 (Pomponius):[9] si quis ita in testamento scripserit "si quid filio meo acciderit, Dama servus meus liber esto," mortuo filio Dama liber erit. licet enim "accidunt" et vivis, sed vulgi sermone etiam mors significatur.

If someone included a clause in his will in these words, "if anything happens to my son, let my slave Dama be free," if the son dies, Dama will be free. For, although things "happen" even to the living, in common parlance one means death.

As shown in Ferri-Probert 2010, *vulgus* does not as a rule entail a substandard evaluation, unless proved explicitly by some other explicit comment, and here Pomponius clearly speaks of a euphemism for "death" in informal speech, in which *accido* "to happen" signifies an individual's demise.[10] Minor

---

[9] Early second century CE.

[10] On *si quid acciderit* and similar turns of phrase with *accido* referring euphemistically to death see Uría (1997, 232, 234). Uría quotes another parallel from Cicero, also discussing this formula in wills: *inv.* 2.64 *cuius heres non illo in testamento quisquam scriptus erat, si quid pupillo accidisset* ("no other heir was provided for in that will, in the event that anything happened to the minor").

206 SCHOLARS AND INTELLECTUALS

accidents, such as the son breaking a leg, by implication do not satisfy the testamentary condition and do not warrant enfranchisement of the slave.

In (11), also from a discussion of testamentary documents, Pedius (second century CE, in an extract from Paulus' *Ad Vitellium libri*) argues against an absolute, blind reliance on the abstract lexical meaning of a word, pleading instead for the reconstructable intention of the writer. To establish that, one should look at the *praesumptio*, or "agreed understanding," of his particular place of origin. Although it is not explicit, the statement must include language, typically regional differences in usage (in this specific case the regional understanding of what constitutes an *instrumentum fundi*):

(11)   *Dig.* 33.7.18.3 (Paulus): optimum ergo esse Pedius ait non propriam verborum significationem scrutari, sed in primis quid testator demonstrare voluerit, deinde in qua praesumptione sunt qui in quaque regione commorantur.

Pedius says that it is best not to scrutinize the precise meaning of the words but above all what the testator wanted to designate, and then the natural assumptions of those who reside in each region.[11]

Awareness of the distinction between linguistic sign and material referent is common, and the pragmatic attitude adopted by jurists can be appreciated in (12), where the third-century jurist Ulpian elaborates on the lexical meaning of *lignum*, which can be analyzed, almost from a lexicographic perspective, into timber (*materia*) and firewood (*lignum*). Also interesting is the remark that geographically the notion of *lignum* covers different realities. In a land such as Egypt, where the landscape is more barren and high-rise trees less dense, the word is understood to include shrubbery and other plants not generally called *ligna* by other peoples:

(12)   *Dig.* 32.55 pr. (Ulpianus): ligni appellatio nomen generale[12] est, sed sic separatur, ut sit aliquid materia, aliquid lignum . . . . (5) lignorum

---

[11] In Schipani's translation (2005–14) "che significato diano alle parole usate coloro che dimorano in ciascuna regione." Lenel (1889, I:1303) interprets the phrase *deinde in qua praesumptione . . . regionis commorantur* as an interpolation, but no reasons are offered. For a discussion of the reasons (mostly stylistic) adduced by earlier scholarship in support of the deletion see Bonin (2019, 63 n. 71).

[12] The distinction between *generalia, specialia, propria* and other minor categories proceeding from comprehensive to more specific is common to several grammatical writers, from where jurists must have taken it: Consent. *gramm.* V 341.23–5 *plerique grammatici eius modi divisionem fecerunt, ut alia generalia nomina dicerent, ut corpus animal, alia specialia, ut lapis homo.*

LANGUAGE VARIATION AND GRAMMATICAL THEORY 207

appellatione in quibusdam regionibus, ut in Aegypto, ubi harundine pro ligno utuntur, et harundines et papyrum comburitur et herbulae quaedam vel spinae vel vepres continebuntur. quid mirum? cum ξύλον hoc et naves ξυληγὰς appellant, quae haec ἀπὸ τῶν ἑλῶν deducunt.

Wood is a general name, but one distinguishes between timber, which is one thing, and firewood, which is another.... (5) In certain regions, such as Egypt, where reeds are used instead of firewood, the term firewood will include reeds and papyrus plants and certain kinds of grasses and thorns or briars. This is not surprising since they call it by the Greek word for wood, and call the boats which bring it from the marshlands "wood transports."[13]

The informality of language used in everyday conversation is referred to with several metalinguistic expressions revealing the jurists' receptiveness toward diastratic variation. In (13) the Augustan writer Alfenus names the spoken language of everyday as the appropriate context in which the phrase *Romam ire* "to go to Rome" includes any part of the urban sprawl, not simply the city center, because "Rome" in the commonly accepted sense includes even buildings outside the city walls.

(13)   *Dig.* 50.16.87 (Marcellus): ut Alfenus ait, "urbs" est "Roma," quae muro cingeretur, "Roma" est etiam, qua continentia aedificia essent: nam Romam non muro tenus existimari ex consuetudine cotidiana posse intellegi, cum diceremus Romam nos ire, etiamsi extra urbem habitaremus.

As Alfenus said, *urbs* means that part of "Rome" which was surrounded by the wall, "Rome," however, also covers the neighboring built-up area; for one can see from daily usage that Rome is not regarded as extending only as far as the wall, since we say that we are going to Rome even if we live outside the *urbs*.[14]

---

[13] More specific reference to the local variation of names for types of trees can be found in the works of land surveyors, not strictly jurists or lawyers, but a category of professionals who lived in close contact with the law and the controversies arising from boundary disputes: Agenn. *grom.* p. 34.13–17 *qui autem appellent arbores notatas, scire debemus idioma regionis. quidam plagatas vocant quas finis declarandi causa denotant, ut in Bruttiis, alii in Piceno stigmatas, in aliis regionibus insignes aut notas* ("We ought to know the terminology of a region in respect of what people may call marked trees. Some describe as *plagatae* trees that they mark in order to denote a boundary, as happens among the Bruttii, while others, for example, in Picenum, call such trees *stigmatae*; in other regions they call them 'denoted' or 'marked.' "; transl. Campbell 2000, 31). Cf. Fögen (2014, 223).

[14] Cf. Paul. *sent.* 3.6.91: when a carriage with its belongings is bequeathed, mules are also included in the legacy but the muleteer does not seem to be, according to the everyday manner of speaking.

208 SCHOLARS AND INTELLECTUALS

Alfenus' *ex consuetudine cotidiana* parallels similar expressions found in grammatical and rhetorical writers and commentators (e.g., *consuetudo communis, vulgaris* or the bare *in consuetudine*), and modelled in turn on the Greek συνήθεια.[15] In fact *consuetudo* is often interchangeable with *sermo cotidianus, consuetudo loquendi, consuetudo locutionis nostrae*. Reference to *usus* or *consuetudo* serves as guidance to assess the individual testator's intention, since he or she was necessarily using words and idioms shared with the community of other speakers.

An important discussion relevant to the topic of linguistic variation in jurisprudents' writings is offered by a fragment of Cascellius, a Republican jurist contemporary with Cicero. The fragment was transmitted by Celsus, a third-century author in the Digest collecting earlier legal opinions, in this case on the interdict *De glande legenda*, the right to collect fruit fallen onto a neighboring property. The use of a collective singular, *glans*, in the wording of the interdict may have elicited Aulus Cascellius' observation about this identifying feature of "legal usage" (14), if this is how the fragment is to be read:

(14) *Dig.* 50.16.158 (Celsus): in usu iuris frequenter uti nos Cascellius ait singulari appellatione, cum plura generis eiusdem significare vellemus: nam "multum hominem venisse Romam" et "piscem vilem esse" dicimus.

In the practice of law, Cascellius says, we often use a singular appellative when we mean to signify several of the same kind; for we say that "many a man has come to Rome" or that "fish is cheap."[16]

The crucial phrase here is *in usu iuris* because it seems to acknowledge a level of linguistic analysis in which the language of the jurists is recognized as a distinct subset of the language. Cascellius also uses first person plural pronouns and verbs (*nos . . . vellemus . . . dicimus*) to identify such technical language, but the examples he uses in support are idioms taken from everyday language situations or conversations, so that the drift of the argument seems to aim at identifying a parallel between the two language varieties, that of law

---

[15] Probert and Ferri (2010, 36); Müller (2001, 190–207).

[16] Gebhardt (2009, 21) interprets Quintilian's *magis ab usu dicendi remota* as "different from the common language," but the context clarifies that here Quintilian (*inst.* 11.2.42) speaks of the style of *iurisperiti* as distinct from that of the orators, for example in its lack of attention to rhythmic features.

LANGUAGE VARIATION AND GRAMMATICAL THEORY 209

and that of current usage (something along the lines of *nam et in communi
consuetudine... dicimus). Indeed the collective singular with common nouns
is a known feature of informal speech,[17] as well as of legal usage.[18] There
seems therefore to be a leap between the referent of *nos*, the jurists, using the
singular number, *singulari appellatione*, with a collective meaning, and the
subject of *dicimus*, who are chatting about the price of fish and complaining
about the crowd in Rome. Perhaps the editing of the Digest was the cause of
some compression or some further material was deleted from the fragment.

4. Use of Greek for Rhetorical and Grammatical Expressions

In (15), *consuetudo* is mentioned disapprovingly (grandsons are called
"relatives" even if conceived after the death of their grandparent), because the
common language here deploys a trope, a catachresis, or rather an *anaphora*,
an *ad sensum* agreement:

(15)   *Dig.* 38.16.8 pr. (Iulianus): quod in consuetudine nepotes "cognati"
       appellantur etiam eorum, post quorum mortem concepti sunt, non
       proprie, sed per abusionem vel potius ἀναφορικῶς accidit.[19]

       Although their grandsons (i.e., of the deceased) are commonly called
       the cognate relatives even of those after whose death they have been
       conceived, such usage is not proper and occurs through misuse or
       rather by analogy.

Julian deploys here a relatively infrequent Greek rhetorical and grammatical term, meaning "in relative terms rather than absolutely," "by proximity,"

---

[17] Prisc. *gramm.* III 269.21 *similiter dicimus "cenatur piscis, prandetur holus."*

[18] Guzman Brito (1999, 59) suggested *iuris* is an interpolation in view of the lack of parallels for
the phrase (only *in usu iudiciorum* is attested, but more a reference to "custom" than "language"), but
the conclusion is not certain. The Greek translation of this passage in the *Basilica* seems to reinforce
Guzman Brito's suggestion: *Bas.* II 2.152 τὰ τοῦ αὐτοῦ γένους ὄντα δυνατὸν καὶ πολλὰ ὄντα ἑνικῶς
ἐκφωνεῖσθαι, ὡς ὅταν λέγωμεν "πολὺς ἄνθρωπος," "πολὺς ἰχθύς," ἢ ὅτε "ἐμοὶ καὶ τῷ κληρονόμῳ
μου ἐπερωτήσω"· καὶ οἱ πολλοὶ γὰρ περιέχονται. Another passage, Sergius (= ps. Cassiod.) p. 77.10
Stock *produxit iure loquela*, discussing the adoption of a non-current form such as *equabus* to avoid
ambiguities regarding gender in the text of wills, may hint at "the language of law" (no discussion in
Stock's notes).

[19] Translated in *Sch. Bas.* 45.1.19 τὸ γὰρ λέγεσθαι ἐν συνηθείᾳ τοὺς ἐκγόνους κογνάτους εἶναι καὶ
ἐκείνων, ὧν μετὰ τὴν τελευτὴν συνελήφθησαν, οὐ κυρίως, ἀλλὰ καταχρηστικῶς λέγεται, ἢ μᾶλλον
ἀναφορικῶς.

210 SCHOLARS AND INTELLECTUALS

that is a word that is understood in a given context by means of another word in relation to which it is being used. Here Watson's translation is slightly misleading since it confuses *anaphora* with "analogy," which has a different meaning in ancient sources. Dionysius Thrax *Ars* 40, defines "anaphora" and "anaphoric" as "what denotes a resemblance" (ἀναφορικὸν δέ ἐστιν . . . τὸ ὁμοίωσιν σημαῖνον), as for example the pronouns τοιοῦτος τοσοῦτος τηλικοῦτος. Whatever the exact reasons for Julian's adoption of the term, its connection with grammatical thought and analysis of sources is easy to recognize.

Greek is sometimes suspected to be an interpolation from the eastern compilers of Tribonian's team, who might have snuck in a Greek word or two for the comprehension of contemporary eastern readers. But the use of Greek meta-language is common in the practice of Roman grammatical writers. For example in (16) Ulpian, in a commentary on the Edict, remarks that *persuadere* is an ambivalent expression since there can be persuasion to good or bad actions. The label Ulpian uses to define the ambivalent nature of this word is a Greek expression, τῶν μέσων, with parallels in literary commentators (18 and 19, on *ornatus* and *coniuro* respectively):

(16)   *Dig.* 11.3.1.3 (Ulpianus, ad edictum): persuadere autem est plus quam <suadere: nam qui persuadet, tamquam> compelli<t> et cogi<t> sibi parere. sed persuadere τῶν μέσων ἐστιν, nam et bonum consilium quis dando potest suadere et malum: et ideo praetor adiecit "dolo malo, quo eum deteriorem faceret."

Persuading is more than suggesting; for to persuade is virtually to compel and enforce obedience. But persuasion is a neutral concept, for one can persuade by giving good advice or by giving bad; therefore, the praetor adds: "fraudulently, in order to make him worse."

(17)   Don. Ter. *Eun.* 237 QVID ISTVC INQVAM ORNATI EST] "ornatus" τῶν μέσων est: ad decus et ad turpitudinem.

"Adornment" is a neutral expression; it can said of a decent and of a shameful get-up.

(18)   Serv. *Aen.* 8.200 CONIVRAT] nota de re bona coniurationem dici posse: nam coniuratio τῶν μέσων est.

LANGUAGE VARIATION AND GRAMMATICAL THEORY 211

Observe that *coniuratio* "conspiracy" can be used of a good thing, for *coniuratio* is a neutral expression.

In (19), another discussion of the Urban Praetor's Edict—a clause authorizing seizure of goods when the defendant does not turn up at the trial nor finds a guarantor to speak up for him—Ulpian uses yet another Greek grammatical expression, found in Greek scholarly sources to indicate either an imperfect tense or the imperfective, durative aspect of an expression. This is probably the correct meaning for this passage, in which Ulpian seems to defend the choice of tense in the Edict and its aspectual nuance, in spite of the odd *consecutio*, where a future tense in the main clause would have required a present or perfect. As seen in (20) and (21), the adverb is used in Greek scholarship to describe aspectual connotations:

(19) *Dig.* 42.4.2.4 (Ulpianus): haec verba "defenderetur" παρατατικῶς scripta sunt, ut neque sufficiat umquam defendisse, si non duret defensio, neque obsit, si nunc offeratur.

The term "defended" is given a wide interpretation so that it is not enough that he enter a defense if he does not persist in it, and equally it will not go against him if, having previously failed to do so, he does now present a defense.

(20) Eustath. *Comm. Od.* 2.296 (referring to *Od.* 23.86): ὀκνηρίαν δέ τινα δηλοῖ τὸ κατέβαινε παρατατικῶς φρασθέν. Εὐρύκλεια μὲν γὰρ πιστεύσασα ἔνδον εἶναι τὸ φίλον αὐτῇ τέκος ἐρρωμένως ἀνέβαινεν, ἡ δὲ γυνὴ ἐνδοιάζουσα σχολαίως κάτεισιν.

The verb κατέβαινε in the imperfect reveals a certain hesitation. Euryclea had come up the stairs energetically since she is convinced that her dear charge has now returned, but [Penelope], unconvinced, comes down without haste.

(21) Ammonius *diff.* 75: παρὰ δὲ τοῖς Ἀττικοῖς ἀρτίως σημαίνει αὐτῆς τῆς ὥρας. τὸ δ᾽ ἄρτι παρατατικῶς καὶ ἐπὶ τοῦ παρῳχηκότος.

The adverb ἀρτίως in Attic means "right now," whereas *arti* is durative and refers also to something which happened in the past.

212 SCHOLARS AND INTELLECTUALS

Other Greek expressions used by jurists and conjuring up the language of Greco-Roman scholarship are ἐν πλάτει "broadly" (*Dig.* 22.3.28 Paulus), καταχρηστικῶς "improperly" and τῇ ἀνάρθρῳ φωνῇ "inarticulate sound."

(22) *Dig.* 50.16.18 (Gaius): licet inter "gesta" et "facta" videtur quaedam esse suptilis differentia, attamen καταχρηστικῶς nihil inter factum et gestum interest.[20]

Although there seems to be a certain subtle difference between *gesta* and *facta*, nonetheless, there is improperly no difference between something which is done and something which is carried out.

(23) Serv. *Aen.* 10.681 MVCRONE INDVAT] aut καταχρηστικῶς dixit "induat" pro "feriat": aut hypallage est pro "mucronem suo induat corpore."

TO THROW HIMSELF ON THE SWORD] either the poet used *induat* in the place of *feriat* ["wound"] with a catachresis, or he used the figure hypallage, instead of "to put the sword's point inside his body."

(24) Sex. Emp. *Pyrrh.* 3.119: τόπος τοίνυν λέγεται διχῶς, κυρίως καὶ καταχρηστικῶς, καταχρηστικῶς μὲν [ὡς] ὁ ἐν πλάτει, ὡς ἐμοῦ ἡ πόλις, κυρίως δὲ ὁ πρὸς ἀκρίβειαν κατέχων, ὑφ' οὗ περιεχόμεθα πρὸς ἀκρίβειαν.

Space, or place, then, is used in two senses, strictly and loosely— loosely of place taken broadly (as "my city"), and strictly of an exactly containing place whereby we are exactly enclosed.

(25) *Dig.* 33.10.7.2 (Celsus): nemo sine voce dixisse existimatur: nisi forte et eos, qui loqui non possunt, conato ipso et sono quodam καὶ τῇ ἀνάρθρῳ φωνῇ dicere existimamus.

Nobody is reckoned to have spoken without use of speech, unless perhaps we also reckon that those who cannot talk speak by virtue of the mere attempt and their sounds and inarticulate cries.

---

[20] Cf. *Dig.* 50.16.19 (Ulpianus) "Labeo, in the first book of the Urban Praetor's Edict, lays down that some things *agantur*, some things *gerantur*, some things *contrahantur*; and indeed, *actum* is a general word (*generale verbum*) whether something is done verbally or executed."

LANGUAGE VARIATION AND GRAMMATICAL THEORY 213

The Greek expression ἄναρθρος φωνή (in Latin *inarticulata vox*) occurs in grammatical sources with reference to non-phonematic utterances or sounds, such as animal sounds and voices, even if some of them can be written:

(26) Prisc. *gramm.* II 5.7–6.2 inarticulata (*sc.* vox) est . . . quae a nullo affectu proficiscitur mentis. . . . aliae autem sunt, quae, quamvis scribantur, tamen inarticulatae dicuntur, cum nihil significent, ut "coax," "cra." aliae vero sunt inarticulatae et illiteratae, quae nec scribi possunt nec intellegi, ut crepitus, mugitus et similia.

An inarticulate sound is . . . one that does not proceed from an emotion of the mind . . . Some [i.e., voices], although they can be put in writing, are nevertheless called inarticulate, since they have no meaning, such as *coax, cra* [i.e., the croaking of frogs and bird sounds]. Others still are at the same time inarticulate and illiterate, since they cannot be written down nor understood, such as the crackling of fire and the bellowing of cows and such like.

5. Grammatical Analysis of Documentary Evidence

At the opposite end of *consuetudo* we find *ratio*. The pair *ratio/usus* or *consuetudo* are a long established binomial opposition from Varro onwards to signify the conflict between the opposing principles of analogy and anomaly, primarily in the field of inflection, but extending to all other areas of linguistic analysis. In (27) *ratio,* or "correct norm," is invoked in support of the view that an adjective can only modify the nominal closest to it:

(27) *Dig.* 34.2.8 (Plautius): mulier ita legavit: "quisquis mihi heres erit, Titiae vestem meam mundum ornamentaque muliebria damnas esto dare." . . . Iavolenus scribit, quia verisimile est, inquit, testatricem tantum ornamentorum universitati derogasse, quibus significationem "muliebrium" accommodasset: accedere eo, quod illa demonstratio "muliebria" neque vesti neque mundo applicari salva ratione recti sermonis potest.

A woman left a legacy in the following terms: whoever shall be my heir, let him be obliged to give my clothing, toilet equipment, and female

214 SCHOLARS AND INTELLECTUALS

jewelry to Titia." . . . Iavolenus: . . . It is probable, he says, that the testatrix had segregated from the whole of jewelry only that to which she had applied the label "female"; there is also the fact that the description "female" cannot be applied to the clothing or toilet equipment without damaging the correct order of the language.

Plautius (second century CE) seems to contend that the adjective (here called *demonstratio*, "qualification")[21] *muliebria* cannot be tied to *vestis* or *mundus* (toiletry, objects used for personal hygiene), but only to *ornamenta* (jewelry). The "rule" or "idiomatic" usage here advocated by Iavolenus is in fact dubious at best, since grammatical agreement with the nearest of several predicates even when of different grammatical genus is common, if nowhere stated as the rule.[22] Therefore Iavolenus' comment must be a subjective, native speaker intuition, but by no means a generalizing assessment of the real linguistic situation. For *ratio sermonis* as a linguistic criterion to assess correctness see Consentius:[23]

(28)   *gramm.* V 394.1–3 = *barb.* 15.2–4 (Mari): fient barbarismi huius modi, cum aut pinguius aliquid aut exilius sonabit, quam ratio Romani sermonis exposcit.

Errors of pronunciation are committed in this way, when something is pronounced in a manner which is either too full or too thin than the correct rule of the Roman language requires.

The deictic meaning of *demonstratio*, typical of grammatical discussion, occurs in another commentary on wills at *Dig.* 34.2.7, a passage concerning the definition of the expression "my clothing" or "my silver":

(29)   *Dig.* 34.2.7 (Paulus): si ita esset legatum: "vestem meam, argentum meum damnas esto dare," id legatum videtur, quod testamenti tempore fuisset, quia praesens tempus semper intellegeretur, si aliud comprehensum non esset: nam cum dicit "vestem meam," "argentum

---

[21] Adjectives were not identified as a distinct part of speech before Priscian, who was the first to use the definition *adiectiva* as a calque of the Greek ἐπιθετικά. For *demonstro* used in reference to the function of adjectives see Sacerdos *gramm.* I 463.8 *epitheton est dictio propriis adiecta nominibus vel demonstrandi vel ornandi vel vituperandi <causa>*.

[22] Pinkster (2015, 1273–5) on adjectival modifiers agreeing with the gender of the nearest noun.

[23] This passage is discussed by Mari (Chapter 6, §4.1).

LANGUAGE VARIATION AND GRAMMATICAL THEORY 215

meum," hac demonstratione "meum" praesens, non futurum tempus ostendit.

If a legacy has been left in the following terms, "let my [heir] be obliged to make a gift of my clothing [and] my silver," the legacy is regarded as comprising property that existed at the time of his will, since the present time would always be understood, if nothing else had been included; for when he says, "my clothing," "my silver," by the description "mine" he indicates present, not future, time.[24]

The notion that a pronoun or adjective entails "present knowledge" occurs in Apollonius:

(31) *De pronominibus* = *GG* II.1 61.3–5 Schneider ἡ μὲν ἐκεῖνος καὶ ἡ οὗτος, δεῖξιν σημαίνουσαι, τὴν ὑπόγυιον γνῶσιν τοῦ προσώπου παριστᾶσιν, ἡ δὲ αὐτός ἐπ' ἀναπολούμενον πρόσωπον φέρεται.

The pronouns ἐκεῖνος and οὗτος, which have a deictic function, represent the cognition of a person who is close at hand, while the pronoun αὐτός refers to a person already mentioned.

Discussions about gender are also common, mainly because disputes arose concerning the inclusiveness of masculine nouns. The most typical discussion is ascribed to Servius, an authoritative Republican source, who deemed that a will leaving a gift of mules also included she-mules, because the masculine gender is "always" inclusive of the feminine, by which he meant that the masculine could be generalizing in Latin (32):

(32) *Dig.* 32.62 (Iulianus = Lenel 1889, I:317): respondit Servius deberi legatum, quia mulorum appellatione etiam mulae continentur, quemadmodum appellatione servorum etiam servae plerumque continentur. id autem eo veniet,[25] quod semper sexus masculinus etiam femininum sexum continet.

---

[24] Similar is a fragment of Mucius Scaevola, the Republican jurist, at *Dig.* 34.2.34.1 (= Lenel 1889, I:758) *articulus "est" praesentis temporis demonstrationem in se continet (continens* trad.).

[25] Perhaps an error for *ex eo venit* "it comes from this." The passage is also discussed by Battaglia (2017, 164–5).

216 SCHOLARS AND INTELLECTUALS

Servius replied that the legacy was due, for she-mules are included under the term *muli*, just as *servae* (female slaves) are mostly included under the term *servi* (male slaves). This comes from the usual practice of including the feminine in the masculine.

(33) *Dig.* 50.16.195 pr. (Ulpianus = Lenel 1889, II:722): pronuntiatio sermonis in sexu masculino ad utrumque sexum plerumque porrigitur.

The use of a word in the masculine gender is usually extended to cover both genders.[26]

(34) *Dig.* 50.16.101.3 (Modestinus = Lenel 1889, I:706): servis legatis etiam ancillas deberi quidam putant, quasi commune nomen utrumque sexum contineat.

Some people think that when slaves are bequeathed, female slaves ought to be included since a single name covers both sexes.

The issue comes to prominence several times in the extracts concerning wills and legacies in the Digest and it must have been a frequent matter of dispute. The resolution is not always in favor of Servius' solution, especially when persons rather than animals were the object of a will. In (34) *quasi commune nomen* conjures up a specific grammatical category, that of nouns in which grammatical genus is not fixed, but can be treated as masculine or feminine depending on the identity of the (generally animate) referent, for example *sacerdos* "the priest/ priestess."[27] On the analogy of *sacerdos*, what Modestinus seems to have had in mind is to treat *servus* as a *commune nomen*, capable of including both masculine and feminine *genera*. The grammarians' definition of *nomina communia* and *epicoena* has been referred to in this context by Pavese (2013, 76). However, there are even more specific parallels for the use of generalized and inclusive masculine nouns when speaking of persons rather than objects. The prevailing notion is not that of treating nouns as *communia* or *epicoena*, but of seeing the

---

[26] *Pronuntiatio* is usually "delivery" in rhetoric; in jurisprudence, the word refers to a judge's verdict, or statement or pronouncement. Perhaps in the context from which the excerpt was taken *pronuntiatio* referred to a judge's verdict, which would provide a setting for this inclusive use of the masculine.

[27] Grammarians distinguished *nomina communia* from *nomina epicoena*, a class of nouns with a stable grammatical *genus* but including both masculine and feminine referents, for example *aquila*, always feminine but referring also to male eagles (Schad 2007, 66–7).

LANGUAGE VARIATION AND GRAMMATICAL THEORY 217

masculine as always superior and inclusive of the feminine. This "sexist" notion is also frequent in grammatical writers and commentators. Didymus, a grammarian-turned-biblical-exegete, expatiates on this in a note on *Ecclesiastes*:

(35) Didymus Caecus, *Commentarii in Ecclesiasten* 11.9a ἐάν τις ἅμα ἀνδρῶ(ν) καὶ γυναικῶν μνημονεύῃ, εἰς τὸ ἀρρενικὸν συνπεραίνει τὸν λόγον· λέγομεν ὅτι πάρεισιν ἄνδρες καὶ γυναῖκες ἀκροασόμενοι, οὐκ ἀκροασ<ό>μεναι· ὕβριν γὰρ φέρει τὸ συναπενεχθῆναι τὸν ἄνδρα τῇ γυναικί, τὴν δὲ γυναῖκα τῷ ἀνδρὶ ἀποδοθῆναι μᾶλλον ἔπαινον φέρει.

When someone mentions man and woman in the same group, the phrase is in the masculine: for example we say that men and women will be in the audience using a masculine participle, because it is offensive for a man to be referred to together with a woman without distinction between them, whereas for a woman it is a reason for pride to be addressed jointly with men.

The idea that the masculine *genus* prevails over the feminine when the two are grouped together by coordination is common in commentators (and of course reflects both shared social prejudice and common idiom in all written sources from antiquity).[28]

A fragment from Proculus' *Epistularum libri* (first century CE) included in *Digesta* 50.16 uses language that places his discussion at the intersection between the discourses of philosophical dialectic and that of grammatical analysis of speech parts. It addresses ambiguous phrasing in wills, for example when two people are named as possible heirs with a disjunctive particle (e.g., *ille aut ille*).[29] In such cases did the first heir exclude all heirs named subsequently in the document? Or were they all to be considered as beneficiaries?

(36) *Dig.* 50.16.124 (Proculus): haec verba "ille aut ille" non solum disiunctiva, sed etiam subdisiunctivae orationis sunt. disiunctivum est, veluti cum dicimus "aut dies aut nox est," quorum posito altero necesse

---

[28] Eustath. *Comm. Iliadem* 2.830.23 Van der Valk τὰ πολλὰ μέντοι ἐν συντάξεσιν ἀρσενικῶν καὶ θηλυκῶν ἐπικρατεῖν φασι τὸ ἀρσενικόν, Plut. *De Homero* 2.42 Kindstrand σύνηθες γὰρ ἦν τοῖς παλαιοῖς, καὶ μάλιστα τοῖς Ἀττικοῖς, χρῆσθαι τοῖς ἀρσενικοῖς καὶ ἀντὶ τῶν θηλυκῶν ὡς κρείττοσι καὶ δυνατωτέροις . . . καὶ ὅταν κοινῶς ἀρρενικῷ καὶ θηλυκῷ ὀνόματι ἐπιφέρηται ῥῆμα ἢ μετοχή, τὸ ἀρρενικὸν ἐπικρατεῖ, Herod. *De figuris* 3.7 Hajdú. In Latin sources: e.g., Don. Ter. *Ad.* 894; Don. Ter. *Eun.* 189, 1065; Serv. *Aen.* 4.95; Aug. *civ.* 16.8; Aug. *quaest. hept.* 7.49.

[29] Such a context is suggested by *Cod. Iust.* 6.38.4 (from 531 CE), which discusses cases of wills involving the ambiguous phrasing *ille vel ille heres mihi esto* or *ille aut illi do lego*.

218 SCHOLARS AND INTELLECTUALS

> est tolli alterum, item sublato altero poni alterum. ita simili figuratione verbum potest esse subdisiunctivum. subdisiunctivi autem genera sunt duo: unum, cum ex propositis finibus ita non potest uterque esse, ut possit neuter esse, veluti cum dicimus "aut sedet aut ambulat": nam ut nemo potest utrumque simul facere, ita aliquis potest neutrum, vel uti is qui accumbit.[30]

> The words "one or another" are not only disjunctive but also belong to subdisjunctive speech. Disjunction is if we say "it is night or day" where if one is true the other is not. So in a similar construction,[31] a word can be subdisjunctive. But there are two kinds of subdisjunctive, one when of two possible conclusions both cannot be true and neither need be true, as when we say, "either he is seated or he is walking," for just as no one can be doing both at the same time, so someone can be doing neither, for instance someone who is lying down.

As in many passages in the Digest, editing by the compilers may explain some awkwardness in the phrasing, for example the transition from the nominative, *verba ... disiunctiva* to a genitive construction, *subdisiunctivae orationis*, probably indicating that *subdisiunctiva* is understood as a subgroup of *disiunctiva*, even if this notion is not correct according to ancient linguistic doctrine. The term *disiunctivus* (here *disiunctivum* with *verbum* understood) is a calque on the Greek διαζευκτικός and in Latin it is used mainly in reference to conjunctions.[32] Even if a philosophical coloring can be recognized, influence from grammarians' teaching should not be disregarded.[33] Dialectic and grammar were closely linked, and Roman scholars such as Varro and Aelius Stilo discussed dialectic in depth. Moreover, Proculus does not

---

[30] A Greek translation of this passage is found in *Liber iuridicus sigma* 57.4.

[31] *Figuratio* also is an obvious term of ancient linguistic analysis, mainly indicating morphological phenomena but also used to describe syntactical constructions: e.g., Prisc. *gramm.* III 38.4–5 *aliis rebus ad eandem figurationem omnia localia possunt adiungi* "prepositions used for place and motion can be combined with other elements creating similar figures" (i.e., *per virtutem* formed on the model of *per medium forum*).

[32] However, Gellius used the variant form *diiunctiva* in reference to a proposition in a syllogism (5.11.9 *in proloquio diiunctiuo* "in a disjunctive proposition"). In Gellius 16.8 an important discussion is devoted to διεζευγμένα (*disiuncta*) and παραδιεζευγμένα ἀξιώματα, "disjunctive" and "subdisjunctive propositions," although no Latin translation is offered for the latter.

[33] Hülser (2015) places Proculus' argument in the context of Stoic dialectic, and quotes two fragments of Chrysippus (*SVF* II 217 and 218 Arnim = *FDS* 973 and 976 Hülser, neither explicit quotations, in which disjunction is discussed. In particular *SVF* II 217 = *Epimerismi Homerici* η 20 Dyck is a piece of Byzantine Homeric scholarship discussing the three meanings of the particle ἤ (ἤ διαζευκτικός ἐστιν ἤ ὑποδιαζευκτικὸς ἤ διασαφητικός "it is either disjunctive or subdisjunctive or declarative").

LANGUAGE VARIATION AND GRAMMATICAL THEORY   219

elaborate a syllogistic, deductive argument, but an explanation of a well-defined linguistic category, that of subdisjunctive conjunctions, which made it possible to understand the phrase *illi aut illi do lego* in a will as inclusive rather than exclusive, and that therefore both legatees were to be included in the estate. The Latin word *subdisiunctivus* occurs only here and in Priscian (*gramm.* III 98.3, 17), where it is used of conjunctions as a calque on a Greek grammatical expression from Apollonius Dyscolus, ὑποδιαζευκτικός. Priscian, following Apollonius, uses examples very similar to Proculus' (compare Proculus' *aut dies aut nox est* to Priscian *gramm.* III 98.1–2 *aut lux est aut tenebrae*).

(37) Prisc. *gramm.* III 98.16–19 si dicam "vel tunicam mihi accommoda vel etiam paenulam," subdisiunctivum est; videor enim in alterius petitione libenter utrumque accipere. sed potest hic etiam disiunctiva esse, aliud est enim alterutrum petere, aliud utrumque.

If I say: "give me my tunic or even my cloak," *vel* is used as a subdisjunctive conjunction, for in asking for just one of the two I say that I would like to receive both. But in the same phrase, *vel* can also be taken as disjunctive, since there is a distinction between asking for one or the other and asking for both the tunic and the cloak.

Another explicit reference to the conjunction as a grammatical part of speech occurs in a fragment of Paulus *Ad legem Iuliam et Papiam* (*Dig.* 50.16.142). Of particular interest here is the equivalence established between different linguistic ways of representing a *coniunctio*, not only with the particles *et* and *-que*, but also using the preposition *cum* and asyndeton.

5. Wills as Performatives

Discussions of valid or invalid wills were a frequent occasion for recourse to law and sometimes jurists were sought to express their views. People usually wrote their wills on sealed tablets, and pronounced a "nuncupation" or a fixed proclamation formula, before witnesses in a ceremony which made the specific contents of the tablets valid and legally binding (a procedure described at Gaius *inst.* 2.104, but probably relaxed after the second century). The level of formality was considerable, and it included a series of performative formulae pronounced in the presence of the witnesses and other participants

220 SCHOLARS AND INTELLECTUALS

required by law, the *familiae emptor* and the *libripens*. The *nuncupatio* did not necessarily disclose the contents of the written will itself, but some wills were delivered only orally (a famous case was that of the poet Horace, who dictated his will *in extremis*, and this may have been common: cf. *Cod. Iust.* 6.23.15.1 *nec necessaria sint momenta verborum, quae forte seminecis et balbutiens lingua profudit*). But even when the will was a written document prepared in advance, the grammar or the language used could be defective and give rise to dispute. Also testators tampered with such documents in the course of their lives, sometimes adding postscripts (called *codicilli*) or deleting names and legates, and perhaps some oddities of phrasing were the result of such repeated interventions.[34] All these were situations where jurists had to address speech that might differ from or be defective compared to standard usage.

The most important act in the *testamenti factio*, the making of one's will, was the naming of an heir, the *institutio heredis*, and this point is mentioned as a specific ground for dispute and lack of validity of a will:

(38)   *Dig.* 28.5.1.3–7 (Ulpianus) quinque verbis potest facere testamentum, ut dicat: "Lucius Titius mihi heres esto": haec autem scriptura pertinet ad eum qui non per scripturam testatur. qui poterit (*sc.* facere testamentum) etiam tribus verbis testari, ut dicat: "Lucius heres esto": nam et "mihi" et "Titius" abundat. . . . (7) idem Iulianus "illum heredem esse," non putavit valere, quoniam deest aliquid: sed et ipsa valebit subaudito "iubeo."

[He who makes a will] . . . can make his will in five words, as by saying, "Lucius Titius be my heir"; however, what is written here relates to someone who is not making his will in writing. And he will be able to make his will even in three words, as by saying, "Lucius be heir"; for both "my" and "Titius" are superfluous. . . . (7) The same Julian did not think that "so-and-so to be heir" was valid because something is lacking; but that too will be valid, since "I authorize" is implied.

The extract from Ulpian refers explicitly to oral testaments, perhaps taken down at a testator's deathbed while they were uttered half audibly and in the few remaining moments of lucidity. How many words are enough to make a will valid? What makes a sentence meaningful? The linguistic

---

[34] On the ceremonial and formal aspects of the Roman procedure of making a valid will see Amelotti (1966, 111–23); Meyer (2004, 118, 265–76).

LANGUAGE VARIATION AND GRAMMATICAL THEORY 221

material they draw on are phrases such as *Lucius heres esto*, with an incomplete name (assuming the heir was identifiable as *Lucius Titius*) and the lack of an indirect object, *mihi*. Here the linguistic commentary clearly echoes grammatical discussions about ellipsis and pleonasm in poetry (*deest . . . subaudito . . . abundat*; equivalent to Greek παρέλκει). These are topics of grammatical and pragmatic correctness which are also the purvey of commentators, for example Donatus on Terence's comedies, but also the expansive rewriting of Justinian's *Institutes* prepared by the jurist Theophilus for his university course, the so-called *Paraphrasis Institutionum* (42):

(39) Don. Ter. *Phorm.* 255 SALVVM TE VENIRE] ἔλλειψις vel ἀποσιώπησις: "gaudeo" enim subauditur; quod nisi acceperis, non intelleges cur hic responderit "credo."

YOUR SAFE RETURN] an ἔλλειψις or ἀποσιώπησις, for the word *gaudeo* ["I rejoice"] should be understood; if we don't understand the passage in this way, the other character's answer *credo* ["I'm sure of this"] makes no sense.

(40) Don. Ter. *Ad.* 28.2 SI ABSIS VSPIAM] abundat "uspiam" aut deest "profectus" aut quid tale.

IF YOU'RE NOT PRESENT, SOMEWHERE] the word *uspiam* ["somewhere"] is pleonastic, unless we supply a word such as *profectus* ["having gone"].

(41) *Schol.* Arist. *Eccl.* 209 σωθήσεσθ' ἔτι] παρέλκει τὸ ἔτι παρὰ τοῖς Ἀττικοῖς.

YOU SHALL STILL BE SAFE] The word *eti* ["still"] is an Attic pleonasm.

(42) Theophilus Antecessor, *Paraphrasis* 2.1.36: τὸ fere δὲ ἤτοι σχηδὸν παρέλκεται.[35]

The word *fere* ["practically"] is really superfluous.

---

[35] The Greek verb παρέλκεται is also used by Latin commentators such as Donatus (on Ter. *Andr.* 579). As D. Mantovani pointed out to me, Theophilus is also making a point about a factual inaccuracy of the adverb "almost" (*fere*) in this passage of Justinian's *Institutes* 2.1.36 since possession of unplucked fruit by the heirs of usufructuaries and tenants is disciplined by identical, and not "almost" identical, rules.

222 SCHOLARS AND INTELLECTUALS

Metalinguistic descriptions of some interest for the study of the awareness of speech pragmatics in Latin sources are found in texts containing commentaries on the linguistic acceptability of *fideicommissa* "trust-legacies," a Roman practice whereby a trust could be made over to any beneficiary, asking him or her to transfer all or part of what they had received under the testament to a third person. While legacies were formulated in the imperative, *fideicommissa* were requests, not binding dispositions, addressed to the beneficiary. The distinction between true legacies and trusts was manifold. Trusts were exempt from the formalities of legacies proper, and not legally binding. Therefore their form varied, and jurists describe how their language could be different from that of wills, where the imperative mood was mandatory.[36] Testators used instead forms of begging and asking, called in our legal sources *precativis (precariis) verbis, precativo modo*. A constitution issued by the emperor Constantine in 339 CE uses interesting analytic language to describe *fideicommissa* as opposed to *legata*:

(43)   *Cod. Iust.* 6.23.15 pr.: placuit . . . institutioni heredis verborum non esse necessariam observantiam, utrum imperativis et directis verbis fiat an inflexa. (1) nec enim interest, si dicatur "heredem facio" vel "instituo" vel "volo" vel "mando" vel "cupio" vel "esto" vel "erit," sed quibuslibet confecta sententiis, quolibet loquendi genere formata institutio valeat, si modo per eam liquebit voluntatis intentio.

It is determined that no particular words are required for designating an heir, whether this is done by imperative, direct or indirect words. (1) For it makes no difference whether it is worded "I make an heir" or "I designate" or "I wish" or "I charge" or "I desire" or "let him be" or "he will be." But a designation will be valid by whatever wording it is accomplished and in whatever mode of speech it is formed, provided only that the intended disposition is comprehensible through it. (transl. Frier et al. 2016)

Imperativus is an obvious grammatical word here, presupposing no specific doctrine. An opposition is set up in the constitution between legacies, couched

---

[36] For example of indirect language used in the phrasing of trusts cf. *Dig.* 30.115 (Ulpianus) *etiam hoc modo: "cupio des," "opto des," "credo te daturum" fideicommissum est*; *Dig.* 30.118 (Neratius) *et eo modo relictum: "exigo," "desidero, uti des," fideicommissum valet: sed et ita: "volo hereditatem meam Titii esse," "scio hereditatem meam restituturum te Titio."* On the evolution of wording in *fideicommissa* see Johnston (1988, 156–80; 213–21), where it is argued that the phrasing with *precaria* or *precativa verba* is a post-classical development in Roman doctrine.

as binding dispositions by means of performative verbs (*mando, volo, instituo*), and requests expressed in the form of prayers and wishes (*cupio des, opto des,* or *rogo, heres karissime, manumittas* in the repertoire of formulae found in *P. Hamb.* 1.72 line 6), a form reserved for *fideicommissa*. Other sources mention an even more indirect formula, *credo te daturum*. Especially interesting here is *inflexa* (*sc. institutio*), which is clearly a word to describe more indirect forms of expressions (literally "curved, oblique"), not explicit or binding. Descriptions of indirectness are relatively rare in ancient grammatical sources, and neither *directis verbis* nor *inflexus* seem to occur.[37] A Greek scholion on Aristophanes (*Schol. Plut.* 23) uses the adverb ἀορίστως with the meaning "with no explicit addressee," implying that the remark is only obliquely aimed at an interlocutor, and Donatus on Terence uses once *implicatio* to describe the tortuous manner of expression used to soften an offensive remark:

(44) Don. Ter. *Eun.* 139 SE IRI PRAEPOSITVM TIBI APVD ME] ἀναστροφή in verbo "praepositum iri." necessaria implicatio in his, quae dura dictu sunt.

HE WOULD BE PREFERRED TO YOU IN MY EYES] there is an instance of anastrophe in the verb *praepositum iri*. The complicated circumlocution is necessary in order to say things that are difficult.

6. Conclusions

The familiarity of jurists with the grammatical tools of language analysis goes back to the unity of the educational curriculum in the Roman world with its emphasis on the literal and figural interpretation of the literary texts. As Mantovani (2018) showed for other intellectual discourses such as philosophy and history, legal writers adapt the tools and strategies of other disciplines to the purpose at hand. Some grammatical vocabulary is precise and technical.[38] At other times some vagueness seems to be sought, and clearly grammatical topics and concepts are discussed with non-standard terminology,[39] perhaps an intentional distancing from the technical precision of

[37] Studied in Zago 2022, 362–4, especially with regard to formulas of politeness.

[38] E.g., in example 37: *subdisiunctiva, figuratio,* and *demonstratio*; in example 34 *commune nomen*. Similarly the use of Greek phrases in legal texts are not necessarily an indication of Greek education or origins, but part of the technical jargon of grammar.

[39] E.g., *articulus* for "particle" or "verb" (see n. 25); *pronuntiatio* for "usage" (n. 27).

224 SCHOLARS AND INTELLECTUALS

the experts. At the moment the nature of the evidence does not make it possible to establish parallels with the evolution of grammatical and linguistic study as we know it from the Republic to Late Antiquity. Nevertheless, the surviving discussions show jurists making use of grammatical analysis to describe and analyze Latin speech that differs in significant ways from standard usage: this includes unusual lexical usage, which may arise from personal idiosyncrasies (no. 9), regional differences (nos. 10–13), colloquial or relaxed forms of popular speech (nos. 2–4, 8, 14, 16), and technical jargon (no. 15). In other situations, they are forced to confront speech that falls below the ideal standard of clarity and results in different kinds of ambiguity (nos. 29–30, 32, 36), particularly in the context of oral rather than written utterances (no. 38), where they also distinguished different pragmatic situations. All this shows Roman legal writing as an important site for creative reflection about language in general and linguistic difference in particular.

Epilogue

Robert A. Kaster

The (Very Fragile) Origins of *Guardians of Language*

When Adam Gitner suggested that I say a few words about the genesis of *Guardians of Language* by way of an epilogue to our gathering, I gladly accepted, and I was fairly confident that I knew where in general terms this excavation of my memory would lead.

Some scholars have the ability to see the shape of their research program stretching out before them for many years, encompassing multiple books. My friend and former colleague the Greek historian and political scientist Josh Ober has that gift: he once startled me by recalling that very early in his career he saw that the story he wanted to tell about Athenian democracy would need to have four components—each of them a book—and that the telling would take about thirty years. And that is almost exactly how the project unfolded, starting in 1983 with his early work on *Mass and Elite in Democratic Athens* and ending with the publication of *Democracy and Knowledge* in 2008 (yes, he did it in twenty-five years, not thirty).

But as I have known for some time, I do not have that gift and am not that kind of scholar. Instead, my scholarly path has more nearly resembled that of a pinball in mid-play—or perhaps better yet, it has more nearly resembled the path that Dexter, my late Labrador retriever, used to take on his morning walk, rejoicing in the pleasures of the moment, bouncing happily from one promising patch to another, ears flapping, tail wagging. My pattern has been no pattern, and my work overall gives emphatic testimony to the power of mere contingency. I knew that *Guardians* fit the general picture, since its proximate cause—as I'll soon explain—was a chance question raised in a faculty seminar. But before Adam's invitation I did not fully appreciate that in the case of *Guardians*, the picture is such that the book really should not exist at all.

Robert A. Kaster, *Epilogue* In: *Roman Perspectives on Linguistic Diversity*. Edited by Adam Gitner, Oxford University Press. © Oxford University Press 2023. DOI: 10.1093/oso/9780197611975.003.0013

226   EPILOGUE

When I emerged from the graduate program in classical philology at Harvard in 1975, a book on the social and intellectual history of education in Late Antiquity was the last thing I would have expected to write, for the very good reason that I knew nothing whatever about social history, or intellectual history, or the history of education, or Late Antiquity. My training at Harvard, in ancient Greek and Latin and the literatures written in those languages, was very effective and very, very focused: it concentrated wholly on— and I've always been grateful that it concentrated wholly on—developing philological expertise, in my case epitomized by the topic of my doctoral dissertation, the ninth-century manuscripts of the *Aeneid*. There was no historical component or requirement, nor so far as I recall was it ever suggested that a course or two in ancient history might be a good investment; as for the history of Latin literature—as represented by the quite formidable graduate reading list—it stopped at Juvenal.

The story of how I came to write that improbable book entails a long series of events and circumstances that were mostly the product of chance and were in any case almost entirely beyond my planning or control. But the story's precise starting point involves no random chance at all, but was instead entirely foreseeable, if not foreordained: in March of 1975, three months before I was to receive my degree, I had no prospect whatsoever of employment in my chosen field. The reason for this was clear: the previous December, in interviews with prospective employers—eleven of them, quite a healthy number for that hiring season in Classics—I was able to persuade exactly none of them that further acquaintance would serve their interests. This in turn doubtless had something to do with the fact that I could not speak about my dissertation without causing their eyes to roll back in their heads as they fell into a coma.

At that point, in a way that to this day makes me shake my head in disbelief, I received a telephone call from Peter White of the University of Chicago: would I be interested in discussing the possibility of an appointment to their faculty? Why, yes, thank you, Professor White, I would indeed. It emerged that the Chicagoans had offered a position to my graduate school friend and our present keynote speaker, Jim Zetzel; and when he declined the appointment, to take a job at Princeton instead, they had asked if he knew of anyone who was any good but still unattached. That was how my name came up and how I found myself flying to Chicago, where my future colleagues were eerily tolerant of my dissertation topic and seemed primarily concerned to assure themselves that I had only one head. On that basis I got the job.

EPILOGUE   227

My first year at Chicago was spent the same way that 99 percent of new assistant professors in the American system spend their first year, beyond getting a grip on their teaching and their new circumstances: they try to develop a plan to turn their dissertations into the published books that will meet the minimum requirement for a permanent appointment, when they are considered for tenure six years further on. This meant that my wife, Laura, and I did not see much of each other: she was beginning the partnership track at a large law firm, often working well into the evening and most weekends, while I went every Saturday and Sunday to my small study in the great Regenstein Library. There I would look over what I had written and the notes cards on which it was based, moving the cards around to see what interesting new patterns might emerge. 1975 became 1976, and the interesting patterns remained hidden; winter became spring, and not much had changed. It must have been the 29th or 30th of May—I know the date because it was the last weekend in May, America's Memorial Day holiday—when I realized that the interesting patterns were not going to emerge, at least not for me or not without much new work, and perhaps not even then. I had wasted one of the years I had to prove my worth—if not a disaster then something that looked and felt very much like one—but I saw no sense in wasting more. Walking home from the Regenstein along 57th Street, I must have looked as stricken as I felt, because Peter White, working in his garden, spotted me, hauled me into his backyard, and put a strong drink into my hand.[1]

"What now?" was the question of the day, and the answer emerged gradually over the summer, taking the form—still very hazy in my mind—of Servius. In working on the transmission of Vergil I had necessarily become acquainted with the Servian commentaries—in fact I had shlepped the three thick volumes of Thilo-Hagen around much of Europe in the summer of 1973, as I visited libraries and collated manuscripts—but I had not yet read them attentively. That was my work for the summer, and by the time the new academic year began in late September, I had drafted a paper—on Servius and "suitable authors," *idonei auctores*, and the reception of Lucan, Statius, and Juvenal into the late antique canon—which seemed much more like the sort of thing I should be doing, and certainly more promising than anything

[1] When the unrevised dissertation was subsequently published in a series of Harvard dissertations in the Classics (*The Tradition of the Text of the "Aeneid" in the Ninth Century* [1990]), Michael Reeve (1991, 59) justly remarked in a review that one of its two main conclusions was "broad and dull," the other "specific and interesting." The early medieval manuscripts of Vergil were by then the subject of two fine studies by Louis Holtz (1985; 1986).

228   EPILOGUE

I had done so far.[2] But it cannot be said that I had more than a hunch about the general direction, and certainly nothing resembling a plan.

But a catalyst for a plan soon appeared, in the person of Arnaldo Momigliano, who in the fall of 1976 happened to begin a series of visits to Chicago that would extend for ten years, during which he led a faculty seminar on a topic of his choosing every fall and gave a series of lectures on a different theme each spring. It is a mark of how blinkered my exposure to my field had been that I had at first only a very vague notion of who he was, and it is a mark of his humanity and the interest he took in other scholars—younger ones especially—that I soon came to know him well and before very long could count him a friend. He was also, for me, a completely transformative influence. He hugely enriched my conception of what classical studies could be, from archaic Greece to the history of classical scholarship in the nineteenth and twentieth centuries, showing me the broad field on which I could deploy the philological skills I had developed at Harvard. He also played the part of intellectual matchmaker, introducing me to other scholars in person or through their publications, including the person and publications of Carlotta Dionisotti and Peter Brown. And most consequentially for the present purpose, he invited me to give a paper in his first faculty seminar, which took as its theme "The Author and His Audience in Antiquity": my specific remit was "The Grammarian and His Audience."

There was more than one way I could have approached the topic, for example by considering the implied audience of the Vergilian commentaries, something in fact that I would later do. Instead, for reasons I cannot now securely reconstruct, I chose Macrobius' *Saturnalia* as my key text. I say "for reasons I cannot now securely reconstruct" primarily because at the time I made my choice I had not yet read Macrobius' *Saturnalia*, in fact knew next to nothing about the work beyond three basic details: it was a dialogue of sorts, it was much concerned with Vergil, and one of the secondary characters in the dialogue was Servius himself. I suppose that last consideration was pivotal, insofar as the dialogue depicted the grammarian as he was conceived by a man who was indubitably a member of his audience.

Be that as it may, I came to be fascinated by an apparent tension in the grammarian's way of being in the dialogue, and by a key virtue that was attributed to him. On the one hand, as a young man of no great social status joining the company of his elders and aristocratic betters, he is described

---

[2] Published as Kaster 1978.

EPILOGUE 229

as almost painfully recessive on his first entrance, "both marvelous in his *doctrina* and likable in his *verecundia*, with his eyes upon the ground and looking as though he were trying to hide" (*Sat.* 1.2.15).[3] On the other hand, he is made to take stage-center and play a leading role later in the dialogue, when he holds forth for much of book 6 on figurative usages in the Vergilian corpus that the poet did not model on his predecessors but fashioned on his own. Of course it could simply be the case that Macrobius was not concerned to construct a consistent characterization for his grammarian. But by investigating the meaning of *verecundia*, in the *Saturnalia* and beyond, I became convinced that there was a more interesting answer.

Though conventionally translated as "modesty" or the like in English, *verecundia* entails a disposition that more accurately can be called "circumspection," a sense consistent with the root it shares with the verb *vereor*, which more commonly denotes "wariness" than outright "fear." People who are *verecundi* are disposed to engage in any personal transaction in such a way that they gauge their own standing relative to the other party and what respect they owe the other, and at the same time gauge what amount of attention and respect they can rightly claim for themselves. Understanding *verecundia* in this way—as a disposition conducive both to hierarchy and to social equipoise and reciprocity—made plain why the character of Servius should yield to his elders and betters in any ordinary social setting, and at the same time why he could claim the spotlight in a setting that called for a display of his professional expertise. And not just that: one could reasonably hold that *verecundia*, thus understood, was the animating force of the *Saturnalia* itself, a dialogue whose participants pay massive respect not just to Vergil but to the entire Roman cultural tradition and yet are confident in their own cultural competence, which makes them worthy of respect, each in his own field.[4]

That in a nutshell was the argument that my paper made, and it must be said that the argument left Momigliano underwhelmed: isn't it simply the case, he asked, that *verecundia* was a young person's virtue, something that the young person could be expected to outgrow in time? I was fairly certain that the answer was "no," but I could not at the time make an adequate case. And so I decided to start doing the work needed to make that case as soon as the seminar

---

[3] Also discussed by Holford-Strevens in this volume (Chapter 11).

[4] My fascination with *verecundia* went underground for some years, only to re-emerge in my later work on the Roman emotions of self-restraint: *Emotion, Restraint, and Community in Ancient Rome* (2005, 13–27, 61–5).

230 EPILOGUE

session ended that day in November 1976. The work continued through the balance of that academic year and into the summer of 1977, and by the autumn I had drafted what were to become my first two substantial papers, "The Grammarian's Authority" and "Macrobius and Servius: *Verecundia* and the Grammarian's Function," both eventually published in 1980. I also had fairly clearly in mind the book that I now wanted to write, one that would comprise a global study of the grammarian and society in Late Antiquity and address such questions as these: what was the range of the grammarians' social circumstances? (The answer to that question demanded the prosopography that is the book's second half.) What was the place of literacy and literary learning in that world? What did it mean to practice what we would call a profession in Late Antiquity? And what were the sources of the grammarian's authority as a cultural figure worthy of respect?

By the fall of 1977, then, I saw much of what I needed to do spread out before me, and I spent the next four years doggedly trying to do it—reading the sources and secondary literature, reading around the edges in the history of education and the sociology of professionalism—with the help of a fellowship from the National Endowment for the Humanities that allowed me to spend a full academic year, in 1980–81, doing nothing else. But by the fall of 1981 it seemed that I still had come up short, in part because of that first, wasted year. The deadline for the decision on my tenure was near, and a negative decision would almost certainly mean that I would be exploring a different line of work, since the academic job market in Classics had entered one of the great depressions it has experienced over the last four decades, and a fired assistant professor six years beyond his PhD would not be an attractive commodity. Yet my dossier at that point would have needed to double in bulk to count as slender: it could show only three articles published in those first six years, and only one half of a first book—and not even the discursive, analytical half, but the prosopography, the collection of data on which the main text of the book would be based, if it were ever written. The case looked weak by the standards of American research universities in 1981, and laughably weak by the standards applied today. And yet my colleagues—in a way I still find staggering—thought they saw some talent, and their recommendation to keep me on was accepted by dean, provost, and president.

I said at the outset that *Guardians* was the product of mere contingency. To fully appreciate that fact, let us now review the bidding:

had Jim Zetzel not received the offer of a job at Princeton;

EPILOGUE 231

had he not accepted it in preference to Chicago;

had he not been asked to suggest an alternative candidate;

had he suggested a different candidate with the normal complement of
heads;

had Peter White and his colleagues not accepted his suggestion;

had I decided to persist in developing my dissertation instead of setting
it aside;

had I not then turned to some vague idea involving Servius;

had Arnaldo Momigliano started his visits to Chicago a year later, or not
at all;

had he chosen a different topic for his first seminar;

had he not invited me to speak on "the grammarian and his audience";

had I chosen an approach to the topic that did not lead through
Macrobius;

had I not been captured by the idea of *verecundia*;

crucially, had Momigliano simply let the point go without raising his
question;

and had the colleagues at Chicago not made the decision they did,
none of us would be here today.

In fact, the utter outlandishness of our being here today can be roughly gauged as a matter of simple probability. I just enumerated fourteen junctures at which events could easily have taken a different course, and that number could probably be increased with a bit more thought: in only a small minority of those junctures was the course taken the result of my own decision; some of those decisions—for example, the choice of Macrobius as a lens—I can barely begin to explain; and if a different course had been taken at any one of those fourteen junctures, the entire sequence would have been broken. So let us suppose that in each case the odds were fifty-fifty that matters would take just the turn they did: that is an absurdly liberal supposition in most cases (e.g., that Momigliano would have chosen just that topic for his first seminar) but let it stand that at each juncture there was a one-in-two chance—a mere coin toss—that what we now know happened would happen. If that were the case, the odds that the story would unfold as it did would be one in two to the fourteenth power. Or to put it another way: if we had the godlike ability to replay the sequence until it turned out just as it did, we would arrive at this outcome only once every 16,384 tries.

232   EPILOGUE

Myself, I am unspeakably grateful that we seem to have beaten the odds, and I close with thanks, again, to Adam Gitner for conceiving this occasion and bringing it off so wonderfully, to all the speakers for their marvelous papers, and to all of you for listening now.

Prosopographical Addenda to Known Ancient Grammarians

At Adam's urging I have compiled the following bibliographic supplement to the prosopography of late antique grammarians in *Guardians of Language*, organized by entry number and name. As before, it covers the period from roughly 250 to 565 (on the scope and parameters of the prosopography see *Guardians* 233–5). Readers will see at once that the job has been made immeasurably easier by Part II—"A Bibliographic Guide"—of Jim Zetzel's monumental *Critics, Compilers, and Commentators: An Introduction to Roman Philology, 200 BCE—800 CE* (New York: Oxford University Press 2018), which provides up-to-date surveys for all the Latin *grammatici* represented by extant writings, and which I gratefully cite in the form "*CCC* [page-reference or §section number]." Papyri and inscriptions, where it seemed useful, have been equipped with Trismegistos numbers to facilitate consultation in online databases (e.g., http:// papyri.info, produced by the Duke Collaboratory for Classics Computing, and the Clauss-Slaby Epigraphik Datenbank at http://www.manfredclauss.de/). Beyond that, references are limited to the individual's identity as a *grammaticus* (or not, in the case of *dubii* and *falsi*) and other aspects of his life and work covered in *Guardians*. I have not tried to be exhaustive; citations concerning the more shadowy figures gathered in the prosopography's second half, "*Dubii, Falsi, Varii*," are, understandably, rather sparse.

"*Grammatici*, Γραμματοδιδάσκαλοι, *Magistri Ludi*, and the Like"

No. 2 Adamantius: cf. no. 95 Martyrius (his son).

No. 3 Agathodaemon: Évieux (1995, 144–7), places Agathodaemon and three other *grammatici* (nos. 71, 107, 109) in Pelusium. Of the five-book edition of Isidore's letters published in *Patrologia Graeca* 78, books 4 and 5 are now available in the critical edition prepared by Pierre Évieux

EPILOGUE 233

(completed by Nicolas Vinel; 1997–2017) for the series *Sources chrétiennes* (containings letters 1214–2000): for Agathodaemon, *Ep.* 5.55 = 1297, 334 = 1671, 439 = 1824, 444 = 1829, 454 = 1850.

No. 9 Ammonius and no. 11 Anastasius: Green (1985, 503).

No. 14 Apollinarius (of Laodicea): Speck (1997, 362–9); *Brill's New Pauly* "Apollinarius (2)" (Savvidis). Faulkner (2020, 1–31) now supports the older attribution of the *Metaphrasis psalmorum* to him, suggesting composition in the 360s.

No. 16 Arcadius: *Brill's New Pauly* "Arcadius (2)" (Montanari); *LGGA* "Arcadius" (Ercoles).

No. 19 Asmonius (Apthonius): the portion of a metrical work quoted by Priscian at *gramm.* III 420.2–7 and ascribed to Asmonius resembles— but is by no means identical with—a passage (*gramm.* VI 80.30–1.2) in the metrical work of Aphthonius transmitted under the name "Victorinus": see *CCC* 185–6, 280 (= §12.2 Apthonius). See also *Brill's New Pauly* "Asmonius" (Schmidt)."

No. 20 Aur. Augustinus: *CCC* 284–5 (= §12.8).

No. 21 Decimus Magnus Ausonius: Green (1985); Sivan (1991); Bajoni (1996); Pucci (2003); Lolli (2006); *PCBE* IV 287–97. See also no. 166 Ursulus.

No. 22 Bonifatius: the inscription *CIL* VI 9446 has been republished, with the supplement *Benemerenti Bonifatio sc[ribae librario]* (vs. *sc[holastico]*) *grammatico,* by Di Stefano Manzella (1997, 229–30); see also Agusta-Boularot (1994, 668–9).

No. 23 Calbulus: *PCBE* I 182 (assigned to Vandal Africa). The poems have been edited in D. R. Shackleton Bailey, *Anthologia Latina: Carmina in codicibus scripta* (Berlin, 1982), nos. 373–4.

No. 25 Calliopius: Cribiore (2007, 33–5).

No. 26 Cassianus: Gärtner and Gärtner (2004).

Nos. 29–30 Clamosus: Gemeinhardt (2008, 38 n. 63).

No. 31 Cledonius: *CCC* 291 (= §12.14).

No. 32 Cleobulus: Cribiore (2007, 33–4, 65).

No. 34 Cominianus: *CCC* 188–90.

No. 35 Concordius: Green (1985, 501).

No. 37 Corippus: cf. *PLRE* III Fl. Cresconius Corippus "poet M/L VI."

No. 39 Crispinianus: Carletti (1986, 116–17 = no. 107); Agusta-Boularot (1994, 672); the inscription *AE* 1969–70, no. 71 = Trismegistos no. 264362.

234   EPILOGUE

No. 41 Aur.(?) Cyrus: cf. *PLRE* III Cyrus 2 "(E/M VI)." Pap. 1 (P.Cair. Masp. II 67134) = Trismegistos no. 18879; Pap. 2 (P.Cair. Masp. II 67135) = Trismegistos no. 23712; Pap. 3 (P.Cair. Masp. II 67139) = Trismegistos 18888; Pap. 4 (P.Cair. Masp. III 67326) = Trismegistos no. 18451; Pap. 5 (P.Cair. Masp. III 67327) = Trismegistos no. 18452.

No. 42 Damocharis: Merkelbach (1977); *Brill's New Pauly* "Damocharis" (Degani); cf. *PLRE* III Damocharis "(M VI)."

No. 44 Deuterius: *PCBE* II.1 558; Barnish (2003).

No. 45 Deuterius: the inscription *CLE* 1964 also published as *ICVR* IV 10888, dating it to the fourth century (Epigraphik-Datenbank Clauss–Slaby EDCS-35100458). Discussed by Gemeinhardt (2008, 38).

No. 47 Diomedes: *CCC* 294–5. Isid. Pel. *Ep.* 5.125 = 1392 Évieux.

No. 50 Domitius: *PCBE* IV 584; Mathisen (2020, 90: "probably a *rhetor* rather than a *grammaticus*").

No. 51 Donatianus: *CCC* 295 (= §12.19).

No. 52 Aelius Donatus: *CCC* 190–7, 296–7 (= §12.20).

No. 53 Dositheus: *CCC* 297–8 (= §12.21).

No. 54 Evanthius: *CCC* 255–6 (= §11.1.4); *Brill's New Pauly* "Evanthius" (Gatti).

No. 55 Eudaemon: *Brill's New Pauly* "Eudaemon" (Fornaro); Cribiore (2007, 76, 165); Meinel (2011); *LGGA* "Eudaemon" (Meliadò).

No. 56 Eugenius: *Brill's New Pauly* "Eugenius (2)" (Fornaro); Ercoles (2015).

No. 57 Eutyches: *CCC* 298 (= §12.22).

No. 58 Faustus: on Luxurius' dedicatory poem to Faustus (*anth.* 287 Riese = 284 Shackleton Bailey), cf. Happ (1985–6, II:14–15); Giovini (2003, 327–36).

No. 60 Iunius Filargirius: *CCC* 265 (= §11.3.4).

No. 62. Fl. Fortunatus: add Brusin (1993, 1032 no. 2931), dating the inscription to 326/400 (= Trismegistos no. 562083).

No. 63 Georgius: Lauxtermann (2005).

No. 64 Acilius Glabrio: Green (1985, 499–500, 503); Sivan (1991; a connection with the Italian Acilii Glabriones is rejected).

No. 65 Harmonius: see no. 166 Ursulus.

No. 67 Helladius: *Brill's New Pauly* "Helladius (2)" (Fornaro); *LGGA* "Helladius (3)" (Meliadò).

No. 68 Fl. Her...: *BGU* XII 2152 = Trismegistos no. 16108.

No. 69 Heraclammon: *P.Ross.Georg.* V 60 = Trismegistos no. 17537.

No. 70 Pomponius Maximus Herculanus: Green (1985, 492, 502–3).

EPILOGUE 235

No. 71 Hermias: prob. to be located in Pelusium, see no. 3 Agathodaemon.

No. 72 Hermolaus: cf. *PLRE* III Hermolaus "M VI or L VII/E VIII" (registering uncertainty whether he was active under Justinian I or Justinian II).

No. 73 Hesychius: *Brill's New Pauly* "Hesychius (1)" (Tosi); *LGGA* "Hesychius" (Valente).

No. 75 Hierius: Passalacqua and De Nonno (2007, 326).

No. 76 Hierocles: *Brill's New Pauly* "Hierocles (8)" (Brodersen); cf. *PLRE* III Hierocles "(VI)."

No. 78 Fl. Horapollon: Pap. (*P.Cair.Masp.* III 67295) = Trismegistos no. 26528; *Corpus dei papiri filosofici greci e latini* I.2.2 (2008) no. 19.

No. 80 Ioannes: *PCBE* IV 1060–1; Mathisen (2020, 102).

No. 82 Ioannes (of Caesarea): *Brill's New Pauly* "Iohannes (15)" (Markschies).

No. 83 Ioannes (of Gaza): Cameron (1993): before 526 and after Nonnus of Panopolis, s. V med.; *Brill's New Pauly* "Iohannes (25)" (Schmidt).

No. 84 Ioannes: cf. *PLRE* III Ioannes 61 "M VI."

No. 87 L. Terentius Iulianus *signo* Concordius: Agusta-Boularot (1994, 685–7); inscription *AE* 1978 no. 503 = Trismegistos no. 208067.

No. 88 Iulius: Cribiore (2007, 33); *LGGA* "Iulius (1)" (Novembri).

No. 89 Leontius *signo* Lascivus: Green (1985, 501, 503).

No. 90 Lollianus *signo* Homoeus: Agusta-Boularot (1994, 706–8); Connolly (2010); Pap. (*P.Coll.Youtie* II 66) = Trismegistos no. 20885.

No. 91 Lupercus: *Brill's New Pauly* "Lupercus" (Baumbach); LGGA "Lupercus" (Ucciardello).

No. 92 Ioannes Lydus: Maas (1992); *Brill's New Pauly* "Iohannes (3) Lydus" (Tinnefeld); Nicks (2000); Kaldellis (2003); Dubuisson (2006).

No. 93 Macrinus: Green (1985, 503).

No. 94 Marcellus: Green (1985, 492, 503–4).

No. 95 Martyrius: *CCC* 304–5 (= §12.28).

No. 97 Melleus: *CIL* XI 3568 = Trismegistos no. 200118.

No. 101: Metrodorus (of Tralles): cf. *PLRE* III Metrodorus "M VI."

No. 102 Musaeus: *Brill's New Pauly* "Musaeus (4)" (Fornaro); Dümmler (2012).

No. 103 Annius Namptoius: Inscr. a + b (*Inscr. Afr.* Cagnat no. 273) = Trismegistos no. 200529.

No. 104 Nebridius: Folliet (1987); *Brill's New Pauly* "Nebridius (3)" (Schindler); Bermon (2009).

No. 105 Nepotianus: Green (1985, 500, 502–3).

236   EPILOGUE

No. 106 Nicocles: *Brill's New Pauly* "Nicocles (5)" (Matthaios); Martin (1998); Martin (2009); Cribiore (2007, 60–1, 313); Cribiore (2013, 165–6, 177, 179).

No. 107 Nilus: prob. to be located in Pelusium, see no. 3 Agathodaemon.

No. 109 Ophelius: prob. to be located in Pelusium, see no. 3 Agathodaemon; Isid. Pel. *Ep.* 4.105, 162, 200 = 1814, 1275, 1332 Évieux; 5.66, 121, 133, 245, 317, 430, 439, 517, 544, 558 = 1314, 1389, 1401, 1543, 1652, 1815, 1824, 1929, 1962, 1979 Évieux.

No. 110 Orion: *Brill's New Pauly* "Orion (3)" (Tosi); manuscript excerpts from an epitome of his *Anthologion* (Vienna, gr. 321, ff. 63–8; erroneously titled *Antholognomicon*) have been edited by Haffner (2001), who defends the authorship; *LGGA* "Orion" (Ippolito); cf. Piccione (2002; 2003).

No. 111 Orus: *Brill's New Pauly* "Orus" (Alpers); Billerbeck (2011); Xenis (2013).

No. 112 Aur. Oursenouphius: Pap. (*Stud.Pal.* XX 117) = Trismegistos no. 18740.

No. 113 Palladas: *Brill's New Pauly* "Palladas" (Albiani). The important article by K. W. Wilkinson (2009) argued that Palladas' most prominent activity should be down-dated from the age of Theodosius to that of Constantine and relocated from Alexandria to Contantinople, with Palladas himself dated to 259–340 (vs., e.g., "Ca. 320?—s. IV ex." in *Guardians*): subsequent scholarship has either explored the revision's implications (Wilkinson 2010a; 2010b; 2012a; with edition of new papyri epigrams id., 2012b; Woods 2016) or regarded it skeptically (Cameron 2015; Benelli 2015; 2016).

No. 114 Pamprepius: *Brill's New Pauly* "Pamprepius" (Fornaro); Feld (2002); Cameron (2007); Livrea (2011).

No. 117 Philagrius: *Brill's New Pauly* "Philogelos" (Fornaro).

No. 118 Ioannes Philoponus: *Brill's New Pauly* "Philoponus, Iohannes" (Savvidis and Wildberg); on his status as a grammarian cf. Fernández (1989); on his career, context, and chronology: MacCoull (1995; 2005; 2007); Perkams (2009).

No. 119 Philtatius: *LGGA* "Philtatius" (Regali).

No. 121 Phocas: *CCC* 307–8 (= §12.33; "a later date seems more likely").

No. 122 Phoebicius: Green (1985, 503).

No. 123 Placidus: Stok (1987); *CCC* 239.

No. 124 Iulianus Pomerius: *Brill's New Pauly* "Pomerius, Iulianus" (Pollmann); *PCBE* IV 1497–1500. Translation of *De vita contemplativa* by Jobard and Gagliardi (1995).

EPILOGUE 237

No. 125 Pompeius: *CCC* 308–9 (= §12.34).

No. 126 Priscianus: *CCC* 197–200 (= §8.8), 309–11 (= §12.35).

No. 127 Probus: *CCC* 183–7 (= §8.4), 312–16 (= §12.36); see also no. 242 Palladius.

No. 128 Fl. Pythiodorus: cf. no. 68 above.

No. 130 Rufinus: *CCC* 316–17 (= §12.37).

No. 131 Domitius Rufinus: de Bohec (2013, 98); for the inscription (*ILS* 7762), cf. *AE* 2013, no. 2153.

No. 132 Marius Plotius Sacerdos: *CCC* 317–18 (= §12.38).

No. 133 Sarapion: *P.Oxy.* XXIV 2422 = Trismegistos no. 16933.

No. 135 Sergius: Torrance (1988).

No. 136 Servius: *CCC* 319–21 (= §12.40).

No. 138 Speciosus: cf. *PLRE* III Speciosus 1 "(532)."

No. 140 Staphylius: Green (1985, 502–3).

No. 144 Stephanus: *Brill's New Pauly* "Stephanus (7)" (Gärtner); Hemmerdinger (1997); Billerbeck (2008); Neumann-Hartmann (2014; 2016); *LGGA* "Stephanus" (Billerbeck and Clerc).

No. 150 Aur. Theodorus: Pap. (*P.Oxy.* XXIV 2421) = Trismegistos no. 16933.

No. 152 Theodosius: *Brill's New Pauly* "Theodosius (I.3)" (Matthaios); van Elst (2011). In her edition of the Epitome of Herodian's *De Prosodia Catholica*, Roussou (2018, 20–5) does not regard the attribution of the work as settled. *LGGA* "Theodosius" (Pagani) accepts the identification of this Theodosius with Theodosius ὁ θαυμάσιος γραμματικός, a friend of Synesius of Cyrene (= *Guardians* no. 151), and accordingly accepts a date of "4th–th c. CE."

No. 153 Theodosius: Pelsmaekers (1988); inscription = Trismegistos no. 102812.

No 156 Timotheus: Schneider (1999, 15–71); *Brill's New Pauly* "Timotheus (14)" (Matthaios).

No. 157 Triphiodorus: *Brill's New Pauly* "Triphiodorus" (Fornaro).

No. 159 Verecundus: *PCBE* II.2 2265–6.

No. 161 Victor: Duval (2001); Gemeinhardt (2008, 38).

No. 162 Victorius: Green (1985, 501, 503).

No. 166 Ursulus: Dräger (2012).

No. 173 Anonymus 7: *SB* XII 11084 = Trismegistos no. 35025.

No. 174 Anonymus (Anonymi?) 8: *PSI* VIII 891 = Trismegistos no. 35091.

No. 175 Anonymus 9: *P.Cair.Masp.* I 67077 = Trismegistos no. 36819.

238   EPILOGUE

"Dubii, Falsi, Varii"

No. 179 Aegialeus: on the historical setting of the *Acta Archelai*, cf. Scopello (2020).

No. 181 Agroecius: *CCC* 279–80 (= §12.1); *PCBE* IV 95.

No. 183 Alethius: Moroni (2002).

No. 184 Antiochus: Cribiore (2015, 136–52: translation of Libanius' *Oration* 39, addressed to Antiochus).

No. 185 Elius Aprilicus: Noy (1993–5, no. 85); Rossi and Di Mento (2013, no. 34; by A. Negroni).

No. 187 Aresthusius: *P.Ant.* II 93 = Trismegistos no. 32723.

No. 190 Audax: *CCC* 283–4 (= §12.7).

No. 193 Cabrias: see no. 198 Chabrias.

No. 195 Carminius: Jakobi (2018, 178) is skeptical that Carminius' *De elocutionibus* was an important source for the rhetoriscian Arusianus Messius' glossary.

No. 197 Arruntius Celsus: Stok (1994).

No. 198 Chabrias: *P.Berl.Bork.* = Trismegistos no. 32643.

No. 199 Ioannes Charax: *PLRE* III (Ioannes Charax 120) dates Charax to the sixth century because he was cited by Georgius Choeroboscus (no. 201), who is however incorrectly dated ad loc. as "M/L VI."

No. 200 Fl. Sosipater Charisius: *CCC* 186–90 (= §8.6), 289–90 (= §12.13).

No. 201 Georgius Choeroboscus: *Brill's New Pauly* "Choiroboskos Georgios" (Montanari), accepting the ninth-century dating.

No. 203 Consentius: *CCC* 291–2 (= §12.15), supporting identification with the elder Consentius; Mari (Chapter 6) supports the younger Consentius, who had a mobile career. Both listed in Mathisen (2020, 88).

No. 204 Coronatus: *CCC* 293–4 (= §12.17).

No. 205 Fabius(?) Demetrius: Agusta-Boularot (1994, 683) reading: *D(iis) M(anibus) S(acrum)* | *[De]metri[o] [ma]gistr[o]* | *[gramma(?)]tico C(aius) [F]abius* | *piiss[imo] et [b]eneme[renti]*, and dating "au plus tôt IIe siècle ap. J.-C."

No. 208 Ti. Claudius Maximus Donatianus: see no. 51 Donatianus.

No. 209 Ti. Claudius Donatus: *CCC* 266 (= §11.3.6).

No. 210 Eudaemon: Cribiore (2007, 33–4).

No. 211 Fl. Eugenius: *Brill's New Pauly* "Flavius Eugenius (1)" (Portmann).

No. 214 Eutyches: *P.Berl.Bork.* = Trismegistos no. 32643.

No. 217 Filocalus: cf. De Nonno (2010).

EPILOGUE 239

No. 218 Firmianus: *CCC* 186–7 (accepting identification with Lactantius).

No. 220 Flavius: *SB* I 5941 = Trismegistos no. 23278.

No. 221 Atilius Fortunatianus: *CCC* 283 (= §12.6).

Nos. 222 T. Gallus and 223 Gaudentius: see no. 60 Iunius Filargirius.

No. 224 Gorgon(i)us: inscription now dated to 290 / 324 by the Epigraphic Database Bari (*ICVR* IV 9894 = Epigraphic Database Bari no. 18916 = Trismegistos no. 308537).

No. 225 Grillius: *Brill's New Pauly* "Grillius" (Gatti); *CCC* 260 (= 11.2.6).

No. 226 Harpocration: Cribiore (2007, 33–4, 65). Baldwin (1992, 103 n. 4) follows *PLRE* I in possibly identifying this Harpocration with the late antique author of a work on the δυνάμεις of plants, animals, and stones (= *LGGA* "Harpocration (3)" [Meliadò]).

No. 227 Helladius: *Brill's New Pauly* "Helladius (1)" (Fornaro).

No. 228 Aur. Herodes: *P.Cair.Isid.* 3 = Trismegistos no. 10359; and *P.Cair.Isid.* 4 = Trismegistos no. 10369 (both now dated to "299?").

No. 229 Hesperius: *PCBE* IV 984; Mathisen (2020, 100): "rhetor."

No. 230 Hierocles: *Brill's New Pauly* "Philogelos" (Fornaro).

No. 232 Hieronymus: *CCC* 357 (= §13.35 on *Ars Ambrosiana*), 360 (on [Hieronymus] *de pedibus*).

No. 233 Hoën(i)us: cf. Mathisen (2020, 101: "grammaticus").

No. 235 Luxurius: *Brill's New Pauly* "Luxurius" (Lausberg).

No. 236 Manippus or Marsipus: cf. no. 179.

No. 237 Nonius Marcellus: *CCC* 98–9 (= §6.2), 231–2 (= §10.2).

No. 238 Marcianus: *Brill's New Pauly* "Marcianus (5)" (Leppin).

No. 239 "Metrorius": *CCC* 333–5 (= 12.46.7 on *De finalibus*).

No. 240 Nepos: on *Dub. Nom.* C 55 *culmus gen. neu., ut Nepus vult* see Spangenberg Yanes (2020, 178–9 *ad loc.*), preferring a reference to a literary source rather than a grammarian.

No. 242 Palladius: *CCC* 306–7 (= §12.33 Phocas); see also no. 127 Probus.

No. 244 Papirianus: *CCC* 307 (= §12.32 Papirius).

No. 245 Phalerius: Cribiore (2007, 71–2).

No. 248 Aur. Plution: *P.Ryl.* IV 656 = Trismegistos no. 13047.

No. 249 C. Iulius Romanus: *CCC* 85–8.

No. 252 Marcius Salutaris: Pap. 1 (*P.Lond.* III 1157va) = Trismegistos no. 22808; Pap. 2 (*P.Wisc.* II 86) = Trismegistos no. 29469; Pap. 3 (*P.Oxy.* XVII 2123) = Trismegistos no. 17504; Pap. 4 (*P.Oxy.* XXXIII 2664) = Trismegistos no. 16869; Pap. 5 (*P.Oxy.* I 78) = Trismegistos no. 20737.

240 EPILOGUE

No. 253 Seleucus: *Brill's New Pauly* "Seleucus (14)" (Matthaios); *LGGA* "Seleucus (2)" (Ucciardello).

No. 254 Vibius Sequester: *Brill's New Pauly* "Vibius (II 14) Sequester" (Sallmann); Gautier Dalché (2014).

No. 255 "Sergius": *CCC* 321–4.

No. 260 Sosistratus: *SB* VI 9270 = Trismegistos no. 17883.

No. 262 Ter(r)entius (better, Terrentius): *CCC* 354 (= §13.30 discussing Virgilius Maro Grammaticus).

No. 264 Theodoretus: cf. *PLRE* III Theodoretus 2 "?M VI."

No. 265 Theodoretus: *Brill's New Pauly* "Theodoretus (2)" (Baumbach).

No. 266 Theodorus: cf. *PLRE* III 53 "? grammaticus (East) M VI."

No. 267 Theon: *P.Berl.Bork.* = Trismegistos no. 32643; for "col. 12.34" read "col. 12.433."

No. 271 Curtius Valerianus: *CCC* 288 (= §12.11.2)

No. 273 Victorinus and no. 274 Maximus(?) Victorinus: *CCC* 328–9 (= §12.35).

No. 277 Anonymus 13: *P.Oxy.* XXIV 2425 = Trismegistos no. 30451.

No. 278 Anonymus 14: *P.Cair.Isid.* V 45 = Trismegistos no. 10369.

No. 279 Anonymus 15: *SB* VI 9191 = Trismegistos no. 17883.

No. 280 Anonymus 16: *O.Petr.* 450 = *O.Petr.Mus.* 575 = Trismegistos no. 75606.

Add:

Add. 1. Aristophanes. γραμματικός. Oenoanda (area of). s. III/IV.

$\qquad$ *SEG* LXIII 1330: Γραμματικῶν | ἐπέων ὁ διδάσκαλος | ἐνθάδε κεῖμαι | ἠδὲ Μενανδρείων | ἐπέων ἴδρις ἐν θυ|μέλαισι [vacat]| καὶ μελέων τραγι|κῶν οὐκ ἄλαλος λα|λιᾷ | οὔνομα δ᾽ Ἀριστο||φάνης, κύριον εὐ|λογίης· χαίρετέ | μοι πάροδοι· vacat | τοῦτο μόγον· πάριτε).

Add. 2. Maximus. grammaticus. late s. VI.

$\qquad$ See *PLRE* III Maximus 6.

Add. 3. Milichus 'Romaicus' East s. V?

$\qquad$ *Explicit de pronomine feliciter bono Milicho romalco* [= *romaico*, with *i longa*]: the subscription to the fragmentarily preserved treatise *De nomine et pronomine* (*gramm.* V 555–66 = Passalacqua [1984, 3–19]), which was probably composed and certainly transmitted in the East, where *Romaicus* commonly denoted not just *Latinus* but *Latinus grammaticus*: Dionisotti

EPILOGUE   241

(1984, 207–8), Passalacqua and De Nonno (2007, 324–8), *CCC* 331–2 (= §12.46.4b).
and more doubtfully:

Add. dub. 1. Theodorus son of Domitius γραμματικός Byzantium s. III/ IV? s. II?

Kaibel no. 534 = *GVI* 1479 = Łajtar (2000, 114–15 no. 120), with Agusta-Boularot (1994, 704–6). Kaibel dated the stone to s. III/IV, followed by Agusta-Boularot (on the basis of the bas-relief accompanying the inscription); s. II according to Peek (in *GVI*) and Łajtar ("wohl 2. Jh. n. Chr.").

Add. dub. 2 Athenades son of Dioscourides γραμματικὸς Ῥωμαικός Marseille

IG XIV 2434, with Agusta-Boularot (1994, 689–90); the inscription is undated.

Add. dub. 3 Valerius γραμματικὸς Ῥωμαικός Thyatira (Lydia)

CIL III 406, with Agusta-Boularot (1994, 700–1); the inscription is undated.

Bibliography

Abbott, F. F. 1909. "Vulgar Latin in the *Ars Consentii de Barbarismis*." *CPh* 4:233–47.

Adams, J. N. 2003. *Bilingualism and the Latin Language*. Cambridge: Cambridge University Press.

Adams, J. N. 2007. *The Regional Diversification of Latin 200 BC–AD 600*. Cambridge: Cambridge University Press.

Adams, J. N. 2013. *Social Variation and the Latin Language*. Cambridge: Cambridge University Press.

Adams, J. N. 2016. *An Anthology of Informal Latin 200 BC–AD 900*. Cambridge: Cambridge University Press.

Agusta-Boularot, S. 1994. "Les références épigraphiques aux *grammatici* et γραμματικοί de l'empire Romaine (Ier s. av. J.-C.—IVe s. ap. J.-C.)." *MEFR* 106:653–746.

Amelotti, M. 1966. *Il testamento romano attraverso la prassi documentale*. Milan: Le Monnier.

Ammirati, S. 2015. *Sul libro latino antico: Ricerche bibliologiche e paleografiche*. Pisa: Fabrizio Serra.

Ando, C. 2015. *Roman Social Imaginaries: Language and Thought in Contexts of Empire*. Toronto: University of Toronto Press.

Ando, C. 2016. "Sovereignty, Territoriality and Universalism in the Aftermath of Caracalla." In *Citizenship and Empire in Europe 200–1900: The Antonine Constitution after 1800 Years*, ed. C. Ando, 7–27. Munich: Franz Steiner.

Arena, V., and F. Mac Góráin, eds. 2017. *Varronian Moments*. Bulletin of the Institute of Classical Studies. Oxford: Wiley.

Astbury, R. 2000. Review of Willis 1997. *Gnomon* 72:309–13.

Ax, W. 2011. *Quintilians Grammatik* (Inst. orat. *1.4–8*): *Text, Übersetzung und Kommentar*. Berlin: De Gruyter.

Babusiaux, U. 2014. "Funktionen der Etymologie in der juristischen Literatur." *Fundamina* 20:39–60.

Bajoni, M. G. 1996. *Professori a Bordeaux = Commemoratio professorum Burdigalensium*. Florence: Le Lettere Editrice.

Baldwin, B. 1992. "*Cyranidea*: Some Improvements." *ICS* 17:103–7.

Baratin, M. 1988. "Remarques sur la place et le rôle du concept de latinité dans les grammaires latines antiques." *Ktèma* 13:187–93.

Baratin, M. 1994. "Sur la structure des grammaires antiques." In *Florilegium Historiographiae Linguisticae: Études d'historiographie de la linguistique et de grammaire comparée à la mémoire de Maurice Leroy*, ed. J. De Clercq and P. Desmet, 143–57. Louvain-La-Neuve: Peeters.

Baratin, M. et al., eds. 2009. *Priscien: Transmission et refondation de la grammaire*. Turnhout: Brepols.

Barnish, S. J. B. 2003. "Liberty and Advocacy in Ennodius of Pavia: The Significance of Rhetorical Education in Late Antique Italy." In *Hommages à Carl Deroux*,

244 BIBLIOGRAPHY

5: *Christianisme et Moyen Âge, néo-latin et survivance de la latinité*, ed. P. Defosse, 20–8. Brussels: Latomus.

Barwick, K. 1922. *Remmius Palaemon und die römische* Ars grammatica. Leipzig: Dieterich.

Basset, L. et al., eds. 2007. *Bilinguisme et terminologie grammaticale gréco-latine*. Peeters: Leuven.

Battaglia, F. 2017. *Iuliani de ambiguitatibus liber singularis: Una monografia romana di lingua del diritto tra esegesi e storiografia*. Pavia: TCP.

Beck, J. W. 1883. *Specimen litterarium de differentiarum scriptoribus Latinis*. Diss. Groningen.

Bellandi, F. 2008. "Intellettuali e insegnanti in Giovenale. La satira 7." In *Aspetti della scuola nel mondo romano: Atti del Convegno (Pisa, 5-6 dicembre 2006)*, ed. F. Bellandi and R. Ferri, 49–79. Amsterdam: Hakkert.

Benelli, L. 2015. "Osservazioni sul P. Ct. YBR Inv. 4000 e sulla sua attribuzione a Pallada di Alessandria." *ZPE* 193:53–63.

Benelli, L. 2016. "The Age of Palladas." *Mnemosyne* 69:978–1007.

Bermon, E. 2009. "Un échange entre Augustin et Nebridius sur la phantasia: (Lettre 6-7)." *ArchPhilos* 72:199–223.

Bernabé, A. 1987. *Poetarum epicorum Graecorum testimonia et fragmenta*. Pars I. Stuttgart and Leipzig: Teubner.

Billerbeck, M. 2008. "Sources et technique de citation chez Étienne de Byzance." *Eikasmos* 19:301–22.

Billerbeck, M. 2011. "The Orus Fragments in the *Ethnica* of Stephanus of Byzantium." In Matthaios, Montanari, and Rengakos 2011, 429–47.

Bischoff, B. 1998–2014. *Katalog der festländischen Handschriften des neunten Jahrhunderts*. 3 vols. Wiesbaden: Harassowitz.

Biville, F. 2008. "Les *Institutiones* de Priscien, une grammaire et une culture bilingues." In *Des formes et des mots chez les Anciens: Mélanges offerts à Danièle Conso*, ed. C. Brunet, 31–50. Besançon: Presses Universitaires de Franche-Comté.

Blank, D. 2008. "Varro and the epistemological status of etymology." *HEL* 30:49–73.

Blank, D. 2019. "What's Hecuba to Him? Varro on the Natural Kinship of Things and Words." In Pezzini and Taylor 2019, 121–52.

Bohec, Y. de, ed. 2013. *La société de l'Afrique romaine*. Bulletin archéologique du Comité des travaux historiques et scientifiques 37. Paris: Éd. du CTHS.

Bonin, F. 2019. "Note per un'indagine intorno alla struttura e alla forma dei frammenti dei 'libri ad Vitellium' di Paolo." *Rivista di diritto romano* 19:61–88.

Bonnet, G. 2005. *Dosithée: Grammaire latine*. Paris: Les Belles Lettres.

Bonnet, G. 2007. "La version grecque de l'*Ars* de Dosithée." In Basset et al. 2007, 191–9.

Bonnet, G. 2011. "Syntagms in the Artigraphic Latin Grammars." In Matthaios, Montanari, and Rengakos 2011, 361–74.

Brandenburg, P. 2014. "Case (πτῶσις), Ancient Theories of." S.v. in *Encyclopedia of Ancient Greek Language and Linguistics*, ed. G. K. Giannakis, online. Leiden: Brill.

Braund, S. 2004. *Juvenal and Persius*. Cambridge: Cambridge University Press.

Brugnoli, G. 1955. *Studi sulle Differentiae verborum*. Rome: Signorelli.

Brusin, J. B. 1993. *Inscriptiones Aquileiae* 3. Udine: Dep. di Storia Patria per il Friuli.

Burman, A. C. 2017. De Lingua Sabina: *A Reappraisal of the Sabine Glosses*. Diss. University of Cambridge.

Butterfield, D., ed. 2015. *Varro varius: The Polymath of the Roman World*. = *CCJ* Supplement 39. Cambridge: Cambridge Philosophical Society.

BIBLIOGRAPHY 245

Calcante, C. M. 2007. "L'antico come categoria stilistica: la teoria dell'arcaismo nell'Institutio oratoria di Quintiliano." In *Dialogando con il passato: Permanenze e innovazioni nella cultura latina di età flavia*, ed. A. Bonadeo and E. Romano, 108–23. Florence: Le Monnier.

Cameron, A. 1993. "On the Date of John of Gaza." *CQ* 43:348–51.

Cameron, A. 2007. "Poets and Pagans in Byzantine Egypt." In *Egypt in the Byzantine World, 300-700*, ed. R. S. Bagnall, 21–46. Cambridge: Cambridge University Press. (repr. in id., *Wandering Poets and Other Essays on Late Greek Literature and Philosophy*, 147–62. New York: Oxford University Press).

Cameron, A. 2010. "The Date of the *Scholia Vetustiora* on Juvenal." *CQ* 60:569–76.

Cameron, A. 2011. *The Last Pagans of Rome*. Oxford: Oxford University Press.

Cameron, A. 2015. "Palladas: New Poems, New Date?" In id., *Wandering Poets and Other Essays on Late Greek Literature and Philosophy*, 91–112. New York: Oxford University Press.

Campbell, B. 2000. *The Writings of the Roman Land Surveyors: Introduction, Text, Translation, and Commentary*. London: Society for the Promotion of Roman Studies.

Cardauns, M. 1976. *M. Terentius Varro, Antiquitates Rerum Divinarum*. Mainz: Akademie der Wissenschaften/Steiner.

Carletti, C. 1986. *Iscrizioni cristiane a Roma: Testimonianze di vita cristiana (secoli III-VII*. Florence: Nardini.

Cary, E. 1937. *Dionysius of Halicarnassus: Roman Antiquities*, Volume 1: *Books 1–2*. Cambridge, MA: Harvard University Press.

Caston, R. and R. A. Kaster, eds. 2016. *Hope, Joy, and Affection in the Classical World*. New York: Oxford University Press.

Cavenaile, R. 1958. *Corpus papyrorum latinarum*. Wiesbaden: Harrassowitz.

Ceci, L. 1892. *Le etimologie dei giureconsulti romani*. Turin: Loescher.

Chahoud, A., M. Rosellini, and E. Spangenberg Yanes, eds. 2019. *Latin Grammarians Forum 2018-2019*. = *Rationes rerum* 14. Rome: Edizioni Tored.

Cioffi, C. 2017. *Aeli Donati quod fertur commentum ad Andriam Terenti*. Berlin: De Gruyter.

Cioffi, C. 2018. *Prolegomena a Donato, Commentum ad Andriam*. Berlin: De Gruyter.

Clackson, J. 2015. "*Latinitas*, Ἑλληνισμός, and Standard Languages." *Studi e Saggi Linguistici* 53:309–30.

Clarke, M. L. 1968. "Juvenal 7. 150-53." *CPh* 63:295–6.

Clausen, W. and J. E. G. Zetzel. 2004. *Commentum Cornuti in Persium*. Leipzig: K. G. Saur.

Collart, J. 1954. *Varron: Grammairien Latin*. Paris: Les Belles Lettres.

Connolly, S. 2010. "A Grammarian Honors the Emperors." *AHB* 24:113–25.

Corbeill, A. 2015. *Sexing the World: Grammatical Gender and Biological Sex in Ancient Rome*. Princeton: Princeton University Press.

Corbett, G. G. 2000. *Number*. Cambridge: Cambridge University Press.

Corcoran, T. H. 1972. *Seneca: Natural Questions, Volume II*. Cambridge, MA: Harvard University Press.

Courtney, E. 1980. *A Commentary on the Satires of Juvenal*. London: Athlone.

Courtney, E. 1993. *The Fragmentary Latin Poets*. Oxford: Clarendon Press.

Cribiore, R. 2007. *The School of Libanius in Late Antique Antioch*. Princeton: Princeton University Press.

Cribiore, R. 2013. *Libanius the Sophist: Rhetoric, Reality, and Religion in the Fourth Century*. Ithaca, NY: Cornell University Press.

246 BIBLIOGRAPHY

Cribiore, R. 2015. *Between City and School: Selected Orations of Libanius*. Liverpool: Liverpool University Press.

Dahlmann, H. 1932. *Varro und die hellenistische Sprachtheorie*. Berlin: Weidmann.

Dahlmann, H. 1935. "M. Terentius Varro." S.v. in *RE* Supplement volume 6:1172–277.

Dahlmann, H. 1940. *Varro: De lingua Latina Buch VIII*. Hildesheim: Weidmann.

Dammer, R. 2001. *Diomedes grammaticus*. Trier: Wissenschaftlicher Verlag.

Davies, M. 1988. *Epicorum Graecorum fragmenta*. Göttingen: Vandenhoeck & Ruprecht.

Della Corte, F. 1937. *La filologia latina dalle origini a Varrone*. Turin: F. Casanova &c.

Della Corte, F. 1954. *Varrone: Il terzo gran lume Romano*. Genoa: Pubblicazioni dell'istituto universitario di magistero.

Della Corte, F. 1976. "L'idea della preistoria in Varrone." In *Atti del congresso internazionale di studi varroniani*, 111–36. Rieti: Centro di Studi Varroniani.

de Melo, W. D. C. 2009. "*Scies (Mil.* 520) e *scibis (Mil.* 1365): Variazione accidentale?" In *Lecturae Plautinae Sarsinates XII: Miles gloriosus (Sarsina, 27 settembre 2008)*, ed. R. Raffaelli and A. Tontini, 41–52. Urbino: Quattroventi.

de Melo, W. D. C. 2019a. "Naturalism and Morphology: Varro on Derivation and Inflection." In Pezzini and Taylor 2019, 103–20.

de Melo, W. D. C. 2019b. *Varro: De lingua Latina. Introduction, Text, and Translation*. 2 vols. Oxford: Oxford University Press.

Dench, E. 2005. *Romulus' Asylum: Roman Identities from the Age of Alexander to the Age of Hadrian*. Oxford: Oxford University Press.

Denecker, T. 2017. *Ideas on Language in Early Latin Christianity: From Tertullian to Isidore of Seville*. Leiden: Brill.

Denecker, T. 2019. "*Ambo legēre*? The 'Dual Number' in Latin Grammaticography Up to the Early Medieval *artes*." *Glotta* 95:101–34.

Denecker, T., and P. Swiggers. 2018. "The *articulus* according to Latin Grammarians Up to the Early Middle Ages: The Complex Interplay of Tradition and Innovation in Grammatical Doctrine." *Glotta* 94:127–52.

De Nonno, M. 1982. *La grammatica dell' Anonymus Bobiensis (GL I 533-565 Keil): Con un'appendice carisiana*. Rome: Edizioni di storia e letteratura.

De Nonno, M. 1990. "L'*Auctor ad Caelestinum* (*GL* IV 219-264 Keil): Contributi al testo e alla caratterizzazione." In *Dicti Studiosus: Scritti di filologia offerti a Scevola Mariotti dai suoi allievi*, [no editor], 223–58. Urbino: QuattroVenti.

De Nonno, M. 2010. "*Et interrogavit Filocalus*: Pratiche dell'insegnamento 'in aula' del grammatico." In *Libri di scuola e pratiche didattiche: Dall'Antichità al Rinascimento. Atti del Convegno Internazionale di Studi (Cassino, 7-10 maggio 2008)*, ed. L. Del Corso and O. Pecere, 169–205. Cassino: Editrice dell'Università degli Studi di Cassino.

De Nonno, M. 2017. "*Vetustas* e *antiquitas*, *veteres* e *antiqui* nei grammatici latini." In Rocchi and Mussini 2017, 213–48.

De Paolis, P. 1990. *Macrobii Theodosii De verborum Graeci et Latini differentiis vel societatibus excerpta*. Urbino: QuattroVenti.

Desbordes, F. 1988. "La fonction du grec chez les grammairiens latins." In *L'héritage des grammairiens latins de l'Antiquité aux Lumières: Actes du Colloque de Chantilly (2-4 septembre 1987)*, ed. I. Rosier, 15–26. Louvain: Peeters (repr. in Desbordes 2007, 107–19).

Desbordes, F. 1991. "*Latinitas*: constitution et évolution d'un modèle de l'identité linguistique." In Έλληνισμός: *quelques jalons pour une histoire de l'identité greque. Actes du Colloque de Strasbourg, 25-27 octobre 1989*, ed. S. Saïd, 33–47. Leiden: Brill (repr. in Desbordes 2007, 91–105).

BIBLIOGRAPHY 247

Desbordes, F. 1995. "Sur les débuts de la grammaire à Rome." *Lalies* 15:125–37 (repr. in Desbordes 2007, 217–33).

Desbordes, F. 2007. *Idées grecques et romaines sur le langage: travaux d'histoire et d'épistémologie*. Lyon: ENS Éditions.

de Vaan, M. 2008. *Etymological Dictionary of Latin and the Other Italic Languages*. Leiden: Brill.

Dickey, E. 2002. *Latin Forms of Address*. Oxford: Oxford University Press.

Dickey, E. 2007. *Ancient Greek Scholarship: A Guide to Finding, Reading, and Understanding Scholia, Commentaries, Lexica, and Grammatical Treatises, from their Beginnings to the Byzantine Period*. New York: Oxford University Press.

Dickey, E. 2012–15. *The Colloquia of the Hermeneumata Pseudodositheana*. 2 vols. Cambridge: Cambridge University Press.

Dickey, E. 2016a. "The Authorship of the Greek Version of Dositheus' Grammar and What It Tells Us about the Grammar's Original Use." In Ferri and Zago 2016, 205–35.

Dickey, E. 2016b. *Learning Latin the Ancient Way: Latin Textbooks from the Ancient World*. Cambridge: Cambridge University Press.

Dickey, E., and A. Chouhoud, eds. 2010. *Colloquial and Literary Latin*. Cambridge: Cambridge University Press.

Diederich, S. 1999. *Der Horazkommentar des Porphyrio im Rahmen der kaiserzeitlichen Schul- und Bildungstradition*. Berlin: De Gruyter.

Dierschke, P. 1913. *De fide Prisciani in versibus Vergilii, Lucani, Statii, Iuvenalis examinata*. Diss. Greifswald.

Dionisotti, A. C. 1984. "Latin Grammar for Greeks and Goths." *JRS* 74:202–8.

Di Stefano Manzella, I. 1997. *Le iscrizioni dei Cristiani in Vaticano*. Città del Vaticano: Monumenti, Musei e gallerie pontificie.

Dräger, P. 2012. "Ein Brief des Ausonius an den Trierer Grammatiker Ursulus." *KurtJb* 52:43–68.

Drummond, A. 2013. "M. Terentius Varro." In *The Fragments of the Roman Historians*, ed. T. J. Cornell, 1:412–23. Oxford: Oxford University Press.

Dubuisson, M. 2006. "Rhétorique et histoire chez Jean le Lydien." In *Approches de la Troisième Sophistique: Hommages à Jacques Schamp*, ed. E. Amato, A. Roduit, and M. Steinrück, 441–8. Brussels: Latomus.

Dubuisson, M. and J. Schamp. 2006. *Jean le Lydien: Des magistratures de l'État romain* (I.1-2, II, III). Paris: Les Belles Lettres.

Dümmler, N. 2012. "Musaeus, 'Hero and Leander': Between Epic and Novel." In *Brill's Companion to Greek and Latin Epyllion and Its Reception*, ed. M. Baumbach and S. Bär, 411–45. Leiden: Brill.

Dufallo, B. 2005. "Words Born and Made: Horace's Defense of Neologisms and the Cultural Poetics of Latin." *Arethusa* 38:89–101.

Duval, Y. 2001. "Le clergé de Cirta au début du IVe siècle: notes de prosopographie et d'histoire." In *"Ubique amici": Mélanges offerts à Jean-Marie Lassère*, ed. C. Hamdoune, 309–40. Montpellier: Université Paul-Valéry, CERCAM.

Eden, P. T. 2008. *Seneca: Apocolocyntosis*. Cambridge: Cambridge University Press.

Eisenberg, P. 2012. *Das Fremdwort im Deutschen*. 2nd ed. Berlin: De Gruyter.

Elst, V. van. 2011. "Theodosius and His Byzantine Successors on the Participle: A Didactic Approach." In Matthaios, Montanari, and Rengakos 2011, 405–28.

Encuentra Ortega, A. 2004. "Mitacismo, eclipsis, aféresis: sobre la pronunciación de 'm' final latina en la Antigüedad Tardía y su reflejo en la literatura." *MLatJB* 39:1–19.

248 BIBLIOGRAPHY

Ercoles, M. 2015. "Alcuni scolî 'metrici' pre-tricliniani a Eschilo e la loro possibile fonte." *Eikasmos* 26:319–32.

Eveuc, P., and N. Vinel. 1997–2017. *Isidore de Péluse: Lettres.* 3 vols. Paris: Les Éditions du Cerf.

Évieux, P. 1995. *Isidore de Péluse.* Paris: Beauchesne.

Faulkner, A. 2020. *Apollinaris of Laodicea:* Metaphrasis Psalmorum. Oxford: Oxford University Press.

Fehling, D. 1957. "Varro und die grammatische Lehre von der Analogie und der Flexion. Schluss." *Glotta* 36:48–100.

Feld, K. 2002. "Pamprepius: Philosoph und Politiker oder Magier und Aufrührer?" In *Gelehrte in der Antike: Alexander Demandt zum 65. Geburtstag,* ed. A. Goltz, 261–80. Cologne: Böhlau.

Fernández, G. 1989. "Was John the Grammarian a Philoponus?" In *Studia Patristica, XXIII: Papers presented to the 10th International Conference on Patristic Studies held in Oxford, 1987,* ed. E. A. Livingstone, 17–20. Leuven: Peeters.

Ferri, R., ed. 2011. *The Latin of Roman Lexicography.* Pisa: Fabrizio Serra.

Ferri, R. and A. Zago, eds. 2016. *The Latin of the Grammarians: Reflections about Language in the Roman World.* Turnhout: Brepols.

Ferriss-Hill, J. L. 2014. "Varro's Intuition of Cognate Relationships." *ICS* 39:81–108.

Flach, D. 2006. *Marcus Terentius Varro: Über die Landwirtschaft.* Darmstadt: Wissenschaftliche Buchhandlung.

Flammini, G. 2004. *Hermeneumata pseudodositheana Leidensia.* Munich: Saur.

Fögen, T. 1997–98. "Der Grammatiker Consentius." *Glotta* 74:164–92.

Fögen, T. 2000. Patrii sermonis egestas: *Einstellungen lateinischer Autoren zu ihrer Muttersprache.* Munich: Saur.

Fögen, T. 2014. "Die Traktate römischer Agrimensoren im Kontext antiker Fachliteratur." In *In den Gefilden der römischen Feldmesser,* ed. E. Knobloch and C. Möller, 215–39. Berlin: De Gruyter.

Folliet, G. 1987. "La correspondance entre Augustin et Nébridius." In *L'opera letteraria di Agostino tra Cassiciacum e Milano: Agostino nelle terre di Ambrogio,* ed. G. Reale, 191–215. Palermo: Editrice Augustinus.

Fortenbaugh, W. W. 2005. *Theophrastus of Eresus: Sources for His Life, Writings, Thought, and Influence,* Volume 8, *Sources on Rhetoric and Poetics* (Texts 666–713). Leiden: Brill.

Fortes, F. da Silva. 2014. "Comparaçónes e contrastes entre o grego e o latim como estratégia explicativa no 'De constructione' de Prisciano (séc. VI d.C.)." *Classica(Brasil)* 27:31–51.

Frede, M. 1994. "The Stoic Notion of a Grammatical Case." *BICS* 39:13–24.

Fressura, M. 2017. *Vergilius Latinograecus: Corpus dei manoscritti bilingui dell'Eneide.* Parte Prima. Pisa: Fabrizio Serra.

Freudenburg, K. 1993. *The Walking Muse: Horace on the Theory of Satire.* Princeton: Princeton University Press.

Friedländer, L. 1895. *D. Junii Juvenalis Saturarum libri V.* Leipzig: Herzel.

Frier, B. W. 1985. *The Rise of the Roman Jurists: Studies in Cicero's Pro Caecina.* Princeton: Princeton University Press.

Frier, B. W. et al. 2016. *The Codex of Justinian: A New Annotated Translation, with Parallel Latin and Greek Text.* 3 vols. Cambridge: Cambridge University Press.

Fritz, M. 2011. *Der Dual im Indogermanischen: Genealogischer und typologischer Vergleich einer grammatischen Kategorie im Wandel.* Heidelberg: Winter.

BIBLIOGRAPHY 249

Fuhrmann, M. 1987. "Erneuerung als Wiederherstellung des Alten: Zur Funktion antiquarischer Forschung im Spätrepublikanischen Rom." In *Epochenschwelle und Epochenbewusstsein*, ed. R. Herzog and R. Koselleck, 131–51. Munich: Fink.

Gabba, E. 1963. "Il latino come dialetto greco." In *Miscellanea di studi alessandrini in memoria di A. Rostagni*, [no editor] 188–94. Turin: Bottega d'Erasmo.

Gärtner, H., and H. A. Gärtner. 2004. "Das Martyrium eines Lehrers: Zur Passion des hl. Cassianus bei Prudentius (perist. 9)." In *Studia humanitatis ac litterarum trifolio Heidelbergensi dedicata: Festschrift für Eckhard Christmann, Wilfried Edelmaier und Rudolf Kettemann*, ed. A. Hornung, C. Jäkel, and W. Schubert, 73–82. Bern: Lang.

Garcea, A. 2012. *Caesar's De Analogia: Edition, Translation, and Commentary*. Oxford: Oxford University Press.

Garcea, A. 2019. "Diomedes as a Source for Pliny's *Dubius sermo*: Some Editorial Problems." In A. Chahoud, M. Rosellini, E. Spangenberg Yanes 2019, 53–71.

Garcea, A., and V. Lomanto. 2004. "Gellius and Fronto on Loanwords and Literary Models: Their Evaluation of Laberius." In *The Worlds of Aulus Gellius*, ed. L. Holford-Strevens and A. Vardi, 41–64. Oxford: Oxford University Press.

Gautier Dalché, P. 2014. "L'enseignement de la géographie dans l'Antiquité tardive." *Klio* 96:144–82.

Gebhardt, U. C. J. 2009. *Sermo iuris: Rechtssprache und Recht in der augusteischen Dichtung*. Leiden: Brill.

Gemeinhardt, P. 2008. "Dürfen Christen Lehrer sein? Anspruch und Wirklichkeit im christlichen Bildungsdiskurs der Spätantike." *JbAC* 51:25–43.

Giovini, M. 2003. "*Velut iocosa si theatra pervoles*: Dichiarazioni programmatiche in Lussurio, carmi 282, 283, 284, 285 Sh. B." *Maia* 55:325–59.

Gitner, A. 2014 [seen in manuscript]. "Creeping Roots: Varro on Latin across Space and Time." Presented at the APA Annual Meeting. Chicago.

Gitner, A. 2015. "Varro *Aeolicus*: Latin's Affiliation with Greek." In Butterfield 2015, 33–50.

Gitner, A. 2019. "Imagining an Archetype of the *Idiomata Generum*." In A. Chahoud, M. Rosellini, E. Spangenberg Yanes 2019, 221–38.

Glover T. R., and G. H. Rendall. 1931. *Tertullian: Apology, De Spectaculis. Minucius Felix: Octavius*. Cambridge, MA: Harvard University Press.

Graver, M., and A. Long. 2015. *Lucius Annaeus Seneca: Letters on Ethics: To Lucilius*. Chicago: Chicago University Press.

Grazzini, S. 2011–18. *Scholia in Iuvenalem recentiora*. 2 vols. Pisa: Edizioni della Normale.

Grebe, S. 2001. "Views of Correct Speech in Varro and Quintilian." In *Papers on Grammar VI*, ed. G. Calboli, 135–64. Bologna: CLUEB.

Green, R. P. H. 1985. "Still Waters Run Deep: A New Study of the *Professores* of Bordeaux." *CQ* 35:491–506.

Guzmán Brito, A. 1999. "El communis *usus loquendi* en el derecho romano." *Revista de Estudios Histórico-Jurídicos* 21:37–64.

Haffner, M. 2001. *Das Florilegium des Orion*. Stuttgart: Steiner.

Hagen, H. 1870. *Anecdota Helvetica*. (= *Grammatici Latini*, Volume 8). Leipzig: Teubner.

Haltenhoff, A., A. Heil, and F. H. Mutschler, eds. 2003. *O tempora o mores! Römische Werte und römische Literatur in den letzten Jahrzehnten der Republik*. Munich: Saur.

Happ, H. 1985–6. *Luxurius: Text, Untersuchung, Kommentar*. 2 vols. Leipzig: Teubner.

Haspelmath, M. 2009. "Lexical Borrowings: Concepts and Issues." In *Loanwords in the World's Language*, ed. M. Haspelmath and U. Tadmor, 35–54. Berlin: De Gruyter.

250 BIBLIOGRAPHY

Hemmerdinger, B. 1997. "Ľἀκμή d'Étienne de Byzance (Stephanus Byzantius)." *BollClass* 3rd ser. 18:53.

Highet, G. 1954. *Juvenal the Satirist*. Oxford: Oxford University Press.

Hitchner, R. B. 2005. "Meridional Gaul, Trade and the Mediterranean Economy in Late Antiquity." In *Fifth-Century Gaul: A Crisis of Identity?*, ed. J. Drinkwater and H. Elton, 122–31. Cambridge: Cambridge University Press.

Holford-Strevens, L. 2003. *Aulus Gellius: An Antonine Scholar and His Achievement*. Oxford: Oxford University Press.

Holford-Strevens, L. 2017. "Fronto's and Gellius' *Veteres*." In Rocchi and Mussini 2017, 199–211.

Holtz, L. 1971. "Tradition et diffusion de l'oeuvre grammaticale de Pompée, commentateur de Donat." *RPh* 97:48–83.

Holtz, L. 1981. *Donat et la tradition de l'enseignement grammatical: Étude sur l'Ars Donati et sa diffusion (IVᵉ-IXᵉ siècle) et édition critique*. Paris: Centre National de la Recherche Scientifique.

Holtz, L. 1985. "La redécouverte de Virgile aux VIIIᵉ et IXᵉ siècles d'après les manuscrits conservés." In *Lectures médiévales de Virgile: Actes du Colloque organisé par l'École française de Rome: pubblicazioni del bimillenario virgiliano promosse della regione Campania*, [no editor] 9–30. Paris: de Boccard.

Holtz, L. 1986. "Les manuscrits carolingiens de Virgile (Xᵉ et XIᵉ siècles)." In *La fortuna di Virgilio*, [no editor] 125–49. Naples: Giannini.

Holtz, L. 1992. "Continuité et discontinuité de la tradition grammaticale au VIIᵉ siècle." In *Le septième siècle: changements et continuités / The Seventh Century: Change and Continuity*, ed. J. Fontaine and J. N. Hillgarth, 41–57. London: The Warburg Institute.

Holtz, L. 2005. "Prolégomènes à une édition critique du commentaire de Pompée, grammairien africain." In *The Origins of European Scholarship: The Cyprus Millennium Conference*, ed. I. Taifacos, 109–19. Stuttgart: Franz Steiner.

Holtz, L. 2007. "Transcription et déformation de la terminologie grammaticale grecque dans la tradition manuscrite latine." In Basset et al. 2007, 37–56.

Horak, F. 1969. *Rationes decidendi: Entscheidungsbegründungen bei den älteren römischen. Juristen bis Labeo, I*. Innsbruck: Scientia Verlag.

Hülser, K. 2015. "Proculus on the Meaning of 'or' and the Types of Disjunction." In *Past and Present Interactions in Legal Reasoning and Logic*, ed. M. Armgardt et al., 7–30. Cham: Springer.

Humbert, M. 2018. *La loi des XII tables: Édition et commentaire*. Rome: École française de Rome.

Jahn, O. 1868. *A. Persii Flacci, D. Iunii Iuvenalis, Sulpiciae Saturae*. Berlin: Weidmann.

Jakobi, R. 2018. "Das Lexikon des Arusianus Messius." *Glotta* 94:166–95.

Jobard, R., and L. Gagliardi. 1995. *Julien Pomère: La Vie contemplative*. Paris: Migne.

Johnston, D. 1988. *The Roman Law of Trusts*. Oxford: Clarendon Press.

Jones, A. H. M. 1964. *The Later Roman Empire 284-602: A Social, Economic and Administrative Survey*. Oxford: Oxford University Press.

Joseph, J. E. 1987. *Eloquence and Power: The Rise of Language Standards and Standard Languages*. London: Pinter.

Kaibel. G. 1899. *Comicorum Graecorum fragmenta*. Berlin: Weidmann.

Kaldellis, A. 2003. "The Religion of Ioannes Lydos." *Phoenix* 57:300–16.

Kaster, R. A. 1978. "Servius and *idonei auctores*." *TAPhA* 99:181–209.

Kaster, R. A. 1980a. "The Grammarian's Authority." *CPh* 75:216–41.

BIBLIOGRAPHY 251

Kaster, R.A. 1980b. "Macrobius and Servius: *Verecundia* and the Grammarian's Function." *HSCPh* 84:220–62.

Kaster, R. A. 1990. *The Tradition of the Text of the* Aeneid *in the Ninth Century*. New York: Garland.

Kaster, R. A. 1992. *Studies on the Text of Suetonius* De grammaticis et rhetoribus. Atlanta, GA: Scholars Press.

Kaster, R. A. 1995. *C. Suetonius Tranquillus: De grammaticis et rhetoribus. Edited with a Translation, Introduction, and Commentary*. Oxford: Clarendon Press.

Kaster, R. A. 2005. *Emotion, Restraint, and Community in Ancient Rome*. New York: Oxford University Press.

Kaster, R. A. 2006. *Cicero: Speech on Behalf of Publius Sestius*. Oxford: Clarendon Press.

Kaster, R. A. 2010. *Studies on the Text of Macrobius'* Saturnalia. Oxford: Oxford University Press.

Kaster, R. A. 2011a. *Macrobii Ambrosii Theodosii Saturnalia*. Oxford: Clarendon Press.

Kaster, R. A. 2011b. *Macrobius: Saturnalia*. 3 vols. Cambridge, MA: Harvard University Press.

Kaster, R. A. 2012. *The Appian Way: Ghost Road, Queen of Roads*. Chicago: Chicago University Press.

Kaster, R. A. 2016a. *C. Suetoni Tranquilli: De vita Caesarum libros VIII et de grammaticis et rhetoribus*. Oxford: Clarendon Press.

Kaster, R. A. 2016b. *Studies on the Text of Suetonius'* De vita Caesarum. New York: Oxford University Press.

Kaster, R. A. 2020. *Cicero: Brutus and Orator. Translated with Introduction and Notes*. New York: Oxford University Press.

Kaster, R. A., and M. C. Nussbaum. 2010. *Anger, Mercy, Revenge*. Chicago: University of Chicago Press.

Knoche, U. 1939. Review of Wessner 1931. *Gnomon* 11:590–603.

Kohlstedt, H. 1917. *Das Romanische in den Artes des Consentius*. Erlangen: Junge.

Kumaniecki, K. 1962. "Cicerone e Varrone: storia di una conoscenza." *Athenaeum* 40:221–43.

Kunkel, W. 1967. *Herkunft und soziale Stellung der römischen Juristen*. 2nd ed. Graz: Böhlau (repr. 2001).

Lacerda Faria Rocha, E. and F. Fortes. 2016. "Análises translinguísticas na *Ars grammatica* de Diomedes: ocorrências de code-switching e *utraque lingua*." *Estudos Linguísticos e Literários* 55:235–49.

Łajtar, A. 2000. *Die Inschriften von Byzantion*. Inschriften griechischer Städte aus Kleinasien, 58. Bonn: Habelt.

Lallot, J. 1998. *La grammaire de Denys le Thrace: Traduite et annotée*. 2nd ed. Paris: CNRS.

Langslow, D. 2000. *Medical Latin in the Roman Empire*. Oxford: University Press.

Lauxtermann, M. 2005. "All about George." *JÖByz* 55:1–6.

Lavan, M. 2019. "The Foundation of Empire? The Spread of Roman Citizenship from the Fourth Century BCE to the Third Century CE." In *In the Crucible of Empire: The Impact of Roman Citizenship upon Greeks, Jews and Christians*, ed. K. Berthelot and J. Price, 21–54. Leuven: Peeters.

Law, V. 2003. *The History of Linguistics in Europe from Plato to 1600*. Cambridge: Cambridge University Press.

Lemerle, P. 1971. *Le premier humanisme byzantin: Notes et remarques sur enseignement et culture à Byzance des origines au Xe siècle*. Paris: Presses universitaires de France.

252 BIBLIOGRAPHY

Lenel, O. 1889. *Palingenesia iuris civilis: iuris consultorum reliquiae quae Iustiniani Digestis continentur ceteraque iuris prudentiae civilis fragmenta minora secundum auctores et libros.* 2 vols. Leipzig: Tauchnitz.

Lenoble, M., P. Swiggers, and A. Wouters. 2000. "L'enseignement grammatical entre grec et latin: le manuel de Dosithée." In *The History of Linguistic and Grammatical Praxis. Proceedings of the XIth International Colloquium of the Studienkreis "Geschichte der Sprachwissenschaft" (Leuven, 2nd—4th July, 1998)*, ed. P. Desmet et al., 3–22. Leuven: Peeters.

Leonardis, I. 2014. "*Vetustas, oblivio* e crisi d'identità nelle *Saturae Menippeae*: il risveglio di Varrone in un'altra Roma." *Epekeina* 4:19–58.

Leonardis, I. 2019. *Varrone, unus scilicet antiquorum hominum: senso del passato e pratica antiquaria.* Bari: Edipuglia.

Leonhardt, J. 1989. *Dimensio syllabarum: Studien zur lateinschen Prosodie- und Verslehre von der Spätantike bis zur frühen Renaissance.* Göttingen: Vandenhoeck & Ruprecht.

Lewis, R. G. 2006. *Asconius: Commentaries on Speeches of Cicero.* New York: Oxford University Press.

Lindsay, W. M. 1894. *The Latin Language: An Historical Account of Latin Sounds, Stems, and Flections.* Oxford: Oxford University Press.

Lindsay, W. M. 1916. "The Latin Grammarians of the Empire." *AJPh* 37:31–41.

Livrea, E. 2011. "The Last Pagan at the Court of Zeno: Poetry and Politics of Pamprepios of Panopolis." In *New Perspectives on Late Antiquity*, ed. D. Hernández de la Fuente, 2–30. Newcastle: Cambridge Scholars Publishing.

Lloyd, R. B. 1961. "Republican Authors in Servius and the Scholia Danielis." *HSCPh* 65:291–341.

Löfstedt, B. 1982. *Ars Ambrosiana: Commentum anonymi in Donati partes maiores.* Corpus Christianorum, Series Latina 133C. Turnhout: Brepols.

Löfstedt, B., L. Holtz, and A. Kibre. 1986. *Smaragdus, Liber in partibus Donati.* Corpus Christianorum, Continuatio Mediaevalis 68. Turnhout: Brepols.

Löfstedt, E. 1959. *Late Latin.* Oslo and Cambridge: Instituttet for sammenlignende kulturforskning.

Lolli, M. 2006. "Ausonius: Die *Gratiarum actio ad Gratianum imperatorem* und *De maiestatis laudibus*: Lobrede auf den Herrscher oder auf den Lehrer?" *Latomus* 65:707–26.

Maas, M. 1992. *John Lydus and the Roman Past: Antiquarianism and Politics in the Age of Justinian.* London: Routledge.

Maas, P. 1973. *Kleine Schriften.* Munich: C. H. Beck.

MacCoull, L. S. B. 1995. "A New Look at the Career of John Philoponus." *JECS* 3:47–60.

MacCoull, L. S. B. 2005. "The Historical Context of John Philoponus' *De opificio mundi* in the Culture of Byzantine-Coptic Egypt." *ZAC* 9:397–423.

MacCoull, L. S. B. 2007. "Philosophy in its Social Context." In *Egypt in the Byzantine World, 300-700*, ed. R. S. Bagnall, 67–82. Cambridge: Cambridge University Press.

MacDonald, C. 2016. "Rewriting Rome: Topography, Etymology and History in Varro *De Lingua Latina* 5 and Propertius *Elegies* 4." *Ramus* 45:192–212.

MacDonald, C. 2018 [seen in abstract]. "Going Underground: Linguistic Metaphors and the Politics of Varro's *De lingua Latina*." Presented at the SCS Annual Meeting. Boston.

Macleod, H. D. 1858. *The Elements of Political Economy.* London: Longman, Brown, Green, Longmans and Roberts.

MacRae, D. 2016. *Legible Religion: Books, Gods, and Rituals in Roman Culture.* Cambridge, MA: Harvard University Press.

BIBLIOGRAPHY   253

Malloch, S. J. V. 2013. *The* Annals *of Tacitus: Book 11.* Cambridge: Cambridge University Press.

Maltby, R. 1993. "Varro's Attitude to Latin Derivations from Greek." In *Papers of the Leeds International Latin Seminar,* Volume 7, *Roman Poetry and Prose, Greek Rhetoric and Poetry,* ed. F. Cairns and M. Heath, 47–60. Leeds: Leeds University Press.

Maltby, R. 2012. "The *De barbarismis et metaplasmis* of Consentius as Evidence for Late and Vulgar Latin." In *Latin vulgaire—latin tardif* IX; *Actes du IXe Coloque international sur le latin vulgaire et tardif, Lyon, 2–6 septembre 2009,* ed. F. Biville, M.-K. Lhommé, and D. Vallat, 727–37. Lyons: Maison de l'Orient et de la Méditerraneé Jean Pouilloux.

Mantovani, D. 2018. *Les Juristes écrivains de la Rome antique: les œuvres des juristes comme littérature.* Paris: Collège de France and Les Belles Lettres.

Mari, T. 2016. "I metaplasmi in Consenzio." In Ferri and Zago 2016, 277–89.

Mari, T. 2017a. "Centro vs. periferia nel latino parlato: la testimonianza di Consenzio." *Linguarum varietas* 6:109–23.

Mari, T. 2017b. *Pauca de barbarismo collecta de multis.* Pisa: Edizioni ETS.

Mari, T. 2019. "Foni e terminologia fonetica nel *De barbarismis et metaplasmis* di Consenzio: il caso della *i.*" In Chahoud, Rosellini, and Spangenberg Yanes 2019, 127–40.

Mari, T. 2021. *Consentius' De barbarismis et metaplasmis: Critical Edition, Translation, and Commentary.* Oxford: Oxford University Press.

Martin, J. 1998. "Nicoclès de Sparte, maître de l'empereur Julien." In *Curiosité historique et intérêts philologiques: Hommage à Serge Lancel,* ed. B. Colombat and P. Mattei, 87–98. Grenoble: Université Stendhal-Grenoble III.

Martin, J. 2009. "Julien dit l'Apostat, écrits autobiographiques." *AntTard* 17:17–78.

Mathisen, R. W. 2020. "Sidonius' People: A Prosopography of Sidonius." In *The Edinburgh Companion to Sidonius Apollinaris,* ed. G. Kelly and J. van Waarden, 76–154. Edinburgh: Edinburgh University Press.

Matras, Y. 2009. *Language Contact.* Cambridge: Cambridge University Press.

Matthaios, S., F. Montanari, and A. Rengakos, eds. 2011. *Ancient Scholarship and Grammar: Archetypes, Concepts and Context.* Berlin: De Gruyter.

Matthews, P. H. 2019. *What Graeco-Roman Grammar Was About.* Oxford: Oxford University Press.

Mauss, M. 1990. *The Gift.* Trans.W. D. Halls. New York: Norton.

Mazhuga, V. I. 1998. "Quand vivait et travaillait le grammairien Diomède?" *Hyperboreus* 4:139–66.

McNamee, K. 2007. *Annotations in Greek and Latin Texts from Egypt.* New Haven: American Society of Papyrologists.

Meier-Brügger, M. 1992. *Griechische Sprachwissenschaft.* 2 vols. Berlin: De Gruyter.

Meinel, F. 2011. "A Note on Libanius Ep. 1057 ed. Foerster." *CQ* 61:766–7.

Meiser, G. 1998. *Historische Laut- und Formenlehre der lateinischen Sprache.* Darmstadt: Wissenschaftliche Buchgesellschaft.

Merkelbach, R. 1977. "Ephesische Parerga: (6). Fragment eines Epigramms auf Damocharis." *ZPE* 24:256.

Merry, D. 2016. *Ancient Greek and Roman Methods of Inquiry into the (Human) Good.* Diss. Humboldt-Universität zu Berlin.

Meyer, E. A. 2004. *Legitimacy and Law in the Roman World: Tabulae in Roman Belief and Practice.* Cambridge: Cambridge University Press.

Moatti, C. 1997. *La Raison de Rome: Naissance de l'esprit critique à la fin de la République (IIe-Ier siècle avant Jésus-Christ).* Paris: Éditions du Seuil (Engl.: 2015. *The Birth of Critical Thinking in Republican Rome,* trans. by J. Lloyd. Cambridge: Cambridge University Press).

254 BIBLIOGRAPHY

Mommsen, T. 1871–88. *Römisches Staatsrecht*. 3 vols. Leipzig: Teubner.

Monno, O. 2009. *Iuvenalis docet: Le citazioni di Giovenale nel commento di Servio*. Bari: Edipuglia.

Montanari, F., ed. 2020. *History of Ancient Greek Scholarship: From the Beginnings to the End of the Byzantine Age*. Leiden: Brill.

Montanari, F., S. Matthaios, and A. Rengakos, eds. 2015. *Brill's Companion to Ancient Greek Scholarship*. Leiden: Brill.

Moroni, B. 2002. "La *Deprecatio in Alethium quaestorem* di Claudiano (*Carm. min.* 23)." In *Tra IV e V secolo: Studi sulla cultura latina tardoantica*, ed. I. Gualandri, 75–96. Milan: Cisalpino.

Mountford, J. 1934. *The* Scholia Bembina. Liverpool: University Press of Liverpool.

Müller, R. 2001. *Sprachbewußtsein und Sprachvariation im lateinischen Schrifttum der Antike*. Munich: C.H. Beck.

Müller, R. 2003. "Konzeptionen des Sprachwandels in der Antike." *Hermes* 131:196–221.

Müller, R. 2005. "Verba peregrina: Von der Interdiktion zur Integration." In *Papers on Grammar*, ed. G. Calboli, 9.1:371–81. Bologna: CLUEB.

Murgia, C. E. and R. A. Kaster. 2018. *Serviani in Vergili Aeneidos Libros IX–XII Commentarii*. New York: Oxford University Press.

Nelsestuen, G. A. 2015. *Varro the Agronomist: Political Philosophy, Satire, and Agriculture in the Late Republic*. Columbus: The Ohio State University Press.

Nelsestuen, G. A. 2017. "Varro, Dicaearchus, and the History of Roman *res rusticae*." In Arena and Mac Góráin 2017, 21–33.

Neumann-Hartmann, A. 2014. "Die 'Ethnika' des Stephanos von Byzanz im Lichte von Querverweisen in der Epitome seines Werkes." *Eikasmos* 25:263–90.

Neumann-Hartmann, A. 2016. "Stephanos von Byzanz und seine Tätigkeit als Lexikograph." In *Munera Friburgensia: Festschrift zu Ehren von Margarethe Billerbeck*, ed. A. Neumann-Hartmann and T. S. Schmidt, 89–110. Bern: Lang.

Nicks, F. 2000. "Literary Culture in the Reign of Anastasius I." In *Ethnicity and Culture in Late Antiquity*, ed. S. Mitchell and G. Greatrex, 183–203. Swansea: Classical Press of Wales.

Niedermann, M. 1937. *Consentii Ars de barbarismis et metaplasmis. Victorini fragmentum de soloecismo et barbarismo*. Neuchâtel: Sécretariat de l'Université.

Nocchi Macedo, G. 2016a. "Juvenal in Antinoë: Paleographic and contextual observations on *P.Ant. s.n.*" In *Proceedings of the 27th International Congress of Papyrology (Warsaw, 29 July—3 August 2013)*, ed. T. Derda, A. Łajtar, and J. Urbanik, 167–83. Warsaw: University of Warsaw.

Nocchi Macedo, G. 2016b. "Il *fragmentum Antinoense* e la fortuna di Giovenale nel mondo grecofono." In *Giovenale tra storia, poesia e ideologia*, ed. A. Stramaglia, S. Grazzini, and G. Dimatteo, 213–19. Berlin: De Gruyter.

Norden, E. 1901. "Vergils Äneis im Lichte ihrer Zeit." *NJb* 7:249–82, 313–34.

Novák, J. 1985. *Cantica Latina: poetarum veterum novorumque carmina*. Munich: Artemis Verlag.

Noy, D. 1993–5. *Jewish Inscriptions of Western Europe*. Volume 2. Cambridge: Cambridge University Press.

Ober, J. 1989. *Mass and Elite in Democratic Athens: Rhetoric, Ideology, and the Power of the People*. Princeton: Princeton University Press.

Ober, J. 1996. *The Athenian Revolution: Essays on Ancient Greek Democracy and Political Theory*. Princeton: Princeton University Press.

BIBLIOGRAPHY 255

Ober, J. 1998. *Political Dissent in Democratic Athens: Intellectual Critics of Popular Rule.* Princeton: Princeton University Press.

Ober, J. 2008. *Democracy and Knowledge: Innovation and Learning in Classical Athens.* Princeton: Princeton University Press.

O'Sullivan, N. 2018. "Manuscript Evidence for Alphabet-Switching in the Works of Cicero: Common Nouns and Adjectives." *CQ* 68:498–516.

Panayotakis, C. 2010. *Decimus Laberius: The Fragments. Edited with Introduction, Translation, and Commentary.* Cambridge: Cambridge University Press.

Parker, H. N. 2012. "Manuscripts of Juvenal and Persius." In *A Companion to Persius and Juvenal*, ed. S. Morton Braund and J. Osgood, 137–61. Malden, MA: Wiley & Sons.

Passalacqua, M. 1984. *Tre testi grammaticali bobbiesi (GL* V 555–566; 634–654; IV 207–216 Keil). Rome: Edizioni di storia e letteratura.

Passalacqua, M., and M. De Nonno. 2007. "'A Long Way to the Truth': A proposito di una sottoscrizione del ms. Napoletano Lat. 1." *RFIC* 135:321–8.

Pavese, M. P. 2013. *Scire leges est verba tenere: Ricerche sulle competenze grammaticali dei giuristi romani.* Turin: Giappichelli.

Pecere, O. 1986. "La tradizione dei testi latini tra IV e V secolo attraverso i libri sottoscritti." In *Società romana e impero tardoantico*, ed. A. Giardina, Volume 4, *Tradizione dei classici, trasformazioni della cultura*, 19–81. Rome: Laterza.

Pecere, O. 2016. "Libri e percorsi tardoantichi delle Satire di Giovenale (e di Persio)." In *Giovenale tra storia, poesia e ideologia*, ed. A. Stramaglia, S. Grazzini, and G. Dimatteo, 231–52. Berlin: De Gruyter.

Peglau, M. 2003. "Varro, ein Antiquar zwischen Tradition und Aufklärung." In Haltenhoff, Heil, and Mutschler, 137–64.

Pelsmaekers, J. 1988. "Een kirte bemerking bij de vertaling van de term μακάριος." *BIBR* 58:5–9.

Pelttari, A. 2011. "Approaches to the Writing of Greek in Late Antique Latin Texts." *GRBS* 51:461–82.

Perkams, M. 2009. "Zwei chronologische Anmerkungen zu Ammonios Hermeiou und Johannes Philoponos." *RhM* 152:385–91.

Pezzini, G. 2018. "Caesar the Linguist: The Debate about the Latin Language." In *The Cambridge Companion to the Writings of Julius Caesar*, ed. L. Grillo and C. B. Krebs, 173–92. Cambridge: Cambridge University Press.

Pezzini, G., and B. Taylor, eds. 2019. *Language and Nature in the Classical Roman World.* Oxford. Oxford University Press.

Piccione, R. M. 2002. "In margine a una recente edizione dell' *Antholognomicon* di Orione." *MEG* 2:141–53.

Piccione, R. M. 2003. "Le raccolte di Stobeo e Orione: fonti, modelli, architetture." In *Aspetti di letteratura gnomica nel mondo antico*, Volume 1, ed. M. S. Funghi. 241–61. Firenze: Olschki.

Pinkster. H. 2015. *The Oxford Latin Syntax*, Volume 1, *The Simple Clause*. Oxford: Oxford University Press.

Piras, G. 2017. "*Dicam dumtaxat quod est historicon*: Varro and/on the Past." In Arena and MacGóráin 2017, 8–20.

Poucet, J. 1967. *Recherches sur la légende sabine des origines de Rome.* Louvain and Kinshasa: Éditions de l'Université Lovanium.

Powell, J. G. F. 2011. "The *Appendix Probi* as Linguistic Evidence: A Reassessment." In Ferri 2011, 75–119.

256 BIBLIOGRAPHY

Prinz, X. 1867. "Quelques passages de Juvénal, encore inexpliqués ou dont le texte n'est pas encore rétabli [4]." *Revue de l'Instruction publique en Belgique* 10:85–103.

Probert, P. 2019. *Latin Grammarians on the Latin Accent: The Transformation of Greek Grammatical Thought.* Oxford: Oxford University Press.

Probert, P., and R. Ferri. 2010. "Roman Authors on Colloquial Language." In Dickey and Chahoud 2010, 12–41.

Pucci, J. 2003. "A Reading of Ausonius, *Professores* I." In *Gestures: Essays in Ancient History, Literature, and Philosophy Presented to Alan L. Boegehold,* ed. G. W. Bakewell and J. P. Sickinger, 88–99. Oxford: Oxbow Books.

Pugliarello, M. 1978. *Agroecius: Ars de orthographia.* Milan: Marzorati.

Rackham, H. 1914. *Cicero: On Ends.* Cambridge, MA: Harvard University Press.

Rawson, E. 1972. "Cicero the Historian and Cicero the Antiquarian." *JRS* 62:33–45

Rawson, E. 1985. *Intellectual Life in the Late Roman Republic.* London: Duckworth.

Reeve, M. D. 1971. "Eleven Notes," *CQ* 21:324–329.

Reeve, M. D. 1991. Review of Kaster 1990. *CR* 41:59–60.

Reinhardt, T., and M. Winterbottom. 2006. *Quintilian: Institutio oratoria, Book 2.* Oxford: Oxford University Press.

Reynolds, L. D., ed. 1983. *Texts and Transmission: A Survey of the Latin Classics.* Oxford: Clarendon Press.

Roberts, C. H. 1935a. "A Latin Parchment from Antinoë." *Aegyptus* 15:297–302.

Roberts, C. H. 1935b. "The Antinoë Fragment of Juvenal." *JEA* 21:199–209.

Robins, R. H. 1993. *The Byzantine Grammarians: Their Place in History.* Berlin: De Gruyter.

Rocchi, S., and C. Mussini, eds. 2017. *Imagines Antiquitatis: Representations, Concepts, Receptions of the Past in Roman Antiquity and the Early Italian Renaissance.* Berlin: De Gruyter.

Rochette, B. 1996. "Les ξενικὰ et les βαρβαρικὰ ὀνόματα dans les théories linguistiques gréco-latines." *AC* 65:91–105.

Rochette, B. 2009. "Les noms de la langue en latin." *HEL* 31:29–48.

Rochette, B. 2015. "L'enseignement du latin à Constantinople: une mise au point." In *Latin Linguistics in the Early 21th Century: Acts of the 16th International Colloquium on Latin Linguistics, Uppsala, June 6th-11th, 2011,* ed. G. V. M. Haverling, 626–39. Uppsala: Uppsala Universitet.

Rodríguez-Noriega Guillén, L., and J. Uría. 2017. "Ibycus and Diomedes: On the Reception of a Greek Poet by a Late Latin Grammarian." *Mnemosyne* 70:450–75.

Roesch, S. 1999. "*Res* et *verbum* dans le *De lingua Latina.*" In *Conceptions latines du sens et de la signification,* ed. M. Baratin and C. Moussy, 65–80. Paris: Presses de l'Université de Paris-Sorbonne.

Rösch-Binde, C. 1998. *Vom δεινὸς ἀνήρ zum diligentissimus investigator antiquitatis: Zur komplexen Beziehung zwischen M. Tullius Cicero and M. Terentius Varro.* Munich: Utz.

Rolfe, J. C. 1927. *Gellius: Attic Nights,* Volume 2, Books 6–13. Cambridge, MA: Harvard University Press.

Rolle, A. 2017. *Dall'Oriente a Roma: Cibele, Iside e Serapide nell'opera di Varrone.* Pisa: ETS.

Romano, E. 2003. "Il concetto di antico in Varrone." In *Memoria e identità: la cultura romana costruisce la sua immagine,* ed. M. Citroni, 99–117. Florence: Università degli Studi di Firenze.

Rosellini, M. 2021. "Da Persio allo Pseudoacrone: *rancidus* nella terminologia linguistico-letteraria e grammaticale." *ASNP* 13:151–65.

BIBLIOGRAPHY   257

Rossi, D., and M. Di Mento. 2013. *La catacomba ebraica di Monteverde: Vecchi dati e nuove scoperte*. Roma: [s.n.].

Roussou, S. 2018. *Pseudo-Arcadius' Epitome of Herodian's De Prosodia Catholica*. Oxford: Oxford University Press.

Russell, D. A. 2001. *Quintilian: The Orator's Education*. 5 vols. Cambridge, MA: Harvard University Press.

Saalfeld, G. A. E. A. 1884. *Tensaurus Italograecus: Ausführliches historisch-kritisches Wörterbuch der griechischen Lehn- und Fremdwörter im Lateinischen*. Gerold's Sohn: Wien.

Sacerdoti, A. 2007. "L'area semantica di *squaleo* nell'epica latina imperiale." *InvLuc* 29:229–40.

Scappaticcio, M. C. 2015. *Artes grammaticae in frammenti: I testi grammaticali latini e bilingui greco-latini su papiro*. Berlin: De Gruyter.

Scappaticcio, M. C. 2020a. "Verrius Flaccus, his Alexandrian Model, or just an Anonymous Grammarian? The Most Ancient Direct Witness of a Latin Ars Grammatica." *CQ* 70:806–21.

Scappaticcio, M. C. 2020b. "Virgilianisti antichi, e anonimi. Su un commento e un *argumentum* alle *Georgiche* dall'Antinoupolis della Tarda Antichità (Schol. Verg. *frg. georg.* 3 e Anon. *argum. georg.* 3—*P.Ant.* I 29)." *InvLuc* 42:357–68.

Scappaticcio, M. C. ed. Forthcoming. *The Corpus of Latin Texts on Papyrus*. Cambridge: Cambridge University Press.

Schad, S. 2007. *A Lexicon of Latin Grammatical Terminology*. Pisa: Fabrizio Serra.

Schamp, J. 2009. "Pour une étude des milieux latins de Constantinople." In *Autour de Michel Lejeune*, ed. F. Biville and I. Boehm, 255–72. Lyon: Maison de l'Orient méditerranéen.

Schenkeveld, D. M. 1998. "The Idea of Progress and the Art of Grammar: Charisius Ars Grammatica 1.15." *AJPh* 119:443–59.

Schenkeveld, D. M. 2004. *A Rhetorical Grammar: C. Iulius Romanus, Introduction to the Liber de adverbio*. Leiden: Brill.

Schenkeveld, D. M. 2007. "Charisius und Diomedes: Writing a Latin Grammar for Greeks." In Basset et al. 2007, 181–9.

Schipani, S., et al. 2005–14. *Iustiniani Augusti Digesta Seu Pandectae: Testo e Traduzione*. Books 1–34. Milan: Giuffrè. Accessed March 2021: http://dbtvm1.ilc.cnr.it/digesto/Digesto_Home.html.

Schironi, F. 2007. "Ἀναλογία, *proportio, ratio*: Loanwords, Calques, and Reinterpretations of a Greek Technical Word." In Basset et al. 2007, 321–38.

Schironi, F. 2018a. "Aristarchus, Greek Dialects and Homer." In *Language, Grammar, and Erudition: From Antiquity to Modern Times. A Collection of Papers in Honour of Alfons Wouters*, ed. P. Swiggers, 167–85. Leuven: Peeters.

Schironi, F. 2018b. *The Best of the Grammarians*. Ann Arbor: University of Michigan Press.

Schneider, J. 1999. *Les traités orthographiques grecs antiques et byzantins*. Turnhout: Brepols.

Schöpsdau, K. 1992. "Vergleiche zwischen Lateinisch und Griechisch in der antiken Sprachwissenschaft." In *Zum Umgang mit fremden Sprachen in der griechisch-römischen Antike*, ed. C. W. Müller, K. Sier and J. Werner, 115–36. Stuttgart: Steiner.

Scholz, U. W. 2003. "Varros Menippeische Satiren." In Haltenhoff, Heil, and Mutschler 2003, 165–85.

BIBLIOGRAPHY

Schröter, R. 1963. "Die varronische Etymologie." In *Varron* (= *Entretiens Hardt* 9), ed. C. Brink. 79–100 (discussion 101–16), Vandoœuvres-Geneva: Fondation Hardt.

Scopello, M. 2020. "Les *Acta Archelai* et ses principaux personnages: Notes historiques et lexicales." In *Manichaeism and Early Christianity: Selected Papers from the 2019 Pretoria Congress and Consultation*, ed. J. van Oost, 152–85. Brill: Leiden.

Seider, R. 1972–81. *Paläographie der lateinischen Papyri*. 3 vols. Stuttgart: Hiersemann.

Sherwin-White, A. N. 1973. *The Roman Citizenship*. 2nd ed. Oxford: Oxford University Press.

Siebenborn, E. 1976. *Die Lehre von der Sprachrichtigkeit und ihren Kriterien: Studien zur antiken normativen Grammatik*. Amsterdam: Verlag B. R. Grüner B.V.

Sivan, H. 1991. "A Late Gallic Branch of the Acilii Glabriones? Notes on Ausonius' *Professores* 24 (Peiper)." *Mnemosyne* 44:435–9.

Sogno, C. 2012. "Persius, Juvenal, and the Transformation of Satire in Late Antiquity." In *A Companion to Persius and Juvenal*, ed. S. Morton Braund and J. Osgood, 363–85. Malden, MA: Wiley & Sons.

Spangenberg Yanes, E. 2017. *Prisciani Caesariensis ars liber XVIII. Pars altera: Commento*. Hildesheim: Weidmann.

Spangenberg Yanes, E. 2020. *De dubiis nominibus cuius generis sint. Introduzione, testo critico e commento*. Hildesheim: Weidmann.

Speck, P. 1997. "Sokrates Scholastikos über die beiden Apolinarioi." *Philologus* 141:362–9.

Spencer, D. 2011a. "Ῥωμαΐζως...*ergo sum*: Becoming Roman in Varro's *De lingua Latina*." In *Cultural Memory and Identity in Ancient Societies*, ed. M. Bommas, 43–60. London: Continuum.

Spencer, D. 2011b. "Movement and the Linguistic Turn: Reading Varro's *De lingua Latina*." In *Rome, Ostia, Pompeii: Movement and Space*, ed. R. Laurence and D. J. Newsome, 57–80. Oxford: Oxford University Press.

Spencer, D. 2015a. "Urban Flux: Varro's Rome-in-progress." In *The Moving City: Processions, Passages and Promenades in Ancient Rome*, ed. I. Östenberg, S. Malmberg, and J. Bjørnebye, 99–110. London: Bloomsbury Academic.

Spencer, D. 2015b. "Varro's Romespeak: *De lingua Latina*." In Butterfield 2015, 73–92.

Spencer, D. 2019. *Language and Authority in the De lingua Latina: Varro's Guide to Being Roman*. Madison, WI: University of Wisconsin Press.

Stein, P. 1971. "The Relations between Grammar and Law in the Early Principate: The Beginnings of Analogy." In *La critica del testo: Atti del secondo congresso internazionale della Società Italiana di Storia del Diritto*, ed. B. Paridisi, 757–69. Florence: Olschki.

Stevens, B. 2007. "Aeolism: Latin as a Dialect of Greek." *CJ* 102:114–44.

Stevens, B. 2008. "The Scent of Language and Social Synaesthesia at Rome." *CW* 101:159–71.

Stok, F. 1987. "Su alcune glosse di Placido." *Orpheus* 8:87–101.

Stok, F. 1994. "Celso e Virgilio." *Orpheus* 15:280–301.

Stoppacci, P. 2010. *Cassiodoro De orthographia: Tradizione manoscritta, fortuna, edizione critica*. Florence: Edizioni del Galluzzo.

Stoppie, K. 2005. "The Role of the Greek in Charisius' *Ars grammatica*." *Annales de lettres et sciences humaines: Philologie classique (Lublin)* 53:123–38.

Stramaglia, A. 2008. *Giovenale, Satire 1, 7, 12, 16: Storia di un poeta*. Bologna: Pàtron.

Swiggers, P. and A. Wouters. 2007. "Transferts, contacts, symbiose: l'élaboration de terminologies grammaticales en contact bi/plurilingue." In Basset et al. 2007, 19–36.

BIBLIOGRAPHY 259

Tarver, T. 1997. "Varro and the Antiquarianism of Philosophy." In *Philosophia Togata II: Plato and Aristotle at Rome*, ed. J. Barnes and M. Griffin, 130–64. Oxford: Clarendon Press.

Taylor, B. 2020. *Lucretius and the Language of Nature*. Oxford: Oxford University Press.

Taylor, D. J. 1974. *Declinatio: A Study of the Linguistic Theory of Marcus Terentius Varro*. Amsterdam: John Benjamins.

Terrosi Zanco, O. 1961. "Divinità sabine o divinità etrusche?" *SCO* 10:188–208.

Thomson, H. J. 1928. "Lucan, Statius, and Juvenal in the Early Centuries." *CQ* 22:24–7.

Thorp, J. 1989. "Standing Up Falling Down: Aristotle and the History of Grammar." *EMC* 33:315–31.

Thurmond, D. L. 2017. *From Vines to Wines in Classical Rome: A Handbook of Viticulture and Oenology in Rome and the Roman West*. Leiden: Brill.

Torrance, I. R. 1988. *Christology after Chalcedon: Severus of Antioch and Sergius the Monophysite*. Norwich: Canterbury Press.

Townend, G. 1972. "The Earliest Scholiast on Juvenal." *CQ* 22:376–87.

Turner, E. G. 1977. *The Typology of the Early Codex*. Philadelphia: University of Pennsylvania Press.

Uría, J. 1997. *Tabú y eufemismo en latín*. Amsterdam: Hakkert.

Uría, J. 2006. "Consideraciones sobre el prefacio del Arte gramática de Carisio." *Studium: Revista de Humanidades* 12:113–25.

Uría, J. 2007. "Charisiana II (Char. *gramm*. p. 149.22-28 y p. 62.2-8 Barwick)." *Exemplaria classica* 11:133–44.

Uría, J. 2009. *Carisio: Arte Gramática Libro I*. Madrid: Editorial Gredos.

Uría, J. 2017. "*Septimus casus*: The History of a Misunderstanding from Varro to the Late Latin Grammarians." *Journal of Latin Linguistics* 16:239–266.

Vainio, R. 1994. "On the Concept of Barbarolexis in the Roman Grammarians." *Arctos* 28:129–40.

Vainio, R. 1999. *Latinitas and Barbarisms According to the Roman Grammarians*. Turku: University of Turku.

Visser, L. 2011. "Heritage and Innovation in the Grammatical Analysis of Latin: The *Ars Ambrosiana* Commentary (6th/7th century) on Donatus (ca. 350 A.D.)." *Historiographia Linguistica* 38:5–36.

Volk, K. 2016. "A Wise Man in an Old Country: Varro, *Antiquitates rerum divinarum* and [Plato], *Letter* 5." *RhM* 159:429–33.

Volk, K. 2019. "Varro and the (Dis)order of Things." *HSCPh* 110:183–212.

Volk, K. 2021. *The Roman Republic of Letters: Scholarship, Philosophy, and Politics in the Age of Cicero and Caesar*. Princeton: Princeton University Press.

Vottero, D. 1974. "La grafia dei termini d'origine greca nelle opere filosofiche di Seneca." *AAT* 108:311–39.

Wallace, R. E., and B. D. Joseph. 1991. "On the Problematic *f/h* Variation in Faliscan." *Glotta* 69:84–93.

Wallace-Hadrill, A. 2008. *Rome's Cultural Revolution*. Cambridge: Cambridge University Press.

Watson, A. 1985. *The Digest of Justinian*. 4 vols. Philadelphia: University of Pennsylvania Press.

Wessner, P. 1929. "Lucan, Statius und Juvenal bei den römischen Grammatikern." *Philologische Wochenschrift* 49:296–303, 328–35.

Wessner, P. 1931. *Scholia in Iuvenalem vetustiora*. Leipzig: Teubner.

260 BIBLIOGRAPHY

West, M. L. 2003. *Greek Epic Fragments: From the Seventh to the Fifth Centuries BC.* Cambridge, MA: Harvard University Press.

Wieacker, F. 1989. *Römische Rechtsgeschichte, Erster Abschnitt: Einleitung, Quellenkunde, Frühzeit und Republik.* Munich: C. H. Beck.

Wilkinson, K. W. 2009. "Palladas and the Age of Constantine." *JRS* 99:36–60.

Wilkinson, K. W. 2010a. "Some Neologisms in the Epigrams of Palladas." *GRBS* 50:295–308.

Wilkinson, K. W. 2010b. "Palladas and the Foundation of Constantinople." *JRS* 100:179–94.

Wilkinson, K. W. 2012a. "The Sarmatian and the Indians: A New Satirical Epigram on the Victory Titles of Galerius." *ZPE* 183:39–52.

Wilkinson, K. W. 2012b. *New Epigrams of Palladas: A Fragmentary Papyrus Codex (P. CtYBR inv. 4000).* Durham, NC: American Society of Papyrologists.

Williams, G. 2005. "Seneca on Winds: The Art of Anemology in Natural Questions 5." *AJPh* 126:417–50.

Willis, J. 1997. *Iuvenalis Saturae.* Stuttgart: Teubner.

Wiseman, T. P. 2009. *Remembering the Roman People: Essays on Late-Republican Politics and Literature.* Oxford: Oxford University Press.

Woods, D. 2016. "Palladas, Constantine, and Christianity." *JThS* 67:576–93.

Wright, R. 1982. *Late Latin and Early Romance in Spain and Carolingian France.* Liverpool: Francis Cairns.

Xenis, G. A. 2013. "An Unnoticed Fragment of Orus' Treatises Περὶ ὀρθογραφίας and Ἀττικῶν λέξεων συναγωγή, and Phrynichus' Σοφιστικὴ προπαρασκευή?" *Mnemosyne* 66:122–8.

Zago, A. 2016. "Iotacism in the Latin Grammarians." In Ferri and Zago 2016, 291–308.

Zago, A. 2017a. "Labdacism: a *vitium* 'from the provinces'?" *Linguarum varietas* 6:93–107.

Zago, A. 2017b. *Pompeii commentum in artis Donati partem tertiam.* 2 vols. Hildesheim: Weidmann.

Zago, A. 2018. "Mytacism in Latin Grammarians." *Journal of Latin Linguistics* 17:23–50.

Zago, A. 2019. "The (New) Prologue to Pompeius' *Commentum.*" In Chahoud, Rosellini, and Spangenberg Yanes 2019, 141–92.

Zago, A. 2022. "Politeness in Ancient Scholarship." In *Politeness in Ancient Greek and Latin,* ed. L. Unceta Gomez, and L. Berger, 341–365. Cambridge: Cambridge University Press.

Zair, N. 2019. "Reconstructed Forms in the Roman Writers on Language." *Language & History* 62:227–46.

Zanker, A. T. 2016. *Greek and Latin Expressions of Meaning: The Classical Origins of a Modern Metaphor.* Munich: C. H. Beck.

Zetzel, J. E. G. 2015. "The Bride of Mercury: Confessions of a 'Pataphilologist." In *World Philology,* ed. S. Pollock, B. Elman, and K. Chang, 43–62, 339–43. Cambridge, MA: Harvard University Press.

Zetzel, J. E. G. 2019. "Natural Law and Natural Language in the First Century BCE." In Pezzini and Taylor 2019, 191–211.

General Index

For the benefit of digital users, indexed terms that span two pages (e.g., 52–53) may, on occasion, appear on only one of those pages.
References to the names discussed in the Prosopography are not included here.

ablative case
  vs. Greek genitive: 92–93
  with *opus est*: 191–92
  see also de; declensional morphology
abusque, improperly formed: 198
Academics: 118
accentuation
  indicated by diacritics: 148
  see also Greek (accentuation of Greek
    words in Latin); *triginta*; *Valerius*
accentus: 96
accersere, vs. *arcessere*: 11
Achilles, inflection of: 109–10
acinacis, as Medean: 109
adjective, agreeing with nearest predicate:
  213–14
advocate: 74–75
Aelius Gallus: 201n.6, 202
Aelius Stilo: 39, 97, 181–82, 195–96,
  201n.6, 218–19
Aeneas, inflection of: 109–10
Aeolism: 94n.48
Africa, North: 38, 40, 115, 187n.43
  African loanwords in Latin: 109
  Africans' Latin: 100–1, 105–6, 108–9, 113
agrimensores: *see* land surveyors
Agroecius: 10–11
Alcaeus: 78–79
Alcuin: 137
Alfenus: 207–8
algero (?): 155
ambiguity: 217, 223–24
ambivalence: 210–11
Ammianus Marcellinus: 145–46
analogy (*analogia*, ἀναλογία): 79n.22,
  93, 101, 179–80, 182–83, 189; *see*
  also ratio

anaphora (ἀναφορά), denoting
  resemblance: 209–10
ἄναρθρος φωνή (*inarticulata vox*): 212,
  213
anceps: 16–17
Anonymus Bobiensis: 73, 76–77
Antinoöpolis (Antinoë): 145–46
antiquitas: 119; see also *vetustas*
  licentia antiquitatis: 127n.19
Antonius Rufus (?): 132–33, 141–42
ἀορίστως "with no explicit addressee": 222–23
Apollonius Dyscolus: xiii–xiv, 97, 218–19
apud, usage of: 125–27
Apuleius: 192, 195–96
Arbogastes: 108–9
Arcadian: *see* Greek
archaism: 43, 104–5, 192
Arctinus of Miletus: 78–79
Aristarchus: 135n.7
Aristophanes *comicus*: 78–79, 185–86,
  222–23
Aristophanes of Byzantium: 79n.22
Aristotle: 83n.27
Armenian: 37–38
Arnobius: 195–96
Ars Ambrosiana: 139–41
Asper, Aemilius
  "Asper": 125–27
  Grammatica Vergiliana: 8–9, 15
aspiration, errors in: 104, 111–12
assibilation, of *ti* as correct: 112, 124n.16
asta, as Oscan loanword: 41–42
Ateius Capito: 169, 186
Atellan farce: 41–42
Athenaeus: 196–98
Attic: *see* Greek
auctores idonei: 125n.18, 227–28

262 GENERAL INDEX

auctoritas: 17–18, 101–4, 129–30, 145–46, 187–88, 200–1
Augustine: 112
Augustus Caesar: 8–9, 28n.19, 187, 192
aurum, as *singulare tantum*: 102
Ausonius: 195–96
Avienus: 196–97

b and *v* confusion: 9–10, 106n.14, 111–12
barbarism: 4–5, 6, 99–100, 104–9; *see also* semantics
barbarolexis: 109; *see also* loanwords
Bavius and Maevius: *see* Vergiliomastix
Bede: 137
bibliotheca, literal vs. extended meaning: 201–2
Bobbio: 139–40, 143n.1, 145–46
Bordeaux: 195–96
BR-uncial ("juridical"): 144n.2
branches: 54–56
Britons: 176

c, errors in pronunciation: 108
cacozelia: 8–9
Caesar: *see* Augustus; Claudius; Hadrian; Julius Caesar; Marcus Aurelius; Tiberius
Callimachus: 78–79
camelus, as Syriac loanword: 37–38
Caper, Flavius: 14, 18–19
    Ps.-Caper: *see* Index locorum
carmen Saliare: 31
Carolingian: 84–85, 140–41, 147n.24
Cascellius: 208–9
cascus, cognate with Oscan: 41–42, 43–44
casnar, as Oscan loanword: 41–42
Cassiodorus: 120n.7, 123–24, 137
    Ps.-Cassiodore: 138–39
Cassius Dio: 170–71
casus, as metaphor: 47–48, 56–57, 58, 67
    as calque on πτῶσις: 83
catachresis (καταχρηστικῶς): 209, 212
cateia, as Gaulish: 109
Cato the Elder: 17, 25, 68, 79n.22
catus, as Sabine: 41
cenatio "refectory": 155–56, 162
Charisius: 12, 13, 14, 15, 16–17, 73–74, 75–79, 81–82, 83, 93–94, 96–98, 122, 123, 133, 189–90

Christianity: xiv, 195; *see also* Gospels
Chrysippus: 23n.3, 93, 118, 182n.31, 218n.33
Cicero, M. Tullius: 4–5, 24, 25, 28, 31–32, 81–82, 102, 117–19, 129, 143n.1, 156, 171–72, 182n.31, 192–93, 197–98, 200n.4, 205n.10, 208; *see also* Varro
cilliba, etymology of: 36
citizenship, Roman conception of: Chapter 10 *passim*, esp. 173–76, 181
    ius Latium, 181, 182–83, 187
    ius Latium maius: 187n.42
class: *see* grammarians (social class), senatorial class
Claudius Caesar: 175–77
Claudius Didymus: 97
Claudius Quadrigarius: 191n.1
Cledonius: 7, 145–46
clipeus, semantics and etymology: 12–13
code-switching: *see* Greek
Codex Theodosianus: 195n.14, 199n.1
cognatio, as metaphor: 50
cohors, vs. *c(h)ors*: 11–12
collective singular: *see glans*
coniunctio (conjunction): 90, 219; *see also* syntax
conjugation, as part of *declinatio*: 56–57
    4th conj. in *-ibam* not *-iebam*: 104n.11
    "dual" verb forms: 131 and Chapter 8 *passim*
Consentius: 93, Chapter 6 *passim*, 137–38, 139–40, 214
consonant length, errors in: 105n.13, 111–12
Constantinople: 73, 75n.7, 98, 100–1, 113, 145–46, 155–56, 192n.3
Constitutio Tanta: 195n.14
consuetudo: 17–18, 101–4, 128–29, 177–78, 209, 213
    cotidiana: 208
    as different from literary language: 192, 195–96
    eruditorum, nostra, vetus, vulgaris: 101
    see also ratio; usage
Consus: 39
Cornelianus: 194
Cornelius: 40; *see also* Fronto
Cornificius Gallus: *see* Vergiliomastix

GENERAL INDEX 263

Cornutus: 111–12
crambe: 146
crepusculum, as Sabine: 41
critical signs: 146–47
cuprum, as Oscan: 41, 46
cura palatii: 100–1
Cynics: 196–97

dative: *see* declensional morphology;
    fraudem facere
de, with the abl. for gen.: 110–11
De ceremoniis aulae Byzantinae: 155–56
De finalibus treatises: 6
De nominibus dubiis: 15
declensional morphology
    3rd decl. abl. sg.: 102
    3rd decl. acc. pl. of *i*-stems: 14, 103
    3rd decl. gen. pl. of monosyllables: 14
    3rd decl. nom. sg. in -*is*: 15–16
    4th decl. gen. (-*us* vs. -*uis*): 35
    4th decl. dat./abl. pl. (-*ibus* vs. -*ubus*):
        104–5
    5th decl. dat. and gen. endings, no
        longer monosyllabic: 192–93
    gen. of noun in -*es*: 15
    gen. sg. not longer than nom.: 16–17
    of loanwords: 109
    see also accentuation; derivational
        morphology; heteroclisy; -*m*;
        vocative
declinatio: 29 (*voluntaria*), 31, Chapter 4
    passim (esp. 48, 56–61, 66), 98
demonstratio "adjective": 214
Demosthenes: 79n.22
deprecor, of cursing or averting: 192–93
derivational morphology
    adverb formation (no adverbs in -*er* for
        adjectives in -*us*): 15
    -*īcula* vs. -*icula*: 102
diacritical signs: 148
dialectic: 118, 218–19
Diana: 44–45, 50–52
Didymus the Blind: 216–17
differentiae or synonyms: 9–10; *see also*
    accersere; *clipeus*; *cohors*; *ferre*;
    insomnia; *manducare*; *oliva*; *robur*
Digest: Chapter 12 *passim* (*see esp.* 199n.1)
diiunctivus "disjunctive": 218n.32

Dio Cassius: *see* Cassius Dio
Diomedes *grammaticus*: Chapter 5 *passim*,
    111n.25, 123, 133
Dionysius Thrax: 61n.24, 83, 92n.39, 98,
    131–32, 209–10
diplai obelismenai: 146, 148
disiunctivus (διαζευτικός): 218–19
distinctio: 148
Dius Fidius: 39
diversitas linguarum: xn.3, xi–xii,
    5–6, 34–35, 143; *see also* Greek;
    Latin; loanwords; plebeian Latin;
    regionalisms; vulgarisms
dole ticket (*tessera frumentaria*): 148–53,
    157–58, 162
domus, as heteroclite: 102–3
Donatus: 6, 8, 18–19, 76–77, 115–16, 133,
    136–41, 145–46, 197, 198, 200,
    220–21, 222–23
Dositheus: 73, 76–77, 81–82, 96
dual number: 75–76, 91–92, 124–25,
    Chapter 8 *passim*
duovicesimus, as obsolete: 192–93

e for *a* substitution: 106n.14
Edict of Caracalla: 188–89
egregius, vocative of: 197–98
Egyptian language: 37–38
elegans, no longer pejorative: 192–93
elegantia (of Caesar): 119
ellipsis: 220–21
eloqui, used in Sabine shrines: 42–43, 46
emendatio, as grammatical practice: 145–46,
    148
Empedocles: 78–79
ἐν πλάτει "broadly": 212
Ennius: 15, 53, 195–96, 198
Erucius Clarus: 193
Etruscan: 10, 42, 44–45, 53, 174–75, 175n.18
etymology: 11, 13, 14, 29, 31, Chapter 3
    passim, Chapter 4 *passim*, 82–83
    in analysis of proper meaning: 200–1,
    202
    see also: *cilliba*; *clipeus*; *miles*; *oratio*;
    pauper; solecism; *syllaba*
euphemism: 205n.10
euphony (*euphonia*): 102–3, 109–10
Euripides: 78–79

264 GENERAL INDEX

Eurus: 178–79
Eutyches: 73

f- and *h-* confused: 41, 46
facies, semantic change: 192–93
Faliscan: 41, 46
Favorinus: 193, 197–98
februm, as Sabine: 43
fedus: see *haedus*
ferre, vs. *portare*: 203
ferrum, as *singulare tantum*: 102
Festus, Pompeius: 17n.40, 201n.6, 202
Festus, Postumius: 185, 193
fideicommissa: 222–23
Fides: 44–45
figura: 198
figuratio: 218n.31
fircus: see *hircus*
floridity, as late antique style: 195–96
fluctus, gen. sg. in *-us* or *-uis*: 35
flumen, proper meaning of: 202
foetutinae: 122
Fons: 44–45
fraudem facere, with dat.: 110–11
frons, formerly masc.: 191–92
Fronto, Cornelius: 18–19, 185–88, 192,
    193, 194–96, 197–98
future tense
    invariable infinitive not recognized: 192–93
    synthetic forms for simple future
        (*futurum ulterius*): 110–11

Gaius: 53–54, 203, 219–20
Galen: 193
Gaul: 100, 107, 112–13
Gauls: 109, 137–38, 175–76 (admitted to
    Senate), 176
    speaking Latin: 100–1, 107, 108–9, 113
Gaulish language: 33–34, 37–38, 109
    (loanwords into Latin), 174–75
gaza, as Medean: 109
Gellius: 14, 18–19, 35, 93, 121–22,
    182n.28, 185–88, Chapter 11 *passim*
geminate: see *s* letter
gender, of nouns
    commune genus: 216–17
    epicoene genus: 216–17
    imposition of: 103

inclusiveness of masculine: 215–17
    see also clipeus; *frons*; Narbonne
        (*Narbo*); *supellex*; *venenus*
generale nomen, vs. *speciale*: 206n.12
genitive: see ablative case; declensional
    morphology
Germanic: *see reno*
glans, as collective singular: 208
Gospels: 197–98
grammarians (*grammaticus, magister*)
    accepting or forbidding new words: 177–78
    annotations made by: 143n.1,
        Chapter 9 *passim*
    easy-going attitude to grammatical
        tradition: 117
    finitiones, use of: 121–22
    forms of address: 193 (*grammaticus* as
        title): 197
    Latinists, opposed to: 18, 114n.30
    payment: 148–54, 158–59, 163
    pedagogical practice: 13, 113–14, 115,
        162–63
    pedantry: 112
    philosophy, sentiment against: 193–94,
        196–97
    professional status: 74–75, 113–14
    receptivity to linguistic change: 112
    relationship to emperor: 169–70, 176
    scorn for normative grammarians: 191–92
    self-promotion: 113–14
    shyness (*verecundia*): 196–97
    social class: 113, Chapter 11 *passim*, 195n.15
        (descended from republican *nobilitas*)
    squalid style of earlier grammarians:
        Chapter 7 *passim*
    using late Latin: 110–11
    verbosity: 123–24
    see also e.g. Cledonius; Donatus;
        Dositheus; Eutyches; Palaemon;
        Pompeius; Priscian; Probus;
        Romanus; Sacerdos; Servius
grammatical doctrine
    importance of intellectual authority:
        141–42
    influence of socio-linguistic
        environment on: 141–42
    normative grammar (*necessitas artis*):
        125, 126–27

GENERAL INDEX 265

propaedeutic genre: 137
Grammatica Vergiliana: see Asper
grammatical vocabulary
  Greek: 47, 83–88, 154–55
  Latin: 47, 76–77
  see also *analogia; barbarolexis; casus; declinatio; impositio; ratio; syllaba*
grammaticus: see grammarians
Greek
  accentuation of Greek words in Latin: 89–90
  annotation in Latin texts: 147–48
  Arcadian: 46
  article: 91
  Attic: 135
  choice of script: 84–85, 86–87, 89–90
  code-switching: 77–78, 83, 94–96
  contrasted with Latin: 81–82
  diachronic change: 135
  forms of address for grammarian: 197–98
  grammatical framework: 131–32
  interaction with Latin: Chapter 5 *passim*
  Latin grammar for Greek speakers: 75, 76–77, 96–98, 100–1, 107–9, 113, 133
  letters (*Graecae litterae*): 179
  loanwords into Latin: 36, 77, 109–110 (inflection), Chapter 10 *passim* esp.170–71, 186; *see also analogia; barbarolexis; Eurus; lepesta; ovis*
  names, inflection of: 15–16
  people: 176
  preterite active participle (missing in Latin): 93
  quotations: 78–83
  richness compared with Latin: 135–36
  as super-standard in grammatical description: 141–42
  terminology for loanwords: 172
  used as meta-language in Digest: 209–13
  see also grammatical vocabulary
Gregory the Great: 18–19
Gresham's Law: 4–5
gurdus, as Spanish: 174–75

h- and *f-* confused: 41, 46
habet, impersonal use of: 110–11

Hadrian: 192, 193
haedus: 41
Hannibal
  as rhetorical *exemplum:* 148–54, 157–58, 162–63
  oblique cases of: 192–93
harena: 7, 192 (as *singulare tantum*)
Hebrew: 189
Helena, inflection of: 109–10
Heliodorus: 93n.40
Hercules: 39
Hermeneumata Pseudodositheana: 73n.1, 153–54, 156–57, 162–63
Hermes Trismegistus: 79n.22
Herodian: 96–97, 172n.12
heteroclisy: 102–3
hircus: 41
Hispania Tarraconensis: 175
Historia Augusta: 195–96
Homer: 78–79, 97–98, 135
Horace: 177n.22, 189, 219–20
hordeum, -a (pl.): 7, 8–9, 102
hostis: 30
Hypsicrates of Amisos: 94n.48

i vowel, closed and long vs. short and open: 112; *see also* iotacism
i-stem nouns: *see* declensional morphology
Iavolenus: 214
Ibycus: 78n.21

-ĭcula: see derivational morphology
idiomata: 76–77, 94, 97, 207n.13
idonei auctores: 125
idus, as Etruscan or Sabine: 42
imitatio: 129
imperial constitutions, floridity of: 195–96
imperial service or bureaucracy: 74–75, 145–46, 162
implicatio: 222–23
impositio: 63–64, 65–69
imposition of names/words: 103, *see also declinatio; impositio;* name-givers; *primigenia verba*
impudentia: 196–97
in (praepos.): 127–28
indicative in indirect questions: 110–11
inflection: *see* declensional morphology

266   GENERAL INDEX

inlaudatus: 192–93
insomnia, vs. *somnia*: 15
iotacism: 107, 124n.16
Isidore of Seville: 93, 112n.28, 137
Italian Latin: 109n.21
Itus: see *idus*
iuger(um), as heteroclite: 14, 102–3

John the Lydian: 145–46
Julian of Toledo: 137
Julius Caesar: 7, 15, 25, 48–49, 117, 119,
    123–24
Julius Victor: 162–63
jurists: 193–94, Chapter 12 *passim*
Juvenal: Chapter 9 *passim*, 194, 226,
    227–28
    author-specific glossaries: 146n.13
    subscriptions in manuscripts of: 145–46

labdacism: 107–8
Lactantius: 145–46, 195–96
land surveyors, linguistic remarks by:
    207n.13
Lares: 44–45
Latin
    casual or informal speech: 204, 207,
        208–9
    diachronic change: 101–4
    diastratic variation:
    late Latin used by grammarians: 110–11
    "Received Standard Imperial Latin": xi
    regional: *see* regionalisms
    standardization: xi, 4, 5–6
    vulgar: *see* vulgarisms
    see also barbarisms; declensional
        morphology; derivational
        morphology; grammatical
        vocabulary; Greek; letters of
        the alphabet; plebeian Latin;
        pronunciation; syllabification errors;
        usage; vulgarisms
Latinity (*Latinitas*): xi n.5, 17–19, 23–24,
    28, 104–5, 183
    canons of correctness: 101
    as feature of *artes grammaticae*: 200
Latinus (King): 28–29
"layering" as method of propagation:
    68–69

lectional signs: 148
lepesta, as Sabine or Greek: 43, 52–53
letters of the alphabet (not distinguished
    from sounds): 88–89; *see also b* and
    v confusion; *c; e* for *a* substitution;
    f- and *h*- confused; Greek (choice of
    script); i vowel; iotacism; labdacism; -m;
    mytacism; *r* (intervocalic); *s; t; u;
    y; z*
Lex Licinia Mucia: 181
Libanius: 195–96
Libycus: 40
lignum, meaning of: 206–7
Lindsay, Wallace M.: 115
lingua: 94n.47
lingula: 13–14
literary authority: *see auctoritas*
Livy: 174–75, 178–79
lixulae, as Sabine: 41
loanwords: Chapter 3 *passim*, Chapter
    10 *passim*, esp. 171 (terminology
    in Latin); 170–73 (*Fremdwörter*
    vs. *Lehnwörter*); *see also* Africa;
    barbarolexis; Egyptian; Etruscan;
    Faliscan; Gaulish; Germanic; Greek;
    Medean; Phoenician; Sabine;
    Sardinian; Spanish; Syriac
Luca bos: 38, 40
Lucan: 121, 145–46, 227–28
Lucanicus: see *Lucanus*
Lucanus: 38, 39, 40
Lucian: 197–98
Lucina: 44–45
Lucius: 39–40
Lucretius, stylistic imitation of: 195–96, 198
ludi scaenici: 27–28

-*m* (word final): 87 (nasalization), 111–12
Macrobius: 96–97, 135–36, 177n.23,
    196–98, 228–30
magalia, as African: 109
magida: 36
magister: *see* grammarian
malapropism: 200–1
Mamers: 42, 46
manducare, vs. *edere*: 87–88
mannus: 109
mappa, as Punic: 174–75

GENERAL INDEX   267

Marcus Aurelius: 197–98
Mars: 42
Martial: 13–14
mastruca, as Sardinian: 109
mature "quickly": 192–93
Maurice: 38
Medean loanwords: 109
metaphor: *see* semantics
metaplasm: 8–9, 84–85, 99–100, 104,
    110–11
metri causa: 8–9
Mettius Curtius: 39
Middle Ages, early: 138–39
miles, etymology of: 201n.6
Minucius Felix: 195–96
Momigliano, Arnaldo: 228, 229–30
monosyllables: *see* declensional
    morphology
moral vices connected to linguistic errors:
    103
Moselle: 108–9
mos maiorum: 23–24
Myrtilos: 196–97
mytacism: 107

Naevius: 41–42
name-givers: 28–29
nanus, as Greek loanword: 186–87
Narbonne (*Narbo*): 103–104 (gender m.
    to f., 100)
"nationalism": 109–10
natura: 60, 101, 177–78; see also *declinatio*
neptis, as f. of *nepos*: 15
Nerva, jurist: 201–2
Nicaeus: 145–46, 147–48
nominative: *see* declensional morphology
number, of nouns: *see pluralia vel
    singularia tantum*

odium philologicum: 13
oleum: 102
oliva, vs. *olea*: 15
Ops: 44–45
oratio, etymology of: 79
oratorical delivery: 113–14
orthographical treatise (*De orthographia*):
    123
Oscan: 41–43, 46; see also *Oscus*

Oscus (*-e*): 38, 40
ovis, as Greek loanword: 36

paean, inflection of: 109–10
Palaemon: 76–77
Palatine Hill: 186
Pan, inflection of: 109–10
Papirius or Papirianus: 112n.28
παρατατικῶς: 211
paragraphoi, forked: 146
Paris, inflection of: 109–10
partes orationis: 91
Patavinity: 174–75
Paulus: 206
pauper, etymology of: 44–45
pedantry: *see* grammarians
Pedius: 206
peric(u)lum: 11
Peripatetics: 118–19
personae Iuvenalianae: 163–64
persuadere, as ambivalent word: 210
petorritum, as Gaulish: 174–75
Petronius: 193–94
Philoxenus: 94
Phoenician: 37–38, 197n.19
Plato: 190, 193–94, 197
Plautius: 214
Plautus: 34–35
plebeian Latin: 100–1, 105–6, 108–9, 113,
    see also populus
Pliny the Elder: 12, 13, 14–15, 18–19,
    107–8, 189
pluralia vel singularia tantum: 7, 15, 75–76,
    102, see also *glans*; *harena*; *hordeum*
Plutarch: 196–97
poetic license or diction: 7–9, 28–29,
    109–10, 125, 177n.22; *see also*
    metaplasm
Pompeius: 93, 111n.25, 112n.28, Chapter 7
    passim: 138–39
Pomponius Porcellus: 169, 176–77, 186, 190
populus, role in linguistic change: 106n.15,
    177–78; *see also* plebeian Latin;
    vulgarisms
porcus, as Sabine: 42
Porphyrio: 194
posse, lacking participle: 96
praesumptio "agreed understanding": 206

268 GENERAL INDEX

praeterpropter: 198
Praetextatus: 196–97
pragmatics: 222
  imperatives: 222–23
  indirect speech, implicature: 222–23
  performative utterances: 219–23
  precatives for imperatives: 222
prepositions, usage of: 127; *see also apud*;
  in; *praeterpropter*; *sub*; *subter*; *super*
primigenia verba: 28–29, 61–65
prior, used incorrectly: 111
Priscian: xiv, 17, 73, 74–75, 76–77, 81–82,
  83, 96–97, 98, 107–8, 145–46, 218–19
Probus: 117, 121–22, 193
Proculus: 217–19
profligare "nearly finish": 192–93
pronunciation: *see* aspiration; assibilation;
  consonant length; letters of the
  alphabet; spelling pronunciation;
  syllabification; vowel length
pronuntiatio "verdict": 216n.26
propago: 58, 67
prosody: *see* consonant length;
  syllabification errors; vowel length
Ps.-Probus: 76–77
Punic loanwords into Latin: 109, 174–75

quadrigae, plural only: 7
Quintilian: 7–8, 93, 101, 120, 132–33, 141–42,
  159–60, 174–75, 183–85, 200–1
Quirinus: 44–45
quis (interrog.) vs. *qui* (rel.): 15
quod-clause for acc.-inf. construction: 110–11

r (intervocalic) for *d*: 106n.14
Rabanus Maurus: 137
rabbī or *rabbōnī*, represented by
  διδάσκαλε: 197n.19
radix: 49–54
raeda, as Gaulish: 174–75
ratio: 17–18, 101–3, 129–30, 213
  (contrasted with *usus*), 214
  collatio rationis: 182n.31
  recta ratio: 137–38, 139–40
  see also analogia
Reatinus: 38, 39–40
recolere "cultivate" and "polish": 123–24
reduplicating syllable *e*: 192–93

regionalisms: 99, 105–9, 113, 143, 206,
  207n.13, 223–24; *see also* Africa;
  Italian Latin; loanwords
regula (grammatical rule): 102–3, 117
  (notion of), 121, 129–30
  as grammatical genre: 77
reloqui, used in Sabine shrines: 42–43, 46
reno, as Germanic: 37–38
rhetorician: 74–75, 148–53, 157–58,
  159–60
robur, vs. *robor*: 11
Romanus, C. Julius: 13n.28, 14, 15–17,
  18–19, 79n.22, 122
Rome: 145–46, 207 (*Roma* designating
  urban sprawl); *see also* Subura
Romulus: 28–29, 39
roots: 49–54
Rufinus *grammaticus*: 73
russeus, rejected: 15

s letter: 10–11
  geminate *ss* simplified: 108
Sabine: Chapter 3 *passim*, 50–53, 55,
  174–75
Sabinus: 37, 38
Sacerdos: 15–16, 133
Saint-Mihiel monastery: 140–41
sales: 15
Sallust: 24–25, 125–27, 156
Samnites: 43–44
Sancus: 39
sapienter: 15
Sappho: 78–79
Sardinian loanwords into Latin: 109
Saturnus: 44–45, 50–52
scansion: 99–100
Scaurus, Q. Terentius: 93, 193
schemata lexeos: 83–84
schesis onomaton: 128–29
Scholia Bembina: 145–46
"Schulgrammatik": 76–77, 104
semantics
  change or errors as barbarism: 104,
    192n.4; *see also* barbarism
  generalia vs. *specialia nomina*: 206n.12
  grammatical analysis of: 200–5
  metaphorical extension of meaning:
    200–1

GENERAL INDEX   269

"proper" or "correct" meaning of a word: 200–5
semilixulae, as Sabine: 41
senatorial class: 100, 106, 113, 162 (clothing), 175–76 (Gauls admitted); *see also* grammarians
Seneca, attitude to loanwords: 178–83
"Sergius": 138–42, 209n.18
Servius grammarian: 8–9, 93, 112n.28, 115, 138–39, 145–46, 196–98, 200, 227–30
    auctus: 145–46
Servius jurist: 215
Sextus Empiricus: 201n.7
shoots of plants: 56–61
Sidonius Apollinaris: 100–1, 108–9, 112–13, 195–96
Silius Italicus: 121
singularia tantum: see *singularia vel pluralia tantum*
slave, fugitive: 29–30
Smaragdus: 140–41
sofistae: 158–59
sol: 42, 44–45
solecism (*soloecismus*): 87, 104
somnia: see *insomnia*
sordes, as *plurale tantum*: 102
Spaniards: 176
Spanish loanwords in Latin: 174–75
spelling pronunciation: 111–12
squal- (*squaleo, squalidus, squalor*): 117–24, 192–93
Statilius Maximus: 79n.22
Statius: 145–46, 227–28
Stesichorus: 78–79
Stoics: 47, 117–18 (stylistic shortcomings), 172n.13, 180, 182n.31, 218n.33; *see also* Chrysippus
sub (praepos.): 127–28
subdistinctivus (ὑποδιαζευκτικός): 218–19
subter (praepos.): 127–28
subulo, as Etruscan: 53
Subura: 108–9
Suetonius: 195–96
suffixation: *see* derivational morphology
Sulpicius Apollinaris: 185–88, 193, 194–96, 197–98

supellex: 16–17, 122 (as fem. sg.): 204 (used carelessly)
super (praepos.): 127–28
supparus (or *-um*), as Oscan: 42
syllaba: 75–76, 82–83, 98
syllabification errors: 106n.16
Symmachus: 196–97
synonyms: *see differentiae*
syntax (*coniunctio*): 70
Syriac: 37–38

t, errors in pronunciation: 108
Tarpeia: 39
Tatius: 39
Terence: 145–46, 156
Terentianus Maurus: 83n.27
Terminus: 44–45
Tertullian: 121, 195–96
theonyms: 44–45, 50–52
Theophilus Antecessor: 220–21
Theophrastus: 78–79
Tiberius Caesar: 169, 170–71, 186
tigris, as Armenian: 37–38
trees: *see* chapter 4 *passim*
tribunus et notarius: 100–1
Trier: 108–9
triginta, accentuation of: 105n.13
Trimalchio: 193–94, 197–98
triticum, singular only: 7
tubur, as Punic: 109
tyrannicidae for *tyranni*, as barbarism: 104

u semivowel pronounced as *v*: 108
Ulpian: 201, 206, 210, 220
Urban Praetor's Edict: 199, 210–11
usage (*usus*): 200–201n.7, 202 ("current")
    changing over time: 137–38
    legal usage: 208
    not discussed by *artes grammaticae*: 200
    Pompeius's attitude to contemporary usage: 124–27
    see also consuetudo; *ratio*; Virgil (usage of)

Valerius, accentuation of vocative: 192–93
varietas linguarum: see *diversitas linguarum*

270 GENERAL INDEX

Varro, M. Terentius: xiii, 14, 15–16,
   Chapters 2–4 *passim*, 92, 93, 94, 97,
   101, 106n.15, 178–79, 218–19
   Antiquitates rerum divinarum: 25
   correspondence with Cicero: 24
   Menippean Satires: 25
   Res rusticae: 48–49
Varro Atacinus: 35–36
vas, as heteroclite: 103
Velius Longus: 11–12, 13, 112n.27
venenus (m.): 155
verecundia: 196–97, 228–29
Vergiliomastix: 7
Vergilius: 40
Verrius Flaccus: 202
vestibulum: 192–93
Vettius: 158–59
vetustas: 25–26, 28–30, 119–24, 204;
   see also *antiquitas*
vexo: 192–93
vina, in plural: 102
vir clarissimus title: 100
Virgil: 7, 8–9, 15–16, 78–79, 102, 121, 123,
   128, 145–46, 156, 196–97, 198, 226,
   227–28
   usage of, criticized: 192–93

vocative: see *egregius*; *Valerius*
Volcanus: 44–45
Volturnus: 43–44
voluntas scriptoris or *legis*: 200, 204
   (vs. *scriptum*)
Vortumnus: 44–45
vowel length
   errors: 105n.13, 111–12
   no longer contrastive: 139–40, 141–42
   shortening of long vowels: 6–7
   see also *i* vowel
vulgarisms: 205–9; *see also* barbarisms;
      plebeian Latin
   with reflexes in Romance: 105n.13
Vulgate Bible: 18–19
vulgus: 205–6

wills: 204, 219–23
wind names: 178–79
wrestling: 197–98

y letter: 11

z letter: 77, 179
Zeno: 172n.13
Zephyrus: 178–79

Index of Notable Passages

For the benefit of digital users, indexed terms that span two pages (e.g., 52–53) may, on occasion, appear on only one of those pages.

This index includes passages that receive longer discussion or quotation. Authors mentioned in passing or discussed without reference to quotations are mainly included in the General Index. For abbreviations and editions of Latin authors see the *TLL* Index online.

Agroecius, *gramm.* VII
    114.16–17: 9–10
    114.21–115.2: 10n.22
    116.18: 9–10
    118.7–13: 10–11
    118.19: 11n.24
    124.24: 11n.25
Ammonius
    diff. 75: 211
Apollonius Dyscolus
    De pronominibus = *GG* II. 1 61.3–5
        Schneider: 215
Ars Ambrosiana
    p. 49.16–18 Löfstedt: 140n.19
    p. 114.756–768 Löftstedt:
        140n.20
Asconius
    Corn. p. 54.16–18: 181
    Corn. p. 56.24–7: 203–4

Caesar
    anal. frg. 11: 7
    Ps.-Caper, *gramm.* VII
    92.1: 9–10
    105.17: 11
Cassiodorus
    orth. praef. 6 (= *gramm.* VII
        143.9–12): 123
    var. 4.24.1: 120n.7
Ps.-Cassiodorus, *de orat.*
    p. 65.2–6 Stock: 139n.16
    p. 77.10 Stock: 209n.18
Cato
    agr. 51: 68–69

Charisius
    p. 13.29–32 (= Diom. *gramm.* I
        435.24–6): 123
    p. 58.26–30: 16–17
    p. 61.16 + 62.2–10: 189–90
    p. 98.1–16 (from Pliny?): 12–13
    p. 113.8–11 (from Romanus): 15–16
    p. 132.14–16: 14
    p. 181.20–3: 16–17
    p. 182.2–4: 122–23
    p. 182.18–21: 16–17
    p. 182.27–183.4: 17
    p. 246.26–247.3: 90
    p. 335.20–336.7: 11n.26
    p. 380.20–5: 93
Cicero
    ac.
        1.8: 28n.20
        1.9: 31–32
    fin.
        3.40: 173n.15
        4.5: 118–19
    orat.
        115: 118
Codex Iustinianus
    6.23.15 pr.: 222
Columella
    1.1.12: 173n.15
Consentius
    De nomine et verbo = *gramm.* V
        343.20–4: 103
        345.14–19: 102–3
        347.32–348.4: 137n.14
        348.11–13: 102

272 INDEX OF NOTABLE PASSAGES

Consentius (*cont.*)
354.24–30: 103
354.33–355.2: 104–5
355.14–15: 102
356.25–357.4: 103
364.8–11: 109
365.12–13, 25: 109–10
379.3–9: 138n.15
barb. (ed. Mari)
1.10–11: 104
1.18–2.1: 104
2.7–8: 109
3.7–13: 105
11.8–9: 105–6
11.18–19: 105–6
11.23–6: 105–6
15.2–4: 214
15.20–16.5: 112
18.4: 113–14
21.21: 113–14
22.2–18: 104

Didymus Caecus, *Comm. in eccl.*
11.91: 217
diff. ed. Beck
A 5–6: 9–10
A 8: 9–10
A 13: 11n.26
D 32: 9–10
N 14: 9–10
Q 2: 9–10
S 34: 9–10
diff. gramm. suppl.
p. 275.1: 9–10
p. 275.10: 9–10
p. 283.13: 9–10
Digesta
11.3.1.3 (Ulpianus): 210
28.5.1.3–7 (Ulpianus): 220
29.1.1.1 (Ulpianus): 201n.6
32.52.7 (Ulpianus): 201–2
32.55 pr. (Ulpianus): 206–7
32.62 (Iulianus): 215–16
32.69.1 (Marcellus): 204
33.7.18.3 (Paulus): 206
33.10.7.2 (Celsus): 204–5, 212
34.2.7 (Paulus): 214–15
34.2.8 (Plautius): 213–14

38.16.8 pr. (Iulianus): 209
41.1.7.13 (Gaius): 53–54
42.4.2.4 (Ulpianus): 211
50.16.8 (Gaius): 212
50.16.87 (Marcellus): 207
50.16.101 (Modestinus): 216
50.16.124 (Proculus): 217–18
50.12.158 (Celsus): 208
50.16.162.1 (Pomponius): 205
50.16.195 (Ulpianus): 216
50.16.235 (Gaius): 203
Diomedes, *gramm.* I
299.1–8: 74–75
300.20–2: 79
300.26–301.2: 90
302.3–7: 92
311.3–6: 93–94
316.32–5: 81
333.21–2: 78
334.25–30: 91–92
334.25–335.7: 133–35
336.8–10: 95
360.24–7: 95
364.29–31: 86
379.11–13: 11n.26
384.15–16: 93
397.15–20: 81
405.35–7: 80
406.26–34: 80
407.10–15: 79–80
421.32–422.3: 88
422.9–13: 88–89
423.3–5: 85–86
426.15–18: 85
427.12–16: 89
430.30–431.3: 95
433.4–7: 89
435.24–6 (= Char. p. 13.29–32): 123
453.21–8: 86
482.14–17: 85
501.30–2: 85
Dionysius of Halicarnassus, *antiquitates Romanae*
1.9.4: 173–74
Dionysius Thrax, *ars*
GG I. 1 25.3–5: 61n.24
GG I. 1 40.1–3: 209–10
Donatus
gramm. mai.

INDEX OF NOTABLE PASSAGES   273

2.1 p. 613.5 Holtz: 90
2.12 p. 637.3–4 Holtz: 136n.12
Ter.
    Ad. 28.2: 221
    Eun. 139: 223
    Eun. 237: 210
    Phorm. 255: 221

Eustathius, *Comm. Od.*
    2.296: 211

Festus (or Paul. Fest.)
    p. 109.22–3 L.: 201n.6
    p. 378.11–20 L.: 17n.40
    p. 482.34–484.4 L.: 202
Fronto
    p. 131.2–6: 173n.15

Gellius: *see* Ch. 11 *passim*
    4.16.1: 35
    9.1.8: 203
    13.21.1: 121–22
    15.9.6–7: 191–92
    17.2.15: 191–92
    19.13.1–3: 185–88
Greg. M., *moral.*
    epist. 5: 18–19

Horace, *ars*
    51: 189

Jerome, *Gal.*
    2.2 p. 382^C: xin.6
Johannes Lydus, *Mag.*
    2.13.6: 175n.18
Juvenal
    7.149–98: Chapter 9 *passim*,
      esp. 164

Macrobius
    Sat. 1.5.10: 177n.23
    verb. De Paolis
      p. 11.7–13.3: 136–37
      p. 93.21–95.2: 136–37
Martial
    14.120: 13–14

Nonius Marcellus
    p. 302.18: 203

Paul. Fest.: *see* Fest.
Pliny the Elder, *dub. serm.*
    frg. 8 Della Casa = 2 M.: 107–8
Pompeius
    Books I–II (*gramm.* V, ed. Keil)
      prol. p. 158.14–20: 116–17
      135.20–2: 90
      234.17–33: 125
      275.17–25: 127
      277.3–11: 128
    Book III (ed. Zago)
      p. 59.13–60.4: 128–29
      p. 62.14: 129
Priscian, *gramm.*
    II 5.7–6.2: 213
    II 279.15–18: 17n.40
    III 98.16–19: 219
    III 405.14–15: 74–75

Quintilian, *inst.*
    1.5.6: 7
    1.5.11: 7–8
    1.5.55–8: 174
    1.5.42–4: 132n.2
    1.5.58: 171
    1.6.16: 189
    1.7.1: 200–1
    2.5.23–4: 120
    8.1.2–3: 183
    12.10.28: 179

Sacerdos, *gramm.* VI
    432.7–9: 133n.3

"Sergius": *see* Ps.-Cassiodorus
Seneca
    apocol. 3.3: 176
    epist.
      95.65: 182n.28
      120.4: 179–80
    nat. 5.16.4: 178–79
Servius, *Aen.*
    8.200: 210–11
    10.681: 212
Sextus Empiricus, *Pyrrh*
    3.119, 212
Sidonius Apollinaris
    carm. 23.235–6: 108–9

274 INDEX OF NOTABLE PASSAGES

Sidonius Apollinaris (*cont.*)
epist.
  2.10.1: 100
  4.17.1: 108–9
Smaragdus, *Liber in partibus Donati*
  p. 134 lines 701–12: 141n.21
Suetonius
  gramm. 22.2: 169
  Tib. 71: 170–71

Tertullian
  apol. 4.6–7: 121
Theophilus Antecessor, *Paraphrasis*
  2.1.36: 221

Velius Longus, *gramm.* VII
  68.11: 13
  74.16–75.5: 11–12
Varro
  Antiquitates rerum divinarum
    frg. 2a (= Aug. civ. 6.2): 26, 27, 32
    frg. 3 (= Aug. civ. 4.22): 27, 32
  ling.
    5.1: 63
    5.3: 30
    5.5: 25–26, 29, 30
    5.8–9: 31

5.10: 171–72
5.13: 49–50, 62–63
5.41: 39
5.74: 44, 50–52
5.88: 11
5.93: 54–55
5.97: 41
5.123: 52–53
6.36–7: 61
7.2: 63
7.3: 31
7.4: 31, 56
7.5: 63
7.39–40: 40
8.1: 57
8.5: 65–66
8.9: 59
8.21: 60–61
8.59: 56–60
9.5–6: 177n.23
10.16: 66
frg. 5 Kent: 35
rust.
  1.7.2: 64
  1.40.4: 67
Virgil
  georg. 1.120: 7, 8–9